UNDER ARTURO'S STAR

Purdue Studies in Romance Literatures

Editorial Board

UNDER ARTURO'S STAR

The Cultural

Legacies of

Elsa Morante

Edited by
Stefania Lucamante
Sharon Wood

Purdue University Press
West Lafayette, Indiana

∞ The paper used in this book meets the minimum requirements of
American National Standard for Information Sciences—Permanence of
Paper for Printed Library Materials, ANSI Z39.48-1992.

Printed in the United States of America
Design by Anita Noble

Library of Congress Cataloging-in-Publication Data
    Under Arturo's star: the cultural legacies of Elsa Morante / edited by
Stefania Lucamante and Sharon Wood.
        p.   cm. — (Purdue studies in Romance literatures ; v. 34)
    Includes bibliographical references and index.
    ISBN-13: 978-1-55753-407-1
    1. Morante, Elsa, ca. 1912–1985—Criticism and interpretation. I.
Lucamante, Stefania. II. Wood, Sharon, 1957– III. Title. IV. Series.
    PQ4829.O615Z915 2006
    853'.912—dc22
                                    2005026155

To our children—

Lucy, Anna, Lamberto, and Stefano

Contents

Acknowledgments

Stefania Lucamante wishes to thank the Catholic University of America, particularly in the person of Vice Provost for Graduate Studies George E. Garvey, for the generous support and the summer grants, which allowed us to do the work. Sharon Wood thanks the University of Leicester for grants which helped toward travel expenses. We would like to thank also Jeffrey Popovitch at the Lauinger Library at Georgetown University and Kevin Gunn at the Mullen Library at the Catholic University of America for their invaluable help. Many thanks to Saveria Chemotti of the University of Padova and of *Studi novecenteschi* for kindly giving permission to use earlier versions of some of the essays in this volume. Our gratitude goes to many friends and colleagues as well as the contributors to this volume, and a particular thank you goes to Roberto Coroneo, of the University of Cagliari, for his generous help with the pragmatics of printing the essays on which we worked during long Sardinian days and nights. A special note of gratitude goes, also, to Susan Clawson, production editor at Purdue Studies in Romance Literatures, for her invaluable assistance in seeing this project through.

Stefania Lucamante
Sharon Wood

Introduction

Life and Works

Elsa Morante has long been recognized internationally as one of the most significant innovative writers of twentieth-century Italy. Nonetheless, there has to date been no full-length study in English dedicated to her work, and indeed this volume proposes to offer the first comprehensive evaluation of Morante to appear outside Italy. Perspectives on Morante's literary achievement have shifted dramatically in recent years, and the contributors to this volume take full account of the recent course of Morante criticism, locating Morante's work within modern critical and theoretical paradigms. These essays thus work across a range of transcultural disciplines; indeed, one of our aims is to underline Morante's centrality in a broader context which goes beyond Italian national borders, departing from the traditional realm of philological analysis to encompass approaches informed by cultural, feminist, and interdisciplinary studies. Scholars contributing to this volume are writers and critics from America, Italy, the UK, and Poland, each offering their own particular and specific perspective on Morante's work within this broader interdisciplinary and international framework.

Elsa Morante was born in Rome on August 18 in 1912—not 1916, as sometimes stated in American translations.[1] She was the second daughter of Irma Poggibonsi, a Jewish schoolteacher, and Francesco Lo Monaco, while her legal father was Augusto Morante, a social worker in the Istituto Aristide Gabelli. Elsa received little formal education and was largely self-taught at primary level. During these years she spent time in the house of her godmother, Donna Maria Guerrieri Gonzaga, where she became acquainted with more privileged social groups and became acutely aware of class difference, a theme

1

that was to emerge particularly in her early stories and first novel, *Menzogna e sortilegio*. The principal reason for her extended stays at Donna Maria's was her precarious health, suffering as she did from anemia. Indeed illness emerges as a trope throughout her work, where it takes not only a physiological but an existential and epistemological dimension. After 1922 the Morante family moved from the working class Testaccio district of Rome, to the Monteverde Nuovo area on the other side of the river. This was a considerable change for Elsa, who now began to attend school regularly. At this time she also began to write regularly for several children's magazines, contributing short stories and poems to *Il Corriere dei piccoli* among others.[2]

Morante never finished her university degree; having decided to live independently from her family, she had to find the means to support herself. Indeed, money was a constant problem for Elsa, who found financial security only in 1941, with her marriage to Alberto Moravia, a novelist and journalist with an already substantial reputation. The experience of war touched the couple closely: with the fall of Mussolini, the armistice of 1943, and the Nazi occupation of Rome, Morante and Moravia escaped south to Ciociaria, living for several months in the small village of Fondi. While this experience led directly to Moravia's novel *La ciociara* (1957), later filmed with Sophia Loren in the lead role, Morante spent these years writing her first novel *Menzogna e sortilegio*. Indeed, she undertook a dangerous, if brief, return to Rome from Fondi in order to rescue the manuscript abandoned in the urgency of departure. The novel, set in Sicily at the beginning of the twentieth century, follows the experience of three generations, filtered through the memory and imagination of the narrator Elisa. In this novel the commonplaces of popular and romantic fiction—love across the social divide, a sequence of unrequited passions, country versus city—are transformed into a narrative of intense tragic drama, while, as narrator, Elisa offers a self-consciously literary framework that reflects continuously on the process of writing itself. A realist novel, *Menzogna e sortilegio* simultaneously derails the conventions of realist fiction in a text of almost postmodern irony. Published in 1948, the novel was awarded the Viareggio Award *ex-aequo* with Aldo Palazzeschi, but Morante was frequently accused, in a spirit of partisan and superficial criticism, of anachronism, of writing a great nineteenth-century novel when there were more pressing concerns in the re-establishment of the nation and of a national culture.

In this same year of 1948 Morante and Moravia moved to via dell'Oca, where Morante was to remain until her suicide attempt in 1982, immediately following the publication of *Aracoeli*. After an accident, her last three years were spent in the Villa Margherita, a private clinic near via Nomentana, where Morante died of a heart attack on the 25th of November, 1985. Like Elisa, the narrator of *Aracoeli* seeks a healing for his damaged psyche through the recovery of his family history and memories. Middle-aged, homosexual, and self-hating, Manuele is tied to the memory of his mother by bonds of simultaneous hatred and adoration. While Elisa stays in her tiny room throughout, Manuele undertakes a journey from Italy to Andalusia in order both to rediscover Aracoeli and to free himself of her. In her first novel as in her last, from *Menzogna e sortilegio* to *Aracoeli*, Morante explores the deepest recesses of eroticism, sexuality, identity, and trauma. Her texts consistently avoid sentimentalisms; they deploy psychological insights gained through Freud and others, and vary in tone from witty and knowing humor, to ironic and comic pastiche, to dark despair. Morante's publications, in between *Menzogna e sortilegio* and *Aracoeli*, were not numerous, but highly respected or controversial. The novel *L'isola di Arturo* won the prestigious Premio Strega in 1957. This is her second full-length novel, narrated by an adult Arturo, who speaks of his blissful childhood on the wild island of Procida. The young boy is ignorant of the world in his isolation, and of women following his mother's death in childbirth. When his adored father, the willful, bisexual, and capriciously godlike Wilhelm, brings home a new wife—a simple young girl from Naples—Arturo is compelled to confront the transition from idyllic childhood to the complexities and uncertainties of adulthood.

A year later, Morante's collection of poems, *Alibi,* was published, while *Il mondo salvato dai ragazzini* won the Brancati-Zafferana Award in 1968. During these years Morante made frequent trips abroad, with Moravia, Pasolini, and others. While

3

in the United States in 1959, she met Bill Morrow, a young painter from Kentucky. Their friendship opened a new path in the author's sentimental life, which ended with Morrow's tragic fall from a New York City skyscraper in 1962. The following year Morante published *Lo scialle andaluso,* a collection of stories including some first published in *Il gioco segreto* (1941).

In 1974, Morante published her third novel, the highly controversial *La Storia,* closely based on the unfinished *Senza i conforti della religione. La Storia* confronts the official history of war and battle with individual, subjective experience and the struggle for survival. Ida Ramundo, a fearful and timid schoolteacher, is raped during World War II by a German soldier passing through Italy on his way to die in Africa. She is left pregnant, and she seeks to conceal this second, illegitimate child, Useppe, just as she conceals her epilepsy and her partly Jewish heritage. Each chapter deals with a year of the war and is prefaced by a brief "official" history of events during that year, while the main part of Morante's text describes the war of an ordinary woman whose elder son becomes first a Fascist, then a partisan, then a black-marketeer. Her younger son, by contrast, epileptic like Ida herself, exhibits an unsentimental but touching innocence, a sympathy for the natural and animal world. Useppe cannot survive in the world in which he lives. For Morante, to be human is to be outside history, and her sympathies are quite clearly ranged with those of the popular classes as yet unaffected by the rapid advance of a new technological and bureaucratic age. And indeed, ordinary people were the intended readership for this book. In her desire for *La Storia* to achieve a wider readership than the cultural elite, Morante urged her publisher Einaudi to produce a paperback edition, priced at 2000 lire, for the work's first publication. This pricing policy, together with Einaudi's aggressive marketing strategy, produced sales of over 100,000 in the first month alone.

Critical Reception: From Marxism to Feminism

Until recent years, the only one of Morante's works to be widely read by the public was, indeed, *La Storia,* while *L'isola di Arturo* remained a cult-book for a few intellectuals; other than the *querelle* following the publication of *La Storia,* which briefly polarized Italian academic opinion and provoked wide-spread controversy, she has been relatively ignored by the critical and academic establishment alike. Certainly her works have always raised problems for those bent on inserting them within specific trends and schools of Italian literature. Critics were divided by *La Storia*, which awkwardly and problematically adopted the rhetoric of the novel in a manner quite out of sympathy with the dominant Marxist ideology of the times, but which nonetheless contained elements of value and interest in the treatment of the round-up of Jews in the Roman Ghetto, of the notion of Power, of aggressor and victim, even if such elements were not easily accessible to interpretation. Cesare Cases's and Giovanni Raboni's articles in *Quaderni piacentini* illustrate this critical reaction. In the summer of 1974, the literary journal *La Fiera letteraria* devoted two issues to the debate: "*La Storia*: è o non è un capolavoro?" Giacinto Spagnoletti, Angelo Pupino, Renato Barilli, Alberto Asor Rosa, and Giacomo Salinari are among the academics who discuss the novel and answer a set of questions, while in the pages of the independent communist newspaper *il manifesto*—starting with the famous "invective-letter" by Nanni Balestrini, Elisabetta Rasy, Letizia Paolozzi, and Umberto Silva of July 18—extraordinarily negative reviews appeared (Camon 216).

The "Kolossal" as Ferdinando Camon called *La Storia* in his insightful and poignant article "Il test della *Storia*" (186–87), divided Italian intellectuals much as did Lampedusa's *Il gattopardo*, and indeed Gregory Lucente compares for various reasons the upheaval provoked by these two texts (220; 264). As Marino Sinibaldi acutely points out in his discussion of the famous *querelle* twenty-five years later, the publication of the book, also censored in 1976 in Franco's Spain, provoked a storm that, seen with hindsight, reveals a failure to understand Morante and her need to write outside a specific ideology. Any recognition that was offered later was grudging and came with a critical view that, rather than insert Morante at the heart of an eccentric Italian modernism, tended to isolate her, denying her intellectual heritage and her subsequent influence, and delimiting her achievement as a solitary one, thus categorizing her as simultaneously both extraordinary as author and irrelevant as master for future generations. In recent years, Alfonso

Berardinelli has analyzed the hostility and resistance that alienated Morante from Italian critics and the Italian public in general. He has given, almost mockingly, a rapid assessment of the situation. He believes that there were three main "fronts of hostility": critics who favored experimental forms of writing; a populist and super-Marxist front, which considered literature an adjunct of politics; and the "scienziati della letteratura" who no longer believed in either expressions of aesthetics, taste, or value and regarded books as mere expendable merchandise (26).

A powerful and quite isolated voice that rejected these waves of criticism was that of Pier Paolo Pasolini, who understood very clearly the role played by Morante's work in Italian cultural history. In his revised review of *L'isola di Arturo* Pasolini commented:

> [N]on solo si inserisce con una serie di rapporti meccanici, ma lo modifica all'interno con la sua stessa presenza, rappresentando una nuova necessità, che i critici, anche ideologicamente impegnati, non possono ignorare, o respingere secondo schemi valevoli fino a ieri. La presenza dell'*Isola* è lì a dimostrare che una seconda fase del realismo del dopoguerra si sta iniziando, evidentemente, al di qua dello stato di emergenza in cui esso è nato. Ne consegue la riassunzione di forme che solo apparentemente erano superate, ma che in realtà, dentro il neorealismo stesso, si erano tramandate, quale tradizione recente (nella specie l'irregolarità sintattica e narrativa e la squisitezza). (170)

> Not only does she insert herself into the historical landscape through a series of mechanical relationships, but her very presence transforms the landscape from within, embodying a new urgency which even those critics who are ideologically partisan cannot ignore, or dismiss according to criteria which had some value until the very recent past. The very presence of *L'isola* [*di Arturo*] demonstrates that a second phase of postwar realism is beginning, this side, obviously, of the state of emergency from which it sprang. As a result, we see adopted once more those forms which had only in appearance been left behind but which in reality had been passed down through Neorealism itself as recent tradition (in particular syntactic and narrative irregularity, and exquisite beauty).

But Pasolini's understanding of Morante's engagement with traditional and literary forms, in part due to the close personal and professional relationship between the two writers, was destined to remain an almost isolated case. Nor with the advent of a feminist engagement with literary history did Morante fare much better. Her work refused any facile analysis of patriarchy that could be absorbed within a radical feminist cultural agenda and make her a chapter in the millennial history of cultural and sexual oppression. Biancamaria Frabotta, a quarter of a century later, recalls with some disdain Morante's refusal to participate in her collection of women's poems, *Donne in Poesia*. In a 1991 paper Frabotta gave in France, she states that the "*post mortem* total redemption of Elsa Morante," thanks to the chapter in Giulio Ferroni's history of Italian literature, could not find her in agreement for several reasons ("Fuori" 171–72). The feminist poet deconstructs the author's posthumously published autobiographical writings such as *Diario 1938*, claiming to find in these texts evidence of Morante's formidable presumption and arrogance, an irrepressible narcissism:

> A ciascuno il suo Narciso e la vecchiaia è una malattia contagiosa. Anche le divinità ne soffrono, le donne sciocche e barbare fuggite dall'harem, gli angelici efebi derubati, nel corso del nostro secolo impietoso, dell'alibi della poesia. (178)

> To each his or her own Narcissus, and old age is a contagious disease. Even deities suffer from it, the silly barbarian women who have run away from the harem, the angelic and effeminate young men who have been robbed, over the course of our pitiless century, of poetry's alibi.

Such comments, made some thirteen years later, still show the resentment and lack of understanding that Morante's refusal to participate in that anthology provoked in some critics and artists in their own right, such as Frabotta. Like their creator, Morante's female characters resisted a critical approach that saw literature as a correlative to a social and political reality, inscribed within the text. Some critics have been more attuned to understanding the complexity of Morante's world with respect to the construction of female characters and their interaction, or lack thereof, with the world. Emblematic is the criticism of Paola Azzolini, who finds that the "retelling of herself to herself" is for *Menzogna e sortilegio*'s Elisa the only possible form of "dirsi come donna" (151). That is, only "by staging herself as a mask or as a ghost," can Elisa say herself. Our engagement with Morante's texts in this volume wishes to challenge an obsolete feminist reading that condemns the artist for her failure to produce characters who might be marshaled as role models for a younger generation of readers. Morante's constant striving toward a utopian perfection could not allow for such a utilitarian approach to fiction. As Adalgisa Giorgio quite aptly puts it in the case of *Aracoeli*, Morante did not write "emancipatory novels," as is the case with some of Dacia Maraini's more programmatic fiction, such as *Donna in Guerra*, or *La femme rompue* by Simone de Beauvoir, "classic" feminist texts of those years. But Morante's works touch issues that are, nevertheless, linked to women and "their relationship with the symbolic and the imaginary," and resound more universal in their comprehension of such relationships. Giorgio concludes:

> Morante's discourse on women in *Aracoeli* is contradictory and ambiguous, but it is certainly neither misogynist nor sexist: it reflects the complexity of current theoretical discourse on femininity and motherhood, providing a critique of certain notions and stereotypes of our culture, but at the same time exposing the traps of facile idealizations and the delusion of oversimplifications. (116)

The feminist condemnation of Morante in the 1970s and 1980s is largely impervious to this point; its claims of radicalism take us little further on from Cesare Garboli's assertions in "Elsa come Rousseau" of a unique and isolated romantic splendor, even in this paradoxical admission of her influence:

> E nelle pagine di quel bel romanzo di cui tanto si parla, uscito qualche settimana fa, *Passaggio in ombra* di Maria Teresa Di Lascia, non si sentono risuonare i passi, gli echi, le reminiscenze di *Menzogna e sortilegio*, non se ne vedono ovunque i segni e le tracce? *Ma non è la capacità di sedurre ciò che si richiede a una madre.* Per quanto grande possa essere la forza di provocazione e fascinazione dei suoi

romanzi, nessuno dei messaggi della Morante ha per destinatarie le donne, né può essere indiziato di solidarietà con la loro lotta, la loro ideologia, le loro battaglie in favore dell'emancipazione femminile. [...] Se a una madre si chiede di fare da educatrice, da guida, da aiuto nella difesa dei diritti della donna, se a una madre si chiede un atteggiamento solidale nei confronti del maschio, la Morante può essere considerata sì e no una pessima matrigna. Esibire le viscere materne, abbandonarsi al proprio demonio non basta. ("Elsa come Rousseau" 223; emphasis added)

And in the pages of that wonderful novel everyone is talking about, published a few weeks ago, *Passaggio in ombra* by Mariateresa Di Lascia, do we not hear the footsteps, echoes, reminders of *Menzogna e sortilegio?* Can we not see signs and traces of the earlier novel everywhere? But it is not the capacity to seduce that we ask of a mother. However great the power of her novels to provoke and to fascinate, none of Morante's messages are directed towards women readers, nor can they be co-opted in solidarity with their struggle, their ideology, their battles for female emancipation [. . .] If of a mother we ask that she act as teacher, guide, help in the defense of women's rights, Morante can, at best, be considered a step-mother of the worst kind. It is not enough to exhibit maternal innards, to abandon oneself to one's own demons.

We see here an assumption from across the political spectrum, one that we do not share, that women's writing should in conscious, deliberate, and politicized fashion reflect and promote a feminist agenda. If many feminist critics failed to understand the complex motivation and vocation of women's writing, Garboli sought to assimilate Morante to a masculinist perspective and to sever links between her "masterful" work and any other women writers, a connection that this volume, on the other hand, sees as the logical evolution of her ethical and aesthetic legacy. Both feminists and Garboli perceive the role of the woman writer as that of the nurturing "good" mother. Such a view disallows the seduction of the maternal voice and, together with Morante's refusal to fit into an archetypal paradigm of femininity, leaves the author inevitably alienated.

The multiple marginalization by a succession of critical approaches with precise if unstated agendas, determined to corral literature into a specific and reductive intellectual space, is itself indicative of a group of texts whose complexity, subtlety, and refusal to align themselves with established formations whether artistic, cultural, or political, left Morante, over the course of half a century of ideological and teleological criticism, consistently outside privileged and authoritative categories. This continues to be the case in the collected works of the author for the Meridiani Mondadori, edited by Cesare Garboli and Carlo Cecchi. While the two volumes offer a comprehensive and extremely useful examination of Morante's work, the critical perspective remains bound to criteria that, rather than open up new readings of the author, tend toward closure. As late as 1996, in a review of Giovanna Rosa's *Cattedrali di carta* and Cesare Garboli's *Il gioco segreto* in which the critic reiterates the conclusions of his introduction to the first volume of the Meridiani, Carlo Madrignani comments:

> Aside from the appropriateness of the comparison (between Morante and Rousseau), it is right to recall that this great artist had no role in the provincial Italy of poet-bards. Amongst the many disorienting features of this complex and mysterious writer is the fact that Morante's works *seem to have sprung from nowhere*, with no inspiring fathers, with no sisters or brothers from the same cultural genealogy. (10; emphasis added)

It is our belief that only an approach that is inclusive and interdisciplinary, rather than reductively ideological, will bring out those very features of the texts that make them far more radical than many of the past critical and theoretical perspectives allowed.

Until the early nineties, only a few monographs on this author had been published, by Carlo Sgorlon, *Invito alla lettura di Elsa Morante* (Milan: Mursia, 1972, 1988), by Gianni Venturi, *Elsa Morante* (Florence: La Nuova Italia, 1977), and by Donatella Ravanello, *Scrittura e follia nei romanzi di Elsa Morante* (Venice: Marsilio, 1980). A new wave of criticism began with the first feminist readings by the Gruppo La Luna, *Letture di Elsa Morante* (Turin: Rosenberg & Sellier, 1987). Over the course of the next few years, several volumes appeared in Italy. These included *Per Elisa: Studi su "Menzogna e sortilegio,"* ed. Lucio Lugnani and Emanuella Scarano (Pisa: Nistri-Lischi, 1990); Giovanna Bernabò, *Come leggere "La Storia"* (Milan: Mursia, 1991); *Per Elsa Morante* (Various Authors; Milan: Linea d'ombra, 1993); *Cahiers Elsa Morante,* ed. J.-N. Schifano and Tjuna Notarbartolo (Naples: ESI, 1993); the monographic volume of *Studi novecenteschi,* "Vent'anni dopo *La Storia*: Omaggio a Elsa Morante," ed. Concetta D'Angeli and Giacomo Magrini (*Studi novecenteschi* 21.47–48 [1994]); *Cattedrali di carta* by Giovanna Rosa (Milan: Il Saggiatore, 1995); *Cahiers Elsa Morante 2,* ed. Nico Orengo and Tjuna Notarbartolo (Salerno: Edizioni Scientifiche Italiane, 1993); *Il gioco segreto: Nove immagini di Elsa Morante* by Cesare Garboli (Milan: Adelphi, 1995); Stefania Lucamante's *Elsa Morante e l'eredità proustiana* (Fiesole: Cadmo, 1998); *Morante Elsa. Italiana. Di professione, poeta* by Marco Bardini (Pisa: Nistri-Lischi, 1999); *Violenza ed interpretazione: "La Storia" di Elsa Morante* by Drude von der Fehr (Pisa: Istituti editoriali e poligrafici internazionali, 1999); *Narrativa 17,* ed. Marie-Hélène Caspar (Nanterre: C.R.I.X., 2000); *Uscire da una camera delle favole: i romanzi di Elsa Morante* by Hanna Serkowska (Krakaw: Rabid, 2002); *Leggere Elsa Morante* by Concetta D'Angeli (Rome: Carocci, 2003). There is little need to point out that, with the exception of the first three, all of these monographs appeared after Morante's death. Almost all of the above have concentrated on the complex literary and philological aspects of Morante's work, offering acute and insightful readings of the author's individual texts and extensive, invaluable bibliographical and archival research. However, despite the cumulative interest to have been shown in Morante in recent years, there is still a need for a detailed examination of the interface between her literary creations and the much broader cultural perspective embraced by Morante's own writings. We aim to expand the scope of Morante criticism, open up new ways of reading her texts, and establish her critical and cultural legacy. In the light of new theoretical and critical studies, our volume thus looks at the literary structures and strategies adopted by Morante, tracing connections between the literary text and her system of ethics and aesthetics, connections that invite us to view Italian culture through the prism of her kaleidoscopic and multifaceted reflections.

New Approaches

In the monographic issue of *Narrativa*, Jean-Philippe Bareil's article, "Ricomposizione e ridistribuzione nell'opera di Elsa Morante: Svolgimento e concrezione," analyzes the most common critical tenets on Morante's presumed artistic d/evolution and considers her re-working of short stories and novelistic works from the beginning of her career to *Aracoeli*. Bareil focuses on her unfinished *Senza i conforti della religione* as representative of the self-imposed and excruciating task performed by the writer throughout her life, that of doing and undoing the thread of her novels. Cesare Garboli and Giovanna Rosa, in two different ways, organize Morante's career in different periodizations. Garboli, in his entire critical work on Morante, identifies *Menzogna e sortilegio* as a moment of breakthrough, while Rosa posits the fifteen years between *L'isola di Arturo* and *La Storia* as a moment of redefinition for the artist. Bareil notes how the short stories prior to *Menzogna e sortilegio* constitute its preparation, establishing a nexus between the two periods (9), while in the recent introduction to the *Racconti dimenticati* Garboli similarly admits the necessity of such stories to the first novel. Rosa, on the other hand, seems to neglect the presence of *Senza i conforti della religione* between the two novels, and does not fully justify or comment on its presence between 1957 and 1974.

The process of "historicization" of Morante's work thus, in Bareil's view, fails to acknowledge the dynamicity of her work. Rosa and Garboli define Morante's work as progressive, even if according to two different rhythms, and the problem becomes particularly acute when dealing with *Aracoeli*. Rather than progression, in Bareil's view Morante's working system can be more accurately conceived as a "concretion of thematics connected around a basic theme" (11), a way of reading that also permits a better comprehension of the crisis of the novelistic genre. With reference to Angelo Pupino's theories about the fable genre as the one allowing Morante to best express her fundamental philosophy, Bareil delineates, more than a "literary recycling," a circular view of literature in the author's work (12). As Cristina Della Coletta convincingly argues in her 1996 study of this novel, the circularity of the literary project fits the notion of history Morante demonstrates in *La Storia*, as well as time, defined within the circularity of the myth against the logical progression of history. This notion of "concretion" theorized by Bareil also allows us better to understand the autobiographical component in Morante's work, so often misunderstood and manipulated. Finally, as Bareil notes, "the circularity of the work is not, to use a psychiatric terminology, compulsive repetition. By definition, compulsion condemns the subject to death and Morante's work manifests an irreducible vitality" (13). It is this vitality in the face of darkness that younger writers instinctively feel and respect.

About This Book

The influence of Morante's aesthetic and ethics of writing has attracted younger Italian writers and poets, who see in her an alternative both to the orthodox literary establishment, to the dictates of left-wing cultural policy, and to the introversions of the avant-garde. While Morante managed successfully to subvert traditional literary codes without being identified exclusively with any of the artistic trends to dominate the decades during which she was writing, she also absorbed the tradition of literature in a production that is still today unique within the Italian panorama. One of the primary aims of this volume is to demonstrate the unusually canonical aspect of her legacy, capable of meshing the disruptive with the traditional. It is surprising that, in a literary context dominated by male figures such as pertains in Italy, the inheritance of her individual stylistic and thematic signature is becoming increasingly visible. With the decreasing polarization of Italian society and the weakening grip of ideological strictures, younger authors like Enrico Palandri, Fabrizia Ramondino, and Mariateresa Di Lascia see in Morante a figure immersed within a cultural and political position that she subverts from within; the title and epigraph of Simona Vinci's latest work, for example, *Come prima delle madri* (Turin: Einaudi, 2003) is taken from Elsa Morante's *Il mondo salvato dai ragazzini*. While addressing topics grounded in Italian society, such as family, relationships, sexuality, and geographical dislocation, Morante uncovers their distorted underbelly, dealing with themes rarely touched on before, such as homosexuality, incest, the logic of madness, class struggle, drugs, and finally ecology; in other words, the whole structure of the contemporary natural world that overlaps the *naturalità* of her characters, whether human or animal. In all these areas it is our contention that the anachronistic nature of Morante's work places her not behind, but ahead of her time. The almost prophetic quality of her writing is now being recognized and drawn on by younger generations.

While the purpose of this volume is to give readers a comprehensive insight into current thinking on, and understanding of, Morante's work, we also intend to situate this author, too often seen as an isolated genius, firmly within, and indeed at the center of, a range of cultural and intellectual contexts. Some contributors will thus examine Morante's quixotic and transformative adoption of traditional generic forms. Sharon Wood considers the ways in which Morante draws on and transforms earlier genres, such as the feuilleton, the epistolary novel, and that of traditional realism. Hanna Serkowska investigates the concept of the *ragazzo materno*, an expression coined by Morante herself. This search for an androgyny that is inclusive rather than reductive had already begun with her first novels and culminates in the intratextual work of *Aracoeli*, a novel that functions as a "summa" of the author's obsessive explorations of the world of adolescent emotional and sexual desire and excruciating struggle with her own narcissism. As well as novels, stories, and some essays, Morante also wrote prefatory pieces about the visual arts, such as "Il beato propagandista del Paradiso" (*Pro o contro* 119–38), and in this volume Marco Bardini analyses the author's lesser-known early writings on aesthetics and the arts. Starting with the 1938 essay "Mille città in una," Bardini uncovers the author's familiarity with a philosophical tradition in the line of Schopenauer and Nietzsche, as well as her fascination with the work of Sigmund Freud. Her posthumous publications reveal, on the other hand, a more intimate and overtly autobiographical aspect of her writing in which the feminine and the sexual emerge through transcription of dreams, as in *Diario 1938*. Elisa Gambaro discusses the critical difficulties created by the radical nature of this text, which, although published in 1989, has still received little attention. Gambaro suggests a critical approach to the diary, one that illuminates Morante's textual practice in her better-known works while overtly challenging previous feminist reductive readings of her texts. The critic underlines that *Diario 1938* avoids a rigid taxonomy of literary genres, subverting the tradition of autobiographical discourse.

Other contributors examine aspects of Morante's cultural legacy and outline the influence of her literary presence in contemporary Italian artistic culture. We wish, then, to reconsider her textual and intertextual practice, her preoccupation with a deconstruction of traditionalism versus modernism, and her powerful and enduring influence on younger writers through her novels, diaries, essays, and poetry. In 1995 Goffredo Fofi wrote a seminal article that for the first time underlined Morante's canonical importance, indicating those female authors who could be defined as her heirs ten years after her death. These were Mariateresa Di Lascia, Fabrizia Ramondino, and Elena Ferrante. Fofi states:

> Borrowing in particular from *Menzogna e sortilegio*, Di Lascia becomes a "border creature," one of those "unresolved creatures, who announce their hybrid identity from their very first appearance" (p. 22) which the narrator and protagonist evokes for herself at the moment in which she re-evokes, the moment of defeat and decadence [. . .] Di Lascia has chosen extraordinary "mothers," extraordinary and solitary. At the beginning of the novel we feel the weight of the first of these mothers, Morante herself, and we fear an imitation, but then this impression dissolves rapidly in the light of a vision and a way of writing which are completely autonomous. (43–44)

In this volume Concetta D'Angeli deals with the protean character of Morante's work and its subsequent influence. D'Angeli defines two lines of influence: the first is Morante's aesthetics and poetics, which are shared by Giorgio Montefoschi, Enrico Palandri, Patrizia Cavalli, and Carmelo Samonà. The second is a more formalistic *rapprochement* whose nature is more problematic given the extraordinary elements constituting Morante's style. Here D'Angeli discusses those same writers identified by Fofi, with a particular emphasis on the work of Samonà and Di Lascia.

In "*Teatro di guerra*: Of History and Fathers," Stefania Lucamante draws out the importance of the shared Southern origin of Morante and Ramondino, a common geography that underpins the theatrical staging of their family autobiographical fictions. Aside from stylistic and linguistic elements that parallel the two authors' sense of writing, the element of theater and, particularly, of war as an unneeded tragic theater, also perceived in the theater of family, is a common denominator in *Menzogna e sortilegio, La Storia, Althénopis, Guerra di infanzia e di Spagna*. The role of the father in these novels, where the notion of genre appears to be entirely reconceived, becomes a purely walk-on part, if not entirely non-existent, as it is strictly connected to the hypocrisy of patriotism, and a set of values that no longer holds any meaning.

The well-known novelist Enrico Palandri, engaged with Morante's artistic thought and literary practice, deals with the political side of Morante's writing, already in evidence in *La Storia*. It becomes more marked and urgent with the publication of *Pro o contro la bomba atomica e altri scritti*, and Palandri explores the roots of Morante's aesthetics in the philosophy of Plato, paying particular attention to the essays contained in *Pro o contro la bomba atomica* (and it should be emphasized that this is the only posthumous volume to have been approved by the author herself), which he sees as fundamental to a clear understanding of Morante's novelistic practice. With the secularization of thought that Morante recognized so distinctly, he locates the ethical imperative of her work in a metaphysical distinction between reality and unreality, philosophical concepts that have artistic correlatives in authenticity and mannerism. The writer has a clear moral role, a secular mission, in a world that risks losing any source of human value. In the historical context in which Morante found herself, these two parallel systems and possibilities are represented by the book and the bomb.

Walter Siti and Filippo La Porta investigate the intellectual exchanges between Morante and her great friend, the poet, novelist, and filmmaker Pier Paolo Pasolini. While Siti operates more on an intertextual territory that spans from *Edipo Re* to *Medea* but also to the love they share for the *ragazzini* ("kids"), La Porta deals with Pasolini's positive use of the term *barbarie* that the artist shared with Elsa Morante. This term is closely connected to another, fundamental to Pasolini's work, that of "unreality." For Morante, "the dragon of unreality" was an insidious enemy. It can coincide with consumer and materialist society, which aims to fill the void of the modern urban city, and takes on the garb of literature itself. Pasolini writes in fact that Morante's aim is "not literature, but an ethic-fantastic ideal, to which literature is handmaiden." Cristina Della Coletta similarly uncovers a resistance to the dominant humanistic culture in utopian space. Morante's narrative anomalies represent, according to Della Coletta, an alternative epistemology based on the dispersive economy of desire. Moving away from reductive feminist views of Morante's representation of women, Della Coletta investigates fractures and fissures in Morante's utopian space, which constitute a powerful resistance to patriarchal logic.

Morante's difficult rapport with her translations of a selection of Katherine Mansfield's *Collected Stories* is at the core of Nicoletta Di Ciolla McGowan's contribution to this volume. In this essay, Di Ciolla McGowan elicits the problematic deconstruction of gender in Morante's and Mansfield's short stories, and considers thematic and stylistic connections between the two authors. A further contribution by Marco Bardini also unveils the problematics of translation, this time with regard to the 1951 translation of *Menzogna e sortilegio* into English. An examination of *The House of Liars* reveals how gravely such a poor translation affected the reception and understanding of Morante's work in the United States and in the United Kingdom. Indeed it is our contention that Morante has not been particularly well served by her English translators over the years, and that her complete works should be made available in a new English translation.

Clearly it is impossible in a volume such as this to encompass all topics of interest, and points of connection, with Morante's work. Nonetheless, it is our hope that the new readings and approaches offered here, together with the attempt to remove the writer from the margins to the center of twentieth-century Italian literature in a hermeneutics that takes account of the political but eschews the ideological, will mark the beginning of a serious re-evaluation of Elsa Morante in the English-speaking literary and academic world.

Notes

Unless otherwise noted, all translations of quotations in this introduction are by the editors. Similarly, translations of the chapters by Marco Bardini, Concetta D'Angeli, Filippo La Porta, Hanna Serkowska, Enrico Palandri, and Walter Siti are by the editors.

1. We refer to the American translation of *Aracoeli,* where the birth date is given as 1916. See also the recent translation of *La Storia* by William Weaver, in which not only is the date of birth for the writer incorrect ("c. 1912"), but the title of the novel reads "*History: romanza*" in which the change of the final "o" into an "a" makes a substantial difference to the general tone of the novel. Some scholars may be aware of the correct date, but it is nevertheless important to assure exact information to the general readership.

2. For an exhaustive bibliography on Morante's first works, see Bardini 733–40.

Works Cited

Azzolini, Paola. "Mettersi al mondo, Elsa!" *Mettere al mondo il mondo. Oggetto e oggettività alla luce della differenza sessuale.* Diotima. Milan: La Tartatuga, 1990. 135–56.

Bareil, Jean-Philippe. "Ricomposizione e ridistribuzione nell'opera di Elsa Morante: Svolgimento e concrezione." *Elsa Morante: Narrativa* 17 (2000): 5–13.

Bardini, Marco. *Morante Elsa. Italiana. Di professione, poeta.* Pisa: Nistri-Lischi, 1999.

Berardinelli, Alfonso. "Il sogno della cattedrale. Elsa Morante e il romanzo come archetipo." *Narrativa* 17 (Feb. 2000): 15–26.

Camon, Ferdinando. "Il test della *Storia* (Letteratura di massa. Critica delle critica)." *Nuovi argomenti* 45–46 (1975): 186–239.

Cases, Cesare. "Un confronto con *Menzogna e sortilegio*." *Quaderni piacentini* 53–54 (1974) : 177–91.

Della Coletta, Cristina. "Fiction and Women's History: Elsa Morante's *La Storia.*" Ch. 3 of her *Plotting the Past: Metamorphoses of Historical Narrative in Modern Italian Fiction.* West Lafayette, IN: Purdue UP, 1996. 117–52.

Fofi, Goffredo. "I riti della memoria e del futuro: il romanzo di Mariateresa Di Lascia." *Linea d'ombra* 104 (May 1995): 43–44.

Frabotta, Biancamaria, ed. *Donne in Poesia: Antologia della poesia femminile in Italia dal dopoguerra a oggi.* Rome: Savelli, 1976.

———. "Fuori dall'harem: l'alibi di Elsa Morante." *Les femmes écrivains en Italie aux XIXe et XXe siècles. Actes du colloque international Aix-en-Provence, 14,15,16 novembre 1991.* Aix-en-Provence: Publications de l'université de Provence, 1991. 171–79.

Garboli, Cesare. "Elsa come Rousseau." *Il gioco segreto: Nove immagini di Elsa Morante.* Ed. Garboli. Milan: Adelphi, 1995. 221–26.

Giorgio, Adalgisa. "Nature vs. Culture: Repression, Rebellion and Madness in Elsa Morante's *Aracoeli.*" *Modern Language Notes* 109 (1994): 93–116.

Lucente, Gregory. "'Scrivere o fare . . . o altro'; Social Commitment and Ideologies of Representation in the Debates over Lampedusa's *Il Gattopardo* and Morante's *La Storia.*" *Italica* 61 (1984): 220–51.

Madrignani, Carlo. "Elsa l'inattuale." *L'Indice dei libri del mese* (Jan. 1996): 10.

Morante, Elsa. *Aracoeli.* Trans. William Weaver. New York: Random, 1984.

———. *Diario 1938.* Introd. Alba Andreini. Turin: Einaudi, 1989.

———. *History: A Novel.* Trans. William Weaver. South Royalton: Steerforth Italia, 2000.

———. *Opere.* Ed. Cesare Garboli and Carlo Cecchi. 2 vols. Milan: Meridiani Mondadori, 1988 and 1990.

———. *Pro o contro la bomba atomica e altri scritti.* Milan: Adelphi, 1987.

Pasolini, Pier Paolo. "L'isola di Arturo." *Il portico della morte.* Ed. Cesare Segre. Rome: Fondazione Pier Paolo Pasolini, 1980. 167–70.

Patrucco Becchi, Anna. "Stabat Mater: Le madri di Elsa Morante." *Belfagor* 48.4 (1993): 436–51.

Raboni, Giovanni. "Il libro di Elsa Morante." *Quaderni piacentini* 53–54 (1974) : 173–76.

Rosa, Giovanna. *Cattedrali di carta: Elsa Morante romanziere.* Milan: il Saggiatore, 1995.

Sinibaldi, Marino. "La storia e la politica: Gli analfabeti degli anni settanta." *Per Elsa Morante.* Milan: Linea d'ombra, 1993. 205–18.

Elisa Gambaro

Strategies of Affabulation
in Elsa Morante's *Diario 1938*

Elsa Morante's *Diario 1938*[1] was discovered among the
author's private papers and published posthumously in 1989.[2]
It is a text that even more than a decade after its first publication, continues to pose problems, raise questions, and above all
create a certain embarrassment within the Italian literary
establishment. The renewed critical attention Morante's writing has enjoyed in the past few years has not extended to this
text; critical studies of *Diario 1938* remain extremely rare, and
appear exclusively in the work of women scholars.[3] In this
chapter, I will suggest new critical perspectives on *Diario 1938*,
and illuminate some obscure twists and turns in the narrative
work of one of Italy's greatest twentieth-century authors.

Among the difficulties confronted by critics in dealing with
Diario 1938, the text's refusal to conform easily to a specific
genre weighs most heavily. Is it, indeed, a notebook of reflections on life, a book of dreams, or a visionary text? A biographical document, an intimate diary, or perhaps an epistolary
confession, as the apocryphal title restored in the second edition, *Lettere ad Antonio*, would seem to suggest? Indeed, like
much "women's writing," *Diario 1938* does not respect—and
rather deliberately resists—a rigid taxonomy of literary genres,
subverting and eluding the traditions of classic autobiographical discourse. Instead, in its use of metaphor, its nonlinear
structure, and its fragmented style, the oneiric writing of
Morante's diary seems close to the *écriture féminine* theorized
in French feminist thought forty years later, in the 1970s
(Hogan 95–99).

At its most literal, *Diario 1938* is the notebook in which the
twenty-six-year-old Elsa Morante transcribed her dreams. In

21

fact, the dream material powerfully dominates these pages: the sections not devoted to retelling dreams reveal a troubled quest for meaning in Morante's continual interrogation of dream images and figures, and of their disquieting effects. Morante's entries are unevenly distributed between her starting date of January 19 and the end date of July 30: while in the first months she writes regularly, entries become increasingly rare with the passing of time. Yet despite its apparent discontinuity, the *Diario 1938* should not be thought a text without shape or form. From the start, the strategic choices and deletions of the author, calculated to conceal the most awkward and delicate moments in the diary, repudiate any hypothesis of "trance" or automatic writing, bringing to light instead her precise control and organization of the material. This same conscious control over her material is evident in Morante's translation of her dreams into writing: the dream visions return with slight variations throughout the course of the diary, articulated in a tight metaphorical network of parallelisms and repetitions. Exemplary of this strategy are the images of the pink flowers, a feminine archetype, which, first announced in a dream of January 21, reappear in the last entry of July 30 to seal the diary: "Questa notte ho sognato i fiori rosa" ("Last night I dreamed about pink flowers").

This dynamic is evidence of a highly self-conscious narrative project. Yet here the narration of life is not shaped in accordance with a linear diegesis, but rather employs the circularity characteristic of the logic of the psyche. It must not be forgotten, moreover, that the *Diario* dates to a crucial moment in Morante's artistic development: it is precisely at the end of the 1930s that, following a long period of autodidactic apprenticeship, Morante refines a series of stylistic instruments and compositional forms that will prove of great relevance for the future development of her work. Her encounter with Freud's thought, to which the diary unequivocally attests, provides the young author with a fascinating representational strategy and an effective key by which to stylize the existential tensions in her narrative material (Rosa, *Cattedrali* 11). The four short stories published in *Il Meridiano di Roma* between 1937 and 1938[4] represent a first attempt in this direction: in a temporally undefined setting, charged with Kafkaesque allusions, but still retaining the dream-memory, all four texts focus on an epiphany in which the female protagonist becomes aware of her own identity as a woman. As Cesare Garboli has observed, in *Diario 1938* the quest for identity is configured as an investigation "dal e del profondo" ("Cronologia" xxx; "from and of the depths"). Morante resists the linear course of traditional autobiography, founded upon the centrality of a strong and unified subject. Rejecting universal abstracts on principle, she chooses a modality of self-representation that develops through the themes of desire and the discovery of the body. It is this choice that gives rise to the extraordinary fascination of the text, with its language immersed in the materiality of the female body:

> "[S]ento che mi sono sopravvenuti i mestrui. Un peso liquido, molle, caldo, fra le mie gambe, tutto mi pesa [. . .] arrivo, perdendo fiocchi di sangue di fra le gambe che pesano" (19 January); "ma io abbassando gli occhi vedo fra le sue gambe il suo sesso scoperto, dischiuso a causa della posa larga delle gambe, ed esso mi appare simile ad un piccolo campo grigio, un po' vizzo, con un lievissimo alone giallo" (22 January); "Ora anche coi sensi amo terribilmente A. I miei sensi non sono mai stati così, sempre all'erta, sempre morbidi" (24 January); "Negli intervalli svegli, continui pensieri di quella cosa. I miei fianchi si sciolgono per la morbidezza della mia voglia." (24 February)

> "I can feel that my period has started. A soft, hot, liquid weight, between my legs, everything weighs me down [. . .] I come, losing drops of blood from between my heavy legs" (19 January); "but looking down I see his uncovered sex between his legs, which he has spread wide, and it looks to me like a little grey field, a bit withered, with a very slight yellow halo" (22 January); "Now I love A. dreadfully with my senses, too. My senses have never been like this, constantly on the alert, constantly in flux" (24 January); "In the periods when I am awake, constantly thinking about that. My thighs melt with the sweetness of my desire." (24 February)

In consonance with a theoretical approach that values the role of corporeal morphology in the imaginary and the symbolic, Morante's writing seems therefore to evoke the celebrated figures of the viscosity assumed by French feminist thought to signify the specificity of female desire. Nevertheless, a substantial difference is evident: in open contrast with the *jouissance* celebrated by *l'écriture féminine*, the bodily images that recur in these pages possess neither value nor dignity. There is no trace here of any delight in, or veneration for, the experiences of women's bodies. On the contrary, Morante's meticulous deciphering of the incandescent tangle of her own drives is tinged with dramatic accents: anguish, humiliation, constraint and guilt dominate in this darkly shaded picture. Her quest for female identity continually clashes with a violent rejection of the female body and its incarnate materiality. Given the inherent contradictions in Morante's struggle to represent a female identity, it seems worth departing from a critical approach that simply seeks to evaluate Morante's work for its "feminism" or, as some might say, its lack thereof (Jeuland-Meynaud 300–12). Instead, I would argue that it is methodologically more profitable, as well as more rewarding from a critical perspective, to explore the deeper themes, the paradigms and the metaphors through which the female condition is represented in Morante's writing.[5] From this perspective, *Diario 1938* offers us a sort of "degree zero" in her representation of femininity: a femininity painfully wounded and unreconciled within itself, which, when reduced to its most coarse and earthy carnality, verges on anguish.

In Morante's diary, the driving contradiction of the self lies in its inscription: there is a silence in the text even as it speaks of the extremes of desire. This paradox relies for its representation upon the metaphoric formalization of the dream. Thus it is not surprising that, as in Morante's novels, oxymoron is the privileged rhetorical figure employed to articulate the conflicting movements of the psyche. In the same way, the tendency of concepts to find expression within dreams through a visual translation of their formal connections and abstract components unfold in *Diario 1938* as bizarre visions of amphibious creatures, half animal, half divine:

> C'è tutto un passato, una memoria che appartiene al sogno.
> Per esempio, in quello di stanotte io ero in possesso di uno
> strano pesce [. . .] Le specie zoologiche hanno un'altra

gerarchia nel sogno: quel mio pesce era un essere venerabile, quasi divino, mi ricordo che a momenti confondevo la sua persona con quella di Platone. [. . .] Era tutto chiazzato di sangue, e lungo il suo trascinarsi mi pareva dentro di me di sentire gridare che la carne si trascina, gli esseri insanguinati si trascinano. Tutti cosí. "Tutti!". Avevo la sensazione di altri simili a lui che lasciassero strie di sangue, e punture d'odio, di angoscia mortuaria. (23 January)

There is an entire past, a memory that belongs to dream. For example, last night I dreamt I had a strange fish [. . .] Zoological species have a different hierarchy in dream; this fish of mine was a venerable being, almost divine, I remember that at some points I confused it with Plato [. . .] It was splattered with blood, and as it dragged itself along I felt as though inside myself I could hear a voice calling out that flesh drags itself along, bloody creatures drag themselves along. All of them. "All of them!" I had the sensation of other creatures similar to him who left trails of blood, jags of hatred, of deadly anguish.

Here is another image of dreams:

Ieri, sognai Odradek: (novella di Kafka). Ero in una stanza con basse scansie di legno (collegata con la mia casa dell'infanzia, col sogno del pesce. Liana F. viene, le danno un posto in una mansarde, e cioè su un piano della scansia. [. . .] Ma Liana F. è Odradek, un essere piccolo come un gomitolo, e, a differenza di lui, è di carne squamosa, umiliata, senza forma. Mi dà la sensazione dolorosa che può dare un tumore, una crosta [. . .]. (14 February)

Yesterday I dreamed of Odradek (Kafka's novella). I was in a room with low wooden shelves (connected to my childhood home, with the dream of the fish). Liana F. comes, they give her a place in a garret, which was on one of the shelves [. . .] But Liana F. is Odradek, a creature as small as a ball of wool, and unlike him, she has scaly, humiliated, shapeless flesh. I have the same painful sensation that a tumor might give, or a scab.

In a famous essay on Kafka, Walter Benjamin observes that "Odradek is the form which things assume in oblivion. They are distorted" (133). In the same way, the young Morante, an avid reader of Kafka, recognizes in the past, the memory that belongs to dream, the dark nucleus of self. She does so, however, with one notable difference. While in Kafka's short story Odradek represents an ancestral guilt, the roots of which lie buried in the inscrutable depths of family history (to be more precise, ancestral guilt in relation to the Father), in Morante the same motif is instead defined in the feminine. Moreover, in Morante's dream not only is Odradek a woman (Liana F.), but she is no longer, as was the case in Kafka, a being formed from rigid material.[6] Instead, the analogue is a shapeless being. The connotations of viscosity, softness, and fluidity in Morante's account then transfer Odradek's Oedipal guilt to the pre-Oedipal sphere of the maternal.

As is clearly shown by the extraordinary frequency with which she appears in the diary pages, Morante's quest for identity as a woman is achieved through a series of painful confrontations with the mother. Always a cornerstone of Morante's imagination, the maternal figure finds its profound truth in dream, where the mother becomes a potent archetype of femininity. Yet the maternal is not hypostatized. The processes of condensation characteristic of dream logic lead the maternal figure to take on ambivalences and contradictions, resulting in a gender identity that appears perennially unstable.

In a convulsive movement that alternates specular identification with a position of distance, the mother oscillates between affectionate, positive connotations and threatening, castrating ones. On the one hand, she is the consoling, gentle face that bends to watch over her young daughter—on the other, she denies Elsa a symbolic feminine fecundity: "Il mio desiderio aumentava, tanto che ancora da sveglia mi è rimasto il senso della tenerezza molle, del dolce colore di quella pianta. Ma mia madre, avara, scuoteva il capo" (21 January; "My desire was increasing, so much so that even now I am awake I still feel that soft tenderness, the gentle color of that plant. But my mother, ungiving, was shaking her head"). While the dreamer obstinately seeks to appropriate a strong female identity for herself, simultaneously she fears this very identity, perceiving it to be founded in brute matter and, as such, suffocating. Thus it is not surprising that, in a later articulation of the metaphorical chain of the abject, Morante insists upon physical decay in her representation of the mother: she is "piccola, grossa, triste, vestita di nero" (2 February; "small, fat, sad, dressed in black"), her face and skin are tired, there are dark rings under her eyes, her blue eyes have faded, her hair is short, grey and untidy, her lips are pale. The mortuary connotations implicit in this vision of the maternal reach a high point of intensity in a dream of March 7:

> A un certo punto di questi sogni, vedendo nel riquadro di una finestra il corpo enfiato, il viso disfatto di mia madre, io, distesa a terra piú in basso in una specie di cortile, avevo un terrore spaventoso della morte [. . .] La morte mi appariva come un corpo squallido, gonfio e viscoso. Un affetto cupo mi attirava a mia madre, già possesso della bruttezza e del disfacimento che preparano per lunghi anni la fine della morte.

> At a certain point in these dreams, seeing framed within a window the swollen body and wrecked face of my mother, I, who was lying on the ground further down in a kind of courtyard, had a terrifying fear of death [. . .] Death appeared to me like a decayed body, swollen and viscous. A dark affection drew me toward my mother, already domain of that ugliness and falling apart that prepare us over long years for our end in death.

As critics have often noted, in Morante's writing of the maternal is a paradoxical construction: the mother is the source of life, but also a dark threat of death (Patrucco Becchi 436–40). This unresolved contradiction, made so explicit and visible in *Diario 1938*, runs as an undercurrent throughout all of Morante's novels to explode in all its violence at the chronological extremes of her creative trajectory. Thus, forty years after the drafting of the diary, the vicious destruction of Aracoeli's body in the anonymous novel figures the tragic conclusion of this process of the descent to the mothers, in order to discover the self (Rosa, *Cattedrali* 309). At the end of his journey to the Andalusian village where his mother was born, the protagonist Manuele will find only an inhospitable, desert-like expanse of ruins. The question that Morante invests with the supreme contradiction of her femininity ultimately finds only one response—silence and death.

> Di continuo, mi riappariva Aracoeli; anzi non proprio lei,
> ma l'oscuro suo corpo di carne, quale una caverna di stu-
> pendi misteri e di tenebre cruente [. . .] Era un focolaio di
> morbi? era una magione di Dio? forse, come una serpe, vi
> si torceva la morte? (*Opere* 2: 1310)

> Constantly, Aracoeli appeared to me; or rather, not exactly
> she, but her obscure body of flesh, like a cavern of stupen-
> dous mysteries and cruel shadows. [. . .] Was it a hotbed of
> diseases? Was it a house of God? Was death perhaps coiled
> there, like a serpent? (*Aracoeli* 204)

At the time of writing of *Diario 1938*, however, the trajectory of the quest for self is still at its beginning, and still far from the catastrophic results that will be made explicit in *Aracoeli*. Masterfully played out through this constitutive ambiguity, Morante's attempts at self-representation that emerge from the diary's shaded depths permit her to articulate a personal reper-tory of figures at an early point in her career. At the same time, it favors an original reflection on the oneiric roots of her own invention and on the reasons for her own creative writing.

As for many women writers of her time, for Morante, the pairing of femininity and writing is lived out in a dramatic sense—in a continuous tension between the desire for personal expression and overpowering guilt. In its most profound for-mulation, this discord implicates, once more, the figure of the mother: the materiality of the maternal body is sorrowful and mute, and the fantasies of death that surround it seem to pre-clude any attempt at linguistic expression as well as aspirations to an autonomous intellectual path.[7]

It is only by crossing this fantasmatic territory of her own unresolved desires that Morante can reach complete artistic expression. In these terms, the diary clearly marks a crucial point. Thus, the authentic interest Morante's diary holds exceeds mere inferences about the connections between life and art. One need not, in fact, postulate a direct or simple rela-tionship between personal writing and fiction. I would argue, instead, that the relationship between the diary and Morante's later fiction should be explored in terms of the role the precise textual strategies of self-representation play in her poetic development. Through her grasp of consciousness in the "miraculous" functioning of oneiric representation, the young

Morante discovers the specificity of a precocious tension toward literature. Operating on the same level as the dream, her creative writing draws its strength from the imaginative and metaphoric transposition of memory:

> Che miracolo il sogno! Ora capisco da dove è nata la grande e ombrosa cattedrale del mio. Ieri sera discorrendo dell'arte nel romanzo e nell'intreccio con V. ricordo di avere di sfuggita paragonato la costruzione del racconto ad un'architettura, a una cattedrale, le scene isolate alle vetrate. [. . .] Che il segreto dell'arte sia qui? *Ricordare* come l'opera si è vista in uno stato di sogno, ridirla come si è vista, cercare soprattutto di *ricordare*. Ché forse tutto l'inventare è ricordare. (23 January; emphasis in original)

> What a miracle dream is! Now I understand where that great and shadowy cathedral of mine came from. Yesterday evening talking about the art in the novel and in the plot with V. I remember making a fleeting comparison between the construction of a story and architecture, a cathedral, the scenes separated out in the windows. [. . .] Is this then the secret of art? *Remembering* as the work was seen in a state of dream, telling it as we have seen it, trying above all to *remember*. Because perhaps all inventing is in fact remembering.

Within the protean world of the nocturnal imagination, the recurrent figure of the cathedral assumes potent symbolic value, ultimately functioning as a metaphor for the storytelling process. What is a dream, moreover, if not a compact fantastic narrative, with its own rhetorical system, its own particular organization of time and space, its own characters?

From this perspective, *Diario 1938* helps to clarify the genesis of representational paradigms and narrative solutions in Morante's work that would otherwise remain at best eccentric or at worst problematic. It may be worth remembering that contemporary critics and reviewers responded to Elsa Morante's first novel, *Menzogna e sortilegio*, with perplexity and bewilderment, if not with a large degree of incomprehension. As long as the majority of writers and intellectuals remained focused on the concrete problems of Italy's social contradictions and the postwar future, perhaps Morante's fantasy-bound prisoner-characters, her complex narration, and her inscrutable settings,

Elisa Gambaro

suspended as they were somewhere between minute realism and unbridled imagination, were inevitably destined to be perceived as an obscure anomaly.

The representation of space, a category that typically constitutes a privileged axis in the fantastic elaboration of dreams, provides an exemplary case. The frequency with which the description of closed environments occurs as part of the diary's dream topology is striking. Most often, the theater of the dream's action is a room. And yet, what is striking is that the topos of the bedroom circumscribes an intense primary experience—most often, that of the body and of death. In the diary's first dream, transcribed on January 19, the object of desire is

> [. . .] una stanza incantevole, con mobili piuttosto vecchi, un po' provinciali, antichi damaschi, un piccolissimo letto sotto un accenno di alcova. [. . .] Questa camera odora davvero di adolescenza e di morte. Ma è un'ingiustizia che, così bella, rimanga disabitata. [. . .] La confronto con le mie camere buie; perché vivere qui e non là?

> [. . .] a delightful room, with furniture rather on the old side, a bit provincial, ancient damask, a tiny bed under a slight alcove [. . .] This room really has the smell of adolescence and of death; But it is not fair that beautiful as it is it should remain uninhabited [. . .] I compare it with my dark rooms: why live here and not there?

Yet when the legitimate owner of the room appears, the dreamer experiences a painful humiliation: not only has she violated a forbidden space, but also, tellingly, she cannot conceal the signs of her menstrual period.

Something not so different occurs in the dream of Odradek, cited above. There also, a notation of the setting precedes the dreamer's dramatic alignment with the corporeal. Following the same pattern of literary suggestiveness, a dream recorded shortly thereafter focuses on the death of Kafka. Again, the setting is scrupulously delineated: "Ho sognato che ero in una stanza che rassomigliava un poco al mio studio [. . .] contro la stessa parete della biblioteca c'era un letto, o meglio una culla tutta coperta di veli chiari. In quella culla lussuosa moriva Franz Kafka" (25 February; "I dreamed I was in a room that looked a little like my study [. . .] against the same wall of the bookcase there was a bed, or rather a crib, covered over with light voile. In that luxurious crib Franz Kafka lay dying"). Death fantasies connected with the maternal figure also take shape within closed bedrooms: "Ma ora sono in uno strano luogo. È una stanza altissima fra dirupi e precipizi. Siamo in molti, fra gli altri mia madre e mio fratello maggiore. [. . .] Tremo un po' per i miei, per mia madre, che, chi qua chi là, tutti sono tranquillamente sdraiati lungo orrendi dirupi" (2 February; "But now I am in a strange place. It's a very high room, precipices and crags all around. There are a lot of us, including my mother and my older brother [. . .] I fear for my family, for my mother, who are scattered around, lying down along horrendous precipices"). Through this articulated system of metaphoric refrains, the room is not only figured as a site of isolation and of solipsistic withdrawal, but becomes the stage for the mise-en-scène of Morante's most burning interior preoccupations, a sort of memorial to her deepest self.

It is difficult, at this point, not to think of *Menzogna e sortilegio*, where the storytelling process that forms the base for the entire novel takes shape within the closed walls of Elisa's tiny bedroom. Confined within her room for fifteen years, Elisa recalls her turbid family history. Her story, nevertheless, possesses none of the objective impartiality of a chronicle: germinating in the darkest meanderings of the psyche, her narration looks to the past through the subjective filter of memories and dreams.

In this sense, the structure of Morante's first novel exhibits a striking resemblance to her reflections on the analogous nature of oneiric representation and creative writing found in *Diario 1938*. If it is only by means of an investigation into the depths that the narrator can embark upon the backwards course of the quest for her own identity, it is only by lending an ear to the larval whispers of dream memory that Elisa is able to transform the untruthful patrimony of childhood daydreams into writing. In the words of the diary, perhaps invention is nothing other than memory.

It has been observed that Elisa's act of writing in *Menzogna e sortilegio* is a fulcrum for the entire machinery of the novel. The course of narrative and its spatial-temporal structure take shape in close dependence upon the storytelling process. The

claustrophobic plot, dominated by an invincible obsessive compulsion, finds its ultimate reason in Elisa's tyrannical mono-
logism and in her haughty separation from the world: "Il mio
tempo e il mio spazio, e la sola realtà che m'apparteneva, erano
confinati nella mia piccola stanza" (*Opere* 1: 22; "My time and
my space, and the only reality that belonged to me, were
confined within my little room"). Elisa's bedroom is emblematic of a clearly oneiric representational mode, where the
implications of memory reveal themselves to be more topo-
graphical than temporal. The vertical collocation of the room,
which is located within a block of apartments, ten floors high,
around a courtyard with high cement walls, reveals its affinity
with the high room amidsts crags and precipices of *Diario
1938*. Critics have analyzed the explicit psychoanalytic references of the motif of the room (Scarano) as well as its
intertextual derivations from the great Proustian model (Lucamante 58–67). While it condenses within itself a particularly
dense metaphoric weight, the room is a space appointed to the
solitary listening to the voices of the psyche and to their on-
going remembering. On the other hand—and the same will
occur with its variant *en plein air*, the island of Procida
enclosed by an azure sea—the room is also a symbol of the
inexhaustible metamorphic power of art and writing, of its
knowing representation of the deep past, and of the great
themes of existence (identity, the body, death) on the poly-
phonic stage of the novel. The recurring presence of this topos
in the pages of a text as intensely private as *Diario 1938* not
only emphasizes its intimate and primary significance to
Morante's work, but also reveals the way in which the author's
quest for personal identity and her writing are, from the start,
fatally intertwined in a cohesive system of representation.

Moreover, the pages of *Diario 1938* provide important clues
in relation to another structural constant of Morante's narrative: the construction of characters. The nocturnal imaginary
that emerges from the diary is indeed infested by a multiplicity
of figures. If their features are at times weak, at times intensely
vivid, Morante consistently sketches them with analytical
punctiliousness and passionate care. But it is especially the
sheer number of female figures that calls attention to their significance within the text. Among these, the figure of the mother

stands out, the maternal presence dominant in her sequence of guises. But also striking for their insistent recurrence are the visions of pre-pubescent and pubescent girls, marked by a still unripe and yet exuberant sensuality: on January 22 appears a slender, strong girl, leader of her own band, beautiful, her face shining and sharp, two black plaits wound around her head. The character is sketched with the crudity that the oneiric imagination seldom holds back: lowering her eyes, the dreamer can make out "il suo sesso scoperto, dischiuso a causa della posa larga delle gambe" ("her uncovered sex, opened up by her wide-spread legs"). Nor is this an isolated case: in a dream transcribed on March 7, "alcune bambine compaiono per fare un ballo [. . .] Si mettono in pose un po' sfacciate, a momenti anche sguaiate, ridono e fanno esercizi in disordine, sollevano le gambe" ("some girls appear, to have a dance [. . .] they strike poses that are shameless, even whorish at times, they laugh and do their exercise raggedly, they lift their legs").

Once more, the intensity of female erotic desire appears in conjunction with its negation, through the drives of censorship and guilt. On February 18, the disturbing but radiant figure of the sexually uninhibited little girl explicitly reveals its dark side: this time, the young girl who appears to be no more than twelve years old has become, indeed, "una piccola prostituta." It is not by chance that the motif of physical decay returns here. It runs under the surface, threatening the vitality of the woman's body. Expressed in physical terms (her face is a little wizened, ugly) it insidiously returns through the metaphors that form the dream's language, where words and things become one and the same, condensed into images of strong visual impact: "Ma ora vedo che questa ragazza è chiusa dentro una farmacia portatile, una specie di gabbia di vetro con ripiani e bottigliette. ("Per le malattie veneree" penso "Dio mio, dover diventare addirittura una farmacia ambulante")" ("But now I can see that the girl is shut up inside a portable chemist's, a kind of glass cage with shelves and bottle. ["For venereal disease" I think, "My God, the idea of having to become a walking pharmacy."]")

But the critical interest of *Diario 1938*'s female characters lies in more than these expressions of an eroticism as vital as it is ferociously repressed: for, if the discourse were limited itself to the repressed sexual content, it would remain unclear how

Elisa Gambaro

Morante's self-analytic investigation could prefigure such rich and complex narrative developments. *Diario 1938* proves rather that, from the start, Morante's narrative imaginary is deeply grounded in a precise sociohistorical discourse. In these representations of young girls, there is a palpable sense of accentuated malevolence, one might almost say of envy. If the motif of competition with younger women appears frequently in the diary, the spite that animates the description of the little girls in the dream is nurtured not only by Morante's rejection of her own femininity, but also by her acute sense of humiliation and social inferiority. The portrait restored to us by *Diario 1938* is that of a young woman oppressed by solitude and constantly beset by financial worries. Her existence is "wretched," she lives in a rented room (and much more could be said about this isolated space, so characteristic of the writing of much modernist women's literature),[8] she suffers bitterly from her petit-bourgeois condition. The descriptions of "costumi piuttosto rimediati" ("rather shabby dresses") worn by the dancing girls or of the blue fox on the shoulders of the little prostitute (who shows, notably, "quella prosopopea delle donne che hanno vestiti, davanti alle altre che non ne hanno, anche se sono migliori di loro" ("self-importance of women who have clothes in the presence of those who don't, even when these other women are better than them") are marked by the same acrimony that will embitter the voice of the petit-bourgeois Elisa De Salvi's derision of the social ambitions of her parents and of the "provincialnobilucci," the minor provincial aristocrats, the Cerentano family.

This intersection of sexual humiliation and class inferiority, reflected on a biographical level by Morante's troubled love affair with Alberto Moravia,[9] opens up interpretative implications of much greater import and brings into focus the strategic relevance of the diary. Condensed in the dream, repressed sexual content is fused with this social envy. Among the conquests of Morante's painful self-analytical exploration, thus, can be numbered the awareness of the indissoluble connection that ties the self's interior concerns to the historical dynamic of an entire class—and more precisely, to that of the lower middle class, which finds in its condition of socioeconomic inferiority inexhaustible material for its own self-destructive deliriums.

The clues given by *Diario 1938* are particularly helpful in resolving the enigmas *Menzogna e sortilegio* posed its first readers. They may also provide the key to clarifying the terms of a still on-going debate as to the definition (realist or intimate? Nineteenth or twentieth century?) of Morante's masterpiece. The apparent aporia between the obscure psychological mutability of the characters and the rigid social determinism that governs events, so striking to readers in the midst of Neorealism, has the merit of identifying a lack of sense that asks to be filled. This dynamic informs the entire plot of the novel, so that the more the characters are constrained to tragically determined social roles, the more they give free rein to bizarre behavioral metamorphoses, apparently devoid of objective foundation. The author's comments on the manuscript of *Menzogna e sortilegio* attest to her reluctance to give overly explicit explanations as to the ultimate forces driving the story. The unsaid is thus knowingly inscribed in the genesis of the text, governing its creative mechanisms, including the formal shape and structure. It is not surprising, then, that the morphology of the figures reflects this most visibly: the burden of repressed psychic content lies on the shoulders of the troubled characters of the "cronache familiari," as the conflicts of desire are mixed with the impact of a vast historical trajectory.

The hypothesis that the text speaks through that which it denies, through the gaps and silences within its surface, finds corroboration in the way in which a historically marginalized subjectivity like that of the feminine bears witness in writing to a latent conflict that emerges from silence. The "intersubjective, reflexive potency of self inscription" (Donnell and Polkey xxii) is moreover confirmed by the symptomatic presence in Morante's diary of a Catholic symbolism shot through with an acute sense of sin. It is almost superfluous to say that these images are incarnated, once more, in apparitions of women. Nevertheless, like the characters of *Menzogna e sortilegio*, these figures are endowed with a striking figural density, capable of representing not only the explosive content of psychic drives, but also an extraordinary constellation of silenced cultural, social, and personal motifs. This is the enormous responsibility that Elsa Morante assigns to the feminine.

Elisa Gambaro

In the fresco that depicts the female condition in virtually its entire biological trajectory, "dall'infanzia alla decrepitezza" ("from infancy to decrepitude"), repeated visions of old women, and of nuns in particular, stand out in *Diario 1938*. Emblematic of a non-procreative and non-erotic femininity, they are "le addette ai castighi" ("assigned to punishment"), the sadistic representatives of censorship and guilt par excellence.

The typology of *sterilità* will be fully developed in all its devastating implications only in the final phase of Morante's production, in particular in the catastrophic picture of *Aracoeli*. Nevertheless, it already appears crucial from Morante's first writings, where it is figured in the recurrent figures of the crone and the grandmother. Overcome by physical decline and burdened by a *pesanteur* without remedy, the old woman appears at the opposite pole with respect to the grace of adolescence and of femininity in flower in Morante's imaginary. Yet the stringent symmetry of the two figures induces the suspicion that in fact they represent just one archetypal image—a child-crone possessed of an irreconcilable physiognomy. In this contradictory binary that delineates both fecundity and sterility, as well as the antinomy of an expressed and negated desire, the paradox of a feminine identity is embodied without simple resolution.

This schizophrenic modality of self-representation, which regulates the entire diary's discourse, constitutes, on a parallel level, the emerging model of the functioning of the psyche, confirming the constitutive double logic of the unconscious. (Morante, "Una duplicità senza soluzione" 126). Transposed within the socializing coordinates of literary creation, this paradigm will reveal its susceptibility to more subtle and complex imaginative developments, which these elementary psychic schematics here herald. The diary illuminates, in this sense, a genetic nucleus of Morante's fantasy that will see a gradual narrative growth through solutions and figures of increasing complexity. The night scene that opens "Il ladro dei lumi," a short story from 1935 that belongs to Morante's "pre-history," is representative of an initial stage. The dim light that weakly filters in from the outside illuminates two female figures, a child and an old woman. Morante plays on the effects of chiaroscuro: the features of the small protagonist remain indistinct, so that the undercurrent of antagonism in relation to her decrepit, grim grandmother is confounded within the still uncertain focalization of the narrating voice. With a symptomatically circular movement, the story closes by reaffirming the primordial indistinctiveness of the borders of the feminine "I," an "I" that is characterized only by its belonging to a matrilineal genealogy: "e quella ragazzina fui io, o forse mia madre, o forse la madre di mia madre" (*Opere* 1: 1414; "and that small girl was me, or maybe my mother, or maybe my mother's mother").

A later short story, "La nonna," exhibits a narrative construction indicative of the direction Morante's invention will take. In this case, the sadistic and repressive connotations of the Morantian sterile woman are brought into focus by a daring plot, as, consumed by a fierce jealousy of her daughter-in-law, the grandmother murders her two small grandchildren. This murder is most particular, emphasizing the strong meta-narrative component: bewitched by the fantastic stories of the old woman, the two children are pushed to the edge of the river, which drags them away in a tragic epilogue that becomes a metaphor of the literary word's innate power of seduction. The theme of the untruthful sublimation of literature (found once again in "Il gioco segreto") could not be expressed more vividly.[10] Storytelling's consolatory compensations, play and liberation, are revealed to be doubly treacherous as they recall the prohibited weight of a primordial repression. The writing of Elisa, also obedient to the whisper of her ancestors ("il biobiglio degli avi"), will find itself imprisoned within a similar contradiction.

It is not by chance that a figure so rich in connotation as that of the sterile old woman, should surface within the network of the diary's textual refrains and the short stories of "Il Meridiano di Roma" to take up a strategic place in Morante's first novel. In "Via dell'Angelo," a short story composed at the same time as the diary, the convent setting forms the background for the protagonist's first troubled rush of sensual feeling. Morante avails herself here openly of the oneiric memory, as her descriptions of the nuns-jailors who oppress the young Antonia coincide almost literally with the portraits of religious women that appeared in her diary dreams.

Elisa Gambaro

If the Morante of the *Diario 1938* ostensibly exhibits a defensive ignorance of the deeper implications of her dreams ("E la suora? Perché una suora e non un uomo? Perché sempre donne?" ("And the nun? Why a nun and not a man? Why always women?") she asks herself in an entry on January 23, yet she does not disregard the enormous figural potential offered by her own painful investigation of the territory of the unconscious.

> Da dove vengono i personaggi dei sogni? Intendo dire non quelli che, piú o meno vagamente e fedelmente, raffigurano i personaggi della nostra vita diurna, ma gli altri, gli ignoti. Ed alcuni (ad es. quella suora della cattedrale) hanno un carattere ben delineato, umano. Sono vere e proprie *creazioni artistiche*. (25 January; emphasis in original)

> Where do the characters in dreams come from? I don't mean those who more or less vaguely or faithfully act as figures for the characters in our daily lives, but the others, the ones we don't know. And some (i.e., that nun in the cathedral) have a human, well-delineated character. They are really *artistic creations*.

Following this path of maximum semantic approximation between the dreamed and the narrated, it is still the oneiric image of the nun, with her lined face and rapid movements, who is superimposed onto the withered features of the old woman with a "faccia scarna, bruciata e fitta di rughe" ("bony face, sunburned and covered in wrinkles"), with her swift, nervous movements, the protagonist of "La nonna." But in the short story, the portrait of the matriarch appears to be constructed on the constant replication of a detail of her clothing: the "stivalini lucidi" ("shiny little boots") worn "con civetteria" ("coquettishly") under the shapeless country dress. I do not believe that it is by chance that in *Menzogna e sortilegio*, the family chronicles of Elisa that open with the figure of the maternal grandmother, depart from the intense recollection of precisely the same detail: "Debbo ritornare ai miei primi anni per trovarla; e allora, eccola, essa è là seduta sulla sua sedia di paglia in un angolo della cucina. La cosa che prima rivedo sono i suoi stivalini" (*Opere* 1: 42; "I have to go back to my earliest years to find her; and then, see, there she is, sitting in her straw-bottomed chair in a corner of the kitchen. First I see again her high shoes [. . .]"; *House of Liars* 23). It should not be forgotten that the first draft of the novel, begun in 1941, carried the significant title *Vita di mia nonna*.

On the threshold of the imposing novelistic cathedral of *Menzogna e sortilegio*, the anamnesis of the smallest splinter of repression can activate a complex storytelling process, where the movement backwards along a matrilineal genealogy unfolds with an ornate sumptuousness directly proportional to the surfacing of the unsaid. Intimately constructed from "that negation which affirms by negating, that in the very act of defending its secret reveals it" (Orlando 213), Elsa Morante's first novel is nourished by a private model of thought that lacerates the fabric of rational logic in order to explore the unreconciled tensions of the mind.

And yet, it is only by conforming to the exchange implicit in literary mediation that "i personaggi del sogno, [. . .] che sono per me sentimenti" (*Diario* 14 March; "the characters of dream [. . .] which are for me feelings") can be transmuted into figures capable of incarnating the profound concerns of all of us. The capricious protagonists of the epic *Menzogna e sortilegio* figure the radical and uncontrolled explosion of conflicting drives, but this same ambivalence governs the entire system of Morante's work. It asks insistently to fill an emptiness, to bring back to life that which has been oppressed and silenced. It is not for nothing, then, that in *Menzogna e sortilegio* Elisa's appeals for the reader's collaboration grow more dense precisely in those places where the elusive figure of Edoardo Cerentano, the alter ego and desiring projection of Elisa, appears. The spirit that decides the destiny of each character, moving the entire plot of the novel and incarnating "[. . .] la grazia celeste dell'ambiguità" (*Opere* 1: 778; "[. . .] the celestial grace of ambiguity"), he is also the only one of the ghosts to hide his face. In this silence, which conceals "la più generosa, e patetica, anzi teneramente tragica fra tutte le ipotesi possibili" (*Opere* 1: 282; "the most generous, full of pathos, and indeed tenderly tragic of all possible hypotheses") Morante plays out a project of imaginative self-representation, long cherished and developed over time. Before deteriorating definitively into a mistrust of her public, the communicative urge of Morante's

Elisa Gambaro

storytelling was as radical as it was generous, yearning for self-recognition in each reader. It is the same self-recognition process that Morante's characters feel within her fiction: their destiny in "Il gioco segreto" is the most telling epigraph to Morante's diaristic efforts toward self-inscription.

> Egli partecipò ai fratelli la sua scoperta e, tutti e tre, credettero di identificare le persone dei libri con le figure che popolavano i muri e i soffitti del palazzo e che, vive da tempo in loro, ma nascoste nei sotterranei della loro infanzia, ora tornavano alla luce. (*Opere* 1: 1467)

> He let his brothers in on his discovery and they believed, all three of them, that they could identify the characters from the books with the figures that populated the walls and ceilings of the house and that, for a long time alive within them but hidden in the subterranean territory of infancy, were now returning to the light.

Notes

1. I would like to thank Rebecca Wright for her helpful and diligent revision of my study.

2. With the revised (and original) title of *Lettere ad Antonio, Diario 1938* was reprinted in the second volume of Morante's *Opere* (1575–1628). This is the only unified diary of Elsa Morante known to us. For traces of other unpublished diaries, drafted but unfinished, see Garboli, "Cronologia" (Morante, *Opere* 1: ix–xc). Some pages of a 1952 diary, also unfinished, can be found in *Paragone letteratura* 39 (1988), 7 (456): 6–16.

3. See Andreini, Prefazione (vii–xii) to *Diario 1938* and "L'autobiografia di Elsa Morante: tra diario e romanzo." See also Rosa, "*Menzogna e sortilegio*. Il 'libro dei sogni' di Elsa Morante"; Contini, "Il primo diario di Elsa Morante"; and Porciani, "Racconto del sogno e metodo della finzione nelle *Lettere ad Antonio* di Elsa Morante."

4. The four short stories are as follows: "L'uomo dagli occhiali," "La nonna," "Il gioco segreto," and "Via dell'Angelo." The last three will come together in the collection *Il gioco segreto* and all will later be reprinted in *Lo scialle andaluso*. See Contini, "Elsa Morante: autoritratti d'autrice. Dal 'Meridiano di Roma' allo *Scialle Andaluso*."

5. I follow the methodological paradigm elaborated by Sharon Wood: "What interests me about Morante's writing is the possibility of looking at it not as an example of female self liberation, not for its positive images of heroic and self-fulfilling and self-fulfilled women, nor for its gratifying portrait of the female half of the sky. It is more rewarding to look at her work not as feminist but as female narrative, which moves beneath the surface of wish-fulfillment and conscious gratification to reach the deeper territory of unexpressed and inexpressible desire which more often than not cannot speak its own name" ("Bewitched Mirror" 312).

6. "At first glance it looks like a flat, star shaped spool for thread, and indeed it does actually seem to be wound with thread; or rather, with what appear to be just odds and ends of old thread, of the most various kinds and colours, all knotted together and even tangled up with one another. But it is not simply a spool, for projecting from the middle of the star is a small wooden crossbar, and to this another little bar is attached at a right angle. By means of this latter bar on one side and one of the points of the star on the other, the whole thing is able to stand upright as if on two legs" (Kafka, "A Problem for the Father of the Family" 176).

7. "A dead mother is a trope for textlessness, a way of speaking the unspeakable, a way of inscribing a silencing, a failure, or a repression of the female speaking/writing subject" (Kloepfer 15).

8. The topos of the hotel room or rented room, emblem of the precariousness of life and of the social isolation of the woman who writes, is recurrent in the work of modernist authors such as Katherine Mansfield and Jean Rhys. For the relationship between the estranged modality of representation of space and the sociocultural conditions of the woman writer, see Gilbert and Gubar, *Madwoman* 79; Hornel and Zlosnik 13–20.

9. Chronologically, *Diario 1938* covers the beginnings of Elsa Morante's relationship with Moravia. As the diary attests, the sense of social inferiority felt by Morante in relation to her companion is a significant element in the tumultuous course of their love affair: "Ieri dev'essere stata per me una giornata piena di soffocate umiliazioni. In tal modo spiego i sogni stanotte. A. è infatti uno snob, e io vorrei soddisfare con la mia persona il suo snobismo, avendo per esempio, un'alta posizione sociale o essendo illustre. Niente di tutto questo è" (28 January; "Yesterday it must have been for me a day full of repressed humiliations. This is how I explain my dreams tonight. A. is in fact a snob, and I would like to satisfy his snobbery with my person, holding for instance, a high social standing, or being illustrious. Nothing of that sort exists"). On the relevance of this theme in relation to Morante's work, see Rosa ("Ovvero: il romanziere" 72–76).

10. For a different reading of the short story see McDonald Carolan.

Works Cited

Andreini, Alba. "L'autobiografia di Elsa Morante: tra diario e romanzo." *Storia e problemi contemporanei* 17 (Apr. 1996): 91–101.

Andreini, Alba. Prefazione. *Diario 1938*. By Elsa Morante. Torino: Einaudi, 1989. vii–xii.

Bardini, Marco. "Dei 'fantastici doppi' ovvero La mimesi narrativa dello spostamento psichico." *Per Elisa* 173–299.

———. *Morante Elsa. Italiana. Di professione, poeta*. Pisa: Nistri-Lischi, 1999.

———. "Spazi, direzioni e gerarchie in *Menzogna e sortilegio*." *Linguistica e letteratura* 26.1–2 (1991): 123–53.

Benjamin, Walter. *Illuminations*. Ed. Hannah Arendt. Trans. Harry Zohn. London: Collins, 1970.

Benstock, Shari, ed. *The Private Self: Theory and Practice of Women's Autobiographical Writings*. Chapel Hill and London: U of North Carolina P, 1988.

Berardinelli, Alfonso. "Il sogno della cattedrale: Elsa Morante e il romanzo come archetipo." *Per Elsa*. 11–33.

Bunkers, Suzanne L., and Cynthia A. Huff, eds. *Inscribing the Daily: Critical Essays on Women's Diaries*. Amherst: U of Massachusetts P, 1996.

Cixous, Hélène. *"Coming to Writing" and Other Essays*. Ed. Deborah Jenson. Trans. Sarah Cornell. Cambridge: Harvard UP, 1991.

Contini, Gabriella. "Elsa Morante: autoritratti d'autrice. Dal "Meridiano di Roma" allo *Scialle Andaluso*." *Annali della Facoltà di Lettere e Filosofia, Università di Siena* 14 (1993): 163–75.

———. "Il primo diario di Elsa Morante." *Allegoria* 11 (1992): 91–99.

Cordati, Bruna. "*Menzogna e sortilegio*: lo spazio della metamorfosi." *Paragone* 450 (1987): 57–87.

Donnell, Allison, and Pauline Polkey, eds. *Representing Lives: Women and Auto / biography*. New York and London: Macmillan, 2000.

Evans, Annette. "The Fiction of Family: Ideology and Narrative in Elsa Morante." *Theory and Practice of Feminist Literary Criticism*. Ed. Gabriela Mora and Karen S. Van Hooft. Ypsilanti, MI: Bilingual, 1982. 131–37.

Finucci, Valeria. "The Textualization of a Female 'I': Elsa Morante's *Menzogna e sortilegio*." *Italica* 65 (1988) : 308–28.

Gallop, Jane. *The Daughter's Seduction: Feminism and Psychoanalysis*. Ithaca: Cornell UP, 1982.

Garboli, Cesare. "Cronologia." *Opere*. By Elsa Morante. Vol. 1. Milan: Mondadori, 1988. ix–xc.

———. *Il gioco segreto. Nove immagini di Elsa Morante*. Milan: Adelphi, 1995.

Gilbert, Sandra, and Susan Gubar. *The Madwoman in the Attic: The Woman Writer and the Nineteenth Century Imagination*. New Haven: Yale UP, 1979.

————. *No Man's Land: The Place of the Woman Writer in the Twentieth Century*. 3 vols. New Haven: Yale UP, 1988, 1989, 1990.

Hogan, Rebecca. "Engendered Autobiographies: The Diary as a Feminine Form." *Prose Studies* 14.2 (1991): 95–107.

Hornel, Avril, and Sue Zlosnik. *Landscapes of Desire: Metaphors in Modern Women's Fiction*. New York: Harvester Wheatsheaf, 1990.

Irigaray, Luce. *Ce sexe qui n'en est pas un*. Paris: Editions de Minuit, 1977.

Jeuland-Meynaud, Maryse. "Le identificazioni della donna nella narrativa di Elsa Morante." *Annali di italianistica* 7 (1989): 300–24.

Kafka, Franz. "A Problem for the Father of the Family." *Metamorphosis and Other Stories*. London: Penguin, 1992.

Kloepfer, Deborah. *The Unspeakable Mother: Forbidden Discourse in Jean Rhys and H.D. [Hilda Doolittle]*. Ithaca: Cornell UP, 1989.

Lucamante, Stefania. *Elsa Morante e l'eredità proustiana*. Fiesole: Cadmo, 1998.

Matte Blanco, Ignacio. *The Unconscious as Infinite Sets: An Essay in Bi-Logic*. London: Duckworth, 1973.

McDonald Carolan, Mary Ann. "The Missing Mother: Procreation vs. Creation in Morante's Early Fiction." *Rivista di studi italiani* 12.1 (June 1995): 100–17.

Morante, Elsa. *Aracoeli*. Trans. Wiliam Weaver. New York: Random, 1984.

————. *Diario 1938*. Introd. Alba Andreini. Turin: Einaudi, 1989.

————. "Una duplicità senza soluzione. 'Dieci voci per il silenzio.'" *L'Europa letteraria* (1964): 126.

————. *House of Liars*. Trans. Adrienne Foulke with ed. assistance from Andrew Chiappe. New York: Harcourt, 1951.

————. *Opere*. Ed. Cesare Garboli and Carlo Cecchi. 2 vols. Milan: Mondadori, 1988 and 1990.

Nava, Giuseppe. "Il "gioco segreto" di Elsa Morante: i modi del racconto." *Studi novecenteschi* 21.47–48 (1994): 53–78.

Orlando, Francesco. *Per una teoria freudiana della letteratura*. Turin: Einaudi, 1992.

Patrucco Becchi, Anna. "Stabat mater. Le madri di Elsa Morante."
    Belfagor 31 (July 1993): 436–51.

Per Elisa. Studi su "Menzogna e sortilegio." Pisa: Nistri-Lischi, 1990.

Per Elsa Morante. Milan: Linea d'ombra, 1993.

Porciani, Elena. "Racconto del sogno e metodo della finzione nelle
    Lettere ad Antonio di Elsa Morante." *Sogni di carta. Dieci studi
    sul sogno raccontato in letteratura.* Ed. Anita Piemonti and
    Marina Polacco. Firenze: Le Monnier, 2001. 120–35.

Rosa, Giovanna. *Cattedrali di carta. Elsa Morante romanziere.* Milan:
    Il Saggiatore, 1995.

———. *"Menzogna e sortilegio.* Il 'libro dei sogni' di Elsa Morante."
    Linea d'ombra (Jan. 1990): 25–27.

———. "Ovvero: il romanziere." *Per Elsa Morante.* 55–87.

Scarano, Emanuella. "La 'fatua veste' del vero." *Per Elisa.* 95–171.

Simons, Judy. *Diaries and Journals of Literary Women: From Fanny
    Burney to Virginia Woolf.* London: Macmillan, 1990.

Smith, Sidonie. *Subjectivity, Identity and the Body: Women's Autobio-
    graphical Practices in the Twentieth Century.* Bloomington:
    Indiana UP, 1993.

Stanton, Domna C. "Difference on Trial: A Critique of the Maternal
    Metaphor in Cixous, Irigaray and Kristeva." *The Poetics of
    Gender.* Ed. Nancy K. Miller. New York: Columbia UP, 1986.
    157–82.

Wood, Sharon. "The Bewitched Mirror: Imagination and Narration in
    Elsa Morante." *Modern Language Review* 86. 2 (1991): 310–
    21.

———. "The Deforming Mirror: Histories and Fiction in Elsa Morante
    (1912–85)." *Italian Women's Writing. 1860–1994.* London:
    Athlone, 1995. 152–68.

Zago, Esther. "Il carattere di stampa come segno ne lo *Scialle Andaluso*
    di Elsa Morante." *Il lettore di provincia* 81 (1991): 33–40.

Nicoletta Di Ciolla McGowan

Elsa Morante, Translator
of Katherine Mansfield

The year 1948, with the appearance of *Menzogna e sortilegio*, marks a significant turning point in Morante's literary trajectory. It is the year when, after decades of fragmented and often *ad hoc* collaboration with papers and periodicals, to which she contributed articles and short stories, Morante published her first novel. *Menzogna e sortilegio* was an ambitious project, one that revealed to the reader Morante's stylistic maturity and poetic vision, and to Morante herself her own true vocation: indeed, after its publication she effectively disowned all her previous writings.

The decades up to 1948 were referred to by Morante, in the afterword appended to the collection *Lo scialle andaluso*, as "fase preistorica"—hence, a period historically located outside the "officially" recognized boundaries, a kind of laboratory in which the author sharpened and tested her creative tools in preparation for the later display of talent that were the novels. Nevertheless, they contain a number of significant writings that already reveal the author's inventiveness and narrative abilities.

Elsa Morante wrote, in fact, from an extremely young age. Her urge to write, as she significantly stated, "nacque, si può dire, insieme a me" (Garboli and Cecchi, in Morante, *Opere* 1: xx; "was born, we might say, when I was born"). *Le bellissime avventure di Caterì dalla trecciolina*, written when the author was 13, was followed by a vast number of short stories, often appearing, feuilleton fashion, in installments in papers and magazines. The first collection, *Il gioco segreto*, was published by Garzanti in 1941; this was followed in 1963 by a second collection, *Lo scialle andaluso*, which incorporated a selection of the stories of *Il gioco segreto* together with more recent production. In 1945, long after financial constraints had ceased to have an influence on the direction of her literary efforts, Morante cooperated in the translation of an anthology of the short stories and *Journal* of Katherine Mansfield (1888–1923), which were published by Rizzoli and Longanesi respectively, and reappeared together in a single volume in 1957. Although translating foreign authors was not an uncommon practice for Italian writers, I would argue that, in Elsa Morante's case, the transposition of Mansfield's writings into Italian was more than a simple editorial operation. It may have been dictated by an artistic affinity, a shared ethics and aesthetics of literature, as well as an analogous sensibility. Working on this assumption, the instance of a "compulsive" writer such as Morante, who has finally and declaredly rid herself of the necessity for commission work and who has acquired the new luxury of being able to dedicate herself completely to her own creativity,[1] nevertheless taking on the task of translating into Italian the works of an Anglophone writer, begs further investigation. Curiously, neither the 1945 nor the 1957 edition of Mansfield's translations included "The Man without a Temperament," a story that Mansfield wrote in 1920 and which was intriguingly, and explicitly, echoed twenty-one years later by Morante's own "Un uomo senza carattere." Yet "Un uomo senza carattere," which was originally published in *Il gioco segreto*, survived the ruthless decimation operated by Morante on the *fase preistorica* materials, and successfully made it to *Lo scialle andaluso* in 1963. These two short stories will become the focal point of the analysis of the numerous and significant links between Elsa Morante and the writer from New Zealand.

Katherine Mansfield's engagement with the short story form is to a large extent a reflection of the cultural and intellectual climate at the beginning of the twentieth century. The sense of despair and the loss of hope produced by the emerging Schopenhauerian and Nietzschean philosophical currents—Schopenhauer's pessimistic rejection of the value of life and denial of will, Nietzsche's theory of the death of God, among others—and by rapid and radical social, political, and technological changes, had shaken the foundations of a cultural praxis based on certainties and logic. In literature, this new attitude manifested itself in the rejection of the realist novel—representation of a finite, knowable, and inscribable reality, ruled by the tenets of linearity, logic, and causality—in favor of the short story, epitome of the new fragmented subjectivity.[2] The void left by the collapse of axiomatic truths was partly filled by the artist's imagination and insight, which were the means of achieving the only conceivable, if transient, moments of revelation—what Joyce later defined as "epiphany." Built not on actions but on atmospheres, moods, and impressions, with a format inspired by brevity and conciseness, and no longer based on the epic architectures of the tradition, the short story was the narrative form that best expressed the Modernist *Weltanschauung;* here the elusiveness and the immanence of an ever-changing reality can be condensed into nothing more than an epiphany, or, in Mansfield's words, the "one blazing moment" (*Novels and Novelists* 32). Morante similarly believed in the epiphanic character of the short story, which she considered as the representation of *one* moment of reality, one single glimpse, as opposed to the expression of its totality and complexity, that could only find a suitable collocation in the extended space of a novel (*Opere* 2: 1498). And even after abandoning the format in favor of the novel, she reaffirmed the power of short stories to convey progressively and cumulatively a comprehensive image of the writer's world, quoting as a prime example Anton Chekhov's *Tales,* which represented the harmonious and homogeneous development of the author's ideas expressed through a sequence of "moments of reality."[3]

Like Katherine Mansfield, Elsa Morante developed most of her short narrative fiction around the tropes of self-discovery and introspection. Writing at the beginning of the twentieth century, Mansfield was concerned with finding the form of literary expression that would best help her define her role and assert her voice as a woman writer. A few decades and another world war later, Elsa Morante was more extensively hostile to contemporary society, more eager to express her dissent, and she viewed her writings as a means of exploring alternative possibilities.

If Morante, with *Menzogna e sortilegio*, realized her "dream of the cathedral," as analyzed by Alfonso Berardinelli, by discovering the ambitious and multifaceted structure that would contain her own poetic reality in its entirety, Mansfield never made the leap from the short narrative format to the novel, and never developed themes or sets of characters into the more complex fabric and configuration of a novel. She did, however, produce recognizable narrative cycles, clusters of stories that, although technically and formally independent, were implicitly linked together through ideas, images, themes, characters, or settings, and that virtually coalesced by a process of logical, natural aggregation. The "Burnell cycle" (which includes "Prelude," "At the Bay," and "The Doll's House") and the "Sheridan cycle" (including "The Garden Party," "Her First Ball," "By Moonlight," and "The Sheridans"), with their unity of themes, settings, and characters, constitute a succession of linked epiphanies; and in building upon each other to form a consistent continuum, in capturing the complexity and multi-layered nature of the reality of the two families, they are arguably very close, in structure and concept, to a novel. Searching through the *preistoria,* it is possible to find a similar instance of genre contamination, of coalescence of brief narratives into a kind of literary hybrid—a short story with novel potential: the group of little-known stories that Morante published serialized in the magazine *I diritti della scuola* between September 1935 and August 1936 under the collective title *Qualcuno bussa alla porta—racconto* (Rosa 58–64). These stories share genesis and nature with Mansfield's cycles. As conveyed by the subtitle, the eleven stories were conceived of by the author as one long short story, presented in a sequence of independent narratives in which genres were mixed (sentimental, *Bildungsroman,* gothic, melodrama, magic realism, etc.), and various combinations of settings and narrative techniques were experimented with. *Qualcuno bussa alla porta* represents the embryonic stage of Morante's "history proper," a rudimentary, underdeveloped, and not entirely successful example of those technical and inventive abilities that were later displayed in the complex architecture of the novels.[4] And it is significant that, although Morante recognized the limited vision of *Qualcuno bussa alla porta* and incorporated a reference to what she intended its genre to be in the title (*racconto*), the editors of the magazine were more audacious and considered the eleven stories to possess enough cohesion and continuity for them to be presented simply as chapters of "un romanzo."

In Morante and Mansfield's short stories the narrative is sustained, held together, and carried forward not so much by events as by dominant moods and atmospheres, conveyed through a style and narrative strategies that suggest a shared aesthetics. Although they were both experimentalists, dedicated to the exploration of new narrative paths and forms of expression, they exercised their experimentalism firmly within the boundaries of a "classical" prose style. Mansfield's classicism was inspired by her belief in the stylistic perfection of the work of art, where every detail, from the choice of a word to the position of a punctuation mark, was the result of the artist's straining toward the perfect balance. Her comments on stories like "Miss Brill" or "Daughters of the Late Colonel," annotated in the *Journal*, are clear statements of her position in this respect. Yet hers was not a passive acceptance of tried and tested styles. Instead of subverting the canons of prose writing, an operation in which some of her contemporaries engaged—Joyce in *Finnegan's Wake*, among others, but also Dorothy Richardson with a gender-specific poetic aim in mind—Mansfield's interest in extending the boundaries of prose writing involved an exploration of the physicality of language, its acoustic properties, or its powers to resonate in other senses and faculties. Thus "Miss Brill" is compared to a piece of music, its structure paralleled to that of an aria, the result of the perfect orchestration of form and content, with all the components operating synergetically in order to reach impeccable stylistic equilibrium. In a letter dated January 17, 1921, Mansfield explained how "In Miss Brill I chose not only the length of every sentence, but even the sound of every sentence. I chose the rise and fall of every paragraph to fit her [. . .] After I'd written it I read it aloud—numbers of times—just as one would *play over* a musical composition—trying to get it nearer and nearer the expression of Miss Brill—until it fitted her" (*Letters* 2: 88–89).

Morante equally pursued classical stylistic modes, similarly in a period dominated by totally dissonant tendencies. The 1930s, the decade when most of the stories were written, were the years of the *Vociani* and of "prosa d'arte" experiments; the years when many writers privileged the briefness and instantaneity of the fragment, expressions of fleeting intuitions, never elaborated further. Morante's prose, on the contrary, vatic, visionary, and evocative, was remarkably reminiscent of nineteenth-century styles, of the rhythms of opera, as one can see, for instance, in this description of Antonietta, one of the protagonists of "Il gioco segreto": "Ella portava le trecce sulle spalle e un grembiule nero così corto che, se si piegava troppo vivacemente, si scorgevano le sue mutande di tela, strette e lunghe fin quasi al ginocchio, adorne di una fettuccia rossa" (*Lo scialle andaluso* 81; "She wore plaits down her back and a black pinafore so short that if she bent down too suddenly, you caught a glimpse of her linen knickers, tight and long almost down to her knees, adorned with a red ribbon")[5] or in the narrative of the tragic death of the two children in "La nonna":

> A un tronco magro e nerastro era legata una rozza barca dalla vernice screpolata; ed appena i fanciulli, dopo un'ardua scalata, ci furono dentro, non reggendo al piccolo peso, il ramo dalla corda attorta si spezzò. Essi salutarono con grida di giubilo, agitando le mani minuscole e tozze, il principio del loro viaggio. (*Lo scialle andaluso* 57)

> A dingy boat with peeling paint was tied to a narrow, blackened tree-trunk. No sooner had the children jumped into it after a difficult climb, than the branch with the cord wrapped round it snapped, unable to sustain even their light weight. They bade farewell with cries of joy, waving their tiny, rough hands. Their voyage had begun.

From the very early writings, Elsa Morante explored the function of language as a means of evoking mysterious and magical atmospheres. Overcoming, as Mansfield had similarly done before her, the norms of both Realism and Neorealism, reality and its representation became in her hands a mere pretext to disclose the virtues of words (Manacorda 412). Through the power of words, she strove to re-create in her writings the lost world of myths and fables, to oppose it to the ephemeral nature of the modern world as the archetypal background of all humankind, and to lead the reader across its threshold. Her prose, which is lyrical, solemn, often magniloquent, in the short stories as well as in the novels, which evokes alternative worlds and times that only obey their own internal logic, subtracting themselves from the strictures of natural laws, is nevertheless controlled, measured; the decadent overtones of some of her passages are solidly underpinned by authorial detachment and irony.

Katherine Mansfield and Elsa Morante were similarly involved in challenging and extending the expressive boundaries of their language—the former to discover perfect stylistic equilibrium, the latter for ideological and artistic reasons, to rescue literary Italian from the relentless deterioration it was undergoing. The evocative and creative potential of language fascinated the two writers, who similarly exploited the visual and tactile properties of words to convey feelings, atmospheres, and images, and to create a "literary reality," that is to say, to bring the artist's own world into this world.[6] That both were somehow atypical, on the fringes of the mainstream debates and groups that dominated their cultural periods, that they both diverged from the leading literary vogues, also constitutes a strikingly similar set of circumstances, as does the fact that they both died just as they felt they had found their true nature and purpose as artists.[7]

A feature that becomes visible when one considers the two collections of short stories, is the similar role reserved by the authors to male characters.[8] Not only do they rarely feature in the foreground as major players in the diegesis, but they tend to be negatively connoted, being depicted alternatively as authoritarian and domineering—such are Stanley Burnell in "Prelude" and "At the Bay," the Colonel in "Daughters of the Late Colonel," the boss in "The Fly," the Jewish father in "Il ladro dei lumi," or the co-narrator in "Il soldato siciliano"; or as disturbed individuals, as is the case of the old man in "The Little Governess" and of the protagonist of "L'uomo dagli occhiali." The majority of female characters, in particular the younger ones, show a tendency toward self-analysis, an enhanced tendency toward introspective thought, and consequently feature in stories where prominence is given to processes of self-development. The men, on the other hand —whether relegated to minor and marginal roles or excluded altogether from the diegesis—appear well settled in their status quo, self-possessed, content, and unquestioning. And even when they do appear in the foreground alongside the female characters, as in the case of "The Little Governess" and "L'uomo dagli occhiali," they are portrayed as one-dimensional figures, whose role is mainly contrastive, to highlight the experiences undergone by their female counterparts.

"The Man without a Temperament" (1920) and "Un uomo senza carattere" (1941), however, present a notable exception to this pattern, introducing for once a different kind of male figure, at variance with the classification sketched above. Although the titles explicitly point to lack of "character" as the most salient trait of the two protagonists, the stories focus specifically on two young male protagonists, exploring their personalities through their relationships with themselves, with a woman, and with the world around them; and these stories progressively disclose a problematic reality that appears to challenge the cultural construction of gender dynamics.

In both stories the protagonist is the eponymous man, identified by his full name, Robert Salesby, in Mansfield's story, and with a nickname, Poeta, in Morante's. Although the two authors deploy different narratorial strategies—Mansfield uses a third-person extradiegetic narrator, whereas Morante lets Poeta perform an autodiegetic function—the effect achieved by the narrating voice is similar. Mansfield's narrator, in fact, by remaining almost constantly within the experiential and emotional orbit of the protagonist, never displays the omniscience and objectivity that his extraneity to the events narrated would technically grant him. This manipulation, or distortion, of a classic narrative strategy, generates an effect of estrangement and imposes a deliberate limit on the decipherability of the story: the readers' expectations of a standard omniscient commentary are subverted, and the events in the story are subject to the same cognitive limitations usually presented by first-person narration. Both authors, therefore, appear to control the narrative point of view in ways that engender a similar sense of the unfathomability of human character: both the first-person narrative of Poeta and the third-person narrative of Robert Salesby allow a similar, limited degree of reader penetration, and infringe on the canonical axiom of authorial—or "narrauthorial"—control.

"The Man without a Temperament," originally to be titled "The Exile," was written by Katherine Mansfield in just over twelve hours as a conciliatory gesture toward her husband and editor, John Middleton Murry, and has a documented autobiographical genesis. After contracting pulmonary tuberculosis in 1917, Mansfield started a wandering life in search of congenial foreign climates and miracle therapies, sometimes accompanied by her husband. In retaliation, however, for Murry's refusal to leave London and his work to follow her to Ospedaletti for a period of convalescence, she wrote an angry and indignant poem called "The New Husband." The abrasive tones obtained the desired effects: Murry hastily abandoned his commitments and, if only for a brief period, joined his wife in Italy. Regretting the harshness of "The New Husband," Mansfield wrote "The Exile," to show Murry that she was aware of the implications of her sickness for their relationship, and understood any feelings of resentment he might be harboring.[9] In the throes of the incurable form of consumption of which she would eventually die in 1923, Mansfield created in the Salesbys a reflection of herself and Murry, focusing almost entirely on the latter and his condition of captivity inside a watertight mechanism of dependency and duty of care.

Robert Salesby is an Englishman from London in enforced exile in an unidentified, warm country because of his wife's precarious health. Taken out of his home environment and constrained by his wife's subtle but nevertheless unrelenting demands, Robert is seen in the narrative as unable to construct any meaningful new relationship or to acquire any independent sense of purpose in the new location. Not only is he isolated as a consequence, he is also an oddity who attracts attention. To the fellow guests of the Pension Villa Excelsior—who judge him upon what they see as his inability to stand up to a whining and manipulative woman—he is an object of ridicule; to the local children—who run in fright at the sight of the bizarre, solitary "Englishman"—he is the epitome of mystery and danger. On the surface Robert appears unperturbed by either attitude, and dutifully attends to his wife's wishes and needs. Behind his collected exterior, however, he shows from the outset imperceptible signs of discomfort, such as the almost ritual, nervous twisting of his signet ring that marks the incipit of the story:

> He stood at the hall door *turning the ring, turning the heavy signet ring* upon his little finger while *his glance travelled*

> *coolly, deliberately* over the round tables [. . .] He pursed
> his lips—he might have been going to whistle—but he did
> not whistle—only *turned the ring—turned the ring* on his
> pink, freshly washed hands. (129; emphasis added)

There is in the story an evident contrast between appearance
and reality, between sense of duty and real feelings, which is
conveyed predominantly through objective descriptions, with
only three brief introspective, and retrospective, inserts. Hence
the pension is connoted as a dark and oppressive space, peopled
by still objects and one-dimensional figures, all constituting a
background of static "types" among whom Robert, the man
without a temperament, is the only real, "live" individual.[10] The
pension's guests are in fact identified by nicknames, titles, or
roles—the Two Topknots, the Honeymoon Couple, the General and the Countess, the American Woman, Antonio the fac-
totum—and are associated with their idiosyncrasies: the frantic
knitting and compulsive gossiping of the Topknots, the hype
and excitement of young love of the Honeymoon Couple, the
senile regression of the General, the obsession with her lapdog
of the American Woman, the nonchalance and carelessness of
Antonio the waiter, and the self-centeredness and hypochon-
dria of Mrs. Salesby. Robert, on the contrary, is not *de-scribed*,
in the sense of "written about," with the result that his most
characteristic feature is the absence of any particular characteristics. The narratorial gaze that holds Robert Salesby—his
actions, the variations in his movements—registers and emphasizes the fact that he does not belong. Unlike the other
characters, he is not exposed or disclosed by his habits or
hobbyhorses, but generally left alone in his private world, of
which we only get brief, but significant, glimpses. And
although memory breaks in only three times,[11] the opposition
between past and present—where past is to happiness what
present "life" is to regret and illusion—is a dominant topos in
the story, where the lack or loss of temperament is posited as
the consequence not only of exile as geographical and emotional displacement, but also of the moral obligations that result
from socialization.

"Un uomo senza carattere," which appears in the 1963 edition of *Lo scialle andaluso,* is similarly based on the notions of

illusion, deception, and conflict between appearance and reality, and on similar motifs. As in Mansfield's story, the setting is a holiday resort, geographically and symbolically distanced from the hometown; an equally colorful set of characters surrounds the protagonists and adds significance to their experiences; the protagonist is another sensitive young male whose commitment to protecting a woman forms the crux of the plot; the main female character is equally somewhat pathetic, self-centered, and a victim of self-deception. The story was written in the style of a memorial, a form that Morante, for whom narrating was an act of remembering, found congenial and adopted extensively both in the stories and, in later years, in the novels. Thanks also to the analeptic character of the narrative, the text strives to communicate a sense of omniscience and control on the part of protagonist/narrator and to enhance the sense of closure attained at the end of the narrative act.

The protagonist and narrator of the story is also the fictional author who supposedly records his narrative years after the events. "Poeta," as he was named by his friends in the village for his fair and delicate appearance, was also often compared to a knight, although—as he regretfully admits in the first paragraph—both epithets were undeserved, as he lacked both the genius of a poet and the courage of a knight. His narrative begins at the end of Poeta's first year at the university, when he has completed his end of year exams and left the city to return to his native village F. for the summer. F. is described as a very conservative environment; with no theaters, little female company (the girls, in the accordance with age-old custom, are said to be reserved, and largely restricted to the four walls of their houses), it offers the young people on vacation few opportunities for entertainment other than card games and practical jokes. Upon his arrival, which is later than usual, Poeta learns that this particular summer the joke is on a newcomer, Miss Candida V., a short and plump thirty-year-old spinster. Brought up in a small provincial town in the South of Italy and having spent years looking after her widowed father, Candida has "mortificato la sua natura esuberante" (126; "mortified her exuberant nature") and lived like a nun in her own home. After the death of her father she moved to the city to stay with her cousins. Anxious to catch up as soon as possible on all that she has missed through her enforced reclusion, she activates a process of accelerated and exaggerated self-emancipation, which, instead of transforming her into a liberated, urbanized female, turns her into a ludicrous caricature. By the time she arrives in F., her metamorphosis is complete: dressed in garish and most unflattering frocks and made up in the brightest and most unsuitable of colors, Candida has achieved total self-assurance, believing in her self-delusion that she is the mistress of every young man's heart. In reality the whole village, not least her own cousins, as Poeta states, laughs at her. Her daily walks become the occasion for collective mockery, and the young men take turns proposing or confessing their love for her, only to laugh among themselves afterwards at her gullibility and self-conceit. Poeta, although declaredly part of the group—he frequently refers to the other characters as his companions, lads of his own age, or more incisively and inclusively "we"—distances himself from this particular collective activity out of respect less for the woman in question, than for the sentiment of love and the words to speak it, which he sees are being abused:

> Presto, tutti le avevano dichiarato amore, fuorché io. Sebbene io non osassi confessarlo, non condividevo il divertimento degli altri; in realtà, quelle parole esaltate da loro usate per illudere Candida, io nel mio cuore le veneravo troppo per farle oggetto di gioco. Le riserbavo, quale offerta sacra, ad una fanciulla ancora non incontrata, ma che vagheggiavo bellissima e semplice. (127–28)

> Soon everybody had proposed to her, except for me. Although I didn't dare confess it, I did not share their amusement; in reality in my heart I had too much respect for those glorious words they were using to fool Candida, to make a mockery of them. I was saving them as a sacred offering to a yet unknown young girl, whom I imagined to be beautiful and unpretentious.

Poeta is in turn singled out by his friends, who publicly and embarrassingly exhort him to "declare himself" to Candida. The latter, fatter, haughtier, and more grotesque by the day, becomes visibly irritated by Poeta's incomprehensible lack of attention for her.

Poeta's "coscienza, l'onore, la verità, la compassione e altre degne cose" (128; "conscience, honor, truth, compassion and other worthy things") finally urge him to expose the deception. He takes Candida outside the local club where all the friends are gathered to play cards, and after revealing to her that all the adulation was in fact deceit, that "nessuno di loro vi ama" (129; "not one of them loves you"), he advises her to apply herself to more becoming activities, such as reading, sewing, or dedicating herself to good works. Finally, in order to persuade her of his truthfulness, he asks her to remain outside the club and to listen to what his friends inside have to say about her. In a switch of cognitive perspective, Candida turns from a viewed subject into a hearing one, a shift from passive to active role that avails her of the truth. But if Poeta's dominant motive had been an unveiling of the truth and an end to illusion, he begins to doubt the worth of truth as its consequences become painfully clear: not only is illusion destroyed but, as the protagonist later discovers, Candida herself is also destroyed. Fatally weakened psychologically, she dies of typhoid at the end of the summer. To appease his conscience and attempt reparation for the damage he feels he has caused, the protagonist decides to visit her grave and bring her flowers. Spotted by a friend, however, he feels unbearably self-conscious, and hiding the reason for his presence in the cemetery, he throws the flowers to the goats and struts back with him, "ridendo servilmente" (133; "laughing in a servile fashion").

The configurations of gender roles and dynamics presented by Mansfield and Morante in the two stories are equally contentious and subversive. Both protagonists reify an alternative, hybrid notion of masculinity, which is, however, not unproblematically appropriated, and both are portrayed in their interaction with alternative models of femininity, which are equally complex and ambiguous.

Robert's docility, his relinquishment of his roots and his life for the sake of loyalty to his wife have turned him into an ambivalent, "feminized" figure whose sexuality is in doubt. Metaphorically castrated by the illness of his wife (135; "*No* man is he, but an ox," one of the characters says of him), his imprisonment is symbolically represented by the signet ring, which he turns relentlessly and obsessively without, however, being able, or willing, to remove it from his finger. In his refusal of food and drink, suggestive of anorexia, the author has deployed another trope tendentially associated with femaleness, the refusal of nourishment being a prime expression of the typically female sense of discomfort with one's body and one's environment (Gilbert and Gubar 53). In similar fashion, Poeta is given androgynous attributes, from his physical appearance ("ero un giovinetto delicato e timido" ("I was a shy, delicate young man"), distinguished for "[i] miei capelli biondi e lo splendore del sorriso" ("my blond hair and bright smile") that made him resemble "un cavaliere antico" (125; "a knight of old"), to his restrained and idealistic attitude, encapsulated in his feminine-sounding nickname; and he too is explicitly presented as an asexual subject, similarly metaphorically castrated by his circumstances. The sense of sacrifice, of self-immolation shown by both protagonists, in the name of which they have made (Robert) or are prepared to make (Poeta) decisive life choices, is also culturally feminine. As Robert has renounced London, so vividly and painfully present in his memories, to mend his wife's health, so Poeta is ready to mend Candida's dignity by offering her the ultimate and most chivalrous of reparations, marriage. In neither case, however, is the male self-abnegation complete or irreversible, which makes the endings of both stories all the more bitter in their poignancy.

The femininity of the male protagonists is counterpoised by the co-protagonists, Jinnie Salesby and Candida V., who represent the unredeemed negativity of genetic femaleness. Both are infected by a disease, Jinnie suffering from an unspecified but purportedly terminal physical pathology, Candida becoming debilitated by an emotional blow that leaves her physically vulnerable. It is interesting to note the double valency of the name Candida V., which incorporates the antithetical notions of purity and of venereal disease, and which echoes the young girl suffering from a sexually transmitted disease whom Morante had imagined and entered in her diary, dated 18 February 1938.[12] These two female characters are petulant, demanding, self-centered, and self-deluded, and both appear to illustrate the veracity of the classic patriarchal notion that a woman who does not present the requisites of an angel—submissiveness, obedience, and modesty—is by default a monster (Gilbert and Gubar 53). In both women the basic, essential features are distorted: as much as Jinnie is virtually disembodied—in the story she is only named in two of the analeptic interludes, as if she too had lost part of her identity in the uprooting—and seen throughout as a phantasmal presence perceived through the sound of her "dragging steps" and of her "soft voice" and through the ethereal touch of her "hand, like a leaf" (130), Candida is the paroxysm of physicality, but of a physicality so grotesque that it loses human attributes. She is introduced as being "ancora abbastanza fresca; piccola e grassa" (125; "still quite fresh-looking; small and round"), she is heard "cinguettare" ("chirping") and seen "saltellare" ("skipping along"); she moves more "da anitra che da fanciulla" (130; "like a duck than like a girl"). Both women show insatiable voracity, literal and figurative. They hunger for attention, which Jinnie procures with the pretext of her debilitating illness and Candida with the outrageousness of her appearance and behavior; and they consume food and drink with passion, as we see Jinnie do, "[b]ut she—with [. . .] her head tilted back, her lips open, a brush of bright colour on her cheek-bones, sipped, sipped, drank . . . drank . . ." (132). Candida by implication does likewise, becoming: "ogni giorno più grassa e superba" (127; "fatter and haughtier every day"). In the presence of these two devouring figures, the male protagonists become incapacitated. Robert Salesby comes to a virtual standstill—a striking contrast to the physical agility and the mental alertness shown when he moves away from his wife and in her absence—while Poeta "fra l'irritazione, la vergogna e un'incresciosa pietà" (128; "in a mixture of irritation, embarrassment and humiliating sense of pity") either blushes uncontrollably or is seized by "una specie di smarrimento" (129; "a sense of bewilderment") and by an urge to run away.

The model of male presented by the two stories is situated outside the boundaries of the canonic social construction, its distinguishing feature being stated by the authors in the titles as the lack of temperament/personality, which initially would appear to indicate lack of assertiveness. Characteristic in both stories is the "de-masculinization" of the two protagonists, whose experiences are represented through historically feminine metaphors: they feel isolated, trapped, caught in a state of psychological and physical constriction from which there is little hope of escape;[13] and bound by a sense of duty and compassion—induced in Poeta by "la mia coscienza, l'onore, la verità, la compassione e altre degne cose" (128; "my conscience, my sense of honor and truth, compassion and other noble sentiments") and in Robert by his wife's professed ineptitude and emotional blackmail tactics: "Robert the awful thing is—I suppose it's my illness—I simply feel I could not go alone. You see—you're everything. You're bread and wine, Robert, bread and wine. Oh, my darling—what am I saying? Of course I could, of course I won't take you away . . ." (143).

As the narratives unfold, however, what emerges in both protagonists is not a case of lack but rather one of dyscrasia: they make choices and adopt moral stances the consequences of which they are unable to fully accept or incorporate in a novel formulation of male subjectivity, as the concluding scenes reveal, and prove that what they lack is not personality (as masculinity/assertiveness), but a balance of character traits, "temperament" in the etymological sense of Medieval philosophy and physiology, as right proportion of qualities.

Robert Salesby is different, not so much because of his relationship with his wife, which appears based on a reversal of the norm—he performing the role of the "angel," caring and submissive—but because of his relationship with himself. His dominant feature for most of the narrative is the inversion of the masculine/feminine polarity, with the masculine scaled down, sacrificed in the name of marital dedication. But the ostensibly devoted and dutiful husband of the invalid Mrs. Salesby lives alongside the independent man of old, whom Mansfield sketches in the body of the narrative only briefly and almost perfunctorily. Irreconcilable as they may be, Mansfield appears to suggest, these two discrete existences are nevertheless part of Robert's personality and make him more complete and composite a person than any of the other characters in the story, who need to be complemented by somebody else in order to get over their inherent incompleteness, and who therefore always appear in pairs. But the ending suddenly flashes a different picture: "'[. . .] I sometimes wonder—do you mind awfully being out here with me?' He bends down. He kisses her. He tucks her in, he smoothes the pillow. 'Rot!' he whispers" (143). In a monosyllable all the repressed anger and the concealed resentment invade the page, the brevity of the outburst also a sign of its finality, of the unredeemability of the situation. In a conclusion that is rendered all the more vividly cruel by the manifest autobiographical link,[14] the roles revert back to an appearance of conventionality, conclusively confuting the sustainability of a permanent new configuration of gender relations.

Morante's Poeta, despite the story implying his difference from his peers, is ultimately the propounder of a more insidious and conservative model of gender taxonomy. On the surface, the first-person narrative lingers on the internal conflicts and on the ambivalent position between the impulse to obey noble feelings and the instinct to follow the crowd, suggesting a man potentially on the threshold of developing into a new formulation of masculinity: Poeta hesitates, has doubts, he explicitly admits his reluctance to jettison his manhood, already undermined by his feminine, romantic appearance and his sensitivity. Amidst the moral conflicts, however, he liberally administers his received wisdom on gender issues, proving how his uneasiness with the circumstances is not provoked by the malignity of his friends' behavior or indeed by his own lack of honor, but by Candida's persistent failure to operate according to an accepted, or acceptable, model of femininity. Poeta's advice to Candida before she listens in to the men's conversation is, "Su, signorina, è tempo di conoscere voi stessi e la vita. A una donna della vostra classe e della vostra età la vita offre altre cose" (129; "Come now, it's time to know yourself and life. Life offers many other things to a woman of your class and age"). And afterwards, trying to console her, "Le rivelai quanto fossero indecorose le sue maniere, quanto ridicoli i suoi vestiti, quanto sfacciata la sua truccatura, e vana la sua vita stessa. Con ipocrita onestà, la esortai nuovamente alle occupazioni modeste che si addicono alle fanciulle mature" (131; "I pointed out to her how unseemly her manner was, how ridiculous her clothes were, how garish her make-up, how vain her whole life. With hypocritical honesty, I urged her to take up the modest occupations more suitable to mature girls").

Although seemingly experimenting with a progressive and desirable new paradigm of gender dynamics, the bitter endings in both stories reveal the authors' pessimism and lack of faith in any possibility of true communication or equality, and a deep-rooted sense of inferiority. The female co-protagonists are deluded by the apparent "diversity" of the protagonists, which is amplified and carried forward as a dominant motif throughout the narrative, only to be clamorously exploded in the final epiphany. And in a tragic switch of point of observation, the concluding lines of the stories shift the focus completely from the male character to the female, from Robert and Poeta to Jinnie and Candida, exposing, with more than a hint of self-deprecation and a sense of *cupio dissolvi*, their illusion and humiliation.

The autobiographical resonance of the plot, that in the case of Mansfield is clearly documented, can be argued convincingly also for Elsa Morante. The year 1941, the year of "Un uomo senza personalità," is also the year when she married Moravia, of whose social and cultural standing she never ceased to be in awe, and who was the principal source of her tormenting sense of inferiority. Moravia, like Murry, was more than a partner, a source of inspiration, and the epitome of all that was desirable and never fully possessed or equaled. In the concluding part of the narratives of Robert Salesby and Poeta, the two female figures emerge as pitiful creatures, deservedly punished for their *hubris*, one dying and one dead, embodying their authors' own subconscious sense of unworthiness, metaphorized by both as a desire for self-obliteration.

Notes

1. In Morante's *Diario 1938* these achievements were due in part to her relationship with Moravia, which began in 1936 and led to marriage in 1941. Morante talks of "un poco di pace" of "un pavilion tutto per me" and of "tempo Vero" as the mental, spatial and temporal accomplishments which allowed her to focus exclusively on her own materials (Garboli and Cecchi liii).

2. Interestingly, many Modernist novels originated from shorter pieces of narrative. James Joyce's *Ulysses*, for example, was initially entitled "Mr. Hunter's Day" and it was meant for inclusion in *The Dubliners* (Hanson 56).

3. "gran parte delle singole narrazioni di Čechov sono, a sé stanti, dei racconti, ma la raccolta cekoviana dei Racconti [. .] senza dubbio ha valore di romanzo: giacché presenta un intero sistema (il sistema cekoviano) delle relazioni umane e dell'universo reale" (Morante, *Opere* 2: 1498–99; "many of Chekov's single stories are tales in their own right, but the collection of the Tales [. . .] undoubtedly could be valued as a novel in that it shows a whole system (the Chekovian one) of human relations and the actual universe"). Note how Mansfield, referring to Dorothy Richardson's *Pilgrimage,* used a similar image to refer to novels, which she described as "nests of stories" (Hanson 57).

4. Rosa sees in the character of Elena, a disabled old aunt who is bitter and hostile to herself and the world, the blueprint for Cesira in *Menzogna e sortilegio*, and in some of the settings an anticipation of the more celebrated ones in *Menzogna e sortilegio* and *L'isola di Arturo* (61–62).

5. All the page references are from the 1985 Einaudi edition of the collection. All translations are mine.

6. See Mansfield's definition of art, which is "not an attempt of the artist to reconcile existence with his vision; it is an attempt to create his own world in this world" (*Journal of Katherine Mansfield* 273). This is echoed in Morante's definition of the novel: "It is a work of art ("opera poetica") through which the artist provides his own image of the universe" ("l'autore [. . .] dà *intera* una propria immagine dell'universo reale" [*Opere* 2: 1498; emphasis in original; "the author [. . .] gives his/her image of the actual universe in its whole"]).

7. A few days before her death, Morante talked about the novel she intended to write, a novel that was all in her head and that was all that she had always wanted to write (Bompiani 199).

8. I refer to the volume *The Collected Stories of Katherine Mansfield,* which includes the three collections published from 1911 to 1922 (*In a German Pension, Bliss,* and *The Garden Party*) and the two collections published posthumously (*The Dove's Nest* and *Something Childish*); and to *Lo scialle andaluso* (1963), which contains Morante's authorized short stories.

9. See *The Collected Letters of Katherine Mansfield* 3; x–xi; Hanson and Gurr, *Katherine Mansfield* 70.

10. See the description of the pension's hall and stairs at the beginning of the story, and in particular the contrast between the darkness, lifelessness, and immobility of the space and the dynamism depicted in Robert's movements through the sole use of adverbs and a mostly nominal, asyndetic structure: "And he turned and *swiftly* crossed the veranda into the dim hall with its scarlet plush and gilt furniture—conjuror's furniture—its Notice of Services at the English Church, its green baize board with the unclaimed letters climbing the black lattice, huge 'presentation' clock that struck the hours at the half-hours, bundles of sticks and umbrellas and sunshades in the clasp of a brown wooden bear, *past* the two crippled palms, two ancient beggars at the foot of the staircase, *up the marble stairs three at the time, past* the life-size group on the landing of two stout peasant children with their marble pinnies full of marble grapes, and *along* the corridor, with its piled-up wreckage of old tin boxes, leather trunks, canvas holdalls, to their room" (130; emphasis added). It is worth noting that the above scene describes the protagonist moving away from his wife and the other characters, or rather removing himself from their presence.

11. The strength and power of Robert's recollection of England, its weather, its atmosphere, its people, is rendered in the story with the omission of narratorial distinction between first narrative (the present circumstances) and the analeptic narrative of the time in London. Memory irrupts and interrupts the linear narrative flow, triggered by Mrs. Salesby's mention of the word *snow*: ". . . Snow. Snow in London. Millie with the early morning cup of tea. 'There's been a terrible fall of snow in the night sir.' 'Oh, has there, Millie?' The curtain rings apart, letting in the pale, reluctant light. He raises himself in the bed; he catches a glimpse of the solid houses opposite, framed in white, of their window boxes full of great sprays of white coral. . ." (132).

A few pages later, a new, equally brief and equally sudden irruption of memory occurs, triggered by Robert Salesby's leaning against a wall: "He leaned against a wall, filled his pipe, put a match to it [. . .] Leaned across a gate, turned up the collar of his mackintosh. It was going to rain. It did not matter, he was prepared for it. You didn't expect anything else in November. [. . .] By Jove! He had to hurry if he was going to catch that train home. Over the gate, across a field, over the stile, into the lane, swinging along in the drifting rain and dusk. . . . Just in time for a bath and a change before supper [. . .] 'By the way, Dennis, I picked up a very jolly little edition of . . .'" (138). Toward the very end of the story, the analepsis provides information on the reason for leaving London: "Well, my dear chap, that's the whole story. That's the long and the short of it. If she can't cut away for the next two years and give a decent climate a chance she don't stand a dog's—h'm—show" (142).

12. See *Diario 1938* (*Opere* 2: 1575–1628). For a study of Morante's diary, see Gambaro's article in the present volume (21–44).

13. See Mansfield's description of Robert's walk out of the grounds of the Pension Villa Excelsior, where the hill seems to enclose the space surrounding the pension, emphasizing the sense of a no-way-out situation (137). In Morante the reference to the enclosed space of Poeta's dingy rented room is significant: "che costituiva, in città, tutto il mio regno, nella solitudine alla quale il mio carattere schivo mi costringeva" (131; "which constituted, in town, my whole kingdom, in the solitude to which my withdrawn personality forced me"). For an analysis of the metaphoric value of space and of its being a feature of female characters in female-authored fiction, see Horner and Zlosnik.

14. Referring to "The Man without a Temperament," Mansfield wrote: "Finished the story. [. . .] I thought of everything in my life and it all came back so vividly—all is connected with the feeling that J. and I are no longer as we were. I love him but he rejects my *living* love. This is anguish. These are the worst days of my life" (*Journal* 192).

Works Cited

Berardinelli, Alfonso. "Il sogno della cattedrale: Elsa Morante e il romanzo come archetipo." *Per Elsa*. 11–33. (Rpt. in *Narrativa* 17 [2000]: 15–26.)

Bompiani, Ginevra. "Per Elsa." *Per Elsa*. 199–204.

Garboli, Cesare, and Carlo Cecchi. "Cronologia." Morante, *Opere* 1: xix–xc.

Gilbert, Sandra, and Susan Gubar. *The Madwoman in the Attic: The Woman Writer and the Nineteenth Century Imagination*. New Haven: Yale UP, 1979.

Hanson, Clare. *Short Stories and Short Fictions 1880–1980*. London: McMillan, 1985.

Hanson, Clare, and Andrew Gurr. *Katherine Mansfield*. New York: St. Martin's, 1981.

Horner, Avril, and Sue Zlosnik. *Landscapes of Desire: Metaphors in Modern Women's Fiction*. Brighton: Harvester, 1990.

Manacorda, Giuliano. *Storia della letteratura italiana contemporanea 1940–1996*. Rome: Riuniti, 1996.

Mansfield, Katherine. *The Collected Stories of Katherine Mansfield*. London: Penguin, 1981.

———. *The Journal of Katherine Mansfield*. Ed. John Middleton Murry. London: Constable, 1927.

———. *The Letters of Katherine Mansfield*. Ed. John Middleton Murry. 2 vols. London: Constable, 1928.

———. *Il meglio di Katherine Mansfield*. Trans. Marcella Hannau and Elsa Morante. Milan: Longanesi, 1957.

———. *Novels and Novelists*. Ed. John Middleton Murry. London: Constable, 1930.

Morante, Elsa. *Opere*. Ed. Cesare Garboli and Carlo Cecchi. 2 vols. Milan: Mondadori, 1988 and1990.

———. *Lo scialle andaluso*. Turin: Einaudi, 1985.

Per Elsa Morante. Milan: Linea d'ombra, 1993.

Rosa, Giovanna. "Ovvero il romanziere." *Per Elsa*. 58–64.

Marco Bardini

Poetry and Reality
in "The Aesthetics of Our Time"

While the critical essays published by Elsa Morante in her life-time were hardly numerous, they contain, nonetheless, a coherent framework of reflective judgments on aesthetics and on the figurative arts, and demonstrate the same level of clarity, precision, and insight as her writings on literature. Along-side the better-known writings, collected in the posthumous volume *Pro o contro la bomba atomica,*[1] are a number of equally significant essays and reflections on art, dating from the 1930s onward.

Current research suggests that the earliest non-narrative writing by Morante was an article from 1938, when she was twenty-six years old. "Mille città in una" ("A Thousand Cities in One") was published in volume 4–5 of Curzio Malaparte's journal *Prospettive,*[2] in the feature column "Viaggi" ("Journeys"). This article is of particular interest, appearing after the short fairy tales for *Il Corriere dei piccoli* and *Il Cartoccino dei piccoli,* the short fictions for *I diritti della scuola* and the short stories for *Il Meridiano di Roma.* This remarkable piece is clear evidence of a writer whose compositional skills are already highly refined. Despite the occasional flaw, such as the term *razza* ("race"), for example, which is used with regard to culture and in particular the laws of the day, as is, if more blandly, the term *patria,* the text demonstrates the intellectual qualities of the author and the eclectic breadth of her reading. As well as the authors recalled or quoted, whether Pirandello, Balzac, Zola, Proust, or Dante, the piece also points to Morante's knowledge—ingenuous, maybe, but never banal—of philosophical terms and concepts, with particular reference to Schopenhauer's *The World as Will and Representation,* and

Marco Bardini

in more indirect fashion to Nietzsche's *The Birth of Tragedy*. "Mille città in una" opens by describing a viewer's subjective perceptions:

> Esiste davvero *per sé* una realtà concreta del mondo, o di esso non vi sono che infinite apparenze, una per ciascun soggetto che guarda? Così che, spentosi l'occhio, anche la visione si spegne, come i colori dileguano col cadere della luce? O forse ancora il vero aspetto della realtà è inscrutabile, nessuno può vederla *quale essa è*, ma ciascuno porta in sé un'apparenza del mondo, limitata alla sua propria sensibilità, effimera quanto egli stesso, e incomunicabile? [. . .] Ogni nazione o città apre al viaggiatore la sua fisionomia vera, la sua anima ricca di forme, di tempo e di esperienza, o tiene segreta questa sua realtà profonda, e si copre il volto di maschere sempre diverse a seconda di chi guarda? Maschere che sono appunto il riflesso del carattere del viaggiatore, della sua vita, della sua sensibilità. Così che egli non può dire di aver visto Roma o Parigi, ma *una* Roma, *una* Parigi, o meglio la *sua* Roma e la *sua* Parigi. [MC 465; emphasis in original]

> Is there a concrete reality of the world that exists *per se*, or do we have nothing but an infinity of appearances, a different one for each subjective eye? Such that when that eye dies, the vision dies with it, just as colors fade with the light? Or perhaps the true aspect of reality is inscrutable, nobody can see it *as it is*, but each of us carries within an appearance of the world, limited by one's own sensibility, incommunicable and ephemeral as we are ourselves? [. . .] Does each country or city open up its true physiognomy to the traveler, its soul rich in form, time, and experience, or else does it keep this profound reality secret, covering its face with masks that are different according to who is doing the looking? Masks that reflect the character of the traveler, his [*sic*] life, his [*sic*] sensibility. So he [*sic*] cannot say he has seen Rome or Paris, but *a* Rome, *a* Paris, or rather *his* Rome and *his* Paris.

Even in this brief extract it is interesting to note how Morante finds a coherent and logical connection between the Schopenhauerian beginning, which she borrows almost to the letter (Schopenhauer 5), and the later Nietzschean concept of "mask" as transfiguration and antidecadent transposition of the relationship/divide between being and appearance.

In speaking of "Viaggi," of journeys that instantly become an allegory of existence, the author reminds us that even when traveling as part of a group, each tourist develops a personal and distinct impression of the destination, which is only nominally the same for all; each human being possesses a different "gradation of the visual faculty"—whether this has to do with what a person sees immediately before him/her, or what a person preserves in his/her memory. Described or represented by different individuals, the same city exhibits a whole range of faces and features. The same place changes appearance and nature according to the age, mood, and sensibility of the observer, to such an extent that if the observer returns as an adult to a place of his/her childhood, even if the observer has a precise memory of the place as it was, the observer is amazed to discover himself/herself in a space that is completely new. And each individual, seeing what he/she sees alone, will always be blind or insensitive to all other visions, which are nonetheless equally present, "[I]nfiniti sono dunque i travestimenti e le apparenze dei luoghi" (MC 465; "[T]he disguises and appearances of places are, then, infinite").

But the infinitely variable visions of the world are not emphasized in order to point to, and constrain, a reality that can be reached beyond appearance. The problem is not posed in terms of an opposition between the truth of the thing in itself and the ripping off of the mask: "Is there a concrete reality of the world that exists *per se*?" wonders Morante in her opening paragraph. And toward the end of her article she posits the thoughts of a man dazzled by the vision of a sunny, bright Venice after years of remembering the dull, rainy Venice experienced as a child. This other Venice existed too, in some far-off world, "nei vasti e rinchiusi feudi della sua infanzia dove non gli era più permesso di visitarla" (MC 465; "in the vast, enclosed fiefdoms of his childhood, where he was no longer able to visit it").

The aim is perhaps to replace the generic, crystallized, and inhuman representation in which humans mechanically live with a different and more authentic appearance (authentic because individual and our own), with a dynamic of appearances. This is less a tearing off of the mask than a search for genuinely different masks because, among humans, a thousand different appearances have the same right of citizenship, in that they are multiple and parallel realizations of what, when it comes down to it, is the real goal, with all its problematic opacities and misunderstandings: the traveler himself, who "si rispecchia nella città; e da questa riceve solo una immagine di se stesso, arricchita di aspetti nuovi" (MC 465: "is mirrored in the city, and from the city receives only a reflection of himself, enriched with new detail"):

> Nella nostra immaginazione già le città che vorremmo visitare si compongono in un quadro; e quando, compiuto il viaggio, confrontiamo questo quadro con la realtà, ci stupiamo delle differenze e quasi ci sembra che la città reale, sovrapponendosi a quella immaginata, ci defraudi di qualche cosa. Oppure noi cerchiamo viaggiando le immagini dei luoghi quali gli autori più amati ce le hanno descritte; allora compiamo una specie di pellegrinaggio sulle loro orme e quella ci appare è più la *loro*, che la *nostra* città; sebbene non sia propriamente la *loro* città che vediamo, ma un suo riflesso, che da essa differisce come la effige del Santo che il pellegrino è giunto ad adorare dopo una lunga strada differisce dalle sue sembianze reali. (MC 466; emphasis in original)

> In our imagination the cities we would like to visit are composed as in a painting; and when, having visited that place, we compare the painting with the reality we are astonished by the difference. We can even feel that the real city, superimposing itself on the imagined one, has cheated us of something. Or else as we travel we search for the images of places as described to us by the authors we have most loved, in which case we undertake a kind of pilgrimage in their footsteps, and the city appears to us as more *theirs* than *ours*—even though it is not *their* city that we see but a reflection of it and that differs from it, as the effigy of the Saint differs from his real features when the traveling pilgrim finally comes face to face with him.

In allegorical fashion Morante here states, even at this early stage of her career, what was to become one of the fundamental assumptions of her poetics: the aesthetic-existential search moves in space and time by progressive shifts between our "images" and those of others. Highly indicative in this specific text is the evocation of an artistic pilgrimage that is transformed from the lay to the mystical, in an exegetical expectation of signs of transcendence. Evidently, traveling serves to teach us less about the world than about ourselves; the secrets that we discover in each city are our own secrets (MC). This is the fundamental thought that lies behind the concept of "necessary *realism*" that Morante was to elaborate over the coming decades.

It is particularly interesting to note that even at this period in her life (*pace* those who deny the young Morante any originality), two themes that later became fundamental to the major works, even as they run through each work in distinctive ways, are here fused coherently, cohesive within their thematic unity, ancestral and foundational: these are the voyage as existential experience and the exploration of our own inner itinerary. Equally remarkable is the fact that in this text we already glimpse what was to be so important in Morante's great novels, the opposition between an individual and emotive vision of reality, and the outrage of mere unreality. Also foreshadowed here is the Morantian notion of "alibi," not to mention the associated perception of the "diverse." And we cannot pass on without emphasizing that these same concerns resurface almost forty years later in the novel *Aracoeli*: the persistent motif of travel and of the "gradation of the visual faculty" remain two of the key elements around which the multiple levels of significance and functionality are articulated.

During the same period that saw the publication of "Mille città in una," Morante was keeping a private "book of dreams," the *Lettere ad Antonio,* which appeared posthumously with the title *Diario 1938*. In this rough, oneiric, mystical, and self-analytical notebook, we plainly see all the signs of an early, ingenuous encounter between Morante and the theories of Freud. During those months, Morante was reading Freud's *Introduction to Psychoanalysis:* "Ci sono in noi degli intuiti, delle vie psicologiche ignote, e talvolta un sogno può servire a ritrovarli" (21 January, D38 12; "In us there are intuitions, hidden psychological paths, and sometimes a dream can help us to rediscover them"). The text investigates with youthful insistence the erotic valence of some of the dreams, although this generates no particular transparency of sense and meaning: rather, we see an ambiguous and unresolved contempt for a body, which is experienced as an encumbrance, such as the description of the hot, liquid heaviness of her period that weighs her down (19 January, D38 6). Or else the body is perceived as funereal: "Niente mi dà il senso della morte come il mio spirito schiavo per ore e ore di questi piccoli divertimenti osceni" (19 January, D38 5; "nothing gives me so much a sense of death as my spirit enslaved for hours on end to these obscene little diversions"). The body is humiliating and wretched, squalid above all: "I miei sogni continuano a rivelarmi le sudicie correnti della mia vita, i bassi padroni che la tengono preda" (23 January, D38 19; "My dreams continue to reveal to me the sordid currents of my life, the vile masters who keep it in their grasp"). From this specific point of view any therapeutically optimistic interpretation put forward by critics, who have frequently sought to give an inappropriate narrative consistency to the notebook, seems out of place.

More surprising in *Lettere ad Antonio* are the asides and corollaries, personal and undoubtedly rendered extreme by her still youthful age, those reflections on art that have been so substantially influenced by her reading of Schopenhauer and Nietzsche. In this light, Morante attributes an unconscious will to the world and to the myriad of phenomena that make it up. This will, avenging itself for the scant attention and desire shown by the subject, stokes our desire as in a furnace (21 January, D38 12). It is within this sphere of ideas that we should understand the first and only apparition of the interlocutor Antonio, an apparition hitherto insufficiently taken into account by critics. With the aim of offering resistance to the irrational tyranny of the "will," Morante's choice moves under the dialectic sign of the epistolary conversation and of relationships among humans, and thus toward reason. Within this primary structure of communicative fiction (whether Antonio is a real or imaginary referent is entirely beside the point), Morante aims to keep at bay any plunge into introspection or solipsism. The fact that the "alibi" Antonio disappears from the text points even more clearly to the frankness of writing never meant for publication.

In other words, if the visions of reality and of the world (the "representations") are legitimately multiple against the unstoppable sclerotization of the purely intellectual, that life which "diventa ogni giorno più stupida, una schiavitù e un'ansia dei bisogni fisici: materiali e sessuali" (19 January, D38 5; "becomes more stupid by the day, a slavish anxiety for physical needs, whether material or sexual")—a sentence that is at the same time introductory and the apparent reason for the notebook-epistolary—the devotee's perception of transcendent truths springs not from outside but from within each individual. Such perception wells up from the territory of dream that, aside from any physical senses, has its own senses, which give rise to all the joy of satisfaction (21 January, D38 12). It is no accident that Morante regards it as a strange gift of God that when we wake we can recall the different world of dream (2 February, D38 31). The sudden flashes of memory that take us back to landscapes and events dreamed and then forgotten are genuine epiphanies that make us aware of the miracle that is dream (23 January, D38 20).

The "memoria che appartiene al sogno" (23 January, D38: 17; "memory that belongs to dream") is immediately associated with the anamnesis that leads to knowledge of the platonic "idea." In the dream of 23 January, Morante states that she owns a concrete *object* that is familiar to her (and whose symbolic oneiric transparency is so taken for granted that it is almost irrelevant: an alien-fish). Aside from its emblematic function, this entity is also a venerable, almost divine being, even while destined for swift and inevitable physical and physiological decline due to poor environmental conditions. In the eyes of the dreamer, a bizarre antonomasia leads this creature to become confused with the figure of Plato. The dream, then, is a momentary illumination, a briefly permitted glimpse of what resides eternally beneath the moon and, in neoplatonic terms, in divine intelligence.

But a new cognition of the originating vision, and some worthwhile notions to be taken as the act of remembering, are not enough for the restless Morante. Taking Schopenhauer once more as her starting point, she follows the thread of a criterion adequate to such a thought. What's more, this thought is immediately contaminated with the bloody and tragic figuration of the gnosis, which will be her destiny as a poet. Ideas, understood in the Platonic sense, are the first objectification of the universal will, and they make themselves visible particularly through the work of art. Morante wonders, "[c]he il segreto dell'arte sia qui? *Ricordare* come l'opera si è vista in uno stato di sogno, ridirla come si è vista, cercare soprattutto di *ricordare*. Ché forse tutto l'inventare è ricordare?" (23 January, D38 20; emphasis in original; "Is this then the secret of art? *Remembering* how the work has been seen in a dream, saying it as it has been seen, trying above all to *remember*. Maybe all invention is memory").

But in practice, with the adoption of the Schopenhauerian paradigm, the contemplative and ascetic writer places the artist, the pure subject of knowledge, outside of herself. At the same time, within the oneiric dimension of *Diario 1938* (*Lettere ad Antonio*) the Nietzschean inference is utterly pertinent. "Artist of dream and ecstasy" is indeed the figure conceived by the young Nietzsche fascinated by the ideas of Schopenhauer, who dismantles and re-elaborates the components of reality, overcoming every concrete and individual limit to retrace in the dream-delirium the true and unique dimension of authentic life. And it is with an authentic Dionysian spirit (Baudelarian indeed, *mutatis mutandis*) that the writer Elsa Morante ventures forth among nightmares and disorders, between coitus, intoxication, and artificial excitement, seeking out a physiological answer that might, at the same time, be an existential and artistic one.

Thus if, on the one hand, such a search can conclude only with the experience of death, one's own death eternally transfused into that of others (see 15 June, but also 25 February onward, and the lucid reflection of 7 March [D38 48–49]), and with the Silenic question "Perché sono nata così? Perché sono nata?" (27 April, D38 57; "Why was I born like this? Why was I born?"), the artistic dimension of Elsa Morante clarifies itself by virtue of the tie of brotherhood that connects Apollo and Dionysus.

It should not surprise us then that the narrative plot of the novel, the construction of the story, is, under the sign of Apollo, architecture (we might think of the repeated vision of the cathedral as well as the less-soothing one of the film-theater of 20 January [D38 9–10]). But structure and function offer themselves up only when urged into being by the Dionysian creative force of music, by pure will. In the dream, architecture and music are mingled (22 April, D38 55), the dreamer writes explicitly, and she explains judiciously that it is perhaps her compulsive habit of listening to the radio that leads her to dream of cathedrals (22 April, D38 56), even if, in fact, it is in the dream of 20 January that she openly associates music and song with the possibility of giving sense (and content) to her own existential representations:

> Ora capisco da dove è nata la grande e ombrosa cattedrale del mio [sogno]. Ieri sera discorrendo dell'arte nel romanzo e nell'intreccio con V. ricordo di avere di sfuggita paragonato la costruzione del racconto a un'architettura, a una cattedrale, le scene isolate alle vetrate. Da questa parola fuggitiva è nata quell'immensa cattedrale sognata. (23 January, D38 20)

> Now I understand where the great and shadowy cathedral of my own [dream] was born. Yesterday evening while I was discussing the art of the novel with V. I remember suddenly comparing the structure of a story with architecture, with a cathedral, the separate scenes to the cathedral windows. From this fleeting word was born the immense cathedral of my dream.

We should also remember the dream of 22 April (D38 55–56), which is in no way homologous with the previous one. But the cathedral, more than the structural archetype of a novel-form thought through in advance (a superficial and inadequate image that has given rise to the decadent misunderstandings of some critics in dealing with Morante's works), is the primary and mystic manifestation (traditionally recognized, and almost a commonplace in its implication with the divine) of the artistic genius against the tyranny of the causal and necessitating connections of the will. It is not the "cathedral" in itself that wishes to be an object of art or a simulacrum; rather it represents the condition, as well as being the obvious vehicle for the approaching of the sacred, for the formation of the work of art.

It is for this specific reason that the six-month sequence of dreams registers an indecisive and inconclusive relationship with the direct vision of the "cathedral," which occasionally offers itself (23 January [D38 18]; 17 February [D38 34–35]; 22 April [D38 55–56]), or else, while desired, does not give itself up (2 February [D38 29]; 16 March [D38 50]).

The second dream of 20 January (D38 9–10) unequivocally stages the existential condition of the writer. The Luce Institute film at which the dreamer is the only spectator and at the same time absolute protagonist is shown inside the enormous and sumptuous hall of a film-theater which is completely empty: the employees, as if they were part of the decor, are "abbandonati come marionette su qualche poltrona" ("abandoned like puppets on some chairs") or else look half asleep. In the sterile and vacuous luxury of the lighted lamps, the tapestries, the carpeted flooring, and the stuffed armchairs, the woman dreaming is in fact the spectator of herself and that means that "non c'è spettacolo dunque. Butto il biglietto ed esco. *Ma subito sento una musica di orchestrina*. Rientro dall'ingresso a ringhiera, come quello dei musei" (emphasis added: "there is then no show. I throw the ticket away and walk out. *But straight away I hear the music of a small orchestra*. I go back in through the turnstile as in a museum"). Animated and vibrating with the unexpected *inner* music, the writer's feverish expectation of success, passively sick with solitude, is once again set alight, but only to meet with further disappointment: there is no show, the enormous hall is empty. This condition of dissatisfaction and frustration will begin to dissipate only with the later shift toward a more active existential phase: "Stanotte *cercavo* la mia Chiesa [. . .] E poi stanotte *scrivevo* delle canzoni dolcissime, musica e parole" (16 March, D38 50; emphasis added; "Last night *I was looking for* my Church [. . .] And last night *I was writing* beautiful songs, both lyrics and music").

The cathedrals together with the other spaces employed in representation, whether sacred or profane (the film-theater of 20 January, the cinema-train of 22 January [D38 13–14], and so on), are the oneiric scenarios within which the dreamer, totally lost, projects herself, intent on her *recherche*, her aesthetic-existential quest; and it is from these scenarios that a first, partial answer comes to meet her inquiry: the vision of the characters.

> Da dove vengono i personaggi dei sogni? Intendo dire non quelli che, più o meno vagamente e fedelmente, raffigurano i personaggi della nostra vita diurna, ma gli altri, gli ignoti. E alcuni (ad es. quella suora della cattedrale) hanno un carattere ben delineato, umano. Sono vere e proprie *creazioni artistiche*. (25 January, D38 21; emphasis in original)

> Where do characters in dreams come from? I don't mean those who more or less vaguely or faithfully are like the characters in our daily lives, but the others, the ones we don't know. And some of them (such as the nun in the cathedral) have a rounded, human character. They are really and truly *artistic creations*.

These are characters whose mere appearance reveals them to possess a perceptible, typical, and compact essentiality, an exuberance and autonomous substance far removed from mere authorial psychologizing:

> Non so perché i personaggi e le espressioni del sogno mi si imprimano nella mente con più forza di quelli della realtà. Più che paesaggi e creature, le visioni del sogno sono per me dei *sentimenti*. E' il sentimento di un paese che io sogno, il sentimento di una persona. Per questo i tratti e i colori danno una commozione quasi dolorosa. (14 March, D38 49; emphasis in original)

> I don't know why the characters and expressions of dream impress themselves on my mind more strongly that those of reality. More than landscape and creatures, the visions of dream, are for me, *feelings*. It is the feeling of a town that I dream, the feeling of a person. This is why the features and colors move me in a way that is almost painful.

During the following years Morante returned to essay writing rarely, but tellingly. There are the seven short pieces in 1950 for *Il mondo* ("Rosso e bianco," in *Pro o contro* 3–30) in which she ironically and wittily picks up on her aesthetic train of thought, applying it, above all, though not exclusively, to literature. We have to wait until 1955 for a more substantial contribution on figurative art. This is the year in which she wrote the introduction to the catalogue accompanying the exhibition of Renato Guttuso at the Seventh Quadriennale Nazionale d'Arte di Roma (Bardini, *Morante* 704–06).

In describing the paintings of her close friend, Morante puts forward some measured considerations on realism in art, considerations that will re-emerge in more organized form but in more or less the same words in her well-known answers to the survey "Nove domande sul romanzo" ("Nine Questions on the Novel") carried out in 1959 by *Nuovi argomenti* (*Pro o contro* 95–118). From this point of view, the coherent and autonomous introduction can be seen as a first draft, within the domain of painting, of the later contribution. The answers to the *Nuovi argomenti* survey should be seen as the fruit of long reflection over the years and not tied to the instance of this particular survey.

Morante begins by constructing her personal definition of realism, dismissing the other common definitions formulated at the time by both partisans and detractors:

> [S]pesso, all'udire certi *realisti*, o loro avversari, parlare di *realismo*, si ha l'impressione che gli uni e gli altri offendano la realtà, col porle dei limiti veramente troppo soggettivi, e arbitrari. Si avrebbe voglia di rispondere (se anche ciò non fosse stato detto mille volte), che l'arte è sempre realista, o sempre astratta, a scelta: giacché non è mai stato ancora smentito un principio elementare (e continuamante rivoluzionario nei suoi effetti). Che l'arte, cioè, si nutre della realtà (e questo sarebbe il suo necessario *realismo*), per esprimere, attraverso il multiforme, il cangiante, e il corruttibile della realtà, una verità poetica incorruttibile (e questa sarebbe la sua naturale e legittima *astrazione*). E tutto il resto è letteratura, o, nel caso migliore, artigianato.
>
> La ricchezza della realtà è inesauribile, e comprende anche tutti i simboli possibili, tutte le possibili favole. Ma purtroppo, nell'epoca presente, alcuni artisti, esangui, o scoraggiati, negano questa ricchezza. Mentre gli altri, ingannati, forse, dalla loro coscienza rudimentale, riducono il movimento meraviglioso della realtà a una convenzione immobile. (RG 704: emphasis in original)

> Often, listening to certain *realists*, or their adversaries, speaking of *realism*, we have the impression that both camps are offending reality by imposing upon it limits that are too subjective, too arbitrary. We would like to answer, as if it had not already been said a million times, that art is always realist, or always abstract, as you choose, since one elementary principle that is continually revolutionary in its effects has never been found wanting. This is that art feeds on reality (this would be its necessary *realism*) in order to express, through the multifarious, changing, corruptible aspect of reality, an incorruptible poetic truth, which would be its natural and legitimate *abstraction*). And all the rest is literature or, in the best of cases, craft.
>
> Reality holds an inexhaustible wealth that comprises all possible symbols, all possible fables. Sadly, in today's times, some artists, bloodless or discouraged, deny such wealth, while other ones, fooled perhaps by their rudimentary conscience, reduce the marvellous movement of reality to a static convention.

Availing herself of the surprising complicity of Gÿorgÿ Lukács in his *Essays on Realism* and *Marxism and Literary Criticism*, who at several points speaks of the incorruptible aesthetic honesty of the artist, whose entire activity is to be placed on the concrete plane of a constant civil engagement (it would be superfluous here to weigh up the final consequences, which are to be firmly rejected by the author over the coming years), Morante identifies the "necessary realism" of the artist in an overarching act of faith. With absolute trust the artist must feed on the inexhaustible richness of reality. If reality has its own proper and most authentic dimension in multifariousness, in change and incorruptibility (in "Mille città in una" the author was already speaking of "apparenze infinite," of "infinite appearances"), the task of the artist is to operate the transformation, and transubstantiation, of corruptible reality into an "incorruptible poetic truth." The artist achieves this by selecting from an infinity of symbols, plots, and structures. This is an operation that is perfected through a legitimate and natural abstraction. The crisis of current times, however, produces artists who are timid and lack courage, myopically denying any such richness of reality, or else limited and rigid individuals who find their only point of reference in stereotype and convention. And in parallel fashion, in the literary sphere, we find certain small-minded reviewers of novels who take it upon themselves to speak in arbitrary fashion about engagement and evasion, and who believe they can pass judgment on a book simply on the basis of its adherence to a given political program. These people one and all believe themselves entitled to make reference to a standard, to a conventional and always identical "feticcio inerte e rudimentale nel quale essi pretendono di identificare la 'realtà assoluta'" (SR 48–49; "inert and rudimentary fetish in which they claim to identify 'absolute reality'").

Renato Guttuso, on the other hand, possesses the gift of seeing reality and the capacity to be faithful to it: in other words, to create poetry. Morante underscores the need for the writer or artist fully to participate in the human drama, as Guttuso does, and in his works she recognizes an aesthetic choice not dissimilar to her own. Among the infinite *pretexts* (which is, as we know, a deeply Morantian term), the realist artist, by means of his participation, chooses man/character as the essential protagonist of his representations in the firm conviction that every real human drama, even if it is apparently limited and subjective, is a total reflection of authentic reality: the moment of utter bliss, in the destiny of all great artists, is when we see "l'accordo fra la coscienza e il temperamento" (RG 705: "the coming together of conscience and temperament"). Shaken to the core by the appalling events of the twentieth century to which he bears witness, his art goes beyond mere leisure or aesthetic preoccupation: "Gli uomini e le donne di Guttuso [. . .] non si definiscono nelle loro singole persone, o nei loro volti, ma signficano, piuttosto (e quasi gridano) attraverso il movimento della scena, la tragedia comune" (RG 705; "Guttuso's men and women [. . .] do not define themselves through their individuality, or through their faces, but they signify [and almost cry out], through the movement of the scene, a common tragedy"). Fleeing the merely beautiful and consoling, but without sacrificing clarity and with passionate participation, Guttuso bears witness to the common tragedy of his times; first the war with the drawings of the series *Gott mit uns,* then the drama of the proletariat with a cycle of great paintings that seek to participate fully in the life of men and that includes among others *Zolfara*, a work that Morante chooses to read from an unequivocally Marxist perspective:

> Qua l'uomo non è figurato, come altrove (anche nell'opera dello stesso Guttuso), soltanto nel suo movimento e nelle sua vivace struttura; ma proprio nella qualità diversa e ineffabile del suo destino. Dal *caruso*, e dal giovane minatore, e dal trapanatore di roccia a sinistra, alla figura ricurva col fazzoletto rosso e alla figura contratta di destra, che scende nella miniera, *come un topo*, l'uomo è qua rappresentato nella sua grazia e nella sua tragica miseria, nella sua angoscia e nella sua amicizia. E infine (sia ringraziata la poesia) anche nella sua immaginazione, vanto eterno dell'umanità. (RG 705–06; emphasis in original)

> Here man is not depicted, as elsewhere (and even in the work of Guttuso himself) only in his movement and in his living structure, but precisely in the different and ineffable quality of his destiny. Whether the *caruso*, the young miner, the rock driller on the left, the bent figure with the red neckerchief, or the squatting figure on the right, descending into the mine *like a mouse*, man is here represented in his grace and in his tragic wretchedness, in his anguish and in his capacity for friendship. And also (thanks be to poetry) in his imagination, the eternal glory of humanity.

Elsa Morante lends her full support to the uncontested leader of the group of artistic militants who, in the period following World War II, favor a pictorial production that retains a recognizable figurative element, offering to some extent a mimesis of reality, immune from intellectual excess and aestheticizing formalization—legible, above all, in a narrative key. Thus she sets her face resolutely against those who follow the latest international trends of the avant-garde, opting for a so-called informal abstraction, as in the work of Emilio Vedova, or for a provocative and extreme experimentalism, as is the case of Lucio Fontana and Alberto Burri. In 1957 Morante was to write:

> Quei valori che [. . .] potrebbero definirsi *valori della morte,*
> si fanno riconoscere, nelle nostre estetiche contemporanee,
> dallo strano culto che queste hanno dell'informe (e voglia
> pure, questo informe, nascondersi sotto le esteriorità

dell'*astratto* [. . .]). Ora, l'informe, proprio, è il contrario
della poesia, com'è il contrario della vita: giacché (e la cosa,
veramente suona troppo comune per essere detta!) la poesia, come la vita, vuole proprio dare una forma e un ordine
assoluti agli oggetti dell'universo, traendoli dall'informe e
dal disordine, e cioè dalla morte. ("Il poeta di tutta una vita,"
in *Pro o contro* 35)

The values that [. . .] might be defined as the *values of death*
can be recognized within our contemporary aesthetics by
the strange cult of formlessness (no matter how hard this
formlessness tries to hide behind the exterior of *abstraction*
[. . .]). Formlessness is the precise opposite of poetry, as it
is the opposite of life, since—and really this seems too
obvious to have to be said!—poetry, like life, aims to give
form and order to the objects of the universe, drawing them
out of formlessness and disorder, out that is from death.

In her essay on Guttuso, Morante discusses the current use of
the word *modern*, rejecting the cliché that automatically defines
as modern what is iconoclastic and antitraditional:

Dicendo di un pittore che è moderno, intenderei dire ch'egli
possiede, come una naturale ricchezza, le esperienze degli
artisti precedenti a lui (anche se, pari a un gran signore, sa
rivoltarsi a questa ricchezza, e dimenticarla, per guardare
unicamente la realtà). Per lui, le scoperte passate non sono
state inutili. Da quelle più antiche, alle più vicine: le luci
degli impressionisti, e l'espressionismo, le geometrie del
cubismo, e il fuoco e l'eleganza dei *fauves*.
   Tali diverse scoperte, però, non sono finite nel risultato
di disgregare ai suoi occhi la realtà, ma, al contrario in
quello di confermargliene la ricchezza favolosa. E' proprio
una nuova fiducia in questa ricchezza favolosa, la novità che
gli uomini moderni aspettano dai poeti moderni. (RG 706)

In saying of a painter that he is modern I mean that he possesses, as with a natural richness, the experience of artists
who have come before him (even if like a great master he
knows how to rebel against this richness and forget it in
order to gaze solely at reality itself). For him, the discoveries of the past have not been futile, whether those of ancient
or more recent times—the light of the impressionists,
expressionism, the geometry of cubism, and the fire and elegance of the *fauves*.

> But all of these different discoveries do not lead to the
> disintegration of reality in his eyes, but rather they confirm
> to him the fabulous wealth of that reality. It is exactly a
> renewed faith in this wealth of reality that modern men
> expect from modern poets.

As she was to write two years later in an article dedicated to
Umberto Saba, the modernity of the artist lies in his constant
and vital being abstracted from the present, and not in a head-
long determination to keep up to date, which always ends by
translating itself into the loss of all historical memory or into
some defensive form of existential oblivion. And when in 1959
she replies to the "Nine Questions on the Novel" Morante
returns in part to this same essay on Guttuso, once more underlining her total lack of trust in the face of any artistic expression
that manifests itself simply through the automatic registering
of a state or a fact:

> Il nostro secolo è il luogo di un passaggio drammatico: che
> si può tradurre, nella psicologia, in una crisi d'angoscia.
> Così accade che gran parte degli artisti odierni proiettino,
> nel mondo, le proprie immagini reali (che essi chiamano
> astratte) di questa angoscia. Tali, che, molto spesso, per
> quanto si nominino "artisti," essi, invece, abdicano, nell'atto
> stesso di esprimersi, alla prima ragione dell'arte: che è la
> forma della verità, espressa attraverso la realtà delle cose.
> Le loro immagini si limitano a rendere la greggia realtà della
> loro angoscia. E qui, curiosamente, certi *astrattisti* di ogni
> arte si ricongiungono con quelli che essi ritengono i loro
> contrari: e cioè i *naturalisti*, e i *documentaristi*. Difatti, gli
> uni e gli altri significano il medesimo fenomeno: registra-
> zione di una realtà greggia—non importa se soggettiva o
> oggettiva—nella rinuncia al valore della verità, e dunque
> all'arte.
> A una simile rinuncia—benché per altra via—si ridu-
> cono pure i seguaci di un altro (e, in certo modo, opposto)
> *astrattismo*: i quali, fuggendo impauriti dalla pienezza della
> loro coscienza, spettatrice dell'angoscia, si esiliano nel
> deserto estremo dei rapporti matematici e spaziali. Si po-
> trebbe ripetere, per loro, che un esercizio ascetico, in se
> stesso, non significa un risultato artistico; ma, ormai, viene
> il sospetto che tutte queste "ascesi" dell'arte contempora-
> nea s'ingannino, da se stesse, anche nella loro possibile pre-
> sunzione edificante. [. . .] Rimane, in ogni caso, la certezza

che anche questa *astrazione* ascetica, come la precedente astrazione, è una risoluta negazione dell'arte. (SR 64–65; emphasis in original)

This century of ours is the site of a dramatic shift that can be translated into psychological terms as a crisis of anguish. Thus it is that so many of today's artists project onto the world their own real images (which they call abstractions) of this anguish. The result is that often, however much they proclaim themselves to be artists, in the very act of expressing themselves they abdicate the first reason for art, which is the form of truth expressed through the reality of things. Their images limit themselves to rendering the raw reality of their anguish. And here, curiously, certain *abstract* artists of whatever form come round full circle to meet up with those who claim to be their opposite, the *naturalists* and the *documentarists*. In fact, former and latter both imply the same phenomenon—the registering of a raw reality—never mind whether objective or subjective—in the renunciation of the value of truth, and with it the value of art.

The followers of a different and in some senses opposite *abstraction* are reduced to a similar renunciation, although of a different order. Fleeing in fear from the full light of their own conscience as it observes this anguish, they exile themselves in the extreme desert of mathematical and spatial relationships. We might say again that for them an ascetic exercise in itself does not lead to an artistic result, but suspicion is beginning to dawn that all these mystical exaltations of contemporary art are deceiving themselves in their possible edifying presumption. [. . .] What is left is the certainty that even this ascetic *abstraction*, like the previous abstraction, is a resolute negation of art.

Puncturing and cutting the canvas, substituting the oxyacetylene torch for the paintbrush, using bits of string, hurling one's own anguish and dismay onto the canvas, is not making art. The courage passively to recognize this sickness is not sufficient, if this means only an abject abdication to symbols. The therapeutic flight into regression and reductiveness is certainly a fundamental human experience, amenable to psychological and psychoanalytical explanation, but none of this can be defined as "art." Because the first duty of the artist is to have a clear and disinterested awareness of human consciousness; his work must explore psychological reality and human society, it must pass through anguish "in modo da ritrovare, anche in mezzo alle confusioni più aberranti e difformi, il valore nascosto della verità poetica, per consegnarlo agli altri" (SR 67; "in order to discover, even amidst the most aberrant and misformed confusions, the hidden value of poetic truth, in order to pass it on to others").

In a manner not far removed from that of artists such as Francis Bacon, Alberto Giacometti, or Balthus, Morante looks on realism as an existential choice of non-concealment. The work of art is pushed to an endless search for new meanings of reality; and while it remains far off from any passive representation of nature or the daily affairs of human life, its copying of reality is an uncontainable anxiety to unveil what fleeting appearances conceal.

In comparison with a large part of militant criticism, which at the time followed with selective attention particularly those artists of informal and action painting who aimed freely to translate their deepest inner pulses into the sign, Morante was strong in her sacral realist belief and always and ever consistent with her declaration of herself as by habit, nature, and destiny a writer of stories in prose. Morante the novelist, as philosopher and psychologist (SR 46), seems very close to that restricted group of theorists and scholars that includes Roberto Longhi and Cesare Brandi, brought together by their predilection for a modern art of purely figurative type that is deeply rooted in a dialectical relationship with the history of art.

And yet Morante remains strongly critical of the need to take account of the profound shifts in society through expressive means. While abstract-informal trends may have rejected the mimesis of reality, claiming the autonomy of thought and the creative gesture, and while the material processes of formlessness have put into question not only the image (Croce's "form") but also the procedures and tools with which to bring it into being, it does not follow that we can speak simply of the death of the picture, or, to use the more schematic terms of the mass media, of the death of painting. "Morte della pittura?" is indeed the title of a survey to which Morante responds in 1960.[3] In her "Risposta," Morante states that as different materials (rags, rubbish, bits of old ironwork, and so on) used by some artists are not materials suitable for painting, the objects created with these materials do not belong to the realm of art. The widespread use of unusual tools and materials to produce "objects for art shows" leads logically to a blurring of distinctions between painting, sculpture, and installation. But when even the most bizarre mish-mash and the whole gamut of uses to which they are put goes so far as to exclude any pictorial quality, this does not mean that the disappearance of "painting" can be sanctioned:

> Riguardo, invece, all'arte propria del dipingere (pittura), non c'è dubbio che il suo linguaggio si rinnova di continuo, come ogni espressione vivente e vitale; ma si tratta sempre di un rinnovamento *dall'interno* e non *dall'esterno*, e, in tale senso, il rinnovamento del linguaggio pittorico è in atto da molti secoli, e non da dieci anni. Le crisi, cadute e deviazioni che spesso lo accompagnano non negano la necessità della pittura, ma anzi confermano che quest'arte è una naturale espressione umana, nata per accompagnare la vicenda umana fino alla fine. E tanto più illecito, dunque, è il confonderla con la non-arte: la quale, per suo destino, è nata-morta. ("Risposta," in Bardini, *Morante* 715–16; emphasis in original]

> As far as the real art of painting is concerned, there is no doubt that its language is constantly being renewed, like every other living and vital expression; but it is always a question of renewal *from within* and not *from without*, and in this sense the renewal of pictorial language has been going on for several centuries and not just for ten years. The crises, lapses, and deviations that frequently accompany it do not deny the necessity of painting, rather they confirm that this art is a natural human expression, born to accompany the business of being human right to the end. It is therefore even less allowable to confuse it with non-art that is destined to be stillborn.

Even more drastically than in her previous essays, Morante rejects as stillborn what she defines as non-art, that is, as she had written in her 1957 essays on Saba, the series of manufactured goods through which "our contemporary aesthetics," so attached to formlessness, spread the values of *death*, while real poetry, which gives form and order to the universe, is the repository of the values of *life* (see IPTV 34–35). Morante writes on the last page of "Sul romanzo," a real work of art can be recognized simply by the fact that it always provokes, whether in the reader or in the spectator, "un aumento di vitalità" (SR 72–73: "a surge of vitality"). Showing surprising affinities with some of the aesthetic theories of Hans Georg Gadamer, which were appearing at this time, in the 1960s Morante will take these reflections of hers, so grounded in life and in living creatures, to their extreme conclusions. And while it might be possible, if ultimately superfluous, to establish a substantial overlap of ideas with those of the unfortunate young painter Bill Morrow,[4] rather more convincing is what Morante would write in 1965 for the painter Bice Brichetto, for the opening of her first show.[5] First Morante explains, using all the rhetorics of simplicity, what "painting a picture" means to her:

> disporsi davanti a una tela bianca, coi sette colori naturali della scala e le loro combinazioni; e là umilmente, dispera- tamente, cercare di tradurre in linguaggio reale visibile quanto il mondo dei sensi offre alla vista; finché la materia comune e superficiale della tela non si trasformi nella intimità preziosa, tenera e parlante della vita unica e indivisibile. (BB 726)

> Standing in front of a blank canvas with the seven natural colors of the spectrum and their various combinations and there humbly, desperately, seek to translate into real and vis- ible language what the world of the senses offers to our vision, until the common and superficial material of the can- vas is transformed into a precious intimacy, tenderly speak- ing of the one and indivisible life.

The subjects, or in Morante's terms, the *pretexts*, which the world of the senses offers to the vision of the artist can be in appearance the most harmless: a familiar landscape, a trailing vine, a rose. However:

> [q]ual è oggi il pittore che avrà il coraggio di dipingere una rosa? Ci vuol più coraggio a dipingere una rosa che ad affrontare una divisione corazzata. E ciò che fa tanta paura non è la inerme, giovane rosa in se stessa; ma, a schermo di lei, i simulacri di tutte le innumerevoli rose defunte che già furono ritratte nel corso della Storia Universale della pit- tura. I pittori, insomma, si son resi incapaci di guardare

all'oggetto presente con attenzione diretta e libera, emancipata da tutte le convenzioni senili, i pregiudizi e le determinazioni sociali. Mentre che la prima condizione di ogni poesia è proprio questa: di saper sempre guardare il mondo col medesimo interesse con cui lo guarderebbe la prima coscienza umana al primo, drammatico Lunedì della Creazione. Per restituire al tempo, continuamente, lo splendore originario delle cose, in luogo delle apparenze logorate dall'abitudine. (BB 726)

What painter today would have the courage to paint a rose? It takes more courage to paint a rose than to face a heavily armed division of troops. What incites fear is not the harmless, youthful rose itself, but screening it, the simulacra of all the countless dead roses that have been painted in the course of the Universal History of painting. Painters, in other words, have become incapable of looking at the present object with direct and uninhibited attention, free from all decrepit convention, prejudices, and social determinations. While the first condition of poetry is precisely this: to know how to look at the world with the same interest with which the first human consciousness would have contemplated it on the first, dramatic Monday of creation. To continually give back to time the original splendor of the rose in place of the worn out appearances of habit.

While avoiding any fall into retrogressive or conservative equivocations, Morante's position is clear: the only real artist is the person who has faith in his/her personal and authentic capacity to apprehend reality empirically. As a person of sensibility the artist understands, in fact, that the consciousness that accompanies every separate representation of his, releases latent virtualities in the represented object. Finally, the work of art speaks more about the original than the original itself, in its pure and simple showing of itself. Every authentic empirical perception opens up onto transcendental perception.

The parable of the eighth day of creation conjured up in the passage just quoted recalls Russian existentialist metaphysics and the writings of Nikolaj Berdjaev (Bardini, *Morante* 341–44) and is present in Morante's notes as far back as the first draft of *Menzogna e sortilegio*. In short, the artistic ideal of Elsa Morante cannot and does not wish to be merely aesthetic but, expressed by a poetic existence that seeks to recognize itself as founded and anchored in the divine, it reveals itself as it passes to an ethical and religious stage. Hence the passionate tension toward a christological dimension of making poetry that will characterize her entire production of the 1960s and 1970s. But when the artist is reduced to a state of lethargy, reflection and perception cease:

> A questo proposito, mi è caro citare qui l'amato, grande pittore Nicolas De Stäel [*sic*], che ha detto: *Il faut que ce soit donné, donné absolument à propos de tout, un prétexte.* Come ogni oggetto che si propone all'artista coraggioso, naturalmente le rose di Bice non sono che un pretesto, per indagare, lungo la trama mitologica della realtà apparente, fin nel suo ordito acceso, sempre vivente e attuale. (BB 726; emphasis in original)

> I love to quote on this the great beloved painter Nicolas De Stäel [*sic*] who said: *il faut que ce soit donné, donné absolument à propos de tout, un prétexte.* Like every object that offers itself to the artist of courage, Bice's roses are of course nothing more than a pretext to investigate the web and weave of apparent reality.

The quotation from Nicolas De Staël is taken from the *Lettre à Pierre Lecuire*, written in 1949, published in Paris in 1958, in the monograph of Antoine Tudal. The reference to De Staël is a response to Morante's need to valorize every artistic journey that rejects the fascination of formlessness in favor of a search for "truth," and the artistic parabola of Nicolas illustrates the point perfectly. De Staël chose to abandon figuration of the object in its phenomenological appearance, aiming instead at a pure representation of dynamic and formative essence in pictorial metaphor. For the same reason, in the last years of his life, before his suicide in 1955, he turned back to the image of things, to the presence marked by the eternal. In the letter quoted, he writes, "Everything is there, outside of us [. . .] Never think of the definitive without the ephemeral." De Staël too, then, seeks in the image of the world not the reflection of existential anguish; rather, in external reality he looks for the witness of a superior order, and confidence in a redemption of the inner condition of disorientation in the face of the chaotic indeterminacy with which the world presents itself to consciousness. And his anguish, if anything, is that of the enfeebled artist in the face of an infinite search that his long personal labors will never exhaust.

Every real artist then, and each artist in his own way, as he makes poetry in the midst of men with his eyes fixed on reality, realizing works that neither betray, blur, abandon, abjure, or obliterate this reality but feed off it in the name of a "surge vitality," contributes to bringing a little closer an interhuman determination of the meaning of being in general. The poet is the one who can still, messianically, if not save the world, at least alert it to the "collective unreality." And it is in these terms that in the lecture "Pro o contro la bomba atomica" (*Pro o contro* 101–20) from the same period, Morante comes to put forward the same concept. The real poet is fully aware of the destiny of atomic disintegration that moves the person of the twentieth century, infected by the delirious plague of petit bourgeois culture, and trapped in the psychoanalytic scheme of things that opposes the drive toward death to the drive toward life. By his very nature tending toward integrity, as the only joyful, liberating condition of his consciousness, he should take up the fight on behalf of what is for Morante an obvious and elementary definition of both art and poetry:

> *l'arte è il contrario della disintegrazione.* E perché? Ma semplicemente perché la ragione propria dell'arte, la sua giustificazione, il solo suo motivo di presenza e sopravvivenza, o, se si preferisce, la sua *funzione*, è appunto questa: di impedire la disintegrazione della coscienza umana, nel suo quotidiano, e logorante, e *alienante* uso col mondo; di restituirle di continuo, nella confusione irreale, e frammentaria, e *usata*, dei rapporti esterni, l'integrità del reale, o in una parola, *la realtà* (ma attenzione ai truffatori, che presentano, sotto questa marca di realtà, delle falsificazioni artificiali e deperibili). La realtà è perennemente viva, accesa, attuale. Non si può avariare, né distruggere, e non decade. Nella realtà, la morte non è che un altro movimento della vita. Integra, la realtà è l'integrità stessa: nel suo movimento multiforme e cangiante, inesauribile—che non si potrà mai finire di esplorarla—la realtà è una, sempre una. (PC 101–02; emphasis in original)

> *Art is the opposite of disintegration.* And why? Simply because the very reason for art, its justification, its only motive for presence and survival, or if one prefers its *func-*

tion, is exactly this: to prevent the disintegration of human consciousness in its daily, wearisome, *alienating* contact with the world; to continually give back to it, in the unreal, fragmentary, and consuming confusion of external relationships, the integrity of the real, or in a word *reality* (but beware the swindlers, who pass off under cover of reality all sorts of artificial and rotting falsifications). Reality is perennially alive, alight, in the here and now. We cannot cause it to decay, nor destroy it, and it does not perish. In reality, death is but another moment of life. Itself integral, reality is integrity itself: in its multiform and changing, inexhaustible movement, which we will never be able to finish exploring, reality is one, always and ever one. With his own images, which are personal to him and different each time, each authentic artist deals with, defines, and dialogically communicates the truth of the single reality, which unshaken, is a clear cipher of transcendence. The inauthentic artist, on the contrary, repudiates any possibility of truthful readability and communicability of reality, and shows only nothingness.

But it was to be with her essay on Fra Angelico entitled "The Blessed Propagandist of Heaven" that Morante would bring to a close her reflections on figurative art (Morante, *Pro o contro* 121–27). This brief piece appears as a preface to Rizzoli's 1970 volume *L'opera completa dell'Angelico* and inserted posthumously in the collection *Pro o contro la bomba atomica e altri scritti*. Critics have demonstrated the extent to which this essay circles within the orbit of *La Storia,* and it certainly anticipates some characteristic elements of the 1974 novel. But it also picks up and reworks concepts already expressed elsewhere.

Morante observes that an artist such as Angelico (in this case an artist who lived in a past still immune from the brute ugliness of today, which means for Morante precisely the *negation* of reality) has "fortunate eyes" that see only what is beautiful; a natural beauty in which we can immediately recognize a model of Paradise incarnate (BPP 124). Guidolino di Pietro, then known as Giovanni da Fiesole (birth and religious names of the famous Beato Angelico), was gifted with the destiny of the born artist, in love with light from the day of his birth, that light which "lo aspetta ogni giorno, dichiarandogli, con la manifestazione dei colori, la presenza del primo amore in tutte le cose" (BPP 126–27; "waits for him every day, declaring to him, with its show of colors, the presence of the first love in all things"). So he discovered his "calling," and it is for this reason that he cannot but be a "propagandist" of the truth.

The concepts of "born artist" and "calling"-profession, passing through Walter Benjamin and Gadamer, lead us toward Wilhelm Dilthey's *Erlebnis*. An indivisible totality of permanent and stable meaning for consciousness, *Erlebnis* (which besides, as we know, originates and legitimates autobiography in literature) can be taken up as an object of aesthetic experience. The works of art that spring from it have the fullness of a symbolic representation that contains within it the total meaning of life.

In the light of this, Angelico, who is at once born painter and, right to the last, man of deep and sincere faith, serenely accepts the task of preparing and bringing to fruition his work, through the double and cyclical structure of an inexhaustible personal search. Living at one and the same time an active sainthood (in his civil engagement, his sermons to the "idiots," in his confrontation with History, in travel, in the historical poem) and art as prayer (in serene detachment, in solitude, in meditation, in the monastery, in lyricism) allows him to establish in the instant that paradoxical and eternally returning "absence-presence" of/in the world that is the beginning and end of each "FP" ("Happy Few") of the *Mondo salvato dai ragazzini*. Perhaps, concludes Morante,

> le mie resistenze al Beato pittore sono colpa, soprattutto, della mia invidia. In realtà, più che nel significato di *santo*, qui, a me, *beato* suona piuttosto in quello di *fortunato*, o *beato lui*. (BPP 123; emphasis in original)

> my resistance to Beato is the fault, above all, of my envy. In reality, more than the meaning of *Saint*, *Beato*, the blessed, to my ears has more the meaning of *fortunate*, or *lucky him*.

Notes

1. Although it appeared posthumously, this volume of essays respects the wishes of the author, who had long been thinking about such a collection, from the early sixties up to her death. See Bardini's *Morante,* which contains all writings (671–731) appearing in the present study except for "Mille città in una," *Diario 1938,* and *Pro o contro la bomba atomica,* listed separately. It is likely, however, that the essay "Il beato propagandista del Paradiso," published for the first time in *L'opera completa dell'Angelico* and reprinted as a postface by the editor of the Adelphi volume, was not part of the author's original plan.

2. In this essay I use the following abbreviations: "Mille città in una" = MC; *Diario 1938* = D38; "Renato Guttuso" = RG; "Sul romanzo" = SR; "Il poeta di tutta la vita" = IPTV; Prefazione per il catalogo della mostra di Bice Brichetto = BB; "Pro o contro la bomba atomica" = PC; "Il beato propagandista del paradiso" = BPP.

3. "Risposta all'inchiesta 'Morte della Pittura?'" ("Response to the Survey 'Morte della pittura?'"), ed. A. Perilli and F. Mauri, originally published in *Almanacco Letterario Bompiani* 1961, qtd. in Bardini, *Morante* 715–16. The survey invited a broad spectrum of artists and intellectuals to give a brief reply to the following question: "Over the last ten years painting has undergone substantial modifications. Do you think that this modification leads to the death of painting or a new form of language?"

4. Perhaps aside from their real artistic value, the highly colored pictures of the American painter Bill Morrow, who died in 1962 at the age of 26, are famous in Italy thanks to their appearance on the front covers of Elsa Morante's books, by the wish of the author.

5. Preface to the catalogue for Bice Brichetto's exhibition in Galleria S. Croce, Florence, 16–30 January 1965 (Bardini, *Morante* 725–27).

Works Cited

Bardini, Marco. *Morante Elsa. Italiana. Di professione, poeta.* Pisa: Nistri-Lischi, 1999.

———. "Scheda sugli esordi editoriali di Elsa Morante." *Italianistica* 3 (1999): 461–67.

Morante, Elsa. *Diario 1938.* Introd. Alba Andreini. Turin: Einaudi, 1989.

———. "Mille città in una." *Prospettive* 4–5 (undated [Feb. 1938]): 14–15, in Bardini, "Scheda sugli esordi editoriali di Elsa Morante" 465–66.

———. *Pro o contro la bomba atomica e altri scritti.* Introd. Cesare Garboli. Milan: Adelphi, 1987.

Schopenauer, Arthur. *The World as Will and Representation.* Trans. E. F. J. Payne. New York: Dover, 1958.

Sharon Wood

Models of Narrative in
Menzogna e sortilegio

> The novel was to be buried in the name of histori-
> cal justice, like poverty, the ruling classes, obsolete
> cars, or top hats.
>
> Milan Kundera
The Art of the Novel

While the Marxist critic Gÿorgÿ Lukács heralded Elsa Morante's
first novel, *Menzogna e sortilegio* (1948), as one of the most
important Italian works of the century, many subsequent critics decried it as an outpost of classical realism, a late and over-
ripe fruit of nineteenth-century narrative forms, a work that was
out of step, out of time, out of date in its supposed unproblematic reproduction of reality, decidedly unmodern in its unfold-
ing of tormented and tortuous sentimental drama. And a
majority of critics appeared to be aghast at a novel of these
dimensions—at over 700 pages—in an age of increasingly
fractured texts that purported to indicate a reality both shattered and fragmented by the experience of modernity.

It is certainly true that Morante had not the slightest interest
in being "al passo"; indeed, she despised the urgent rush of
many of her contemporaries to appear modern, new, or avant-
garde. But this is far from saying that Morante is a logorrheic
scribbler, unaware that times have moved on. Appearing at a
time when the historical and traditional forms of the novel were
under consistent and persistent ideological attack, whether
from the aesthetic avant-garde or current political orthodoxies,
Menzogna e sortilegio evades any standard definition of the
form, at the same time ambitiously and self-consciously presenting itself as a kind of "summa" of the possibilities of the

novel as genre. The cover of the 1975 edition, written by Morante herself, informs us:

> Il modello supremo di *Menzogna e sortilegio* è stato il *Don Chisciotte*, senza dimenticare, in diversa forma, l'*Orlando furioso*. Difatti, come quegli iniziatori esemplari della narrativa moderna segnavano il termine dell'antica epopea cavalleresca, così, nell'ambizione giovanile di Elsa Morante, questo suo primo romanzo voleva anche essere l'ultimo possibile del suo genere: a salutare la fine della narrativa romantica e post-romantica, ossia dell'epopea borghese. (*Opere* 1: lvi)

> The supreme model for *Menzogna e sortilegio* was *Don Quixote*, while not forgetting, in a different way, *Orlando furioso*. In fact, just as those exemplary initiators of modern narrative marked the end point of the ancient chivalric epic, so, in the youthful ambition of Elsa Morante, this first novel of hers aimed to be the last one possible of its kind: to salute the end of narrative and post-romantic narrative, in other words the bourgeois epic.[1]

Morante remained convinced that despite the opprobrium heaped on it by critics and the *addetti al lavoro*, the novel, and the novel in its most expansive form, was nonetheless the genre best suited to approaching the complexities of the modern world and to encapsulating our obsessive, neurotic, modern selves. With each successive novel she describes herself as "romanziere," or the work as a "romanzo," even when the title would appear to point in a different direction, such as *La Storia*. Like the Czech novelist Milan Kundera, several decades later, Morante saw the novel as defining the modern era in Western culture, the talisman of an age of exploration, both of exterior and inner worlds. Morante, too, lays claim to a wider view of modernity and to what Kundera called "the depreciated legacy of Cervantes,"[2] the store of accumulated wisdom and discovery, the weighing of possibilities, the suspension of transcendental or authoritarian judgments, which the novel has to offer. Her image for the novel, to go down in a final blaze of glory, is that of the phoenix, the "fenice lucente" that appears in the dedicatory poem to this first novel. The image of the phoenix, rooted in poetic tradition (Petrarch's "Questa fenice de l'aurata piuma"),[3] recurs throughout the novel, a symbolic trope of fiery splendor and ashes, of death and resurrection, and, on the level of enunciation and narration, of metamorphosis and transformation.

Morante brings to her novel, then, the weight of tradition, but this too is not enough to dismiss her as unfashionable, to be discarded like one of Kundera's top hats. This first novel is an extraordinary tissue of fabulation, drawing on numerous literary models from Cervantes himself to family sagas, from the epistolary novel to epic poetry to the baroque. What is particularly striking is the inclusive, panoramic nature of the text's literary antecedents, its mixture of high and low cultural reference, which predates some of the more clichéd notions of postmodernism. We might perhaps pause to consider that Morante's immersion in European culture makes her one of the most intellectual writers to have emerged from modern Italy. She is an intensely *modern* writer who is certainly not to be confined within the strait-jacket of a flatly pedantic realist aesthetic. In both *Menzogna e sortilegio*, and *L'isola di Arturo* after it, in 1957, Morante is concerned to explore the ways in which her narrators, Elisa and Arturo, approach the business of writing—what they read, what they write, how they position themselves in relation to the text, the models on which they draw. Morante repeatedly foregrounds and stages the process of writing in these two novels, forming an intradiagetic meta-narrative that comments not only on the text in the making but on the capacity and possibilities of the novel itself to serve as a metaphoric representation of the real. The novels are, and *Menzogna e sortilegio* is particularly so, self-consciously literary. Just as her character/narrators find themselves in liminal border spaces, so the texts offer themselves as marking not just an end but a beginning, a revival and *expansion* of the novel, merging a self-conscious tradition with the insights of the twentieth century into the psyche, both Freud and Jung, into obsession and neurosis on both individual and social scales, the whole framed and contextualized by a keen debate on how the resources, and what we might almost call the unconscious of fiction, can best be deployed to help us grasp the world in which we live.

Menzogna e sortilegio is structured less according to a model of paratactic linearity than around a series of specular tropes or discursive moments, around equivalences and doublings that both echo the parallelism of traditional bourgeois narrative and give it a modernist dimension. The narrative framework gives the text a circularity that brings us back finally to Elisa's "cameretta": we still do not know whether she will leave the room, although we do discover that the mysterious Alvaro alluded to in the opening pages is a cat, a chimerical creature who inhabits the enchanted garden of fable. Situations, images, objects recur and reflect each other throughout the text in a narrative dynamic that is purely internal and that has little reference to external historical events. The topoi of traditional novelistic fiction are absorbed and transformed to reveal not a lack of imagination, nor even an intimation of intertextuality, but ironically, and tragically, to delineate the historical and psychological gulf between the originating texts and Morante's reinterpretation of them. Elisa's grandmother, Cesira, while apparently subject to the same delusions as Emma Bovary, discharges her frustrations not through adultery but through a brutish and brutal adherence to everyday duty; Francesco, the "generoso Hidalgo," is a petit bourgeois Don Quixote who tilts at the windmills of politics and social injustice while envying those more fortunate than himself. Francesco and Edoardo, while specular opposites—poor and rich, dark and fair, scarred and beautiful—taken together, present a picture of masculinity in crisis. Nor does the text fulfill the socially recuperative function of much bourgeois fiction: there are few Italian novels to paint so devastating and chilling a picture of family life. Perhaps even more shockingly, the perennial myth of delighted motherhood, peddled by male and female novelists alike, is demolished in the person of Anna, whose attitude to Elisa, adoring daughter of the dark-haired Francesco rather than the blonde beloved Edoardo, is at best one of indifference and at worst one of unfeeling cruelty. Morante's reading of Freud offers an analytical system by which neurosis can be charted back to early experience; at the same time Jung's insight that the unconscious of the parent can inflict psychological damage on the child lends further weight to a novel where the story across three generations is not a pretext to the description of social and historical change and progress, but rather a presentation of obsessional and neurotic stasis.

The privileging of space over time in Morante's narrative is in direct contrast to the aesthetic of popular fiction and to the family and historical saga with which a partial reading would label this novel.[4] Within theoretical writings on modernism and postmodernism it has been argued that critical and social theoretical developments have been too much in thrall to a historical dimension, to a historicist perspective that is the residue of a largely superseded Marxist analysis. There are those who maintain that academic study has privileged time and history over space, a bias that has led to an overly hasty misinterpretation of modernity as that which destroys what has come before, or tradition, whether in the social, conceptual or artistic sphere. Edward Soja, for example, claims:

> An essentially historical epistemology continues to pervade the critical consciousness of modern social theory. It still comprehends the world primarily through the dynamics arising from the emplacement of social being and becoming in the interpretive contexts of time [. . .] This enduring epistemological presence has preserved a privileged place for the historical imagination in defining the very nature of critical insight and interpretation [. . .] the critical hermeneutic is still enveloped in a temporal master-narrative. (15)

Soja aims to shift the emphasis, interpreting modernity, rather, as the complex reorganization of spatial and temporal relations. This is more than a wry plea from Geography, hitherto the Cinderella of academic disciplines, to join the modern and postmodern bandwagon driven largely by ex-historians. It is also a recognition, however oblique, of a profound shift, both scientific and critical, in the relations between space, time, and matter.

A philosophical conception of space goes back at least to Plato and Aristotle, Newton and Kant.[5] And with the twentieth century, of course, the assumption that space and time were constant or could be measured independently was shattered by the law of relativity. As Herman Minkowski put it, rather dramatically, "henceforth space by itself, and time by itself, are doomed to fade away into mere shadows, and only a kind of union between the two will preserve an independent reality" (72).

Clearly the historical and dialectical philosophies of the nineteenth century privileged the forward movement of time over the perceived stasis of space. "Did it start with Bergson or before," wonders Michel Foucault. "Space was treated as the dead, the fixed, the undialectical, the immobile. Time, on the other hand, was richness, fecundity, life, dialectic" (126). Foucault argues strongly for, as it were, a history of space, a fusion of space and time to bring forth a new kind of knowledge. He notes that "for all those who confuse history with the old schemas of evolution, living continuity, organic development, the progress of consciousness or the project of existence, the use of spatial terms seems to have an air of anti-history" (128).

For Fredric Jameson, the different conceptualization of space, often seen to mark the breakpoint between the modern and the postmodern, is only part of the story. If it has become conventional to see the experience of temporality—existential time, along with deep memory—as a dominant of the high modern, the more correct distinction for Jameson remains that

> between the two forms of interrelationship between time and space rather than between these two inseparable categories themselves [. . .] What one means by evoking (the spatialization of the present) is rather the will to use and to subject time to the service of space, if that is now the right word for it. [. . .] If experience and expression still seem largely apt in the cultural sphere of the modern, they are altogether out of place and anachronistic in a postmodern age, where, if temporality still has its place, it would seem better to speak of the writing of it rather than any lived experience. (154)

Spatial relations are collapsed, as Elisa's existential dilemma is both realized and metaphorized by her inability to leave her room. Her room, long a sanctuary from the gesturing and posturing of polite society to which she was subject while Rosaria was still alive, cut off from the rest of the world, looking onto nothing but emptiness, a little-frequented courtyard, with no direct sunlight, has become a liminal space, at the margins of social intercourse but also a threshold between the dead and the living, reality and fiction. Not only is Elisa, as she describes herself in ironic reference to a topos of nineteenth-century fiction, a "sepolta viva," buried alive, seemingly inside conventional narrative traditions but nonetheless outside conventional spatial and temporal parameters, lingering between life and death. Her room serves as a porous membrane between the living and the dead, between Elisa, one of the few surviving members of her family, and the importunate whisperings and remonstrations of her dead who demand that their story be told. Kept company only by Alvaro, the cat, this is the room where Elisa has begun to write the story of her family, subject to the *menzogne* of self mis-recognition, which Elisa hopes to dispel for herself through the *sortilegio* of the written word, thus freeing herself of both her burdensome family inheritance and the constraints of the room in which she finds herself.

In this context the present tense of the enunciation is constantly brought to the fore, and with it the space—more than just the place—in which Elisa writes. As she relates her family history, the linear sequence of the traditional novel is consistently ruptured by reference to the present time and space itself, which is also the space in which Elisa addresses herself to her reader. The forward dynamic of family history—the progressive motion of temporality and sequentiality—is thus brought to heel by a precise localization of enunciation, a rupture that operates a distancing effect on the *fabula*, shifting our attention from language as creator of images to language as process, to language itself as it is being produced, to the small writing desk where the story is being written.

The structural forms of the text, with its admixture of diegetic and metadiegetic mode, adjuncture of memory and imagination, its constant return to the present tense of writing, tempt a reading of memory on the one hand and imagination on the other as the discursive embodiment of time and space. A reading of this kind would place Morante at the heart of the modernist project as outlined by Jameson, producing a text that tempers the overweening demand of history and the nineteenth-century novel with a spatiality that both thwarts the forward propulsion of the narrative and leads to a decidedly different interrelationship between the two than pertained, for example, in those countless nineteenth-century texts that purported to hinge on memory and recall. And it would simultaneously remove her even further from the contemporary ethos of Neorealism, with its teleological project of historical dynamism. What the critic Giovanna Rosa describes as the dialectic in this text between historical dynamism and anthropological permanence could be seen through a change of terms as the dialectic between time and space. The text superimposes temporal planes whose diachronic flow is interrupted by analepsis, gaps, ellipsis, a kind of stitching together reminiscent of spatial rather than merely temporal organization.

Nonetheless history, *storia* with a capital "S" as Morante would have it, is present in the novel. Scattered clues in the text, the few overt references to external space and time, suggest the spatial and temporal parameters are Palermo at the turn of the century. These then are the years during which Italy began to modernize. With increasing urbanization and the development of a capitalist economy, the old aristocratic, feudal, and peasant culture that dominated the South began to crumble—this is of course the same period covered by Lampedusa's *Il gattopardo*—giving way to what Morante saw as the moral and intellectual squalor of the petite bourgeoisie— the very class that decades later was to provide a bedrock of support for Fascism. Morante's gaze is neither regressive nor nostalgic. Her fascination with the aristocratic Edoardo does not blind her to his despotic cruelty, nor does her sympathy for characters such as Francesco's mother, Alessandra, prevent her from observing a peasant civilization in crisis. The "triste Mezzogiorno" of Elisa's birth and childhood is viewed now from a critical distance—years have passed, and Elisa is now in Rome: not, interestingly enough, in the entrepreneurial, industrialized north, but in the bureaucratic capital itself.

Before beginning her family romance, at the threshold of her own text, Elisa, the narrator of *Menzogna e sortilegio,* describes the route by which she comes to write her narrative, her family romance, the history of the lies and self-deceit that have destroyed her family and that can be traced back down the generations. She recounts her solitude, her separation and reclusion from any form of human or social relations following the death of the woman she describes as her "seconda madre," Rosaria. She inhabits a minimal space with no obvious relation to the external, where time no longer marks change, where duration no longer holds—the last fifteen years have vanished as in a single day. Elisa's name first appears followed by a question mark—"Chi è questa donna? Chi è questa Elisa?" (*Opere* 1: 10; " Who is this woman? Who is this Elisa?"). The only image she encounters, two months following the death of Rosaria, the beginning of her solitude and of her own writing, is that of the schizoid, dissociated self in the mirror: glimpsing her own reflection, "quando mi riconosco, resto immobile a fissar me stessa, come se mirassi una medusa" (*Opere* 1: 19; "when I recognize myself, I stand still and stare at myself, as if I were gazing at a medusa").[6] The narrating "I" doubles and splits off from the pale, ghostly form in the mirror. She is caught between two worlds, uncertain whether or not to recognize herself in the immobility of death.

Elisa's narrative is a teleological act, rooted in a Freudian therapeutic model, designed to liberate the narrator from those same obsessions and neuroses—the *menzogne* of the title—that have led to the obliteration and disruption of her family genealogy and her own incarceration or burial in her room. Her aim is to free herself from the gorgon in the mirror, to reach a sense of her identity both as woman and as writer, independent and free of the mother figure: this is, then, a moment of self-reflection and self-reflexivity. In the three introductory chapters of the novel, before we reach the story proper of Elisa's family romance, Elisa lays out her stall as narrator, as character in her own family drama, determined, as few narrators are, to reveal and display the path which has led her to this point: her sources, her hesitations, her second thoughts about the writing of the text. She warns us that while she is a character in her own story—and therefore, as witness and participant, some sort of guarantor of the text—she is nonetheless a romancer, afflicted by the same *menzogne* as her family. She is not just unreliable but at times willfully so. Elisa recounts two series of events: the story of her family and the story of her own writing, and only of the second can she be regarded as protagonist. Her self-presentation in the introductory chapters, as character rather than narrator, takes the form of disguise, concealment, a theatrical facade of identity. Called to mix with her guests by Rosaria, a woman as cheerful as her reputation is dubious, Elisa, we are told, is covered in false, cheap jewelry, painted, rouged, and combed in an attempt to draw her out of her preferred invisibility. She is required to act according to the conventional "copione" or script of aspiring petit bourgeois society: she is, she states, like a walk-on part onstage, or, in a different cultural sphere, like a rabbit drawn out of the magician's top hat—which as we know once it appears, can swiftly disappear again. Once again the narrating "I" dissolves, withdrawing into its own interior theater.

Elisa tells us of narrative models taken up and discarded. Her own small library, she confesses, consists of books that "appartengono al genere fantastico" (*Opere* 1: 24; "belong to the fantastic genre"), legends, darkly romantic tales predominantly from the North, from Germany or Scandinavia, and the lives of saints. Narrative here takes on an overtone of the sacrilegious, as even religious texts become mere form, stripped of their referent in order to generate not belief in a transcendent reality but other stories, in a syntagmatic chain of narration. Elisa describes herself using these tales as templates for her own fantasies and storytelling—taking on the role less of serious novelist than that of recounter of serialized tales, whose purpose is not closure but the present continuation of reading itself, designed never to end. In these early fantasized and, significantly, *unwritten* stories, the costumes of princes, kings, and saints are draped over the malnourished shoulders of members of her own family or acquaintance, who then proceed to walk onto the stage of her imagination. Storytelling becomes a consolatory, redeeming fiction, escapist theater, a way of bringing her characters to an obligatory happy ending by means of "tracotanza e teatralità" that pushes the genre to its limits. Yet it is a genre with a tenuous grasp on the "real," which abolishes the signified, which is pure dream: and Elisa herself acknowledges that "Dopo essersi fatte credere la mia consolazione, la mia festa e il mio riscatto di contro all'inquietante realtà, le mie maschere m'imposero la negazione d'ogni realtà, in cambio del loro mondo larvale" (*Opere* 1: 25; "after having me believe them to be my consolation, my joy and my ransom against disturbing reality, my masks imposed on me the denial of all reality, in exchange for their larval world").

With the death of Rosaria, Elisa's fictional, self-imposed solitude takes on darker tones. Her characters have abandoned her. She can catch an oblique glimpse of them out of the corner of her eye, "flosce spoglie senza vita. Simili a costumi abbandonati in disordine dagli attori, alla fine dello spettacolo, in un retroscena d'infimo teatro" (*Opere* 1: 26; "flaccid, lifeless remains. Similar to costumes abandoned in a heap by actors, at the end of their performance, backstage in a shabby theater"),[7] a scenario that recalls the costumes and hats littering the stage of Luigi Pirandello's *Sei personaggi in cerca d'autore*. The model of narration settled on by the end of the introduction is that of "memoria" as opposed to "menzogna," with "memoria" doubling as "romanzo'" itself. Elisa becomes faithful scribe to the stories recounted by the importunate, demanding characters who crowd round her—a notion of character, of *personaggio*, again remarkably close to that of the Sicilian dramatist. Deprived of the grand costumes of fantasy borrowed from models of bad literature, her characters undergo what we might call the Cinderella principle: no longer grand princes, they now "vestono per lo più abiti dimessi e consunti" (*Opere* 1: 32; "wear for the most part second-hand, worn out clothes"). But does this mean that the narrative model to be followed is that of nineteenth-century realism, whether of French or Italian derivation, with Elisa as the detached observer engaged in mere reportage, however oneiric? Clearly not. For one thing, the theatrical imagery persists throughout the novel. This is not so much a mixing of genres, for the novel rarely reproduces dialogue, and all the action and emotion, however dramatic, is filtered through the consciousness of the narrator herself. In its diegetic extremism *Menzogna e sortilegio* is light years from the Americanized models of Pavese or Vittorini, or from the colloquialisms of Neorealism.

Theatricality indicates a different kind of modernity that sees the adoption of roles as a Freudian displacement and concealment. In the face of reality, Morante's characters clothe themselves, disguise themselves, mask themselves, fall prey to the *menzogna* of the book's title, in the hope of glimpsing the desired image in the mirror. The mask, as in Pirandello, is the turning away from reality. Elisa's grandfather, Teodoro, conceals his lost fortune; her father, Francesco, his humble background. Nicola Monaco, administrator to the Cerentano estate, plays the part of the grand lord with the peasants. Anna, Elisa's beloved mother, passes herself off as suffering saint in order to disguise her rancorous disillusion. The case of the prostitute Rosaria is diametrically opposite. The only character not afflicted by *menzogne*, her showy, gaudy make-up points only to itself, is all surface. Her sympathetic integrity, her compassionate humanity, is protected by the very excess of the attempt to disguise it, by her "colori teatrali": "Nè i tanti lisci e cosmetici erano spalmati con arte, ma al contrario, in una maniera brutale e primitiva: come se colei si compiacesse di *mascherarsi*, più che di abbellirsi" (*Opere* 1: 822; emphasis added; "And her cosmetics were not applied with any skill but, quite the contrary, in a brutal, primitive manner as if she wished to *disguise* herself rather than make herself beautiful").

Elisa cannot take up the role of omniscient narrator. Her aim is to *ricordare*,[8] "to remember," but this clearly has a different meaning to orthodox autobiography. She inserts herself into her own text, but three-quarters of the text recounts events that took place before Elisa was born, and she is fully conscious that as narrator she must, of necessity, have recourse to fiction. Memory is not enough: Elisa's only hope of reaching reality, or any kind of truth, is "memoria" in conjunction with the imagination. This is true for Elisa as it is true for Morante, for the enunciation as well as the discourse of the text. Elisa's ancestors whisper their stories but they are filtered through the consciousness of the narrator, and the reader is constantly brought back to the moment of Elisa's writing. It is not simply a matter of expedience, but is central to the narrative paradigm of the text, to its ambiguous adoption and enigmatic transformation of literary forms. Oneiric memory transforms the *menzogne* of her family members—almost all now dead—into the *sortilegio* of literary writing, which alone can throw light on the ambiguities that govern our destiny. One of the central characters of the text is the blond, wealthy, enigmatic, and capricious Edoardo, whose idyll with his dark-haired, impoverished cousin Anna dominates the first part of the book, a paradise that once lost, leaves her with nothing but ashes, *menzogne*. Elisa shares her mother's fascinated adoration of Edoardo, the last scion of an aristocratic caste on the verge of extinction, a polysemic character whose precise historical significance in delineating rigid and ruthless class structure sits side by side with the decadent topos of the boy destined to die young. She knows everything about him, yet he remains fundamentally unknowable—to be created through the imagination, through the art of fiction:

> [. . .] mentre conosco a memoria, da mille ritratti, le sue fattezze, al contrario i suoi delicati colori, la sua voce, i suoi gesti, e in breve i suoi piú vivi pregi, tanto vantati da chi li conobbe, son rimasti per me cose ignote e leggendarie. Ed io non posso rappresentarmi l'intero esser suo senza un qualche aiuto dell'immaginazione, allo stesso modo che se dovessi trattare, poniamo, del paladino Rinaldo, o del bruno Medoro, o del principe Enea. (*Opere* 1: 885)

> [. . .] while I know his features by heart, from a thousand portraits, his delicate coloring on the other hand, his voice, his gestures, his most excellent qualities that were so extolled by those who knew him, have remained unknown to me, the stuff of legend. And I cannot picture his entire being to myself without some help from the imagination, in the same way as if I had to picture, let's say, Rinaldo, or the dark Medoro, or the prince Aeneas.

The text of *Menzogna e sortilegio*, with its echoes of romantic, popular fiction, of epic poetry, its unobtrusive drawing on Freud, becomes a workshop in the art of storytelling. The narrative is clearly placed within a framework that overturns any rigid policing of spatial, temporal, and generic boundaries and borders, to be punctuated with metaliterary comments on, and enactments of, the business of writing, and most particularly the business of fiction. As in the opening chapters, models of fabulation are examined, observed, and discarded. The relationship between author and his characters is constantly put before us, and the question of narrative voice—of how to tell a story— is revealed as fundamental for understanding a reality as complex as the one in which we live. Francesco's natural father, the disgraced administrator of the Cerentano estate, *bon viveur* and philanderer Nicola Monaco, is something of a *raconteur:*

> Molti di questi racconti erano inventati, e tutti modificati e coloriti dalla sua fantasia; e ciò non perché la vita di Nicola non fosse ricca, in realtà, d'avventure simili, ma per la ragione ch'era impossibile a Nicola di raccontare un fatto senza aggiungervi alcunché di suo. Carattere precipuo di tal narratore era, poi, la nessuna importanza da lui concessa alla singola sorte dei suoi personaggi. Egli si compiaceva di descriverli con tinte vivaci o fosche allo stesso modo che si descriverebbe un paesaggio o un oggetto; quasi che essi fos-

sero là esclusivamente per fare da specchio o da paragone
alla sua propria gloria. (*Opere* 1: 98–99)

> Many of these tales were invented, and all were transformed
> and colored by his imagination, not because Nicola's life
> did not abound in such adventures but because it was
> impossible for him to speak of a simple event without add-
> ing something of his own. His chief characteristic as a story-
> teller was his total lack of concern for the fate of his
> individual characters. He delighted in painting them in
> simple bright or dark colors, as one might describe a land-
> scape or an object, almost as if they were there exclusively
> as the mirror or the measure of his own glory.

The narrative *tour de force* of the faked correspondence toward
the end of the novel gives a graphic illustration of the way in
which Morante absorbs and transforms traditional narrative
forms in her text, in this instance the epistolary novel. While
letters and correspondence move the plot along at various
points throughout the novel, the writing and reading of these
false letters constitute a *mise en abyme* of the business of writing, a tantalizing, distorting glimpse of the creative process.
Elisa's mother Anna's youthful amorous idyll with her wealthy
cousin Edoardo, though over years ago, has continued to haunt
her imagination, even though she is married with a daughter,
our narrator, Elisa herself. When Anna learns that the fragile,
fascinating Edoardo has died of TB, she not only refuses to give
up her own imaginings, she pushes her neurotic romancing further, writing letters that she pretends are from Edoardo, and
that she then goes to read to Edoardo's mother, Concetta,
whose bigoted religiousness has become almost comically
deranged in grief. In yet a further image drawn from the theater, Concetta is convinced that if she masks and disguises herself with enough paint and rouge, adopts a "maschera grottesca,"
she will be able to slip past the guards at the gate of Heaven
and visit her beloved son. Anna and Concetta spend hours poring over the letters, parodies of themselves, written in poor
style but in a handwriting remarkably similar to that of Edoardo
himself. Anna takes advantage of her husband's night shifts (on
the post train, neatly enough, which finally kills him in an
accident and thus brings us back full circle to the starting point
of the novel as Elisa is taken in by Rosaria), taking advantage

of her husband's absence "per levarsi, e scrivere a se medesima le finte lettere d'un cugino che non esisteva più" (*Opere* 1: 761; "to get out of bed and write to herself the pretend letters of a cousin who no longer existed"). Elisa states that she has these letters by her side as she writes, but refuses to transcribe their contents literally: our knowledge is further mediated by the choices of the fictional narrator with regard to the fictional letters. And she tells us that she will destroy the letters, burn them, once she has finished her writing. The sensible, reasonable, realistic explanation of this episode, that the letters are the product of Anna's unsatisfied obsession, a bodying forth of neurotic fantasy, is unacceptable to Elisa, who as narrator is unwilling to remain impartial and see the letters as merely the reflection or production of a disturbed mind. The letters themselves become a kind of distorting mirror game, yet another *specchio stregato*, a "bewitched mirror." All is false, inverted: the author is fake, the addressee, the message, even the handwriting itself. Yet the drama of the letters emerges from their being read, shared, partially disclosed, partially concealed: for what they disclose and reveal about Anna and Elisa herself. During the reading of these letters where the theater of pretense takes on the intense drama of religious ritual, Elisa is once again mute witness to a farcical but nonetheless lacerating tragedy: "[. . .] taciturna, isolata nel fondo della mia poltrona, contemplavo quel duplice mostro d'amore" (781; "[. . .] without a word, alone in my armchair, I contemplated that double monster of love").[9]

The role of Elisa as observer and commentator on the action, on the stage, deeply involved emotionally but not the protagonist, is reminiscent above all, perhaps, of the Chorus in Greek tragedy. Nietzsche's gloss on Schiller, who viewed the introduction of the Chorus into Greek drama as "the decisive step by which war is declared openly and honestly against all naturalism in art" (59), saw in the Chorus, with its multiple deployment of distancing perspectives, the first possibility of tragedy (63). Morante's perspective resonates with Nietzsche's "mythic" as opposed to "theoretical" view of things, and in a secular, rationalist age her work points toward what Nietzsche termed a "rebirth of tragedy":

> If ancient tragedy was driven from its course by the dialec-
> tical desire for knowledge and the optimism of science, it
> might be inferred that there is an eternal conflict between
> *the theoretic* and *the tragic view of things*, and only after
> the spirit of science has been led to its boundaries, and its
> claim to universal validity has been destroyed by the evi-
> dence of those boundaries, can we hope for a re-birth of
> tragedy [. . .] He who recalls the immediate consequences
> of this restlessly onward-pressing spirit of science will
> realise at once that myth was annihilated by it, and that, in
> consequence of this annihilation, poetry was driven as
> homeless being from her natural ideal soil. (131; emphasis
> in original)

Morante's originality is diametrically opposite to the clichéd
models discarded by Elisa. If Elisa dresses her family in the
clothes of tales of heroic adventure in order to accommodate
them to some model of literature, and thus redeem their
wretched lives, Morante uncovers the tragic in shabby petit
bourgeois flats where decidedly unheroic characters continue
to clash and collide in the manner of tragic myth, in a narrative
that brings the depth of European tradition face to face with
the shabby reality of the immediate postwar period. It is only
now, after some of the shibboleths and shackles of ideologically motivated criticism have rusted away, that we can begin
to see Morante as an artist who was deeply anti-avant-garde
but profoundly modern, and whose modernity is dialectically
rooted in a dialogue with the traditions of Western culture. If
this is so, then Morante's narrative has as its purpose nothing
less than the freeing of the novel from ideological, generic constraints, a drawing together of the multiple forms of fiction in
order to produce a work that stitches together past and future,
looks forward as well as back.[10] Elisa's tale is not simply
hinged onto the opening chapters as some sort of narrative
expedient so common in nineteenth-century narrative. Rather,
the narrator, the one who should be the guarantor of truthfulness, reveals herself once more to be *herself* subject to
menzogne, to the siren call of fiction itself. And if we return to
the dedicatory poem, we see a very modern, indeed postmodern (and certainly very female) image of the writer as
weaver, which at the same time takes us right back to classical

myth: "L'ago è rovente, la tela è fumo" (*Opere* 1: 5; "the needle is burning, the weave is aflame").

Notes

1. Given the difficulties of published translations of Elsa Morante's works as outlined in this volume by Marco Bardini in his essay on the American translation of *Menzogna e sortilegio,* all translations are the author's own.

2. See Kundera's essay of this title in *The Art of the Novel.*

3. Questa fenice, de l'aurata piuma / Al suo bel collo, candido, gentile, / Forma, senz'arte, / un sí caro monile / Ch'ogni cor addolcisce, e'l mio consuma" (Petrarch 250).

4. See Bardini's chapter on the translation of this novel for an account of how the temporal was once more privileged in the American version.

5. Plato's *Timaeus* describes the *khora* as a medium in which simple numerical ratios are represented by tiny polyhedra whose fluctuations constitute the fabric of the perceived world. Aristotle discusses place rather than space, geometry rather than the constitutive nature of space itself. Isaac Newton's assertion that spatial relations are mind-independent is challenged by the idealism of Kant, whose Transcendental Aesthetic argues that space and time are subjective forms of human sensibility, through which the mind makes sense of the world, rather than the self-subsisting realities posited by Newton.

6. On a possible Jungian intertext, see Wood.

7. Missing in the American translation.

8. "Che il segreto dell'arte sia qui? *Ricordare* come l'opera si è vista in uno stato di sogno, ridirla come è vista, cercare soprattutto di *ricordare.* Che forse tutto l'inventare è ricordare?" (Morante, *Opere* 1: xxxiv; "Is this then the secret of art? *Remembering* as the work was seen in a state of dream, telling it as we have seen it, trying above all to remember. Because perhaps all inventing is in fact *remembering*").

9. On the nature of the comedy of these scenes we might recall Nietzsche once more: "Art approaches, as a saving and healing enchantress; she alone is able to transform these nauseating reflections on the awfulness or absurdity of existence into representations wherewith it is possible to live: these are the representations of the *sublime* as the artistic subjugation of the awful, and the *comic* as the artistic delivery from the nausea of the absurd" (96).

10. "The novel's spirit is the spirit of continuity: each work is the answer to preceding ones, each work contains all the previous experience of the novel. But the spirit of our time is firmly focused on a present that is so expansive and profuse that it shoves the past off our horizon and reduces time to the present moment only. Within this system the novel is no longer a *work* (a thing made to last, to connect the past with the future) but one current event among many, a gesture with no tomorrow" (Kundera 18–19).

Works Cited

Foucault. Michel. *Power/Knowledge: Selected Interviews and Other Writings, 1972–77*. Ed. and trans. Colin Gordon. Hemel Hempstead: Harvester Wheatsheaf, 1980.

Jameson, Fredric. *Postmodernism, or the Cultural Logic of Late Capitalism*. London: Verso, 1991.

Kundera, Milan. *The Art of the Novel*. Trans. Linda Asher. London: Faber and Faber, 1988.

Minkowski, Herman. *The Principle of Relativity: A Collection of Memoirs on the Special and General Theory of Relativity by H. A. Einstein, H. Minkowski and H. Weyl*. With notes by A. Sommerfeld, W. Perrett, and G. B. Jeffery. London: Methuen, 1923.

Morante, Elsa. *Opere*. Ed. Carlo Cecchi and Cesare Garboli. Vol.1. Milan: Mondadori, 1988.

Nietzsche, Fredric. *The Birth of Tragedy: Out of the Spirit of Music*. Ed. Michael Zanner. Trans. Shaun Whiteside. London: Penguin, 1993.

Petrarch, Francesco. *Canzoniere*. Vol. 1. Ed. Piero Cudini. Milan: Garzanti, 1977.

Rosa, Giovanna. *Cattedrali di carta: Elsa Morante romanziere*. Milan: Il Saggiatore, 1995.

Soja, Edward. *Postmodern Geographies: The Reassertion of Space in Critical Social Theory*. London: Verso, 1989.

Wood, Sharon. "Jung e l'isola di Arturo." *Narrativa* 17 (2000): 77–88.

Marco Bardini

House of Liars

The American Translation
of *Menzogna e sortilegio*

Elsa Morante was always intensely private about her work and reticent about her own creative process, frequently declaring her disapproval of critical editions. She firmly believed that once a text was released by its author it became an intangible entity, unalterable in time and, above all, inscrutable in its creative development. It was for this reason that in her writings, especially in her later years, Morante went to exhausting and exhaustive lengths to specify the formal and even the typographical aspects of her work, inspired by a genuine terror of the careless and superficial changes introduced by typographers and editors. She insisted, what's more, on the significance of the editorial elements of her work, writing, for example, to her publisher, Einaudi, that these elements "prendono un valore non solo tipografico, ma anche poetico [. . .], così come io li ho indicati [. . .] rispondono, nel mio racconto, a un determinato ritmo narrativo" (Bardini, *Morante* 77n67; "take on a value that is not merely typographical but also poetic [. . .] as I have indicated [. . .] within my story they follow a specific narrative rhythm"). This comment is richly indicative of Morante's fury when confronted with some thoughtless slip.

Perhaps most notable of all her efforts to protect the integrity of her work was her disavowal of the American translation of *Menzogna e sortilegio*, because of the severe distortions she found in it. The episode is remarkable, less for the mediocre standard of the translation as such, than for the reverberations felt for years after by the writer, who continued for many years to recall the incident with heartfelt indignation. After this affair, Morante decided in all her dealings with publishers to include an iron clause prohibiting any arbitrary cut or change in the text, a choice that was to cause her some difficulty and delay in sorting out rights to the text abroad. It is worth remembering here that when the prestigious translation of *La Storia* appeared, published by the First Edition Society, Morante insisted that the bibliographical reference to *House of Liars* be followed by the title *Menzogna e sortilegio—Lies and Witchcraft*, signaling the novel as yet to be translated. Given the extremity of the author's reaction to this translation, it seems worth while to take a closer look at the nature of the betrayal of the original text.

Menzogna e sortilegio appeared at the beginning of the summer of 1948, and thanks to the support of Giacomo Debenedetti, in August of the same year it was awarded the Viareggio prize, shared with Aldo Palazzeschi. The weighty novel had some limited success among a small, elite circle of readers, but after a year or two of fading attention, it was more or less forgotten by the wider public. In October 1948, it was suggested that the novel be translated and introduced onto the international market, and Morante, still at the beginning of her career and always keen for commercial success, agreed with considerable enthusiasm.

The novel was sold through an intermediary American agency, and the date on the contract is November 19, 1948. According to this initial agreement the novel was to have been translated into American English by Frances Lanza, but it was in fact translated by Adrienne Foulke, with the editorial assistance of Andrew Chiappe, and published in 1951 by Harcourt, Brace & Company, New York, with the title *House of Liars*. It is not clear who chose this title, and we can only recall that "La casa dei bugiardi" was one of hundreds of possibilities noted by Morante in her manuscripts. But it is equally clear from these same manuscripts that this title, unlike only a handful of others, was never likely to have found favor with the author and been the final, privileged one.

By January 27, 1949, as we can see from a letter written by Morante to Giulio Einaudi, the American editors had already declared their intention to cut a large part of the novel:

> Ti espressi già a Torino il mio punto di vista sulla questione
> dei tagli, e mi sembra strano che un autore debba difendere

certi diritti così ovvii e naturali. Non so come i suddetti editori stranieri non si rendano conto che la mole e complessità di un'opera (quando non si tratti di letteratura amena ma di libri scritti con impegno d'arte), non sono un caso, ma il frutto di una lunga e meditata fatica, e che solo l'autore ne conosce le ragioni e i fini. Per cui chi si permette di tagliare un libro senza autorizzazione dell'autore procura a questo un danno morale e materiale e cade, quindi, in un abuso punibile dalla legge. Sono certa che tu sei d'accordo con me su questi punti. Ad ogni modo, ti ripeto qui che io non accetterei per nessuna ragione da nessuna casa editrice una simile menomazione del mio libro. Non ho sottoscritto nessuna clausola che parli di una possibilità di questo genere e ti prego di far sapere ad Harcourt and Brace [. . .] il mio punto di vista sulla faccenda. Da parte mia, devo dirti che agirei legalmente contro chiunque fosse responsabile di tagli apportati al mio libro senza la mia autorizzazione. (Bardini, *Morante* 210n2)

I told you in Turin what I thought about cuts, and it seems bizarre to me that an author has to defend rights that are so obvious and natural. I don't see how these foreign publishers fail to realize that the weight and complexity of a work, especially books that are not just light reading but written as works of art, do not come about just by chance but are the fruit of long thought and effort, and only the author can know its reasons and its aims. That is why allowing a book to be cut without the permission of the author damages that author morally and materially and thus becomes an abuse punishable by law. I am certain that you agree with me on these points. Anyway, I am telling you once more that for no reason, and from no publisher, would I accept such a mutilation of my book. I have signed no clause that mentions a possibility of this kind, and I would ask you to let Harcourt and Brace [. . .] know my position on this matter. As for me, I have to tell you that I would take legal action against anybody who introduced cuts into my book without my express permission.

Out of ingenuousness and inexperience Morante had signed a contract that did not contain a specific clause disallowing editorial cuts. And so, despite the remonstrance of Giulio Einaudi himself and the attempt at reconciliation by Natalia Ginzburg, who was at the time an editor at the Einaudi publishing house

in Turin, the American translation of *Menzogna e sortilegio* was
published in 1951 in a drastically reduced version. At first surprised and bewildered, then seriously embittered, Morante was
compelled to admit defeat in another letter to Giulio Einaudi
on January 3, 1952:

> Però il mio libro, in quella riduzione, è irriconoscibile, e
> questo è stato uno dei miei più grossi dispiaceri del 1951
> che, se Dio vuole, è un anno finito. Spero che il 1952 non
> mi porti dei dispiaceri simili. Del resto, la colpa è stata mia
> che ho ceduto con gli americani sulla questione dei tagli—
> almeno, avrei dovuto avere il coraggio di tagliarlo io—loro
> l'hanno massacrato e, quello che è strano, l'hanno appesan-
> tito invece di alleggerirlo. Se, come tu dici, il libro, così mal-
> trattato, ha avuto risalto in America, vuol dire proprio che il
> testo contiene tesori indistruttibili. Ti devo perciò i miei
> complimenti per esserne l'editore. (Bardini, *Morante* 210–
> 11n3)

> In its cut and reduced form my book is unrecognizable, and
> this has been one of the most hurtful things to have hap-
> pened to me in 1951, which is, God willing, finally over. I
> hope 1952 will not bring similar displeasures. Besides, it's
> my own fault because I gave way to the Americans over the
> cuts—I should at least have had the courage to cut it myself.
> They've massacred it, and what is strange is that instead of
> lightening it they've made it heavier. If as you say the book
> has been well noticed in America despite being treated so
> badly, it means that it has within it treasures that are inde-
> structible. I offer you all my compliments for being its
> publisher.

Nonetheless, after accounts with the intermediaries have been
settled, royalties from American sales in 1952 are in fact negative and Morante writes another unhappy letter to her publisher
on March 16, 1952:

> I tagli della traduzione americana mi hanno amareggiato
> molto, e vorrei almeno che la parte finanziaria andasse nel
> modo più semplice e vantaggioso. Nemmeno uno dei miei,
> né dei tuoi dollari deve andare al Sig. Greenburger [an
> American intermediary] né a nessun altro. Mi è estrema-
> mente necessario di guadagnare. (Bardini, *Morante* 211n4)

> The cuts in the American translation have left me very bitter, and I would like at least the financial side to go as simply and as profitably as possible. Not a single dollar of mine or of yours should go to Mr. Greenburger [an American intermediary] or to anybody else. I urgently need to make some money.

Aside from the alarmed and rhetorical lamentation for the "massacred" book, Morante's statement that the cuts made by the Americans have not lightened, but have, rather, weighed down the book, rendering it unrecognizable, offers an interesting clue to follow. The concept of *pesanteur* (in the meaning given the word by Simone Weil) was soon to become an obsession of Morante's, while a consideration of the version rejected by the author can guide us, as in a negative, toward a more appropriate reading of the original.

House of Liars made a meager impact on the Anglo-American market, such that even after the success of *L'isola di Arturo* and the extraordinary international attention given to *La Storia*, it was never republished, far less retranslated. Sales at the time were minimal and critical reception modest in the extreme. Up to now I have found only three reviews, which differ considerably. The first, by Serge Hughes, appeared on October 20, 1951, in the *Saturday Review of Literature* with the title "Human Disintegration." The second, by Frances Keene, appeared in the *Nation* on October 27, 1951, entitled "House of Nightmare." The third appeared in *The New Yorker* on February 9, 1952, by Maeve Brennan and is entitled "Lives in Limbo."

In attempting this comparison between the two books I have used the only existing edition of the American version, *House of Liars*[1] published in New York by Harcourt, Brace and Company in 1951, translated by Adrienne Foulke with the editorial assistance of Andrew Chiappe. The volume is bound, in black cloth, with a colored dust-jacket. Unlike the Italian edition, whose cover presents a suggestive detail of a famous painting by Marc Chagall, the American cover shows a design whose intention is more flatly narrative and representational: a woman dressed in a long, scarlet garment that recalls a Hollywood negligée more than any Italian dress, with an incongruous low neckline far removed from anything Elisa might wear, her black hair piled on top of her head, contemplates herself in a large mirror in a Chippendale-style room. Easily recognizable as the situation in which the narrator describes herself in the opening chapters, what we see is a glimpse of Rosaria's vulgar flat in Rome. As if to confirm this, the caption reads, "Elisa, still in her twenties, is all alone in the house of Rosaria, friend of her father and of many men. What has brought her to Rosaria's empty rooms?" In the foreground we see a decorated oil lamp, an open book, and a monochrome female nude, this last doubtless there to represent all those "statuine le cui figure e atteggiamenti sono spesso tali da fare arrossire ogni persona onorata che vi posi lo sguardo" (MS 10; "statuettes, whose figures and postures are such as to make any decent person blush to see them"; HL 4).[2] The back of the dust jacket bears an old photograph of Elsa Morante. Captions include a brief comment by Robert Penn Warren, an introduction to the novel that recalls the Viareggio prize and a brief note about the author. The frontispiece gives no further information. Nowhere does the volume signal the fact the reader has an abridged version of the original novel.

As for the Italian edition of *Menzogna e sortilegio*, it would have been more correct from a philological perspective to use the first Einaudi edition of 1948, the version obviously used by the American translator. Given, however, the rarity of this edition and the fact that the novel is known above all in its 1975 Einaudi "Struzzi" edition, I have decided to use this later one instead, mainly to facilitate a comparison between the two texts in terms of page numbers. The 1975 text moreover, although revised by the author and reset typographically (in 1961 for the "Supercoralli" reprint), is not substantially different from the 1948 edition except for a few modest variants, which I discuss in *Morante Elsa. Italiana. Di professione, poeta* (209–17).

The American version has 565 pages, as against the 706 of the Italian edition. Given that one page of the American edition has approximately the same number of words as one page of the Italian edition, we can calculate a reduction in the text of around 140 pages. The cuts are of an irregular and unpredictable nature that at first sight follow no logical or coherent process. Cuts range from a single word or phrase, to one of the three poems ("Ai personaggi"; "To the characters"), to an entire chapter, which I shall come to shortly. Sometimes a substantial cut is in part filled by a brief summary. Of less significance are other alterations, some instances of periphrasis that are helpful to the non-Italian reader, or brief additions designed to be explanatory; pleonastic from the point of view of the narrative, they serve to sew together those portions of the text that have survived the cuts (and are indeed themselves not without error).

Clearly it is not my purpose here to pass judgment on the linguistic quality of the translation. Two reviewers at the time expressed different opinions on the matter. While Hughes sees in the "lumpy" translation of Foulke a barrier to the comprehension of the psychological subtleties of Elsa Morante, Keene on the other hand claims that with regard to a novel that she defines as "clumsy," "cumbersome," and "verbose," the translator has performed impeccably and is much to be praised for the improvements she has brought to the readability and flow of the text.

We can accept the premise, as did the author herself, that this act of reduction is not an authoritarian act of censorship but a humiliating trimming. The resigned words of Morante leave us in no doubt, and her reaction would have been far more vehement and insistent had this been a question of genuine censorship, as was to be the case for the Spanish version of *La Storia*. Let us consider, then, how such a faithless translation affects the sense of the novel. Apart from the compromises inevitable in any adaptation, what do we lose of *Menzogna e sortilegio* when we read *House of Liars* (if we lose anything)? What characteristics of the novel are lacking, to the point of rendering it, in its author's words, "unrecognizable"? And finally, how should we interpret Morante's judgment that the novel is made "heavier"?

I will attempt to answer these questions through a brief inventory. As we go down the long list of short cuts (words, phrases, or clauses) we realize that the translator's scissors have chopped away, above all, adverbs of time and manner, adjectives, subclauses, comparisons, and the second term of pairs of synonyms (rarely the first). The evident aim is to simplify (also taking account of the target language) a style perceived as baroque, excessive, overflowing, and awash with superfluity. By operating in this manner, Foulke does nothing other than conform to a widely shared critical judgment of the day. Almost all the Italian reviewers of *Menzogna e sortilegio,* deceived as to the meaning of the "theatricality" that governs Elisa's language, had declared themselves firmly against the overblown exuberance of the young writer.

At this first level, the damage might have been said to have been contained and limited, were it not for the fact that entire metanarrative interventions disappear. The following, for example, serves to clarify the pact between the writer and her readers, not to mention her responsibilities with regard to the macrostructure of the text:

[. . .] chi ignora al par di me, o miei scanzonati lettori, il fasto e la malinconia [. . .] (MS 281)

[. . .] who, like me, do not know the glory and the pain [. . .] (HL 234)

[. . .] e ritorniamo al principio di questa Quarta parte della nostra storia: là dove lasciammo [. . .] (MS 371)

[. . .] let us return now to the moment when [. . .] (HL 301)

Similar criteria of economy can be adduced to the suppression of entire sentences. In order to achieve a presumed objective of narrative flow, many of the comments of the narrator are eliminated:

[. . .] [Teodoro] era non già un traditore o un dongiovanni, bensì l'uomo che si sacrifica perennemente a un ideale (da parte nostra noteremo che, a voler precisare la figura di questo nebuloso ideale, si scoprirebbe soltanto, temiamo, l'effige dell'ozio, dello sperpero e dell'ignoranza). Era il cavaliere di ventura [. . .] (MS 49)

[. . .] [Teodoro] was not the unfaithful lover, nor a Don Juan, but a man who offers himself repeatedly as a sacrifice to an ideal. He was the adventure knight [. . .] (HL 34)

We lose significant comparisons and metaphors, descriptions designed to direct rhetorically the attention of the reader, many of those swift proleptic insertions that are there to chill any momentarily cheerful note of the story by underlining that the destiny of the characters is death. And we lose the fundamental metanarrative clause that ends the "Capitolo primo" of the "Parte prima": "E ora, con le memorie, appunto, di Cesira, diamo inizio al romanzo dei miei" (MS 45; "And now, with the memories, indeed, of Cesira, let us begin this novel of my family"). Anything but pleonastic, this is the sentence in which for the first time, after calling it repeatedly "this book," Elisa attributes the definition of "novel" to her act of writing, just as Morante does in the frontispiece. Yet the term "novel" is placed here side by side with another term that, while belonging to the same cultural sphere, is by definition opposite—that of the memoir. In this structurally privileged place this sentence sets into motion, or rather sanctions once and for all, the referential short-circuit that underpins *Menzogna e sortilegio*: the narrating voice imposes the juxtaposition and mixing of elements that in general would not be permissible, especially when the objective of the narrator is that of her *propria sincerità*, her "own sincerity": here a text that lays claim to truthfulness gives way to the beginning of a text of open invention.

But clearly the most serious gaps derive from the cutting of longer sentences, or indeed entire paragraphs and sections, some of which extend over several pages. It would take too long to give these in detail; a few examples should suffice to make clear the nature of these transformations.

In the "Parte prima," the characters of Teodoro Massia and Nicola Monaco are drastically cut. In the case of Teodoro, disgraced aristocrat and dissolute *bon viveur*, we lose the story of his first wife, especially interesting for the bizarre reflections that spring into the mind of the narrator:

> Detto ciò, e lasciando da parte il passato, per tornare al tempo di cui si parla, e al caso di Cesira saremmo tentati a chiederci quanto potè, sul nobile impulso matrimoniale di Teodoro Massia, la subitanea convinzione di non poter soddisfare che con le nozze il proprio capriccio per la bella donna. In verità, chi conosca, al par di me, Teodoro, è tentato a farsi di queste domande; ma poiché egli era schiettamente convinto delle proprie ragioni virtuose, vorremo noi intorbidare il suo candore con la nostra malizia? (MS 53)

> Having said this, and leaving the past to one side, to return
> to the time we are talking about and Cesira, we might be
> tempted to wonder how much of his noble matrimonial
> impulse came from his sudden conviction that only with
> marriage would he be able to satisfy his whim for this beau-
> tiful woman. In truth anyone who knows Teodoro as well as
> I do would be tempted to ask the same questions, but since
> he was uprightly convinced of his own virtuous reasons,
> why should we go and muddy the waters of his candor with
> our malice?

The narrator's commentary to Teodoro's previous experience
only furthers the notion of her intense knowledge of her *avi* in
all their weaknesses and vices. Among others, we also lose a
sequence on the spectacle of drunkenness witnessed by his
daughter Anna "quali manifestazioni d'una sorta di morbo
sacro, e affascinante" (MS 69; "manifestations of a sort of fascinating, holy sickness"). This is a scene that at a first and
superficial reading may appear pedantic and superfluous, but
that in fact, like many, others, is of extreme importance in the
symmetrical mirroring of the characters. As recent criticism has
pointed out several times, the anecdotes "invented" by the adult
narrator throughout the first half of the novel represent an attempt at therapeutic storytelling for the episodes suffered by
her as a child and related in the second half. Thus the heroic-
esoteric inebriation of Teodoro, like the fabulous and feverish
drunkenness of Edoardo when he kisses Anna in the street (and
indeed like the crazed, visionary, and Dionysian drunkenness
of Gabriele the sacristan, whose story disappears in its entirety
from *House of Liars*) all serve to attenuate and correct in part
the shame of the drunkenness of Francesco, who forces the
young Elisa into the hellish hostelry of Gesualdo. Or rather,
they legitimate *a priori* a sort of narrative alibi for those
moments of rancorous partiality that the narrating voice lets
slip, particularly in the second half of the book.

As for the character Nicola Monaco, numerous episodes and
descriptions that characterize him are suppressed: his passion
for singing and melodrama, his taste for quotes and aphorisms,
his Don Giovanni-like amorous adventures, his prodigality,
arrogance, and sloth. Also to disappear are the character and
story of his wife, Pascuccia Monaco: archetype of all the

"monache di casa," the domestic nuns who populate the novel. All that remains of her is a fleeting and anonymous evocation as unredeemed victim of Nicola's maltreatment.

With regard to melodrama and singing, we should note that Foulke resolves the arduous problem of translating snatches of opera *libretti* almost exclusively with her scissors. As shown by Lucio Lugnani in his study "L'ipotesto melodrammatico come luogo della tracotanza e della teatralità," the narrator closely embroiders her text with elements taken from melodrama at the level of both sign and language, allusion and quotation, character and situation and autonomous narrative motivation. The words from opera arias sung by the characters, or else quoted or evoked by the speech, but still recalled or alluded to or rewritten by the narrator, have an important role that is both connotative and parodic with regard to novelistic writing, with extremely significant results. The pernicious doubleness of Nicola Monaco is nurtured and ethically legitimated by the words of Iago in Verdi's *Otello;* the desire for vengeance on the part of Teodoro, old and sick, appears simultaneously inane and awesome because his words recall those of *Rigoletto*; the gothic bewilderment of perfidious Alessandra is modeled on the character of Azucena in the *Trovatore*; Anna's illness and death emphasize their own inexplicability, fundamental to the ambiguity that is the heart of the novel, by virtue of the madness scene in *Lucia di Lammermoor*. All this, and much more besides, is lost.

The objective difficulties of translation also affect another important code, the religious-devotional one. The constant and systematic recourse, typical of Southern Italian, to a lexis and structure profoundly imbued with expressions of piety and awe, with invocations to the Faith of the Madonna and the saints, to the precepts of the catechism, to devotional practices, symbolic rituals, snatches of prayer, quotations from the Gospels, religious comparisons and metaphors (the equivocal description of Edoardo, for example, as "cittadino del Paradiso Terrestre non ancora acclimatato all'esilio" (MS 164; "citizen of Earthly Paradise not yet acclimatized to exile"), disappears, even though its insidious syllogistic development will condition the text right to its very end: none of this finds a homology in the English version, which nonchalantly eliminates the vast majority of these elements. Also to disappear are the ambiguous rites of Gaudiosa and the overly ornate descriptions of Paradise, the bizarre teachings of the nuns and the anathema of Cesira. But the translation also eliminates sequences frequently vital for a deeper understanding of the text, such as Elisa's willful interpretations of presumed heavenly signs and her suspect oration to "our advocate." Then there is a most singular error: a bigoted term such as *fioretti* (MS 224) is wrongly translated into a literal but incongruous "little flowers" (HL 187).

One of the sections whose loss is felt most keenly is certainly the "Quarta," which deals with Francesco's native village and his childhood. Here the translator works with a decidedly heavy hand, cutting entire pages, including those on Damiano's past and the reasons for his loss of faith, and the exuberance of the administrator Nicola Monaco, his reflections, and his ambiguous behavior toward the child Francesco. Many of the pages that trace Francesco's profound sense of estrangement from the other inhabitants of the village have gone, together with those on Agata and poor Anita. But most remarkable is the cutting of the dreams of Francesco and the entire oneiric episode of Gabriele and Eugenia. This last is particularly important for the meaning of the whole text, as the episode stages and explains through the act of storytelling the very personal concept of *eredità* ("heredity"), poised between eugenics and immanence, which is elaborated by Elisa and evoked at an early stage in the "Introduzione."

And speaking of dreams, the translator cuts them systematically, including those of Elisa, essential in the identification and understanding of the Freudian hypotext (Bardini, "'Fantastici doppi'"). It is interesting in this regard to note a point that can tell us something more about the quality of the translation, and that is that the cuts do not censure the overtly psychological aspect of the novel. It is not by chance that, in his review, Hughes speaks more than once of the "psychology which motivates the characters," underlining its depth and importance. It seems clear that the choices made by Foulke are never motivated by a desire to control elements that are more or less disturbing or risqué—the sadomasochistic games of Anna and Edoardo, for example, are still present. Rather, the cuts, which amputate beyond redemption the possibility of reading the text as "la storia di una nevrosi" ("the history of a neurosis") in Morante's own words, are governed by the translator's inability to identify and hence translate the cultural referent alluded to in the novel. Only this can explain the following omission:

[. . .] Da allora (quindici anni fa), questa fu e rimase la mia camera, e lo è tuttora.	[. . .] This room is my room today, just as it was fifteen years ago.
La congerie d'oggetti che ingombra il ripostiglio ostruisce quasi, a somiglianza d'una barricata, l'accesso alla cameretta, di cui l'uscio può aprirsi soltanto a mezzo. E quest'uscio, e la tenda pesante del mio minuscolo vestibolo attutiscono alquanto ai miei orecchi i rumori delle altre stanze.	One window in the room opens on a court [. . .] (HL 7)
L'unica finestra della cameretta dà su un cortile [. . .] (MS 16)	

The translation ignores completely the subtle allegorical elaboration so carefully executed by Morante but of which Elisa is totally unconscious, which models the typography of the room on the basis of the spatial representation that Freud gives to the concept of repression in the nineteenth lecture of his *Introduction to Psychoanalysis*.

As if this were not enough, the translator regards as justifiable the cutting of an entire chapter of ten pages, the fourth chapter of the sixth part entitled "Le seduzioni romantiche non erano che prose scadenti?" ("Were romantic seductions no more than decadent prose?")

Let us retrace briefly the content of this missing chapter. Addressing herself directly to her readers, Elisa speaks of, and in part describes, the "finte lettere," the fake letters, which her mother claimed to receive from her cousin Edoardo. Edoardo has, in fact, been dead for some time, and the real author of the letters is Anna herself, but since early childhood Elisa has never wished or been able to "rinunciare alla presunzione ch'ella avesse un compagno, quantunque invisibile, nel fantastico gioco" (MS 588; "give up the presumption that she had a companion, invisible though he might be, in her game of fantasy"), an "ispiratore" or inspirer, perhaps disembodied, almost a ghost. Defining it as the "patetico romanzo di Anna" ("Anna's novel of pathos") the narrator reveals that she is still in possession of the letters and she wonders about their documentary value, torn between the desire to keep silent on them and her duty to refer to their content. In this long, metanarrative section, which is deliberately presented in the form of an autonomous chapter, Elisa stops to reflect, entranced, on the captivating and bewitching power of writing even when that writing is ungrammatical, illiberal, and narcissistic. The *mise en abyme* is clear: in showing the mediocre letters, in defining the circumstances that surround them, in specular and elliptical fashion Elisa is speaking of herself and of her own novel: "il finto Epistolario si trasforma per me in uno specchio" (MS 589; "the fake letters are transformed for me into a mirror"). In this neglected chapter Elisa tells us things that are indispensable for a psychoanalytical reading, at least, of the novel, for here Elisa gives us her own "diagnosis":

> Altra risposta non rimane fuor di quella che darebbe un onesto scienziato, un medico, [. . .] questo carteggio [è] ibrido frutto d'una povera mente morbosa, sfogo romantico d'una passione insoddisfatta. (MS 589)

> There is no other answer than that which an honest man of science, a doctor, would give [. . .] these letters [are] the hybrid fruit of a poor sick mind, the romantic release of a passion never satisfied.

But such a diagnosis, doubtless "the most reasonable," causes her such pain that "memoria, volontà e fantasia [le] suggeriscono di scegliere una menzogna" (MS 589; "memory, will, and fantasy suggest choosing a lie").

The suppression of this chapter, mistaken perhaps for mere padding, together with the brutal cuts in the "Introduction," destroys the entire structural mechanism of the text: Elisa's need to write is no longer reflected in Anna's need to write. While they have no immediate influence at the level of the story, these pages reveal themselves to be fundamental at the level of discourse: in a novel where *menzogna*, or "lies," are a determining category from the very title onward, this meditation on the bewitching capacity of language and on its autonomy with regard to some supposed objective truth, becomes also a speculation on the degree of reliability of every specific narrative instance, including the *io*, the "I." But the American Elisa is deprived of this possibility of speculation, with the inevitable result that she becomes merely assertive.

Let us see, then, if it is possible to give some answers to the questions raised above. But before that, we should make a few further remarks. Since there is no evidence that encourages us to speak of revision as censorship, I would not wish to lay particular blame at the door of Adrienne Foulke, or Andrew Chiappe, in so far as he was involved. Faced with the work of a new writer, the translator, presumably under instruction of the publisher, most likely took this approach, which, however unfortunate, certainly chimes with the history of editorial practice. It would be ungenerous to reproach Foulke for failing to see in *Menzogna e sortilegio* what escaped the most diligent of criticism, which was to consider Morante's novel once more only in the second half of the 1960s, and only after the unexpected, and for some still incomprehensible, appreciation of Gÿorgÿ Lukács.

It seems to me more pertinent to inquire into the cultural model that more broadly informed the work of the translator, and more useful perhaps to consider the nature of the novel in its American form, judged "unrecognizable" by its own author.[3]

We can state with reasonable confidence that as well as reducing the bulk of the novel, the cuts that bring *House of Liars* into being—and of this, the translator is only partly aware—serve to curtail the narrative instances of the novel. With the traditional memoir novel as referential model, the cuts effected in the *House of Liars* confer on the narrating voice a strongly assertive tone, stronger at least than the original: that degree of unimpeachable assertion, in other words, that we can expect from a conventionally reliable narrating voice intent on narrating a story from which it is largely absent.

Thus we realize that what is missing are all those elements that make Elisa, and her act of writing, the protagonists of the novel. In the attempt, most certainly influenced by the reviews of the time, to contain the overflowing novel with its self-evident rejection of Neorealism, within the safety of respectable tradition, child of the great season of the late-nineteenth century, between naturalism and a degraded decadentism, the book is ruthlessly axed of everything that cannot be drawn into the ambit of epic novels that narrate lengthy stories about large families. In underlining the assertiveness of the narrating voice, *House of Liars* does indeed narrate the sorrowful history of Elisa's family, the story of the *casa dei bugiardi*, the "house of liars," but it does not relate the story of Elisa herself, a story that, moving constantly between the two poles of *menzogna* and *sortilegio*, is at the same time the history of a neurosis and the history of an existential (and in part existentializing) search in the light of transcendence, as I have argued elsewhere (Bardini, "'Fantastici doppi'"). In spite of those who still make the grave error of speaking of Elsa Morante as the "greatest nineteenth-century Italian writer" of the twentieth century, it seems to me clear that Elsa Morante's dismay in terming her own novel "unrecognizable" and "heavier" lies precisely in the bitter awareness of this forced, humiliating retrogression toward the styles and forms of an obsolete past, thus denying *Menzogna e sortilegio* its status as a novel that, on the contrary, reverberates with the most advanced cultural debates of twentieth-century Europe.

Notes

1. From now on all references to the American translation of *Menzogna e sortilegio* will appear parenthetically as HL.

2. All references to *Menzogna e sortilegio* will be given parenthetically as MS.

3. As Di Ciolla McGowan's study in the present volume shows (45–66), Morante read English well and indeed translated the stories of Katherine Mansfield.

Works Cited

Bardini, Marco. *Morante Elsa. Italiana. Di professione, poeta.* Pisa: Nistri-Lischi, 1999.

———. "Dei 'fantastici doppi' ovvero La mimesi narrativa dello spostamento psichico." *Per Elisa* 173–299.

Lugnani, Lucio. "L'ipotesto melodrammatico come luogo della traco-
    tanza e della teatralità." *Per Elisa* 343–407.

Morante, Elsa. *Menzogna e sortilegio*. Turin: Einaudi, 1975.

———. *House of Liars*. Trans. Adrienne Foulke. Editorial Assistance
    Andrew Chiappe. New York: Harcourt, 1951.

Per Elisa. Studi su "Menzogna e sortilegio." Pisa: Nistri-Lischi, 1990.

Cristina Della Coletta

The Morphology of Desire in
Elsa Morante's *L'isola di Arturo*

It has become almost a cliché to note that when the literary establishment decides to open its ranks to a woman writer, it does so by praising her uniqueness, her absolute originality.[1] Thus, Cesare Garboli places Elsa Morante "fuori da ogni tracciato. Estranea a qualsiasi tradizione consacrata del Novecento, la scrittura della Morante non lascia intravedere modelli" (v; "outside of all categories. Contrary to established twentieth-century traditions, Morante's writing reveals no models"). Because similar statements define many of the currently anthologized women writers, their double edge merits further scrutiny.[2] On the one hand, Garboli identifies a uniquely feminine kind of writing, one that precisely because of its difference has been overlooked by generations of critics, and therefore now demands consideration. On the other hand, claims such as Garboli's inevitably isolate women writers: exceptions as they are, these women are separated from the clusters of recognized authors and schools, and doomed, at best, to follow a bright yet lonely trajectory. Having no models, women writers are bound to leave no legacy of their own. "È nata da se stessa Elsa Morante" ("Morante was born from her own self") Garboli writes, her style being "natural," her narrative movements, "magical," her attitude toward storytelling, "child-like" (v–vi).

A novel such as Morante's *L'isola di Arturo* (1957; *Arturo's Island*, 1959) appeared to give succor to this interpretative approach. Set on an island that has less in common with the geographical Procida than with a mythical, a-temporal island as *axis mundi*, this text has been consistently read as the archetypal story of a *fanciullo divino,* the pure narrative of a universal child's coming of age.[3] While it is true that Morante delves deeply into myth, her rendition of Arturo's initiation into adulthood is far more sophisticated than these interpretations would imply. Morante's narrative strategies can best be defined by Luce Irigaray's notion of "mimicry." In mimicry, a model is repeated in a self-conscious manner in order to expose the citational, distorted nature of the repetition (76). *Arturo's Island* freely borrows from the generic models of the epic and the *Bildungsroman*, repeating and intermixing them with an ironic slant. In blurring conventional genre boundaries, Morante thus creates a hybrid textual space controlled by a narrating "I" who recaptures the mythical world of his past while charting his discovery of the meaning and "dangers" of parody, as applied to that same world. Arturo's estranging narrative journey brings him back to his native island, to the time when his all-consuming and singular passion was forced to confront the collective onslaught of his multiple desires, and when his absolute code crumbled under the pressure of a relative, changing reality.

Borrowing what Mikhail Bakhtin identified as one of the founding elements of the epic—the absolute distance separating the narrated world from the time in which both author and audience live—Morante defines the island's space-time paradigm around the concepts of distance, separation, and self-sufficiency (Bakhtin 13). In spite of its geographical vicinity to the mainland of Campania, Procida appears as different, remote and inaccessible, its atavistic isolation verging on self-imposed captivity. Morante uses the island, mythically, as a distinctive and total space—the space of a unique and exceptional tale:

> Se per caso uno straniero scende a Procida, si meraviglia di non trovarvi quella vita promiscua e allegra, feste e conversazioni per le strade, e canti, suoni di chitarre e mandolini, per cui la regione di Napoli è conosciuta su tutta la terra. I Procidani sono scontrosi, taciturni. Le porte sono tutte chiuse, pochi si affacciano alle finestre.[4]

> A foreigner perchance disembarking at Procida is amazed to find none of the promiscuous and cheerful life for which Naples is famous throughout the world: no parties, no chatting in the streets, no songs, no guitars and mandolins. Procidans are unsocial and silent. All doors remain closed, and few people appear at their windows.

Procida's uncommunicative and secluded inhabitants have no equals elsewhere. Doubling one another in their exotic and solipsistic identities, they are different both physically and psychologically from the mainlanders just a few miles away: "Sono di razza piccola, bruni, con occhi neri allungati, come gli orientali. E si direbbero tutti parenti fra di loro tanto si rassomigliano" (10; "They are small and dark, with long black Asiatic eyes, and they look so much alike that one would think they were all related").

Functioning as our guide into this exceptionally sealed world, Arturo, the first-person narrator, superimposes temporal distance onto spatial distance. His narrative journey explores not only a different land, but also a different "self," that of his own childhood in Procida. Initially, Arturo underscores the distance between narrating and narrated "selves." Critics have duly noted that there is a substantial lack of information about the adult Arturo. We know that he no longer lives in Procida, but know nothing about his present situation—where he lives, what he does, when and why he has decided to commit his memories to the page.[5] Although Arturo's story takes place in the years preceding World War II, no specific information is given as to the time of his writing. If the *story* is circumscribed within the time-space coordinates of the island, the temporal and spatial dimensions of the *discours* are exceptionally open because of their indeterminacy. Lacking any clues to pinpoint, chronologically, the narrative act, the gap between past and present tends to expand into infinity, and becomes absolutized. Like the island, Arturo's childhood and his life with his stepmother, Nunziata, and his father, Wilhelm Gerace, belong to an utterly remote and separate time: "Da questa infinita distanza," Arturo writes, "ripenso a W.G." (427; "From this infinite distance, I think back to W.G.").

The inspiration for Arturo's decision to delve into his past remains equally mysterious. If the more famous Marcel had found in a *petite madeleine* the link between past and present, while Elio Vittorini's Silvestro had to engage in a spatial journey to recover the lost temporal dimension of the past, Morante furnishes no explicit element of contact between the narrator's present situation and his remembrance of times past. Nothing seems to trigger the act of remembrance and therefore mend the broken link between present desires and previous experiences. Memory works in a vacuum, highlighting distances, isolating spaces and altering times: "La mia casa non dista molto da una piazzetta quasi cittadina [. . .] e dalle fitte abitazioni del paese. Ma, nella mia memoria, è divenuta un luogo isolato, intorno a cui la solitudine fa uno spazio enorme" (12; "My house is not far from an almost urban little square [. . .] and the clustering houses of the village. But, in my memory, it has become an isolated space, around which solitude creates an enormous void").

Arturo's "absolute past" corresponds to the temporal dimension that Bakhtin, borrowing Schiller's definition, identifies with epic time (13). The founding norm of the epic demands the transferal of the represented world into a self-contained, vacuum-sealed past:

> [T]he authorial position immanent in the epic and constitutive for it (that is, the position of the one who utters the epic word) is the environment of a man speaking about a past that is to him inaccessible [. . .].
>
> Both the singer and the listener, immanent in the epic as a genre, are located in the same time [. . .] but the represented world of the heroes stands on an utterly different and inaccessible time and value place, separated by epic distance [. . .].
>
> The epic past is called the "absolute past" for good reason: it is both monochronic and valorized [. . .] it lacks any relativity, that is, any gradual purely temporal progression that might connect it with the present. It is walled off absolutely from all consequent times, and above all from those times in which the singer and listener are located. (Bakhtin 13–16)

The time-space paradigm of *Arturo's Island*, therefore, designates the morphology of a genre, the epic, and one of its imaginative components, myth. In spite of his epic-sounding name, however, the narrative's epic center is not Arturo, but his father, Wilhelm Gerace, as seen from young Arturo's worshipping eyes. Wilhelm belongs to a realm beyond relativism, plurality, or doubt. Like the singer of epic tales, Arturo maintains the "reverent point of view of a descendent" (Bakhtin 13) in his narrative of a valorized temporal category, its idealized spatial location, and its superhuman protagonist. The world of the epic is indeed a world of "beginnings," a world of "fathers," of "firsts" and "bests" (Bakhtin 13).

> Per me, che non potevo attribuire, a lui, nessun capriccio umano, il suo broncio era maestoso come l'oscurarsi del giorno, indizio certo di eventi misteriosi, e importanti come la Storia Universale. (29)

> And I, who could not attribute to him any human whim, found his sulks as majestic as the darkening of the day— unmistakable clues of mysterious events, as important as Universal History.

Wilhelm speaks a language endowed with the mystery and power of an original, primordial utterance: "Tutte le parole che lui diceva parevano appena inventate" (31; "All the words that he uttered seemed newly invented"). He thus places himself at the mythic source of both Being and Word, as shown by Arturo's description of the apparently childish game of the echo, in which playful routine is defamiliarized to share the esoteric secrecy of ritual, and the epic code reconnects with its sacred fount. Wilhelm's calls into the echoing vault are no longer merely playful or even angry, but assume the mantle of epic legend:

> [A]scoltavo quegli enigmi in silenzio. Non mi pareva d'as-sistere al solito gioco dell'eco [. . .] ma a un duello epico. Siamo a Roncisvalle, e d'un tratto, sulla spianata, irromperà Orlando col suo corno. Siamo alle Termopili, e dietro alle rocce si nascondono i cavalieri persiani, coi loro berretti puntuti. (30)

> I [. . .] listened to those enigmas in silence. I did not seem to attend to the usual game of echoes [. . .] but to an epic duel. We are at Roncesvalles, and, suddenly, Roland storms into the clearing blowing his horn. We are at Thermopylae, and the Persian horsemen in their spiked helmets are hiding behind the rocks.

Whole unto himself just like the mythical Procida, Wilhelm, in Arturo's eyes, embodies the condition of the epic hero, or the divine Father, that of "authentic essence and significance"

(Bakhtin 16). Unique in his difference, Wilhelm has the value of a prized "original" in both appearance and manner, a difference that in Arturo's eyes is a sign of belonging to a race not of this earth: Wilhelm is "fratello del sole e della luna" (29; "brother to the sun and the moon").

Wilhelm confirms this notion when he explains to Arturo his decision to adopt his father's last name, a decision that, in his case, denies all moral and ontological inheritance: "Che importa il nome? Chiama pur la rosa con altro nome: avrà men dolce odore?" (61; "What's in a name? That which we call a rose by any other name would smell as sweet").[6] By rejecting the patronymic power in the definition of identity, Wilhelm also rejects the idea of having taken after someone else. Authentic and impenetrable, Wilhelm's essence precedes and defies naming, existing independently from it. Wilhelm's linguistic nominalism (names are established by convention, they are not by necessity determined by the objects they name) conceals an essentialist's core—essences are not to be altered by interpretation. Unique in themselves, they are indeed sacred in their defiance of all semantic appropriation. Alone and isolated, Wilhelm remains elusive, and cannot be explained away: he is "*il più misterioso di tutti*" (133; emphasis in original; "*the most mysterious of all*").

In Arturo's eyes, God is dead and Wilhelm has taken His place. Just like the biblical father, Wilhelm's justice is mysterious and indisputable, his interdictions eternal. If the sixth law in Arturo's "Code of Absolute Truth" declares that "LE PROVE PIÙ EVIDENTI E TUTTE LE ESPERIENZE UMANE DIMOSTREREBBERO CHE DIO NON ESISTE" (33; "THE MOST EVIDENT PROOF AND ALL HUMAN EXPERIENCE SHOW THAT GOD DOES NOT EXIST"), this does not mean that Arturo has successfully rid himself of the notion of transcendency. He has simply chosen a substitute god. In fact, Arturo's code can be compared to Moses's tablets, defining Arturo's moral world in light of Wilhelm's universal law:

> Lui era l'immagine della certezza, e tutto ciò che lui diceva o faceva era il responso di una legge universale dalla quale io dedussi i primi comandamenti della mia vita. Qui stava la massima seduzione della sua compagnia. (31)

> He was the image of certainty, and everything he said or did
> was the response of a universal law from which I deduced
> the first commandments of my life. This was the greatest
> seduction of his company.

By bringing God down to earth, and giving Him a human face, albeit the superhuman face of his own father, Arturo transposes God's absolute uniqueness onto Wilhelm. This does not narrow the distance separating Arturo from his transcendental model. In Procida, classical mythology, primitive mysteries, and Christian mysticism conspire in the process of deification of the father by reinstating the sense of the sacred. Self-consciously human, Arturo feels excluded from full participation in the island's sacred rites. "Relentless guardian of a closed garden where only the elect may enjoy eternal beatitude" (Girard, *Deceit* 77), Wilhelm belongs to a distant world of absolute perfection and happiness. From Wilhelm he desires the denied recognition for his faith, a reward that itself would constitute paradise on earth (72–73).

If daily events in Procida become part of a separate, sacred space, replete as they are with taboos, anathemas, terror, and trials, Arturo's role remains that of the pious observer, unable to penetrate the ritual's secrets.[7] When he is finally called to participate in the ritual, Arturo's actions acquire a strange air of fatality. The boy's search for his father's lost watch along the Mediterranean seabed becomes a metaphor for an existential quest reaching universal, timeless proportions, its outcome defining Arturo's final destiny:

> Erravo per quei fondi variegati e fantastici, fuori dai regni
> umani, bruciando, minuto per minuto, questa speranza ine-
> guagliabile: di splendere, come un prodigio, agli occhi di
> Lui! Era questa, la posta grandiosa ch'era in gioco! E nes-
> suno per aiutarmi, né angeli né santi da pregare. (41)

> I wandered around the seabed—varied, fantastic, beyond all
> human realms—consumed, minute by minute, by this
> incomparable hope: to shine like a prodigy in his eyes!
> These were the grand stakes for which to play! And there
> was no one to help me—no angels, no saints to whom to
> pray.

Later, Arturo describes a dream in which his father, immensely tall and wearing shining armor, precedes a puny Arturo, who strives to keep up, encumbered with a recruit uniform, too big for him. When Wilhelm, without even looking at him, orders Arturo to go and buy a packet of cigarettes, Arturo proudly executes his command but, just before handing over the packet, he reverently kisses it. The object of Wilhelm's desire has a sacred value, and Arturo mimics the pious believer's adoration of a relic. By sharing in the divine by synecdoche or proximity, the relic thus allows the faithful to approach divinity.

In terms of René Girard's understanding of mimetic desire, Wilhelm is Arturo's mediator, the model that defines and establishes Arturo's desires. What is it that Wilhelm owns and that Arturo lacks and so desperately desires? Wilhelm clearly represents for Arturo the dream of metaphysical autonomy. Arturo turns passionately toward his father, who "seems to enjoy the divine inheritance: So great is the disciple's faith that he perpetually thinks he is about to steal the marvelous secret from the mediator" (Girard, *Deceit* 77). Arturo's life is confined to the repetition of the same gesture, the feat that will initiate him into the mysterious secrets that continue to elude him, while nourishing his desire. As Girard points out:

> The desire to absorb the being of a mediator [. . .] often takes the form of a desire to be initiated into a new life. The sudden prestige which the narrator gives to an unfamiliar way of life always coincides with his meeting of a being who awakens this desire. (*Deceit* 53)

Arturo's persistent requests to accompany his father in one of his fabled journeys fulfill precisely this function. Travel, Wilhelm's mysterious life outside of Procida, acquires enormous value as Arturo sees it as the way to penetrate Wilhelm's secret, and by thus sharing his essence, assimilate, and, finally, repeat it. Arturo's conviction that Wilhelm is setting off for glamorous adventures is matched by his desire to win his father's admiration and thus one day be permitted to accompany him in his epic travels (38–39).

Arturo's metaphysical desire, in its impossibility, needs Wilhelm's indifference to sustain and thus continually reproduce itself. "Il mare è uno splendore indifferente, come Lui" (41; "The sea is splendid and indifferent, like Him"), argues Arturo while seeking his father's watch. Absence nurtures desire, and desire paradoxically needs to be frustrated in order to thrive. What Arturo desires, his metaphysical dream of absolute originality, is not achievable in a world of copies. Arturo organizes his world around what Gilles Deleuze defines as "Platonic" repetition (*Difference* 8). This repetition "is grounded in a solid archetypal model which is untouched by the effects of repetition. All the other examples are copies of this model" (Miller 6). The assumption behind this approach to repetition is that the copy acquires its value based on its degree of similarity to the original. The original, in turn, cannot be replaced or lessened by the copies, no matter how close they get to the model. Wilhelm thus sets the evaluative standards for judging all that follows based on the copies' ability to reproduce a prized and authoritative original. Arturo thus claims: "S'io fossi stato un pittore, e avessi dovuto illustrare i poemi epici [. . .] credo che, nelle vesti dei loro eroi principali, avrei sempre dipinto il ritratto di mio padre, mille volte" (38; "If I had been a painter and had had to illustrate epic poems [. . .], I believe I would have depicted my father, dressed as the famous heroes, a thousand times over").

In this light, a desire that is both necessary and self-defeating frames Arturo's identity-building process. The imitative nature of Arturo's desires weaves a complex web of recurrences and repetitions upon the novel's narrative progress. Just like Don Quixote toward Amadis, Arturo has completely surrendered to his father the choice of his own desire. Not only does Arturo desire what he thinks his father owns, but he goes a step further: he identifies himself fully with this object, thus underscoring desire's narcissistic thrust. If it is true that "imitative desire is always a desire to be Another" (Girard, *Deceit* 83), the "Self" cannot be obliterated, but simply forced to wear the seductive mask of the "Other." Arturo invents analogies between himself and Wilhelm's fabulous friends. One of them is Romeo, the man from Amalfi. A gift to Wilhelm, the photograph of Romeo standing with a foot forward, holding a cane in one hand and two dogs on a leash in the other, reminds the young boy of the constellation of the Herdsman and his star Arturo. This uncanny similarity explains itself in connection with the novel's opening paragraph:

> Uno dei miei primi vanti era stato il mio nome. Avevo presto imparato (fu *lui*, mi sembra, il primo a informarmene), che Arturo è una stella: la luce più rapida e radiosa della figura di Boote nel cielo boreale! (7; emphasis in original)

> One of my main sources of pride was my name. Early on, I learned (*He* was the first, I believe, to inform me of this) that Arturo is a star—the fastest and brightest light in the figure of the Herdsman, in the northern sky!

When Wilhelm tells Arturo that the watch with the word AMICUS is a present from perhaps the best friend he has, Arturo's first thought goes to "Romeo-Boote" (43), leaving the identification with the constellation unexplained. But since Romeo is long dead, he replaces him with an imaginary and even more extraordinary epic companion, whom he names *Pugnale Algerino* ("Algerian Knife"). Once again, the stellar metaphor clarifies the trajectory of Arturo's desire: from Romeo to *Pugnale Algerino* and from *Pugnale Algerino* to Wilhelm, all the substitutions conceal Arturo's desire to be part of his father's epic firmament.

Similarly, Arturo's wishful description to Nunziata of his relationship with his nurse and "faithful companion" Silvestro, closely reproduces that between Wilhelm and *Pugnale Algerino*, while the German cigarette lighter that Silvestro gives to Arturo mirrors the watch that Wilhelm received from *Pugnale*.

The iridescent web that Arturo imagines is imprisoning him in Procida transforms linear time into cyclical, cosmic time. The island and its archipelago mirror the constellations in the skies, creating a perfectly closed, self-reflective universe: "il firmamento, a guardarlo, mi diventava un grande oceano, sparso d'innumerevoli isole" (202; "the sky, when I watched it, looked like a great ocean dotted with innumerable islands").[8] This *paradiso,* in turn, repeats the divine image: shaped like a dolphin, Procida both hosts and mirrors the sacred, as Arturo reveals when saying that before his father he feels like "un'alìce in presenza di un grande delfino" (28; "an anchovy compared to a great dolphin"). In spite of Arturo's mirroring efforts, no complete and full analogy is ever possible between father and son, and it is this disparity that continues to fuel desire's inexorable drive.

Classical imagery, Christian myth, and epic lore contribute to the construction of Arturo's metaphysical system. Not only do these paradigms "reflect the transcendent as an echo sends back the sound to its point of origin" (Girard, *Deceit* 79) but they also reveal the constructed, mediated nature of Arturo's desire. Arturo desires through the heroes who people his imagination, and like Madame Bovary, "the second-rate books which [he] devoured in [his] youth have destroyed all [his] spontaneity" (Girard, *Deceit* 5).[9] Reading fills Arturo's winter evenings and rainy days, and his carefree, primitive lifestyle on the island, which seems founded on the satisfaction of natural and spontaneous needs, reveals a bookish counter-side. His father is not totally uneducated and owns some books: in his small family library there are children's novels, thrillers, and adventure stories, as well as classical works and textbooks such as atlases, dictionaries, history books, collections of poems, and translations of famous works, all of which Arturo devours (32).

One of these favorite books, *Le vite degli eccellenti condottieri*, very likely an Italian translation of Nepos Cornelius's *De vita excellentium imperatorum (Lives of the Excellent Commanders)*, helps build Arturo's myth of the patriarchal hero, a divine subject in his autonomy, inspiring his peoples to emulate him in his glory. It is through these texts that Arturo transfigures both his model and the objects of his desire, and the type of poetic distortion that they undergo is that wrought by a boy who observes the world through the lenses of his childhood readings. Wilhelm's absolute originality reveals here its paradoxical core: true mythmaker, Arturo has constructed his God in Wilhelm through literary imitation, rather than having discovered the divine *ex nihilo* in his father.

So far Wilhelm's mediation is purely external, and therefore fitting to the mythical island of absolute time. Arturo openly worships his model and proclaims himself as his faithful disciple. The arrival of Nunziata, Wilhelm's new bride from Naples, alters the morphology of desire. Nunziata announces herself as a contradiction in terms, a challenge to Arturo's carefully constructed analogies between books and life. On the one hand, Arturo muses, "Secondo i libri che avevo letto, una matrigna non poteva essere che una creatura perversa, ostile e degna di *odio*" (80; "According to the books I had read, a stepmother must be a perverse creature, hostile and worthy of *hatred*"; emphasis added). On the other hand, Nunziata is bound to mirror, by sheer proximity, Wilhelm's divine essence "come sposa di mio padre, costei, per me era una persona *sacra*!" (80; "as my father's bride, for me she was a sacred being"). Hatred and adoration are thus made to live in uncomfortably close quarters. To further complicate matters, Arturo realizes that books tell him that he should expect to see his father arrive with "qualche essere meraviglioso, che attestasse l'esistenza della famosa specie femminile descritta nei libri" (81; "some marvelous being attesting to the existence of the famous female species described in books"), yet Nunziata, "nei suoi abiti informi, consunti, non appariva molto diversa dalle solite pescatore e popolane di Procida" (81; "in her shapeless and worn clothes, she did not seem to differ much from the usual common people and fisherwomen of Procida"). Wilhelm's open scorn toward his bride seems to preempt all idealization. Wilhelm's marriage, moreover, sharply contradicts his misogynistic views. The mere existence of women challenges Wilhelm's sense of divine autonomy, the narcissistic foundation of his desire, and the very existence of his (and Arturo's) solipsistic utopia:

> L'intenzione delle femmine è di degradare la vita! E questo che ha voluto dire la leggenda degli Ebrei, raccontando la cacciata dal Paradiso terrestre per volontà di una femmina. Se non fosse per le femmine, il nostro destino non sarebbe di nascere e di morire, come le bestie. La razza delle femmine è nemica di tutto ciò che non ha limiti. Vuole il tempo, il decadimento [. . .] vuole la morte! Se non fosse per le femmine, l'esistenza sarebbe una giovinezza eterna: un giardino [. . .] e *amarsi* vorrebbe dire soltanto: *rivelarsi, l'uno all'altro quanto si è belli.* . . . L'amore sarebbe [. . .] come guardarsi allo specchio. (162–63; emphasis in original)

> Women's aim is to degrade life! This is what the Hebrew legend meant in stating men were chased out of Earthly Paradise because of a woman. If it were not for women our

destiny would not be to be born and die, like animals. The
female race hates everything that is not limited. It demands
time, decay [. . .] and it demands death! If it were not for
women, existence would be eternally young: a garden [. . .],
and *loving* would mean *revealing one's beauty, one to
another.* . . . Love would be [. . .] like gazing upon oneself
in a mirror.

While establishing the mesmerizing epic absolutes of timeless
permanence and enduring self-sufficiency, *Arturo's Island* also
charts the young protagonist's identity-formation process along
the *Bildungsroman*'s contrastive paradigm, based on progress,
evolution, and change.[10] Arturo discovers a desire that brings
havoc in the *House of the Guaglioni*—the epic masculine space
from which women are banned—shattering his and Wilhelm's
enclosed hall of mirrors. Ambiguity creeps into Arturo's Code
of Absolute Certainties, and desire takes multiple directions,
revealing its protean nature, its unresolved contradictions.
Nunziata's body becomes the blasphemous temple of these
contradictions. Both child and woman, goddess and beast, and
object of scorn and desire, Nunziata continues to escape single
definitions, as revealed in the difficulty Arturo has in naming
her, either as a boy or now, in writing about her. Arturo resorts
to "N." or "Nunz," a name that "mi piace abbastanza; fa pensare
a un animale mezzo selvatico e mezzo domestico: per esempio
una gatta, una capra" (144; "I rather like; it makes me think of
a half-wild and half-tamed animal: for example, a cat or a
goat").

The absence of naming reveals the underlying taboo.
Nunziata embodies, for Arturo, the impossible target of his
desire, a combined mother and bride. In her hybrid identity,
she forces Arturo's metaphysical system to falter, anticipating
thus the crash of his idol from an increasingly precarious altar.
In spite of her name and her naive religiosity, Nunziata announces the onset of a relative world, marked by the endless
proliferation of signs, a world without God. Her snakelike hair
and wild appearance recall one of the three Gorgons, the only
mortal one, whose destructive powers had already been foreshadowed in Wilhelm's swimming encounter with a medusa:
"al vedersi il petto segnato da quelle striature sanguigne, fu
vinto da un orrore che lo fece impallidire fino sulle labbra [. . .].

Cristina Della Coletta

Sulla spiaggia e per tutto il mare si fece un gran silenzio" (31;
"when he saw those blood-red stripes on his chest, he was overcome with horror, and turned pale all the way to his lips [. . .].
A great silence reigned over the beach and the whole sea").[11]

The threat that Nunziata poses to Arturo's metaphysical system is such that Arturo would rather replace his mediator than
see his system fail. Losing her mediocrity, it is Nunziata herself who metamorphoses into a legendary figure, one that fits
right into the metaphorical coordinates defining the celestial
status of Arturo and his father: "rivedevo i suoi occhi [. . .] dai
cigli raggianti come le punte di una stella" (83; "I saw her eyes
again [. . .], with the eyelashes shining like the points of a
star"), and "[i] suoi occhi [. . .] mi ricordavano [. . .] le notti
stellate dell'isola" (115; "[her] eyes [. . .] reminded me [. . .] of
the island's starry nights"). Contrary to Wilhelm's description
of women as time-bound and harbingers of death and decay, in
one of Arturo's dreams, Nunziata becomes the primeval Goddess, and the priestess of a monumental time:

> Faceva una notte chiara [. . .] io ero un eroe, e camminavo
> lungo la riva del mare. Avevo ricevuto un'offesa, o soffrivo
> di un lutto: forse avevo perduto il mio più caro amico. [. . .]
> Chiamavo qualcuno, e piangevo [. . .] e appariva una donna
> assai grande, che sedeva su una pietra, a un passo da me.
> Era una bambina, ma pure aveva, in tutta la persona, una
> maturità maestosa, e la sua misteriosa infanzia non pareva
> un'età umana, ma piuttosto un segno di eternità. (121)

> It was a clear night [. . .] I was a hero, walking along the
> seashore. I had been insulted, or suffered from some loss;
> perhaps I had lost my dearest friend. [. . .] I was calling
> someone, weeping [. . .], and a very large woman appeared
> and sat on a stone, a step away from me. She was a little
> girl, yet she had a majestic maturity, and her mysterious
> infancy seemed unlike any human age, but was more a sign
> of eternity.

Exactly as he had done with Wilhelm, Arturo borrows mythological and classical imagery to build a sacred figure in which
he can quench his metaphysical thirst, and impose the rule of
eternity upon Time's merciless becoming. As his new mediator, Nunziata now inhabits Wilhelm's epic kingdom, and Arturo

142

compares her to a painting of the Wind-God Aquilo, blowing a fleet of ships along during an episode from the Crusades. Repeating a familiar pattern, Arturo attempts to impress Nunziata with descriptions of his imagined future heroic actions. Imagining that his admiring stepmother looks upon him "come un devoto specchio" (128; "like a devout mirror"), Arturo once again reveals that the working of desire is fundamentally self-reflective and self-idolizing.

In the preceding examples, the shift in mediators from Wilhelm to Nunziata does not alter the functioning of desire, yet other elements intervene in the novel to make desire both dynamic and changeable. Wilhelm and Nunziata's wedding night tilts the scale from external to internal mediation. Wilhelm's (real or imagined) desire for Nunziata inspires an identical desire in Arturo. No longer an unreachable idol, Wilhelm has come down to earth. Model and rival at the same time, Wilhelm forces Arturo to succumb to contrasting feelings. Admiration and hatred, emulation and envy, desire and jealousy mix in an explosive emotional compound:

> Mio padre, in una specie di rabbiosa felicità, mosse verso la sposa e prendendola per il polso, col gesto di un ballerino le fece fare un mezzo giro su se stessa . . .
> —Andiamo! Cammina!—le ingiunse egli con asprezza; e lei, ubbidiente lo seguì. Prima di varcare la soglia, volse indietro il capo, a guardare nella mia direzione; ma, preso da uno strano sentimento d'odio e di rabbia, io distolsi subito le pupille da lei. (143)

> My father went up to his bride in a kind of furious joy, seized her by the wrist and, like a ballet dancer, twirled her around in a half-circle . . .
> "Let's go! Move it!" he urged her harshly, and she followed him obediently. Before going through the doorway, she looked back in my direction, but I felt a strange feeling of hatred and rage, and averted my eyes.

> Pure, in certi momenti, mi pareva quasi d'odiare Wilhelm Gerace. [. . .] Mi accadeva più che mai d'odiarlo, perché, come un invasore, s'impadroniva [. . .] della mia *isola*; ma pure sapevo che l'*isola* non mi sarebbe piaciuta tanto se non fosse stata sua. (215; emphasis added)

> Then, in certain moments. I felt I almost hated Wilhelm
> Gerace. [. . .] I found myself hating him more than ever,
> because he had taken over [. . .] my *island*, like an invader.
> Yet I knew I would not have liked the *island* so much if it
> had not been his own.

As the mediator comes closer to the subject, so does the object, and it is easy to see the body of Nunziata replacing Arturo's careful word-choice, *island*.

The "inhuman offense" that Nunziata suffers on her wedding night disrobes her of the sacred vestments in which Arturo had clad her, plunging her into the flux of change and decay. This loss does not change the intensity of Arturo's desire, but, rather, complicates it. If in external mediation, the subject was openly proclaiming his reverence for his hero, the concrete battlefield of internal mediation stages devious and deceitful moves, thus apparently muddling the trajectory of desire. Arturo has one initial moment of frankness with Nunziata. When he reveals to Nunziata his mediated dreams of epic victories modeled on the heroic *persona* of his father, he is also disclosing a thinly veiled secret, his predisposition to repeat *all* of Wilhelm's desires, including that for Nunziata: "Mi vergognavo d'aver potuto [. . .] abbandonarmi fino al punto di dirle i miei segreti! Sulla panca [. . .] c'era ancora il libro degli *Eccellenti Condottieri*; e quella vista rincrudì la mia onta" (148; "I was ashamed to think [. . .] that I had let myself go so far as to tell her my secrets! My book on the *Excellent Condottieri* [. . .] was still on the bench, and the sight of it increased my shame"). Arturo atones for his infraction with an increase of ascetic dissimulation. He resists the temptation to see Nunziata, spending long days away from the house, pretending indifference. "*Askesis* for the sake of desire is an inevitable consequence of triangular desire" (Girard, *Deceit* 158) and once again it is the mediator who looms large in Arturo's lonely world, his influence felt by metaphoric substitution: "Leggendo, [. . .] tenevo sempre in mostra sul tavolino [. . .] un pacchetto di sigarette Nazionali" (149; "While reading, I always kept a pack of Nazionali cigarettes [. . .] clearly visible on the table"), the same cigarettes that Wilhelm smokes alone in his room (152). Arturo's indifference mimics Wilhelm's persistent *ennui*. Indifference and ennui translate the sense of divine self-mastery that both father and son continue superficially to boast, and for which they secretly long.

Significantly, as Wilhelm's role evolves from that of an external to an internal mediator, Carmine Arturo, Nunziata's newborn baby, is a replica of his blond father and thus fulfills yet another mediating function, as Arturo's acute jealousy indicates. Hated rival, Carmine Arturo has access to Nunziata's idealized maternal body, just as Wilhelm had access to her sexed, bridal body. Arturo imagines the scene of a mother kissing her son "con affetto quasi divino" (266; "with almost divine love"). This son is not Carmine Arturo but his dark, older double, Arturo himself, and the mother is not Arturo's dead mother but Nunziata. On another occasion, Arturo asks a bemused Nunziata to wear her hair in two braided buns pinned up above her ears. This is the same hairstyle that Arturo's mother wears in a cherished photograph. Thus, Nunziata reveals a striking resemblance to Arturo's mother (199). As they mimic each other in Arturo's imagination, Nunziata and Arturo's dead mother reflect the original, mythic Mother:

> [. . .] senza rendermene conto, io, per lei, credevo addirittura in un paradiso. Che cos'altro era, difatti, quella specie di tenda orientale, alzata fra il cielo e la terra, e portata dall'aria, in cui lei dimorava sola, oziosa e contemplante, con gli occhi al cielo, come una trasfigurata? (55)

> [. . .] without realizing it, I actually believed in heaven, because of her. What else could it be, that kind of Oriental tent, floating on air between the sky and the earth, in which she dwelled alone, idly contemplating the sky with upturned eyes like one transfigured?

Arturo's representation of his mother in light of the popular iconography of contemplating Madonnas follows the male child's idealization of woman. This fact, however, is overall less meaningful than its implied corollary, which reveals by implication Arturo's imaginary fulfillment of his innermost metaphysical desire. The adoration of the Mother conceals the adoration of the Self. By implicitly placing himself in Christ's place, Arturo fulfills his dream of colliding selfhood and divinity. His daydream about his mother's love, "[per mia] madre gli altri Arturi esistenti sono tutti imitatori, gente secondaria" (54; "for my mother, all the other existing Arturos are second-class impersonators"), further confirms Arturo's desire to inhabit the point of absolute origin. In this sense, the chart of Arturo's desire for his idealized father repeats exactly that for his idealized mother(s) because both desires spring from the same source. The narrative of Girardian desire's metamorphoses and the *Bildungsroman* of Arturo's adolescence on the island thus coexist with the circular return of the same foundational, metaphysical need.

Arturo's double desire to replace both Wilhelm and Carmine Arturo at Nunziata's side reveals the double essence of Nunziata herself—a mythic mother and earthly lover. The Oedipal contradiction appears untenable, as untenable as the mixture of love and hatred that Arturo feels for Wilhelm:

> Io, a mia insaputa, venivo sottoposto a prove più amare di quelle d'Otello! Giacché quel negro sventurato, almeno nella sua tragedia, aveva un campo segnato, dove combattere: di qua l'amata, e di là il nemico. Mentre che il campo di Arturo Gerace era un dilemma indecifrabile, senza sollievo di speranza, né di vendetta. (165)

> Without realizing it, I was enduring trials more bitter than Othello's! In his tragedy, that unlucky Moor at least had a demarked battlefield on which to fight: the woman he loved on one side, the enemy on the other. While Arturo Gerace's battlefield was an undecipherable dilemma, without the relief of hope or revenge.

Arturo's passionate kiss with Nunziata seems to both break and confirm the taboo against incest. On one hand, no longer Mother, Nunziata, whom Arturo calls for the first time by her proper name, becomes the object of Arturo's adult desire: "Aveva una vesticciola rossa. [. . .] All'impovviso la strinsi, baciandola in bocca. [. . .] D'un tratto la mia voce disse: —Nunziata! Nunziaté!" (289–90; "She wore a little red dress. [. . .] Suddenly I pressed her to me and kissed her on the mouth. [. . .] All at once my voice said, 'Nunziata! Nunziatè!'").

In spite of Arturo's assertion that his kiss responded to a spontaneous impulse of joy, his observation that he had read "il canto di Paolo e Francesca" (297; "the canto of Paolo and Francesca") belies this claim. Not only does Arturo reveal his fear of both the incestuous and adulterous nature of his desire, but he shows that this desire is not spontaneous at all. Mediated once again from his readings, Arturo's story is that of a surprisingly loquacious Paolo. The representation of Nunziata clad in red recalls Beatrice's first encounter with Dante in the *Vita Nuova*. If the trajectory of Dante's desire for Beatrice proceeded from the body to the soul, Arturo's own trajectory is rather more complex. The revelation of transcendental ambition coincides and coexists with the parallel, horizontal revelation of the body's multiple and mediated desires.

This revelation becomes clear in Arturo's subsequent narrative of Wilhelm's love life. The "convict" who disembarks on the Island on his way to the penitentiary and to whom Wilhelm appears to be tied, inspires Arturo's unmitigated hatred. He flaunts the same arrogant and carefree self-sufficiency that Arturo used to identify with his father, and Arturo is horrified to see that it is Wilhelm, now, who plays the role of the victim rather than that of the omnipotent seducer: "Uno sguardo, in risposta al suo sguardo di adorante amicizia, era tutto quanto poteva chiedergli. E quest'unica cosa implorata, che avrebbe potuto dare a mio padre, colui gliela negò" (310; "One look, in response to his gaze of adoring friendship, was all that my father could ask of him. And this single thing that my father implored, and which could have been easily given, was refused"). Wilhelm becomes the unwitting guide of Arturo's ascent to the *Terra Murata* ("The Walled Country"), the medieval district that hosts Procida's penitentiary. If the enclosed garden of Eden becomes a prison, the ascent of the sacred mountain has no vertical thrust, and Arturo compares his father's directionless meanderings to those of a moth beating crazily around a lamp. Once at the top, the revelation that Arturo had desired for such a long time—his final access to Wilhelm's innermost being—takes place indirectly, through the mediation of the hated third party. Privy to the cryptic language that Arturo used to share with his father, the prisoner finally responds to Wilhelm's desperate entreaties. Arturo is quick to decode the message: "VATTENE PARODIA!" (359; "GO AWAY, YOU PARODY!"), but does not understand it. If the signifier is clear, knowing the signified has, so far, been unnecessary in the divine island of absolute space, time, and essence.

Arturo's newly acquired knowledge, that of parody as "IMITAZIONE DEL VERSO ALTRUI, NELLA QUALE CIÒ CHE IN ALTRI È SERIO SI FA RIDICOLO, O COMICO, O GROTTESCO" (359; "AN IMITATION OF OTHER PEOPLE'S ACTS, IN WHICH WHAT IS SERIOUS IN OTHERS IS MADE RIDICULOUS, OR COMIC, OR GROTESQUE"), is the wisdom that this cruel Eden bestows upon him. Arturo's ascent of the forbidden mountain inexorably reveals the flaws in his metaphysics. Originally built on a deviated transcendency that set Wilhelm at the place of the divine, Arturo's absolute system now confronts the rule of the relative. A universe of horizontal proliferation replaces the monolithic island of vertical singularity. Parody is based on imitation, and Arturo now sees that the mediator is a victim of the same imitative desire that had ensnared the mediator's faithful disciple. Once again, but more clearly, the loved object has been invested with all the infernal charms of the written word, as Dante well understood in the episode of Paolo and Francesca in *Inferno V*. In a brilliant *mise en abyme* of the mechanics of mimetic desire, Morante's use of the word *Galeotto* reminds us of how Paolo and Francesca modeled their passion on that of Lancelot and Guinevière as narrated in Galahalt's romance:[12]

> Difatti (adesso me ne rendo conto) la fede di Wilhelm Gerace ambiva, per accendersi, di una qualche seduzione convenzionale: e il personaggio del *Galeotto* si addiceva bene ai suoi sospiri. [. . .] Allo stesso modo il pubblico dei teatri domanda, per accendersi, di fede, eroine convenzionali (la Traviata, la Schiava, la Regina) [. . .] E così in eterno ogni perla del mare ricopia la prima perla, e ogni rosa ricopia la prima rosa. (341–42)

> In fact (now that I think about it) Wilhelm's Gerace's devotion needed something conventionally seductive to be awakened: the character of the *convict* suited his sighs well. [. . .] In the same way, theater audiences want to believe in conventional heroines (The *Traviata, The Slave Girl, The Queen*). [. . .] And thus every pearl in the sea eternally copies the first pearl, and every rose copies the first rose.

Shifting from Dante's lofty shrine to the marketplace of clichéd romances and popular operas, desire's imitative thrust not only proliferates endlessly, as demanded by the law of mass production, but also falls prey to the rule of parody. Rather than trying to reproduce a prized original, parody debases and distorts; it exaggerates and inverts; it zooms in on the dethroned model's flaws and magnifies them. When he sings for his unresponsive lover, Wilhelm's voice becomes sharp, out of tune, almost feminine and unharmonious, and Arturo compares him to a miserable toad croaking at the moon (356). This amphibian depiction of the once princely Wilhelm does not imply Arturo's condemnation of homosexual desire—following a familiar pattern, Arturo both loathes and admires the object of his father's affections. The convict's name, Tonino Stella, and the tiny star tattooed on his arm, give him a lofty place in Arturo's imitative firmament. Wilhelm's bisexuality is a curse just like any other homo- or heterosexual longing, a curse simply and solely because it denies divine independence and speaks for multiple, juxtaposed, proliferating, and nomadic desires (Deleuze and Guattari xiii). Thus defamiliarized and estranged though the merciless filter of parody, Wilhelm's sad love story allows Arturo to reach a wisdom that he had been unable to obtain by self-analysis alone.

By recording the progress of Arturo's childhood perceptions, *Arturo's Island* slowly erodes the epic code that had paradoxically sustained its own narrative. If it is only at the end of the novel that Arturo understands the relative laws of desire, the seeds of this disruption were buried deep within the island. Readers are given brief glimpses of them when the voice or point of view shifts from Arturo to another character or in the rare cases when Arturo the narrator underscores the differences between his childhood perceptions and his current views. The most meaningful example of another character's perspective is probably offered by Wilhelm's report of a statement made by Romeo, the man from Amalfi. Romeo essentializes humankind's sexual economy by using an analogy that takes us back to the image of the rose:

> Dunque, pare che alle anime viventi possano toccare due sorti: c'è chi nasce ape, e chi nasce rosa. Che fa lo sciame

delle api, con la sua regina? Va, e ruba a tutte le rose un
poco di miele, per portarselo nell'arnia, nelle sue stanzette.
E la rosa? La rosa l'ha in se stessa, il proprio miele: miele
di rose, il più adorato, il più prezioso! La cosa più dolce che
innamora essa l'ha già in se stessa: non le serve cercarla
altrove. Ma qualche volta sospirano di solitudine, le rose,
questi esseri divini. Le rose ignoranti non capiscono i propri misteri.

"La prima di tutte le rose è Dio.

"Fra le due: la rosa e l'ape, secondo me, la più fortunata
è l'ape. E l'Ape Regina, poi, ha una fortuna sovrana! Io, per
esempio, sono nato Ape Regina. E tu Wilhelm? Secondo
me, tu Wilhelm mio, sei nato col destino più dolce e col
destino più amaro: tu sei l'ape e sei la rosa." (71–72)

So, it seems that living souls can be subjected to one of two
fates: some are born as bees, and some are born as roses.
What does the swarm of bees do, with its queen? It flies and
steals a little honey from all the roses, and takes it to the
hive, into its little cells. And the rose? The rose has its own
honey in itself: rose honey, the most adored and precious!
The sweetest, most enamoring thing is what the rose already
contains within itself: it needs not seek it anywhere else.
But, sometimes, they sigh in solitude, the roses, those divine
beings. The roses are ignorant; they don't understand their
own mysteries.

"The first of all roses is God.

"Of the two, the rose and the bee, I think the luckier is
the bee. And the Queen Bee is the luckiest of them all! I, for
example, am born a Queen Bee. And what about you,
Wilhelm? I think, dear boy, you are born with the sweetest
destiny, and the bitterest. You are the bee and you are the
rose."

Romeo creatively manipulates information derived from
mythological, literary, and natural-scientific sources to define
human sexuality. Since classical times, roses have been com-
monly equated with feminine beauty or virtue. Sacred to the
Greek goddess of love, Aphrodite, the rose became the floral
symbol of her Roman counterpart, Venus. With the advent of
Christianity, roses became the emblem of the Virgin Mary, as
the tradition of the rosary demonstrates. "Commencing with
the legends of the early Hindus and Greeks," Jean Gordon
writes, "the rose and her human companion, woman, have been

inseparable" (16). While Romeo recovers the traditional link between divinity, love, and roses, he abandons all references to woman. Associated with God, roses become a synonym of a pre-gendered, or non-gendered, self-sufficiency. In the divine rose, subject and object of desire inhabit the same, absolute space, the space preceding all divisions and sexual differences. Perfectly self-contained, the rose does not know the duality of either interior and exterior, self and other, consciousness and self-consciousness, or male and female. The rose becomes the image for the androgyne, the "symbol of supreme identity" (Zolla 5). The androgynous body represents the space where the polarity of being blends and becomes absolute unity—all that precedes divisiveness and contrast.

The idea of an androgynous God is certainly not Morante's invention. What is meaningful here in the light of Arturo's development is that Romeo rewrites the myth of the androgyne by inserting an element of negativity in the apparent perfection of *coincidentia oppositorum* and the absolute balance of a pre-lapsarian unity. If, in the rose, the economy of desire short-circuits, ending precisely where it started, from the perspective of a world marked by the laws of desire, exchange, and becoming, this economy is flawed. Ignorant of its own mysteries, the rose is bound to bitter solitude.[13] Identifying himself with the queen bee, Romeo sees love as a form of trade, ruled by the laws of acquisition and exchange, and nurtured by the hope of wondrous gains, and the fear of sudden losses. In Romeo's natural economy, Wilhelm—who is both rose and bee—stages the clash between the utopia of absolute self-sufficiency and the reality of multiplying and polymorphic desires.[14]

In rare cases in the novel, Arturo the narrator juxtaposes his current views of characters and events with the views he used to hold as a young boy. The sealed world of his epic past is forced to open up to present evaluations:

> [Mia madre], in se stessa, non era altro che una femminella analfabeta; ma più che una sovrana, per me [. . .]. La sola immagine sua ch'io abbia mai conosciuta è stata un suo ritratto su cartolina. Figurina stinta, e mediocre, e quasi larvale; ma proiezione fantastica di tutta la mia fanciullezza. (7)

Cristina Della Coletta

> [My mother] in and of herself, was nothing more than an
> illiterate little woman, though to me, she was more than a
> queen [. . .]. The only picture I have ever seen of her was a
> postcard-size portrait, a faded, mediocre, and almost ghostly
> figure that I projected into fantastic proportions throughout
> my childhood.

In moments like these, time is no longer absolute, but underscores progress and change. Thus, while recording, for
example, his childish reaction to Wilhelm's accusation of jealousy, Arturo also reports a later, deeper revelation—his lucid
understanding that the trajectory of jealousy, like that of desire,
is never linear, and that the roads of passion are multiple and
intersecting: "Può darsi che, nella mia inconsapevolezza, io
lamentassi già, invece, le pretese impossibili del mio cuore. E
le gelosie opposte e intrecciate, le passioni multiformi, che
dovevano segnare il mio destino!" (182; "Perhaps, instead, I
was already unconsciously suffering from my heart's impossible longings, and for the interwoven, contradictory jealousies
and multiformed passions that were to mark my fate!").

After Arturo attempts suicide in order to win Nunziata's
compassionate affection, and Nunziata adamantly rejects his
final, desperate plea, Arturo decides to leave the island forever.
As he waits for the steamer that will take him to the mainland
the next day, Arturo looks for an isolated spot, and finds a natural cave in which to hide and rest. In this secluded, maternal
space, Arturo is surprisingly joined by Silvestro, the servant
from Naples who had nursed Arturo with goat's milk as a newborn baby. Returning to Procida after many years, it is Silvestro
who breaks the island's spell by bringing news from the outside world; namely, that troops are being called up for war.
Arturo is an avid reader of history books but knows nothing of
his own times, as he does not read newspapers: "Non m'aveva
mai incuriosito l'attualità. Come fosse tutto cronaca ordinaria
da giornali, fuori della Storia fantastica, e delle Certezze
Assolute" (415–16; "I never felt the slightest curiosity about
current events. It all seemed ordinary newspaper reportage, far
removed from the fantastic History and from the Absolute Certainties"). Now assuming the role of symbolic mid-wife,
Silvestro brings Arturo out of the womblike cave and into the
ominous light of history at the outbreak of World War II. This

reborn Arturo introduces himself *en artiste*, as he begs Silvestro to go to the House of the *Guaglioni* and fetch all his papers, "perché io sono uno scrittore" (420; "because I am a writer").

Discussing the birth of the artist in Proust, Girard argues that the novelist-narrator in *The Past Recaptured* is "none other than Marcel cured of all his errors, who has overcome his desires and is rich with novelistic grace [. . .] The novelist is a hero cured of metaphysical desire" (Girard, *Deceit* 232–33).[15] While exploiting the death and rebirth paradigm, *L'isola di Arturo* dismantles Girard's notion of artistic transcendency. Morante avoids all clear-cut distinctions between self-deluded hero and "cured" artist. Arturo gains maturity and self-awareness, but he is not, and never will be, free of desire. As he announces his artistic mandate, Arturo also claims that he wants to enlist, in order to become a *true* modern hero, facing the eternal enemy on the concrete stage of history in accordance with the literary fantasies of his childhood. He is rewarded with Silvestro's admiration, which mirrors Arturo's own admiration of Wilhelm.

Ideologically naive, Arturo joins the Fascist war while sharing Silvestro's Marxist belief. Again Arturo searches for a hero who will admire him, and with whom Arturo can identify—a mirror image of his own familiar face. Whatever faith the Absolute Certainties belong to, the final confrontation with death that Arturo seeks reveals desire's ultimate goal: the Self's ever-renewed mirage of effacing death and attaining metaphysical autonomy. Unlike Girard's claim about Marcel, Arturo, the artist, is not immunized from desire's contagion, and his journey out of the island brings no metaphysical freedom, just an ever-increasing awareness of the universality of the disease.

While remaining a victim of desire, the protagonist-narrator of *Arturo's Island* is able to offer a clear glimpse into desire's workings. If transcendence is impossible, the self-awareness gained through the creative process may offer a reasonable palliative after all. In *L'isola di Arturo*, the dynamic world of the *Bildungsroman* does not follow and replace, but rather coexists with the static paradigm of the epic, each one estranging the other. In the same way, Arturo's perspective as older *narrator* both re-creates and self-consciously corrects the childhood

Cristina Della Coletta

point of view of the *character* Arturo. In its hybrid form and deviant reappropriation of conventional genres, *L'isola di Arturo* records Arturo's construction of his personal myth and monitors this myth's progressive disruption; the novel reveals the phoenixlike resurgence of desire in endless permutations and perennial conflict.

Notes

1. I thank my colleague Gustavo Pellón for his insightful comments on this essay and for drawing my attention to René Girard's reading of *Inferno V* in *To Double Business Bound*.

2. Claudio Marabini's evaluation of Anna Maria Ortese's writings, for example, begins with the authoritative "unico è il posto che l'Ortese occupa nel secondo Novecento: unico e netto" (220; "Ortese occupies a unique place in the twentieth century: unique and clear").

3. See Debenedetti (379–96) and Sgorlon (69–87). On the theme of the *fanciullo divino*, see Kerényi (51 and 115–16).

4. Elsa Morante, *L'Isola di Arturo* 8–10. All quotations are taken from the 1969 edition and will be identified in the text by page numbers within parentheses. All English translations are mine.

5. See Ricci, "*L'isola di Arturo*" and "Tra *Eros e Thanatos*."

6. Ironically, Morante has Wilhelm state his absolute originality by borrowing words from one of the world-famous tragedies of mimetic desire, Shakespeare's *Romeo and Juliet*.

7. On the notion of the sacred see Girard, *Violence and the Sacred*.

8. See Cornish's study on medieval literary influences ("A King and a Star: The Cosmos of Morante's *L'isola di Arturo*").

9. For a different interpretation of Arturo's readings, see Bardini (373).

10. On the genre of the *Bildungsroman,* see Shaffner and Moretti.

11. On the topic of Medusa's gaze, see Siebers.

12. See Girard, "The Mimetic Desire of Paolo and Francesca" in *To Double Business Bound*: "The written word exercises a veritable fascination. It impels the two young lovers to act as if determined by fate; it is a mirror in which they gaze, discovering in themselves the semblance of their brilliant models" (2).

13. On the theme of the Androgyne's lack of self-awareness and on that of the Androgyne's solitude see Monneyron (45–46; 67) and Serkowska's study in the present volume (157–87).

14. On Wilhelm as "*figura doppia*" see Wood, "Jung e *L'isola di Arturo*"; and on Arturo's shift from a life built upon absolute certainties to one based on the proliferation of desire and on interpretative ambiguity, see also Wood, "The Bewitched Mirror."

15. For a reading of the influence of Proust on Morante, see Lucamante, *Elsa Morante e l'eredità proustiana (43–58)*.

Works Cited

Bakhtin, M. Mikhail. *The Dialogic Imagination: Four Essays*. Ed. M. Holquist. Trans. C. Emerson and M. Holquist. Austin: U of Texas P, 1981.

Bardini, Marco. *Morante Elsa. Italiana. Di professione, poeta*. Pisa: Nistri-Lischi, 1999.

Cornish, Alison. "A King and a Star: The Cosmos of Morante's *L'Isola di Arturo*." *MLN* 109 (Jan. 1994): 73–92.

Debenedetti, Giacomo. "L'isola della Morante." *Saggi*. Ed. F. Contorbia. Milan: Mondadori, 1982. 379–96.

Deleuze, Gilles. *Différence et repetition*. Paris: P.U.F., 1972.

Deleuze, Gilles, and Felix Guattari. *Anti-Oedipus: Capitalism and Schizophrenia*. Trans. R. Hurley, M. Seem, and H. R. Lane. Minneapolis: U of Minnesota P, 1977.

Garboli, Cesare. "Prefazione." *L'isola di Arturo*. Milan: Einaudi / Club degli Editori, 1969. v–xx.

Girard, René. *Deceit, Desire and The Novel*. Trans. Yvonne Freccero. Baltimore and London: Johns Hopkins UP, 1961.

———. *To Double Business Bound: Essays on Literature, Mimesis, and Anthropology*. Baltimore: Johns Hopkins UP, 1978.

———. *Violence and the Sacred*. Trans. P. Gregory. Baltimore: Johns Hopkins UP, 1977.

Gordon, Jean. *Pageant of the Rose*. New York: Studio, 1953.

Irigaray, Luce. *This Sex Which Is Not One*. Trans. C. Porter and C. Burke. Ithaca: Cornell UP, 1985.

Kerényi, Karoli. "Il fanciullo divino." *Prolegomeni allo studio scientifico della mitologia*. By C. G. Jung and K. Kerényi. Turin: Boringhieri, 1972.

Lucamante, Stefania. *Elsa Morante e l'eredità proustiana*. Fiesole: Cadmo, 1998.

Marabini, Claudio. "Ortese." *Nuova antologia* 559 (Apr.–June 1988): 219–22.

Miller, J. Hillis. *Fiction and Repetition: Seven English Novels*. Cambridge, MA: Harvard UP, 1982.

Monneyron Francois, ed. *L'Androgyne dans la littérature*. Paris: A. Michel, 1990.

Morante, Elsa. *Arturo's Island.* Trans. Isabel Quigly. New York: Knopf, 1959.

———. *L'isola di Arturo.* Milan: Einaudi/Club degli Editori, 1969.

Moretti, Franco. *The Way of the World: The Bildungsroman in European Culture.* London: Verso, 1987.

Ricci, Graziella. "*L'isola di Arturo.* Dalla storia al mito." *Nuovi argomenti* 61 (Jan.–Mar. 1979): 237–75.

———. "Tra *Eros e Thanatos*: storia di un mito mancato." *Strumenti critici* 38 (1979): 126–68.

Sgorlon, Carlo. *Invito alla lettura di Elsa Morante.* Milan: Mursia, 1972.

Shaffner, R. P. *The Apprenticeship Novel.* New York: Lang, 1984.

Siebers, Toby. *The Mirror of Medusa.* Berkeley: U of California P, 1983.

Wood, Sharon. "The Bewitched Mirror: Imagination and Narration in Elsa Morante." *Modern Language Review* 86 (1991): 310–21.

———. "Jung e *L'isola di Arturo.*" *Narrativa* 17 (Feb. 2000): 77–87.

Zolla, Elemire. *The Androgyne: Reconciliation of Male and Female.* New York: Crossroads, 1951.

Hanna Serkowska

The Maternal Boy

Manuele, or The Last Portrait
of Morante's Androgyny

Elsa Morante's last novel, *Aracoeli*,[1] has received the least
amount of critical attention of all her works.[2] Frequently
regarded as a parody or palinode, particularly of *La Storia* but
also in more general terms of her entire production prior to
Aracoeli, the novel has been defined by Franco Fortini as
"definitive," the ultimate and final work, while Cesare Garboli
sees in it a parody of the preceding novels, "sotto le apparenze
di un viaggio immaginario e insieme reale di un figlio alla
ricerca della madre" (*Il gioco segreto* 199; "under the guise of
a voyage, at once imaginary and real, of a son looking for his
mother"). In Garboli's view, the parody inherent in *Aracoeli*
signifies a gesture of extreme masochism by which the writer
destroys all that she loved most, ripping the veil off her own
fables. If the mother-son system can no longer constitute and
legitimate the world, only nothingness is left, for nothing else
can take its place.

For this novel of "corruption and anguish" one could argue,
instead, for a reading that goes beyond the idea of palinode
generally suggested by Morante's critics; a reading that elicits
a remarkable continuity between *Menzogna e sortilegio* and the
later book, through an operation of exquisitely Morantian
intertextuality. Morante consistently revisits previous writings
in her works; novels subsequent to *Menzogna e sortilegio*
repeatedly pick up on names, characters, motifs, and entire stories previously sketched out. This last novel suggests less
nihilism than a spiritual search whose inevitable end is death. I
would argue for an interpretation of the novel as dealing primarily with the myth of androgyny as fulcrum and ideological
center of *Aracoeli*, but also as a fundamental ontological position of Morante's thought. She has a strong predilection for

157

figures marked by marginalization and alterity. Pier Paolo Pasolini is one of her dearest friends, and her revered models include Arthur Rimbaud, Umberto Saba, and Sandro Penna, while the broad category of novelistic outcasts embraces women, Jews, adolescents, and animals. I would also argue that the presumed homosexuality of Morante's characters should be revisited, to see whether this has indeed been the "syndrome" that the previous works have dealt with.

One of Morante's masters is Plato, one of the "Happy Few" listed in the *Mondo salvato dai ragazzini*. As creator of the original myth of androgyny that was later to be picked up and developed by Ovid and Diodorus of Sicily, Plato tells that humans were originally men, women, and androgynes, all with two-faced heads. Having challenged the gods, they were divided into two, and from this point onwards the two divided halves have continued to seek each other out. In *Aracoeli* we witness a case of androgyny in its original Platonic, purely spiritual, form; the goal of Manuele's voyage-quest, which structures the novel, is to regain that primary androgynous unity and completeness, prior to the binary system that holds gender as its goal. My aim in analyzing this voyage is to identify the paths taken by the protagonist, who continues throughout the entire length of the narrative to search in vain for a remedy to his own alterity. The Other is seen here as lack, that which is lacking in the questing "I," and which it is impossible to assimilate. Reconsidering these paths in the light of the androgynous motif or "syndrome," one can see the use that Morante makes of psychoanalysis, as well as her adherence to oriental mysticisms and to her cabalistic and gnostic-platonic sources of inspiration.

Itinerary to *Aracoeli:* The Voyage toward Absence

Aracoeli is, then, structured as a voyage-quest. The goal of the voyage is the absent mother, the mother no longer there. The novel is thus a votive offering to the mother: the "internal" mother who resides in the *Es,* in psychic reality, and also, in the absence of the real mother, the "imaginary" mother, constructed by calling into play fantasy and imagination, by the intersection of desire with the figure of the real mother. Such a dichotomy, produced by the split between psychic reality and the reality principle, constitutes the fundamental motivation of the voyage-quest on which the novel is structured, a perennial voyage in search of the maternal body and language, and angelic children, and the yearned-for heights of androgyny. Manuele has understood, though Arturo still had to learn, that it is impossible to escape the "internal" mother; from behind the face of the father (never more than a stopping point, never the final goal for the protagonist-son) emerges the disquieting face of the mother. The great influence of this first love object, which reigns over all Manuele's subsequent love objects, is manifested along the path followed by the protagonist over the course of his journey, which is anything but sentimental, toward Aracoeli.

Beginning with the actualization of the "internal mother" (hidden behind a mirror, perceived at the back of his eye in a sort of *introspective* voyage), represented as absence, lack, and fissure, Manuele will try to transcend the dichotomy between psychic reality and the reality principle. He will thus embark on a retrospective voyage in search of the real mother's body and language, which can be approached only through the "imaginary" mother, passing through the various requests for love in return for money that he makes to various more or less angelic "*ragazzi di vita*," boys with whom Manuele, mindful of the breast forever denied him, will seek to repeat the unforgettable rite of nursing. Ageing but without maturing, the child who lingers within, remembering the figure of the "coco" with which Aracoeli frightened or extracted obedience from the small Manuele (the "coco" that calls to mind the tattooed Queequeg of Melville's text), he continues to imagine himself sucking at the great maternal breast (*Opere* 2: 1052). Mother and son together form, in fact, a single, androgynous creature, as Garboli observed, two in one, a double. Garboli was the first to identify an androgynous couple in *La Storia*'s Ida and Useppe, a "duo animale, una matrioshka che risucchia il mondo" (Garboli, *Il gioco segreto* 174; an "animal duo, a *matrioshka* sucking up the world"). In support of his argument he draws on the biography of the writer, and her marriage to Moravia, an approach that is not sufficient to explain a "syndrome" that Garboli defines as androgyny while meaning, in fact, homosexuality.[3] It is perhaps more appropriate to put to one side any hypothetical biographical inference, whether a possible but unproven conjugal crisis, or Bill Morrow's suicide in 1962. On the issue of androgyny other comments by Garboli may be more helpful when discussing the maternal figure in *Aracoeli*. The first observation regards Encarnación, who within the economy of the novel and the context of the "syndrome" has not been given due weight; the second concerns the mirror in which the protagonist reflects himself.

Encarnación is the unifying character who represents the change of gender of the narrator, a change that now distantly echoes the first substitution between *Menzogna e sortilegio* and *L'isola di Arturo*. Only by factoring in the motif of Encarnación can we rationalize the situation of androgyny within Morante's work as an ontological one, juxtaposing the search for the mother with what is believed to be homosexuality in many of her characters, and which is, rather, androgyny. Many critics seem to have been caught in a prohibitive sense of embarrassment on androgyny, which they define as homosexuality. Either they write nothing or they engage in lengthy circumlocutions or sybilline statements about Oedipal tragedy.[4] Morante herself shed light on the matter in her interview with Jean-Noël Schifano. Asked about the cutting judgments to be found in her books on women, especially women with male children, and citing as an example Wilhelm Gerace, the writer was quite clear: "he is homosexual, but not only. He is both things" (8). It would be to fly in the face of textual evidence, then, to limit the matter to a question of homosexuality, to be explained away by the failed or at least disturbed identification of the boy (after all, it is only of male heroes that critics have spoken) because of the mother's obsessive love. But it should be remembered that Morante states, "both things." In her novels, then, there is not homosexuality but rather androgyny, understood as spiritual wholeness, the longed-for *Einheit*.

From such a hypothesis it follows that the apparent homosexuals (Silvestro, Stella, Wilhelm, Arturo, Daniele, Manuele) are not, in fact, that. The cabin boy Daniele, the handsome mariner in the kingdom of the father reigned over by Eugenio (*Opere* 2: 1324), to which no women, or short-sighted or bespectacled boys are admitted but only men and sailors, is at the same time the sweet "esteemed nurse" who mothers Manuele. This male nurse is endowed with all the maternal qualities: he dresses and undresses Manuele, takes care of him, bathes and cradles him, and sings him to sleep with lullabies (*Opere* 2: 1367). Spaces and settings become similarly contaminated in a gendered way, juxtaposing the characteristics of one gender onto the other to the point that every rigid opposition fades away: this is the case with the "casa dei guaglioni" in *L'isola di Arturo*, the fashion store "Dalle Sorelle," or the "Sfilata di Sorelle" brothel. In the kingdom of the fathers there are no women, only men, and all sailors. And here, on terra firma, in the kingdom of the mothers, refused entrance to the kingdom of the fathers, Manuele remains on land, holding his handsome sailor hostage: as long as he has him, he will lack for nothing (*Opere* 2: 1342). But Daniele will have to leave, and his desertion will not be the last of the many separations inflicted on the protagonist. Manuele does not understand such autonomous spaces, assigned to only one specific gender, just as he does not accept rigid categorization of gender. To be born female seems to him an impossible wonder (*Opere* 2: 1266). His introspective quest for identity is about to begin.

Encarnación in the Mirror

The advent of Encarnación recalls the character of Elisa in *Menzogna e sortilegio*. As she views herself in the mirror, Elisa, the "sepolta viva" ("one buried alive"), whose pathetic ugliness won her no affection, is more or less turned to stone, as by the gaze of the Medusa. Then Elisa-Medusa wrenches her gaze away from the glass in the hope of seeing a different self. The "antica avversione" ("ancient hatred") of the little Gorgon for her own face, the morbid attachment to her mother, and her desire to be a boy should be seen together in the mirror episode.[5] Her own body and her own sex cannot but be a source of disgust to her. Since her gaze into the mirror causes distress to herself first of all, in later novels the ill-grown child, the old maid Elisa, is rejected and replaced with a series of boys (Arturo, Useppe, Manuele) whose attachment to the maternal body has a long history in mythology and culture and is therefore on more solid ground. In this sense, Arturo's and Manuele's

Hanna Serkowska

gender can become an alibi. Encarnación and her brief life (of only one month) is an echo of the gender substitution that takes place in the final novel too, diminished in comparison to the first novel, so we understand that such a substitution resolves nothing, only reversing the two poles but otherwise leaving them equally imperfect and incomplete. Aside from its androgynous connotations, the episode of Encarnación seems to have little autonomous semantic weight in the novel. Her figure gives us a glimpse of the fusion and metamorphosis that has taken place, together with the problematic gendered identity of the young protagonist, her brother, whose grandparents already harbored doubts that he could behave as a male (*Opere* 2: 1397, 1399).

Manuele, just like the "sepolta viva" before him, will see himself from now on as ugly. Upon his arrival at the hotel, fully aware of the absurdity of someone with shaken nerves and used to a sedentary life making an exhausting trip of this kind, he strips off his clothes and contemplates his body in a mirror:

> E súbito ne ho ricevuto una sensazione già nota, ma pure sempre dubbiosa, disorientata e stupefatta: come all'intrusione di un estraneo. Mi è sempre più difficile (quasi un esercizio innaturale e penoso) riconoscermi nel mio corpo. [. . .] Questo ammasso di carne matura, che oggi mi ricopre all'esterno, dev'essere una formazione aberrante, concresciuta per maleficio sopra al mio corpo reale. (*Opere* 2: 1170)

> [A]nd at once it gives me a sensation, familiar, but still doubting, disoriented and dumbfounded: the intrusion of an alien. It becomes harder and harder for me (as if performing an unnatural and painful exercise) to recognize myself in my body [. . .] This bulk of aging flesh, which today covers me on the outside, must be an aberrant formation, an excrescence that has grown, thanks to an evil spell, over my real body. (99)

Looking at oneself in the mirror represents an act of recognition of one's own androgynous nature, imprisoned in a sexually defined body and perceived therefore with a large dose of malaise. What follows is a detailed description of the defects, deformities, and disproportions that characterize the naked body. As soon as his eyes fall on his genitals, "attributes of virility," Manuele, like Elisa before him, withdraws his humiliated gaze from his own image: the sexed body seems an imposture, seems to belong to someone else. And when the gaze meets the all-too-familiar face, it seems foreign to him, "like a prosthesis" (*Opere* 2: 1171). But Manuele does not give up so easily and tries to rise to the challenge, looking himself in the eye, "[d]icono che immergendosi allo specchio nei propri occhi [. . .] si arriva a distinguere finalmente in fondo alla pupilla l'ultimo Altro, anzi l'unico e vero Sestesso [. . .]" (*Opere* 2: 1171; "They say that, plunging into our own eyes in the mirror [. . .] we can discern in the depth of the pupil the ultimate Other, indeed the one and true Oneself [. . .]"; 100). The final Other that Manuele glimpses deep within his own eyes is the "*niñomadrero,*" the child who has never separated from his mother, who continues to dream of himself as a suckling baby, not yet weaned. But the Other is also the mother herself with whom he forms the androgynous couple (*Opere* 2: 1052) and so the *niñomadrero* will imagine another mirror for himself, constituted by the eyes of Aracoeli. In this mirror he might fall in love with himself:

> C'era una volta uno specchio dove io, mirandomi, potevo innamorarmi di me stesso: erano i tuoi occhi, Aracoeli, che m'incoronavano re di bellezza nelle loro piccole pozze incantate. E questo fu il miraggio che tu mi fabbricasti all'origine [. . .]. (*Opere* 2: 1172)

> Once upon a time there was a mirror where, looking at myself, I could fall in love with myself; it was your eyes, Aracoeli, that crowned me king of beauty in their little bewitched pools. And this was the mirage that you fabricated for me at the beginning [. . .]. (100)

This mirror, which has disappeared with the death of Aracoeli, can give him back nothing more than the image of what he has become, a greying Narcissus, an ugly little man (*Opere* 2: 1128, 1172).

Reading the tourist brochure he found on the plane taking him to El Almendral, he discovers that the name Almeria means mirror in Arabic (*Opere* 2: 1087), and this discovery immediately evokes another maternal association. Even before this, Aracoeli's body, longed for by Manuele as if he were a breastfeeding child, appeared enclosed within the golden frame of the mirror (*Opere* 2: 1149 and 1193). The trip to Andalusia, which will appear to him progressively more and more absurd, will be depicted first as a bizarre, vanished mirror, inside which everything happens. The fact that Manuele's mother was born in a mirror (such that in looking at himself he is also searching for her, or he looks at himself in the hope of finding her) presupposes (the "Once upon a time") a possible intertext in fairy tale. The presence of this genre within the novel is not by chance. The fable is a genre predisposed to the identity itinerary, to the quest for personal individualization. If the mother inhabits the mirror, the *niñomadrero* will have to descend inside it in order to find her, like Alice in Wonderland. Consequently, the mother enclosed within the mirror (the internal mother) turns out to be Manuele's own image, reflected and reversed. Impelled by these first early intuitions, Manuele will gaze at himself continuously, seeking the Other in himself in order to resolve the enigma of his own, barely glimpsed, Other. Thus he will decide to go in search of the maternal body and the maternal language, in the hope of being able to understand the sense of abandon, fissure, and estrangement that assails him.

The retrospective journey thus springs from the introspective journey and the "inner mother." The start of the retrospective journey is not promising: "nessuno può sfuggire alla propria nascita" (*Opere* 2: 1173; "No one can elude the birth sentence"; 102) we read, and later we see his mother's laconic reply to the urgent questions of her son: "[. . .] non c'è niente da capire" (*Opere* 2: 1428; "[. . .] there is nothing to understand"; 292). The condemnation is uttered while the narrator contemplates his forearm marked with "ancient cuts" that remind him of his attempts as a child to commit suicide, and that fuel his desire to regress into the body from which he has been expelled: "Come fanno le gatte coi loro piccoli nati male, tu rimàngiami. Accogli la mia deformità nella tua voragine pietosa" (*Opere* 2: 1174; "As mother cats do with ill-born kittens, eat me again. Receive my deformity in your pitying abyss"; 102).

The "ancient cuts" again recall Queequeg in *Moby Dick*, the tattooed boy with whom he forms a pair of "bosom friends," clinging to his friend in a scene of presocialized eroticism. The reference to the reconstitution of the original androgyne in Melville's text is authorized by Morante herself, in that she considers maternal religion to be the predominant sentiment that inspires Melville. Within the context of my reading of *Aracoeli*, Morante's statements in "Sul romanzo" offer an interpretative key. In the spiritual androgyny that constitutes the ideological axis of the novel, maternal religion appears to have profound implications, while the maternal sentiment is deeply implicated with androgyny (*Pro o contro la bomba atomica* 52).

From now on, birth (separation from the mother and the beginning of "deformity") and death (irremediable absence of Aracoeli and his own death, by now almost sought and invoked by Manuele) will appear side by side, two routes to rejoining the lost *Einheit*. To evoke the mother is to evoke loss, the missing part of the self. Regression into the immense maternal uterus (Zampolini 55) becomes achievable only in the presence of death, and the search for death will be the only means of reconjunction, reunification, and reconquest of the lost unity. Evoking the mother equals evoking the Other in the self, the missing side of the human. Each time she is invoked by the protagonist, the image of the enormous abyss of the uterus appears, infesting the semantic fields of the novel. Within that abnormal uterus, a sort of whale's belly, human limbs float (*Opere* 2: 1166, 1173, and 1274); it is a uterus-cradle (*Opere* 2: 1324) or a uterus-shawl (already seen in the Andalusian shawl), a uterus that enfolds and wraps (*Opere* 2: 1332). Regression into the immense maternal uterus becomes possible only in the presence of death; it is for this reason that scenarios of death are so frequent, displayed in oneiric theaters in which it is plausible that Manuele's body lies resting in a rented room in Milan and that the trip happens only in the dream (*Opere* 2: 1115). To be born sexed is partly also to die, in the sense of having to lose, or fragment, the original unity. After the fissure of birth, the tearing away, only death can be invoked. Reconstructing his own childhood, Manuele identifies the episodes that have accelerated his regressive urgency, his need to return into the protective, and simultaneously deadly, womb of his mother.

Einheit: Before Genesis and after Death

The myth of the androgyne in philosophy and literature has, over the centuries, taken on different forms in accordance with the sociocultural system in which it appears (Pagliano 152). Androgyny may thus summon forth divinatory powers, which allow Manuele to travel freely along the temporal axis, the capacity to reproduce oneself, and the idea of harmony and completeness. This last is the fundamental meaning of *Aracoeli*; androgyny is adopted as emblem of the archaic character of human nature raised to the state of a superhuman being, divine, perfect, and complete, while mortals lose such perfection in the act of being born. The androgynous motif in Morante's thought is of a decidedly spiritual and mental order, light years, for example, from the hermaphroditism typical of decadent poetry. The decadent or symbolist androgynous was conceived as a vulgarized phenomenon, removed from the dimension of common sense, in the pathological and satanic sense of the term. Often hermaphroditism, perceived as exclusively anatomical and physiological, was equivalent to an orgiastic confusion of sexes, promiscuity, and exuberance of erotic experience. The Morantian androgynous re-evokes individual completeness and fullness with which, according to many gnostics (Leone Ebreo and Jakob Boehme, among others), divinity was endowed, and which humans lost in the Genesis. The idea of the androgyny of the divine, a feature of several religions, combines the Platonic conceptualization of hermaphroditism as a perfect being with the biblical tradition of the Fall as motif of the dichotomy of the First Man into two sexes. Hence the metaphysical aim of humanity, still suffering this lack and laceration, will tend toward the reunification of opposites. And it is from the human that the process of reunification must begin:

> Eravamo integri prima della Genesi; e può darsi che la cacciata dall'Eden vada intesa, nel senso occulto, per un gioco

ambiguo e provocatorio: "Avete mangiato il frutto *proibi-to*," dice la sentenza del Signore, "ma non quello *segreto* della vita, che io, Padrone del giardino, vi tengo nascosto, perché vi renderebbe uguali agli dei." (*Opere* 2: 1289; emphasis in original)

We were whole, before Genesis, and perhaps the expulsion from Eden must be understood, in its hidden meaning, as an ambiguous and provocative game: "You have eaten the *for-bidden* fruit," the Lord's command says, "but not the *secret* fruit of life: that I, Master of the garden, keep hidden from you, because it would make you the equal of gods." (189)

While in the above passage the connection between knowledge and sexuality is quite evident, we nonetheless see that in Morante's text the forbidden fruit is that of life, and not that of good and evil. It is the tree of life or fullness, completeness, and wholeness that the androgynous master of the garden has kept hidden from mortals. Androgyny is precluded to mortals, and they feel an unbearable nostalgia for what they have lost. The impossibility of satisfaction is such that Manuele will decide to seek death in order to free himself of it. The call of death is implacable in the Morantian novel: the desire to regress to a time prior to birth, for the one who is alive, can be brought about only by dying.

Manuele, like his mother before him, is looking for death: the novel narrates the desired death that is his goal as he is engulfed by the desert. It is only by dying that one can hope to reconnect with the Other, restoring the shattered unity in order no longer to feel half, nor double, but full and one at the same time (cf. *Opere* 2: 1175). Starting with the absence of the mother, Manuele's split is rendered as mutilation, dismemberment, deformity, and we should add that it is a rigorously dual, binary fragmentation.

Manuele sees himself divided while embarking on his voyage *à rebours* (*Opere* 2: 1057, 1180), as in the case of amputated limbs (1171) or the rags of a disintegrating piece of cloth. With the departure of Aracoeli to the brothel, disintegration spreads to the other characters too. Manuele's father is told that with the disappearance of his beloved wife, he becomes divided as it were into "two selves" a white-faced, rigid puppet in the afternoons, and a tough, unapproachable Commander during the rest of the day (Zampolini 55). Manuele's body appears divided and, as such, appears hybrid (*Opere* 2: 1398, 1406).

The search for androgynous fullness, lost at the birth of a lacerating sexed life, can go through a metamorphosis in which the rite of hybridization is endlessly repeated and celebrated. The split is not healed but indeed reopened and aggravated over the course of a lifetime. In *Menzogna e sortilegio*, Anna was the hybrid: a female centaur, a wild dual figure whose duality was incurable, and who introjected the lessons of Edoardo, that master of ambiguity and duality, dominant and submissive, weak and rash, contemplative and restless, frivolous and a slave to passion (*Opere* 1: 778–79). The metamorphosis is worth the effort to lessen the horror of mutilation. As in the first novel, in *Aracoeli*, too, metamorphosis is persistent and continuous. Only in the beginning was there a close relationship among all things "alberi-foglie-uccelli-foglie" (*Opere* 2: 1185; "trees-leaves-birds-leaves"), "[f]ra unità e i suoi multipli non esistevano confini precisi, così come ancora l'io non distingueva chiaramente dal tu e dall'altro. [. . .] non ebbi nozione di essere maschio, ossia uno che mai poteva diventare donna come Aracoeli" (*Opere* 2: 1186; "For me precise boundaries didn't exist between unity and its multiples, just as the form 'I' was not yet clearly distinguished from the 'you' or any other [. . .] I had no notion of being male, or one who could never become a woman, like Aracoeli"; 112).

The time when Manuele didn't know he could never become the Other belongs to the era of Totetaco, when he would wear a little girl's garment in bed. He still remembers that at the time he was "rather androgynous" (1204). Now, in one of his drugged and frantic visions, Manuele imagines himself to be an Indian girl, then a phoenix (similar to Ovid's Coenis), or the metamorphic figure par excellence (*Opere* 2: 1214). In *Menzogna e sortilegio*, the phoenix was the figure that metaphorically encompassed Anna's character (*Opere* 1: 1186), constituting a promise of perennial transmutation. The perpetual hybrid, all the better if in continuous transit, can take on the appearance characterized by the constant regeneration and vitality, and splendidly embodied in the figure of the phoenix. A hybrid of this kind points to the recomposition of what has been slowly dissolving. It reaches toward the Other from itself in spite of the original imposed by the Genesis. The metamorphosis can further be depicted in the forms of strange animals, made up of the ephemeral union of a camel and an ox. The two beasts lie in wait outside Manuele's door. The camel is now the woman of the *Quinta* who took his mother away from him, becoming Aracoeli herself by metonymy. The ox is the revolution that took Manuele's uncle's life (*Opere* 2: 1190). Both the camel and the ox are figures of death. In this case, the reference to the *Guernica* of Morante's beloved Picasso is mandatory, as the painter is one of the *Felici Pochi*. Searching and death become total and totalitarian.

The androgynous motif bears within it nostalgia for the equilibrium of lost fullness (by which *Einheit* becomes *Ur-Einheit* if it recalls the time before Genesis), while the image of androgynous perfection continues to disturb, positing itself as a mirage of the only possible primary fullness, anterior to any duality. Even in the case of twins, a particularly close pair who walk hand in hand and use their own private language, male and female are destined to remain different. We are inevitably born sexed, generically declined, one of only two, either or.[6] Such a system of primordial twins is desired in the case of Manuele and his uncle Manuel, or Manuele and his mother. Uncle Manuel, his precursor in affinity with Aracoeli, appears in the boy's imagination as a transvestite (*Opere* 2: 1421). Another time Aracoeli and Uncle Manuel Muñoz Muñoz appear to be as identical as twins (1104), and are thus easily able to switch roles. Manuele alludes instead to the *niño-madrero* ("mama's boy") twin of his mother while he dreams of how he was before his birth, before the disappearance of Aracoeli—before the forty-year-old body that is now such a source of shame fell upon him like a theatrical disguise.[7]

The aversion to Eros can be explained by the protagonist's difficulty in dealing with a sexed corporality; declined in the singular, it recalls the split and impels the nostalgia for the unity lost in Genesis. Eros should then be freed of the raw, violent connotations of sexual instinct that litter Manuele's past. Reconstructing his own initiation to Eros, the protagonist recalls in a youth crowded with "amori solitari" ("solitary loves"), only two "avventure di donne" ("adventures with women"), the "avventura di spiaggia" ("a beach affair") and "forfait" ("lump sum"; *Opere* 2: 1117, 1132). Both experiences hold a deadly weight for his future. The first adventure shares with the second a series of characteristics: the disgusting nature of the whole scene, which is compared to the coupling of wild goats and tame monkeys (*Opere* 2: 1121; *Aracoeli* 64); and an enlargement of the female genitals that terrifies the protagonist (*Opere* 2: 1143) and provokes disgust for the unbearable ugliness of the sexed body. The evocation of the first experience with the young prostitute on the beach, who indulges in group sex with a bunch of boys, is swiftly followed by the second: in order not to be sick over the old hag, the decaying old prostitute he throws himself on, Manuele closes his eyes and tries to think of something else. One thing is certain when he draws up the sad balance of his adventures: "sei condannato! Nessuna donna, mai per te! Sei condannato" (*Opere* 2: 1145; "You are condemned! No woman for you! Never! You are condemned!"; 81). The sexual instinct can only divide and reify by subjugation. It is based on overbearing power, while Manuele would like Eros to be platonically able to transcend the abyss between subject and object. Disappointed by his experiences, he will wish not to become a "man" but to stay beardless or even to regress inside the double Calypso, the tender and monstrous lover-mother.

The Retrospective Voyage:
In Search of Our Mothers' Gardens

The retrospective search for the maternal body and language that Manuele undertakes occurs on two parallel levels that flow into a single figure.[8] The figure of the mother, tender and monstrous at the same time, is equivalent to death. The foreground corresponds to the pursuit of the maternal body and stands as remedy to the fragmentation to which Manuele has been exposed at birth, and a second time after Aracoeli's disappearance to the *Quinta* and the hospital. The other pursuit concerns the maternal language sought in the idiom of people in the street, the adventure-seeking truck driver, the maid in the Andalusian inn, but also the residual language in the memory and desire of the now adult protagonist.

Morante's protagonists are ambivalent in their adaptation to corporality.[9] This is most evident with respect to the maternal body, site of the uterus, beginning and omen of death. The symbolic death of the mother in the Irigarayian sense when Manuele was entering the age of reason (*Opere* 2: 1404) and the physical one of cancer that causes Aracoeli's second death. And so it is that the search for the maternal body loses impetus and Manuele hesitates. He gets distracted. He no longer desires to find anything; he knows he is going toward the void, the desert. The more he pursues the maternal body, initially so full of promise ("HODIE MECUM ERIS IN PARADISO"; *Opere* 2: 1196), the more it reveals itself as unknown, as alien as a stellar mass. That body is similar to the sepulcher we carry within ourselves, "di tutte le voragini fra cui ci muoviamo alla cieca [. . .] nessuna è tanto cupa, e per noi stessi inconoscibile, quanto il nostro proprio corpo" (*Opere* 2: 1332; "To tell the truth, of all the chasms through which we move blindly [. . .] none is so dark and so unknowable to ourselves as our own body"; 221–22). Aside from the very possible reading of *Aracoeli* as a parabola of disintegration and the bodily degradation of the mother,[10] we see in the novel a search and recuperation, conceptualized as anamnesis in which the past is approachable only in the act of "apocryphal remembrances." The closer Manuele gets to El Almendral the more authentic seem these apocryphal remembrances, because "apocryphal" means also not written, not yet explained with words, prelinguistic and presymbolic. It becomes possible to trace back Aracoeli and her language in the only way in which the search seems unlikely to succeed; in order to exhume the past, it is necessary to distance oneself from the *hic et nunc*. Having grown inside Aracoeli's body, Manuele should know by heart the pregnant body of his mother: the nipple, the taste and warmth of her milk. A maternal body of scents and flavors, made up of different life-giving fluids, an edible body, capable of satisfying his hunger and thirst. But now this far-off body means that when he arrives in Andalusia, Manuele must face the legendary maternal *Estero* (*Opere* 2: 1063, 1046), a body that harbors a perennial "elsewhere," never destined to be "here," just like the *Estero* pictured by her father to Anna in *Menzogna e sortilegio* and dreamed of by Arturo. Aracoeli, the nomad in no-man's land, on the other side of history, communicates a sense of nonbelonging and denies herself to the son with the peremptory "io non sono più la tua mamita" (*Opere* 2: 1377; "I am no longer your *mamita*").

Different types of metaphors can be identified in accordance with the different phases of the search for the maternal body. The images of El Almendral's garden (almond orchard, and paradise, in Spanish), the Aracoeli-garden, the maternal Eden that welcomes Manuele into her luminous womb, correspond to the remembrance of childhood (*Opere* 2: 1986). It is the Roman Totetaco[11] garden in which Manuele imagined creatures to be living (*Opere* 2: 1177–79 and 1992). Upon his arrival in Aracoeli's village of origin, Manuele discovers, however, that, instead of almond orchards there is a stony desert burnt by the wind, a calcified desert.

The "other" garden, then, that appears during his travels in Spain, is presented alongside apocalyptic motives. The other category of metaphors refers to landscapes of ruins, sterile, spectral lands reduced to deserts. Again, in the middle of such a desert there is a green area, an orchard, an orange tree, an olive tree, a vine (*Opere* 2: 1428). Also the Roman cemetery of Campo Verano, where Aracoeli is buried and where Manuele has never set foot, now seems a live garden to him (*Opere* 2: 1443). The juxtaposition of several typologies of images, endowed with opposite signs, follows the design that Manuele traces during the voyage, a path that is at once concentric and eccentric. Slowly the data of memory, fantasy, and the subconscious bear fruits less and less discernible one from the other, and the regression to Aracoeli is equivalent to the approaching of death. Thus we can explain the seeming confusion between several groups of metaphors: the childhood garden with Campo Verano, with the land of stone, with the almond orchard. The running forward with the going backward:

> [I]l nostro tempo finito lineare è in realtà il frammento illusorio di una curva già conchiusa: dove si ruota in eterno sullo stesso circolo [. . .] e se poi davvero ogni nostra esperienza, minima o massima, è LÀ stampata su quel rullo di pellicola, già filmata da sempre e in proiezione continua. (*Opere* 2: 1406–07)

> [O]ur finite, linear time is, in reality, the illusory fragment
> of an already concluded curve, where we turn eternally on
> the same circuit [. . .] and if then our every experience, mini-
> mum or maximum, is really THERE, printed on that roll of
> film, already shot for all time and in ceaseless projection. (276)

Manuele's retrospective path is an ahistorical, discontinuous,
and cyclical movement, governed by the time of the eternal
return toward the place of origin, capable momentarily of
masking the factual non-existence of the mother. The recuperation of the maternal body (known-strange, green-parched) is
not a search undertaken in order to distance himself, to achieve
some level of autonomy (the Freudian *fort-da*) from the pos-
sessive body, to free himself from the desired object-mother.
The movement of return is not an escape from, but a desperate
rush toward a body that, as Manuele realizes only now, while it
nourished him was also poisoning him, implanting the germ of
death. And it is death that Manuele is searching for in the body
of Aracoeli.

Pursuing the Mother Tongue:
Das Leben hat nur eine schlechte Sprache

Life has just one poor, degraded, worn-out language, says
Ingeborg Bachmann's Franza. It is a language incapable of
expressing individual suffering other than by placing it within
a generalizing category. Suffering is always individual, even
when it is historical. With Manuele's arrival in Andalusia, the
mother tongue, now on everybody's lips, appears to him
strangely incomprehensible, "Ma proprio questa, fra le altre
lingue, suona vuota di significati al mio cervello, riducendosi,
per me, a poco più che un rumore incomprensibile" (*Opere* 2:
1064; "But this one, among all languages, sounds meaningless
to my brain and is reduced, for me, to little more than an
incomprehensible noise"; 22).

This is not what Manuele was expecting: he now realizes he
has committed to memory only a "divine" mixture of Italian
and Spanish, disjointed sentences, expressions, nursery rhymes
from the time of Totetaco (*Opere* 2: 1038, 1099, 1136, 1058,
1086, and 1334), perhaps without ever having really understood,

or understanding them in his own way as he felt them addressed to him. Aracoeli's tongue is foreign, but its foreign nature does not derive from its substratum of Spanish, which must be overcome if she is to master the use of Italian and bring up her son as the child of Italians (*Opere* 2: 1191). Manuele wonders that, "Questa parlata doveva pure suonarmi chiara nei giorni che, analfabeta, imparavo le prime canzoncine di Aracoeli; ma in séguito [. . .] essa è piombata in un qualche impervio, oscuro dirupo della mia conoscenza" (*Opere* 2: 1065; "This language must have been clear to me in the days when, illiterate, I learned my first little songs from Aracoeli; but afterward [. . .] it plunged into some inaccessible dark chasm of my consciousness"; 22). In the attempt to recuperate the maternal tongue, Manuele has sought to approach the body, but in vain. The maternal tongue is irrevocably supplanted by a usured tongue, the language of the truck driver and of the maid in Andalusia. And besides the maternal one, there is no other tongue, "Nessun dialogo possibile. Nessun alfabeto comune [. . . il corpo] ci lega a sé nello stesso rapporto che lega un forzato alla ruota del suo supplizio" (*Opere* 2: 1353; "No possible dialogue. No common alphabet. [. . . I]t binds us to itself in the same relationship that binds a convict to the wheel of his torture"; 236). Later El Almendral (Aracoeli's native town), the mother, and her language will fuse into one. The postal mark of "Gergal" is in fact a name that it would be futile to look up in common atlases. It is a "minimal point": a small center containing his mother and her body. The voice of the maternal call becomes embodied as Manuele approaches the place, regressing toward that center, remembering the very first little songs. It has a tender taste of mouth and saliva, such that the boy-man's manner of speech bears the impression of her skin that "smelled like a fresh plum" (*Opere* 2: 1047). Gergal is the point with a little garden in the center; a garden in which lullabies resonate, goal of his voyage. Birth and death together.

It is precisely here that *Aracoeli* contains a further reference to *Menzogna e sortilegio*. The apparent diegetic division "fin qui/d'ora innanzi" ("until now/from now on") of Morante's first novel is taken up by the last as a quotation: "quando ero un lettore" for "fin qui" and "[d]a quando non sono piú lettore" for "d'ora innanzi"; "When I was a reader" [. . .] "Since I am no longer a reader." Manuele used to read a lot, then he ceased completely (*Opere* 2: 1262; *Aracoeli* 168; emphasis in original). From the age of reading Manuele passes to the phase of memoir, which indeed expands to the entire diegesis: of the former, only a brief narratorial confessional moment remains. If, rather, we consider the two "epochs" as preceding respectively the introspective (medianic) and retrospective (mnestic) phases, the distinction "fin qui/d'ora innanzi" turns out to be as illusory in *Aracoeli* as it was in *Menzogna e sortilegio*. The data provided by the unconscious and imagination are enmeshed with those of memory. Unlike *Menzogna e sortilegio*, the operation of remembrance in *Aracoeli* does not pretend to be an authentic, autoptic, and rigorous rendition but configures itself from the beginning as apocryphal. The illusory nature of the split, so firmly stressed in the first novel, is present not because of the novelistic contagion, as Elisa mentions several times, but by virtue of the mnestic (retrospective) and introspective (psychoanalytic) paths now conjoined in the mind of the protagonist who, as we shall see, defines himself as a fantasist. In *Aracoeli* every memory is fragmented, fractioned, shredded, like a film that has been chopped about and reassembled such that the resulting narrative preserves all the characteristics of a montage that is at once visual (body) and audible (language) (*Opere* 2: 1328). Images and words are superimposed; they dissolve, split off, divide, multiply themselves, and vanish in the great picture of this immense illusion.

The risk of the mendacious syndrome that afflicted Elisa, and which in *Menzogna e sortilegio* metaphorized linguistic lack, seems to have passed. With the lucidity of an expert psychoanalyst Manuele tries to discern and keep distinct from his *nunc* the scraps of the past that for so many years passed themselves off as canceled. As soon as he perceives them, they assail him, endlessly ready to show themselves. Projected once more as on a cinema screen, they are marked "documentari d'archivio" (*Opere* 2: 1344). The film reproduces that interjection of the data of intro- and retrospection, of the subconscious and memory. The present imposes itself by force on the "documentaries" to nurture the doubt that is at once foundation and plot (*Opere* 2: 1344). The data of the unconscious split the mnestic depositions in two each time, obfuscating and complicating the analeptic exposition of the facts of the past (*Opere* 2: 1327). All this is foreseen in the scenario. It is foreseen that each apparent reality is attenuated and erased in the attempt to recompose the two parts into one; that everything tends toward synthesis typical of the androgyne. Birth is united to death, the past is assimilated into the present, the retrospective voyage flows into the introspective one. The end result of the two paths can be identified in the awareness that the psychic reality–reality principle dichotomy can be transcended, accepting its confusion and definitive indistinguishability as in a photomontage.

The Psychoanalytic Paradigm Derided

Framing the Morantian psychoanalytic paradigm within the relative temporal context is important as is also keeping in mind the hostility expressed toward this psychology of the darkest recesses, and to the few paladins who attempted to spread the word in Italy. The observations I wish to make with respect to the psychoanalytic matrix of Morantian novels spring from the polemics about psychoanalysis in Italy and the lack, with the exception of Italo Svevo, of irony in the writings of artists who divulged such theories (Fortini 244; David, *Psicanalisi* 23–28), thus corrupting the myth of "Italian sanity" (Bardini, "'Fantastici doppi'" 175). Morante was one of the few non-ironic readers of Freud in Italy. In her last novel, however, the writer appears to be making fun of the "positive science of the soul" and the conceiver of the specular (pre-Oedipal) phase, typical of early childhood, characterized by primary erotic drives. She settles accounts with psychoanalysis, with which from her first novel onwards she constructed a paradigmatic, sporadic, and unsystematic relationship. In the complex "final" novel, partly constructed around the parody of a psychoanalytic session, the mocking attitude toward the self-confessed "greying Narcissus" and the greying scientific discipline is striking. Morante has never used this psychology in a flat or neutral manner, but only in *Aracoeli* does she unlock all previous uses of psychoanalysis, as if to show that, after all, "La favola mammarola è [. . . un] reperto da seduta psicanalitica" (*Opere* 2: 1172; "The mama's boy fairy tale is [. . . a] typical retrieval of a psychoanalytic session"; 100). In order to outline the writer's attitude

we should recall a note in her own hand written on the manuscript of *Menzogna e sortilegio* and later erased "sopprimere—
troppo apertamente freudiano" ("suppress—too openly
Freudian").[12] This annotation demonstrates the desire to conceal or at the least leave minimal traces and eliminate over-
obvious allusions to Freud's psychological theories. Her
hesitation at appearing "too openly Freudian" can be explained
by the fact that Morante, like so many others, was affected by
the Crocian syndrome by which one could not but refer to
Freud's theories with some degree of irony. *Menzogna e
sortilegio* was constructed like a gigantic, fictitious representation of all the pathological cases that Elsa Morante can imagine for her characters (Bardini, "'Fantastici doppi'" 179–80);
Aracoeli, too, appears to be inspired by the same desecrating
drive: the same phrases, allusions, and metaphors appear. Once
again the writer uses the Freudian paradigm. The narrator is
divided into three persons and speaks in three voices: the
Accused, the Prosecution, and the Defense, or in other words,
clinical case, patient, and psychoanalyst. She insists on the term
enigma, the same one Elisa would use to signify the "mille
fole" ("thousand tales") with which she wanted to replace the
trite bourgeois drama of her parents. In *Aracoeli* the enigma
does not finally find a solution and is not solved by the act of
writing. And if the attempt at writing as therapy fails, it is the
same writing operation, based on the parodic self-analysis of
the narrating "I," that succeeds. Morante concludes the itiner-
ary-narrative toward Aracoeli with a phrase that screams out
its disdain for the "positive science of the soul." The son confesses that only *in extremis* can the "noted enigma" (which now
refers to himself as well as to his mother) be explained by placing, at the center, the figure of the . . . father. The tale of the
mama's boy is a finding of psychoanalytic sessions. The
enigma cannot be explained with what many readers have taken
to be the homosexuality of Manuele (and before him, Wilhelm,
or Arturo). The paternal figure evokes in the end, with an ironic
charge, the Freudian understanding that the homosexuality of
the boy follows from maternal tenderness and the relegation of
the father to a secondary role.

In order to organize the writing act as a psychoanalytical session, the narrator appears in the garb of an expert, whether
playing the part of doctor or patient. A patient who accuses his

mother of the sins of which Freud accused the feminine side: the denied breast and birth as a violent tearing away from the maternal abyss, followed by a wail of mourning. Other pieces of the psychoanalytic mosaic are the threshold of the third year, the pendulum between guilt and shame. The woman/mother is held to be guilty of not having adequate psychoanalytic knowledge and thus not being able to comprehend the damage she has inflicted on her son. The monstrous fruits of the mother's crimes include the need to suck and the morbid attachment of the now adult son to the nipple of the sleeping mother. The parodic intent with respect to the Freudian intertext is particularly salient when Manuele describes himself as a "paziente sapienziale" ("knowing patient," patient and doctor in one) and, while taking hashish, tries to summon up dreams that he hopes will offer him some kind of explanation. Medical science assures him that dreams are necessary. Following such self-prescription, Manuele dreams frequently, and dreams of suggestive Freudian topoi: cradles, wombs, roses, breasts, unsure whether his dreams are plagiarizing his waking life or vice versa. The sickness of the past, ironically called "the enigma," brings with it the need to investigate and meditate on something that can be brought back; the material that the protagonist finds himself working on is made up of dreams, hallucinations, imagination, *déjà vu*, fantasies. During this imaginary trial of himself, the protagonist is guilty of confusing memory (later revealed as apocryphal) with the subconscious: we cannot know, he concludes, if memory is the fruit of fantasy or vice versa. For, to adopt Freudian terms, artistic creation is a daydream that is realized in three moments, here superimposed one over the other. Beginning in the present, a hotel room in Milan, it is later connected to a past experience, generally belonging to childhood: the aging Narcissus begins to mirror himself and starts a "film" of private memories. And finally we see created a vision of the future, representing the satisfaction of desire. In this case, satisfaction must take place while Manuele takes an imaginary trip to the land of his mother. The risk, the contagion, and the *menzogna* emerge from other literary texts, as Elisa claimed in *Menzogna e sortilegio*, but are rooted in our triple psyche. Confusion is the keyword: the psychoanalytic apparatus does not solve the enigma, but on the contrary fuels it;

it is only useful in the operation of writing insofar as it is capable of igniting this enigma. It is precisely this doubt that Manuele turns into a story, a past, a narrative, and a voyage, designed and carried out in intricate detail. What in Morante's first novel might still appear a fragmented, episodic, and chaotic reflection of the Freudian intertext, becomes in *Aracoeli* a skillful and highly ironic reworking.

Morante and Angelology:
Other Androgynous Paths

There is an area firmly ignored by Morantian criticism[13] and by the "greying science" of psychoanalysis,[14] which prefers to carry on spinning the same mama's boy tale, always in the Oedipal key. But together with the search for the real or imaginary mother, Manuele undertakes another quest, seeking out the *fanciulli angelici* ("angelic boys"), of whom the prominent example is Pennati, his "sweet child of one night" to whom the forty-year-old man still feels drawn. An ancestor of these boys can be found in Edoardo-Edoarda of *Menzogna e sortilegio*, the wry and delicate androgynous boy, while it does not seem by chance that a figure of Edoardo's imagination in Morante's first novel is the handsome bullfighter Manuelito. In *Aracoeli* Morante finally translates concretely her androgynous intuitions into what has been circled around but never stated so incisively: the angel as figure of the androgyne.

The self-pleasing in which Manuele indulges at various points takes the form not only of a waking dream or ecstasy as in the first novel, but also of a vision, while the protagonist imagines another self, frequently more handsome; for example, a film actor. Manuele tries to understand who this Other from himself is, an "[. . .] apparizione misteriosa e irriconoscibile, all'aprirsi del mio scenario, lo minacciasse dal fondo: presentandosi come un barlume indistinto, che poteva tramutarsi in una forma umana" (*Opere* 2: 1126; a "[. . .] mysterious and unrecognizable apparition, at the opening of my play, might threaten from the distance, presenting itself in a vague glimmer that could be transformed into a human form"; 67). Its first characteristic is its non-existence: human figures are strictly excluded from Manuele's visions. This is thus an indistinct and non-existing being, "uno di quegli esseri 'portati dal vento' e incamminati sempre all'addio" (*Opere* 2: 1131; "one of those beings 'borne in the wind' and heading always toward farewell"; 70). It seems natural then that one of the interpreters of his private cinema is named Cherubino and that in his desperation Manuele should invoke his double, yet single, Angel magician. In the scene where Mariuccio rejects Manuele's sexual attentions and requests for company, his contempt for Manuele is made manifest by his use of the language of sacred images: "[. . .] coi tuoi occhi di pesce, come la vergine davanti all'arcangelo dell'Annunciazione! Io non sono l'Annunciazione, hai capito?!" (*Opere* 2: 1095–96; "those fish-eyes of yours, like the Virgin looking at the angel of the Annunciation! I'm not the Annunciation, you understand?"; 45). This follows the description of Mariuccio's "scapole sporgenti sotto la maglietta slabbrata" (*Opere* 2: 1097; "shoulder blades protruding under the tattered T-shirt"; 46) resembling two small wings, as he walks away. Those wings will henceforth induce Manuele to seek out their bearer many times, and always in vain.

When referring to these indistinct, double, and yet unique beings, the writer frequently has recourse to a series of oxymoronic adjectives and noun-adjective pairs, abstract with concrete, physical with moral. She describes her characters, for example, as aged children in whom the double aspect still prevails over the single one typical of angelic beings. According to Emanuel Swedenborg,[15] drawing on a previous theory of the coincidence of opposites, in fact, angels are endowed with the highest degree of spirituality and the lowest degree of corporality. Angels remind human beings of their own androgynous origins. Only an angel is spared the bitterness of sexed beings, and does not know the split brought upon other unhappy boys by Adam and Eve with the expulsion from Eden. All boys with feminine traits or effeminate males, who appear alongside beings with inverse gender features (thus the angel appeared to Manuele to be female rather than male), have an angelic appearance. Delicate features, whitish lips, tired but proud, stubborn, these creatures constitute the sick but health-giving, the loving but death-giving, aspect of Morante's work. Eugenio, Daniele, Uncle Manuel, Pennati, and Mariuccio all have upon them, if to different degrees, this primary angelic beauty.[16] Eugenio resembled the Angel de la Guarda who displays unseen his transparent wings; or the angel of the Annunciation, such that when Aracoeli finds out she is pregnant the reflection of the Visitation remains in her eyes. But if angels do have a sex, the Annunciation to Aracoeli was made by a female angel: as the Narrator quietly jokes, it is a well-known fact that angels have no sex. After Daniele's desertion, Manuele is left to sleep alone, as his father claims he is now old enough. When nocturnal fears assail him, he urgently calls his personal guardian angel, who never fails to appear. On waking, Manuele can still sense his presence:

> Non era né maschio, né femmina (ma piuttosto femmina che maschio). Era tutto coperto di piume, e le sue piume sapevano di bagnato, come se, lungo il volo, avessero attraversato una zona di piogge. Rimase pochi secondi, rovesciato su di me; e io sentii nella sua carne, da vicino, una mollezza, quasi di mammelle pendenti. La sua bocca, dal movimento del fiato, sembrava bisbigliare; ma non dava nessun suono, per cui s'intese che il creduto bisbiglio, in realtà, erano baci; e me ne rimase, infatti, un sentore di saliva, ingenuo: da saliva di bambino. (*Opere* 2: 1383)

> The angel was neither male nor female (but more female than male). It was all covered with feathers, and the feathers had a damp odor, as if, during the flight, he had crossed a rainy zone. The angel remained a few seconds, sprawled on me; and I felt in its flesh, close, a softness, as of sagging breasts. Its mouth, in the movement of respiration, seemed to whisper but emitted no sound, so it was clear that the supposed whispering was, in reality, kisses, and they left with me, in fact, a sense, ingenuous, of saliva: a child's saliva. (258–59)

The "supposed whispering," a way of communicating without words, the speaking of the angel that turns into kisses, is, in fact, the angelic language that, according to Swedenborg, is assumed here to be the direct expression of feeling. The angelic language brings us back to the utopian project, already sketched out by Manuele during his search for the maternal language, a presymbolic language that, in accordance with Julia Kristeva's distinction, remains prior to logos in the semiotic.

Aracoeli and her language are anarchic, revolutionary, and barbarian. Such language remains outside the literary in particular, and outside the symbolic in general. The maternal language of Irigaray, tactile and scented, conserves the memory of the maternal skin that exhales a scent of plums. Similarly, the language of the angels is an untranslatable language: the communication between angel and human being can take place only by a direct communication of thoughts. The search for the angelic-maternal language leads to Manuele's desire for perennial boyhood. He wishes never to grow up, if this means he can stay in the realm of his own private cinema and angelic encounters: becoming a man is a scandal, just as it is a scandal that his fragile boy Pennati, companion for one night in 1943, is now surely married with children, and working somewhere as a salesman.

It is androgynous beings who enable Manuele to become a complete being, similar to the gods and the angels, including the angel who brings him the message of death. Death is the only one not to deny him the dream of wholeness, for from the very start his is a voyage in search of death. Having renounced the Christian sky, Aracoeli obeys the call of Andalusia, land of the Muslim religion. Manuele, the desolate bearer of a name meaning God is with us, goes toward death more lightly, toward the divinity that represents the coincidence of opposites. A divinity that is less a catalogue of attributes and qualities than absolute freedom, beyond good and evil, the absolute.

Aracoeli, more even than Morante's other novels, bears witness to the significance in her work of oriental mysticism, to which she was initiated by her readings of Simone Weil and Allen Ginsberg. We should also add cabalistic and gnostic-platonic thought, particularly when we think of how many midrash present Adam as an androgyne, man on one side, woman on the other. Gnostic and para-gnostic sects place androgyny at the heart of their doctrine. Androgyny, as Mircea Eliade notes, is a constant motif of rites, legends, and recurring myths in many oriental religions where one finds a tension toward a unifying principle by which it might be possible to explain a world in which opposites cancel each other out. The revelation that marks the end of Manuele's path echoes the childhood cosmogony of the protagonist. The only primary star, the true

Master of the Garden, is not discernible from the others but replicates himself *ad infinitum*. There is a structural affinity between the myth of androgyny and the myths of cosmogony. Once the original unity disappears, it is impossible to discern one's own *real* body, one's own *real* identity. Everything originates in this one star, multiplied in an endless play of mirrors.

Notes

1. The name "Aracoeli" (which appears already in *Senza i conforti della religione*) refers both to heaven ("altar of heaven," the Roman church) and to the penitentiary (Regina Coeli). The idea of christening her heroine in this fashion may have come from Morante's acquaintance with Aracoeli Zambrano, sister of the Spanish philosopher, who also frequented the circle of Elena Croce during the ten years the Zambranos spent in Rome (1954–64). Aside from physical traits and the name, the empirical Aracoeli shares with the fictional one aspects of their biography such as the revolution and anti-Franco stance. All references and quotations from *Aracoeli* and other novels are taken from her collected works edited by Cesare Garboli and Carlo Cecchi.

2. Even recently there have been few studies of *Aracoeli*, most notably Giovanni Raboni's and Rocco Capozzi's, until some of the papers presented at the Pisa symposium in 1994, "Vent'anni dopo *La Storia*. Omaggio a Elsa Morante" and collected in a special issue of *Studi novecenteschi* (D'Angeli and Magrini). Bruna Cordati follows the escape from power toward innocence. Anna Maria di Pascale reads it as the renunciation of the poetic truth of the word by a failed poet who has not received the gift of grace. In a recent issue of *Narrativa*, Gianni Venturi speaks about the novel. In his reading Venturi sees two journeys of Manuel (that in his own past and that—perhaps oneiric—in Spain), which the critic likens to the Dantesque journey parallel to Ulysses' itinerary.

3. In *Il gioco segreto* Garboli underlines a biographical approach, already defined by Moravia himself, that identifies the security offered by her marriage to him as a factor in her creative development (174).

4. Giulio Ferroni sees in Manuele a sequel and conclusion to the tragic martyrdom of Pasolini (560). See Walter Siti's essay in this volume (268–89).

5. See Bardini's acute concept of Elisa's name being changed from the first to the second novel into a different gender, "Eliso" (*Morante* 41).

6. The theme of male and female twins whose individual edges are fluid and blurred appears in the story "La nonna" (Morante, *Opere* 1: 1440). The theme of the twins is pertinent to that of spiritual androgyny here analyzed. In many oriental religions a pair of twins (Jama and Jami in India, Jima and Jimagh in China) stood in for the first born male as an androgynous equivalent of Adam.

7. We might remember the noted episode of the cross-transvestitism of Anna and Edoardo in *Menzogna e sortilegio*. While the cousins are playing the momentarily reversed roles, they discover themselves to be physically similar and opposite, like two twins. Edoardo, always self-absorbed, calls himself the "bella Edoarda" (*Opere* 1: 217). The motif of transvestitism recalls ritual androgyny, widespread in many cultures, particularly oriental ones. Transvestitism marks the moment of transition and/or dangerous instances in the life of an individual: birth, initiation, matrimony, and death.

8. The term is borrowed from Alice Walker.

9. In his analysis of androgyny in the *Symposium*, Plato, and the gnostics after him, thought of the sexed body as a jail or a sepulcher, fault of a powerful devil, an anti-Christ. In the Christian system, Greek thought was modified, and the mortality of the body compensated with the promise of resurrection in one's own flesh post-mortem. In the treatment reserved to the body, Morantian works reveal a strong pre-Christian component.

10. Fortini (240–41), Fofi (88–92), and Peretti (33) give a negative reading of *Aracoeli*, describing it as a dark and desperate work, while Bardini, in his book (*Morante* 638–42), parallels Pasolini's *Edipo Re* to Morante's *Edipo a Colono*.

11. It is the childish pronunciation of Manuele that turns Montesacro, the name of a Roman neighborhood into Totetaco.

12. See David (*Psicanalisi* 528–29), Bardini (*Morante* 230–31), Scarano (115).

13. Guido Sommavilla analyzes this topic at length.

14. Of the few who have addressed this issue, Lucamante considers Elisa's point of view to be "tinged with androgyny" (181).

15. All my references to Swedenborg's theories are drawn from Guido Sommavilla's study on angelology.

16. Claudia Vannocci locates the figurative hypotext of Morante's first novel in religious iconography. Lorenzo Lotto's *Annunciation* (1527, Pinacoteca of Recanati) does not find a location in Vannocci's inventory, while it could recall *Aracoeli,* in which the angel and Annunciation occupy a significant space (409–38).

Works Cited

Bardini, Marco. "Dei 'fantastici doppi' ovvero la mimesi narrativa dello spostamento psichico." *Per Elisa* 173–300.

———. *Morante Elsa. Italiana. Di professione, poeta.* Pisa: Nistri-Lischi, 1999.

Cacciaglia, Norberto. "L'esperienza materna nella narrativa di Elsa Morante (Osservazioni sulla maternità nella "Storia" e in "Aracoeli")." *Maternità trasgressiva e letteratura.* Ed. Ada Neiger. Naples: Liguori, 1993. 145–52.

Capozzi, Rocco. "Morante's 'Aracoeli': The End of a Journey." In *Donna: Women in Italian Culture.* Ed. Ada Testaferri. Ottawa: Dovehouse, 1989. 47–58.

———. "Scheherazade and Other Alibis: Elsa Morante's Victims of Love." *Rivista di studi italiani* 5–6 (1987–88): 51–71.

Cases, Cesare. "Una pagina della Morante." *L'Indice* 3 (Mar. 1989).

Cordati, Bruna. "'Aracoeli,' L'innocenza punita." D'Angeli and Magrini 277–85.

D'Angeli, Concetta, and Giacomo Magrini, ed. "Vent'anni dopo la Storia. Omaggio a Elsa Morante." Special issue of *Studi novecenteschi* 21. 47–48 (1994).

David, Michel. "Entretien: Elsa Morante." *Le Monde* (13 Apr. 1968). Interview.

———. *La psicanalisi nella cultura italiana.* Turin: Bollati Boringhieri, 1966.

Debenedetti, Giacomo. "L'isola di Arturo." *La stanza separata.* By Debenedetti. Milan: Mondadori, 1969. 56–71.

Ferroni, Giulio. "Elsa Morante e le narratrici." *Storia della letteratura italiana.* Vol. 4. Turin: Einaudi, 1991. 559–61.

Ferrucci, Franco. "Il Mito." *Storia della letteratura italiana. Le Questioni.* Vol. 5. Turin: Einaudi, 1996. 513–49.

Fofi, Goffredo. "La pesantezza del futuro." *Paragone letteratura* 38 (1987): 88–92.

Fortini, Franco. "Aracoeli." *Nuovi Saggi italiani.* Vol. 2. Milan: Garzanti, 1987. 240–47.

Garboli, Cesare. *Il gioco segreto: nove immagini di Elsa Morante.* Milan: Adelphi, 1995.

Gruppo la Luna. *Letture di Elsa Morante.* Turin: Rosenberg e Sellier, 1987.

Lucamante, Stefania. *Elsa Morante e l'eredità proustiana.* Fiesole: Cadmo, 1988.

Mengaldo, Pier Vincenzo. "Spunti per un'analisi linguistica dei romanzi di Elsa Morante." D'Angeli and Magrini 11–36.

Milano, Paolo. "Sull'altare di Aracoeli." *L'Espresso* (28 Nov. 1982).

Morante, Elsa. *Aracoeli*. Trans. William Weaver. New York: Random, 1984.

———. *Opere*. Ed. Cesare Garboli and Carlo Cecchi. 2 vols. Milan: Mondadori, 1988 and 1990.

Morante, Marcello. *Maledetta benedetta: Elsa e sua madre*. Milan: Garzanti, 1986.

Oz, Amos. "Into Mother's Bosom: On Several Beginnings in Elsa Morante's 'History; A Novel.'" *The Story Begins: Essays on Literature*. Trans. M. Bar-Tursa. New York: Harcourt, 1999. 65–87.

Paduano, Guido. "La svolta nella produzione di Elsa Morante: Domande e ipotesi di lavoro (e una verifica su "Aracoeli")." D'Angeli and Magrini 303–19.

Pagliano, Graziella. "Il mito androgino." *Fra norme e desideri*. Rome: Aracne, 1998. 149–58.

Palandri, Enrico. "Alcune notazioni in margine a 'Pro e contro la bomba atomica.'" D'Angeli and Magrini 79–90.

Pascale, Anna Maria di. "Senza i conforti di alcuna religione." D'Angeli and Magrini 287–302.

Patrucco-Becchi, Anna. "Stabat Mater: Le madri di Elsa Morante." *Belfagor* 48 (1993): 436–51.

Per Elisa. Studi su "Menzogna e sortilegio." Pisa: Nistri-Lischi, 1990.

Peretti, Alessandra. "Dalla stanza di Elisa al deserto di El Almendral: Un itinerario." Gruppo la Luna 25–37.

Raboni, Giovanni. "Quella luce tenebrosa." *Il Messaggero* (16 Nov. 1982): 5.

Rosa, Giovanna. *Cattedrali di carta. Elsa Morante romanziere*. Milan: Il Saggiatore, 1995.

Scarano, Emanuella. "La fatua veste del vero." *Per Elisa* 95–171.

Schifano, Jean-Noël. "La divina barbara." *Cahiers Elsa Morante* 1 (1993): 5–13.

Sgorlon, Carlo. *Invito alla lettura di Elsa Morante*. Milan: Mursia, 1972.

Siti, Walter. "Elsa Morante nell'opera di Pier Paolo Pasolini." D'Angeli and Magrini 131–48.

Sommavilla, Guido. "Anarchia e angelologia di Elsa Morante." *Scrittori italiani* 6. By Sommavilla. Milan: Letture, 1976. 79–96.

Vannocci, Claudia. "La pinacoteca di Elisa: per uno studio dell'ipotesto figurativo." *Per Elisa* 409–38.

Venturi, Gianni. "La menzogna della bellezza: *Aracoeli*." *Narrativa* 17 (2000): 123–36.

Walker, Alice. *In Search of Our Mother's Gardens: Womanist Prose.* New York: Harcourt, 1983.

Zampolini, Anna Maria "*Aracoeli*: Morte di Narciso." Gruppo La Luna 55–58.

Concetta D'Angeli

A Difficult Legacy

Morante's Presence in
Contemporary Italian Literature

Critical theory on literary influence, as taught in the university
lecture theater, would frequently have us believe that the connections between an author and his/her successors are more
direct and unproblematic than is, in fact, the case. Indeed, these
connections rarely reveal an illuminated and rational transmission of the cultural legacy in question. While not wishing to
invoke every step of the way the Oedipal model of Harold
Bloom, I am in agreement with his postulation of a large measure of irrationality, pockets of resistance and passions that are
not always decipherable, unexpected byways and epiphanies,
and tortuous meanderings that shape the fundamental operation of constituting a cultural heritage and transmitting it to
future generations.

While these considerations on the transmission of literary or
cultural heritage hold good in any relationship, not just those
within a particular "school," in the case of Elsa Morante there
is a particular rather than general argument to be made, because
of elements specific to her own writing. Morante is, in fact, an
original writer, or rather from the very start an anti-conformist
one, since she came onto the literary scene with a lengthy
nineteenth-century-style novel, *Menzogna e sortilegio* (1948;
House of Liars, 1951), a work utterly counter to the current
trend in the Italian novel. Critics of the time, as at other times,
were decreeing the death of the novel. Her publication of this
rich and convoluted family saga, so at odds with the current
popularity of war memorials, the fascination with American
writers, and the favored dry, spare fictional prose of the times,
marks the beginning of a whole series of anti-conformist gestures Morante was regularly to repeat, most strikingly with the
publication of *La Storia* (1974; *History*, 1977 and 2000). In the

1970s, when writers were engaged in experimental writing, drawing from French writers like Alain Robbe-Grillet, Philippe Sollers, and Italo Calvino and their experience of the *Oulipo*, Morante published this lengthy novel characterized by numerous narrative strategies that would not be out of place, indeed, in a work of Neorealism.

What Morante most clearly transmits to future generations of writers is her faith in the narratability of the world, the recuperation of large-scale narrative structures, attention to psychology, and psychological coherence. These are the techniques and tenets that writers were to turn back to when, at the beginning of the 1980s, they began once more to show interest in novels that exhibit a strong interest in form.

If, on the one hand, Morante found followers, it has to be said that she is only with difficulty "imitable," in the sense that she never adopts a fixed style; neither does she profess an explicit and definite poetics even loosely based on theoretical writings. Her poetics must be deduced from her creative writing, and should be assumed to be in constant evolution, in tune with the evolution of artistic creation. Aside from her famous interview on the novel, "Nove domande sul romanzo," the few theoretical writings by Morante were collected posthumously. Morante refuses to strike the pose of the intellectual, distinguishing herself from numerous writers of her age and times, who tend to accompany their artistic production with a critical reflection that becomes the insuppressible corollary of their creative work. Often this relationship is so evident that the two territories coincide, but not in the sense of making the practice of writing the dominating container enveloping its underlying speculative system: rather, in the sense of creating a sort of hybrid genre, half way between narrative and critical essay, as in the paradigmatic case of Calvino's last works.[1]

Along with recognition by younger generations, the consecration of an author and the defining of his or her role as the founder of a school also comes about through the activity of critics, whose role it is—or which role they take upon themselves—to elaborate genre and literary canons. It is interesting to explore the problem of Morante's critical reception and evaluation on both anthropological and, of course, cultural grounds, as well as for the example of that irrational passion that, according to Bloom, informs the transmission and reception of artistic matter. The gulf between the critics who immediately appreciated Morante's work, and those who rejected it with great hostility, was clear right from the start, and is characterized by a furor and *parti pris* rarely found in the assessment of Italian literary works. Scholars who first manifested interest in the merits of her work include Giacomo Debenedetti and Cesare Garboli, the latter one of the most important and consistent in Morante criticism.[2] The writings of another influential critic, Alfonso Berardinelli, have added to the deep appreciation of the first two.[3] Aside from these isolated demonstrations of admiration and understanding for both her style and her poetics, Morante lacked, for many years, any wider recognition by academics. This absence of interest signified exclusion from the canon, and the consequent exclusion from the cultural transmission usually channeled by the school and academic syllabus. I can attest that, until recently, it was considered an act of cruelty or sabotage to ask even brighter students questions on Elsa Morante's work; literature manuals offered only the briefest and sketchiest of summaries, relegating her work to the space of half a single, miserable page.

There are many reasons for this lack of interest and hostile silence. Above all, Morante was a solitary artist, extraneous to schools and trends, even if she cannot be considered, particularly up to the end of the 1960s, an isolated and marginalized writer: she belonged, after all, to a group of Roman intellectuals who included highly influential artists such as Alberto Moravia and Pier Paolo Pasolini. Nonetheless, Morante's position in the vehement political and cultural discussions that racked Italian postwar literary society needs to be considered. While these debates unquestionably lent this *milieu* great vitality, they also functioned as a bright light illuminating the protagonists of polemics and debates, while casting a shadow over those who did not promote their ideas with the same intensity and visibility. Even while she held firm views on the issues under debate, Morante shied away from discussion, or at least did not participate in a public forum, a situation that served only to sideline her. Not only this, but her manner of working, her craftsmanlike care for her writing, her attentiveness to the documentation of the background of her works, together with the attention bestowed on their form and detail, remove her work from the fads and fashion of the moment. Her faithfulness to the internal and subjective motivations of her own art made her unwilling to reflect the trends and ideas of the dominant cultural groups, with the inevitable result that she was rather less visible as an artist.

Neither did the writer's cultural background, with its many and varied elements extraneous to the more usual cultural baggage of the average Italian intellectual, serve to swing the balance. We might think particularly of her dedication to Simone Weil, overlooked if not ignored by the leftist writers after the war, with the exception of Franco Fortini, although he was interested principally in the class component of Weil's thought. Morante's interest in American 1960s beat poetry, and the oriental religions she so profoundly studied and respected, never brought her close to the generic irrationalism with which the more conformist criticism of the left always tarnished her. A further obvious, but not insignificant, reason lies in the fact that Elsa Morante was a woman, and therefore, in a society strongly sexist even in its intellectual sphere, considered not fit to take on the role of protagonist.

The credit for overturning such an ostracizing verdict must go to Giulio Ferroni, who was the first to give Morante prominence in his *Storia della Letteratura Italiana*. After him, two national conferences, the first in Perugia (1992) and the second in Pisa (1994), marked her definitive academic consecration.

If academic criticism has until recently undervalued Morante's production, militant criticism flowing from the avant-garde has also been violently hostile: the case of Angelo Guglielmi, who on the publication of *Aracoeli* wrote a review tinted with peculiarly aggressive tones, should suffice to prove the point.

The critics of a more decidedly ideological left merit separate consideration. This strand of criticism started with the unconditionally positive judgment of Gÿorgÿ Lukács at the beginning of the 1960s. But in Italy, Cesare Cases introduced a high level of diffidence into his ostensible admiration for Morante's art, thus heralding an attitude that would later characterize the judgments even of the most sensitive and attentive representatives of this critical line. Franco Fortini should be

placed in the same camp. Even though he exhibited considerable perplexity at a political level, nonetheless he published
some of the more illuminating interpretations among essays on
Morante, as in the paradigmatic case of *Aracoeli*. Conversely,
there are examples of critical blindness that verge on the
ridiculous, particularly in the case of the harsh polemics that
followed the publication of *La Storia*. The subtly ideological
discussions, the complex distinctions between artistic and political reason, the harsh condemnation of the emotional
emphasis that characterized the debate following the novel's
publication (Sinibaldi 205–18), nonetheless failed to explain
the great popularity of this novel among a readership significantly different from the one usually interested in Morante's
work, particularly among young readers and people with radical political views and in general with little interest in things
literary.

The vicissitudes of *La Storia* demonstrate another aspect of
the reception of Morante's work. This has to do with reader
response: indeed, reception should play a significant part in
defining the author's canonicity, even if, in practice, it carries a
relatively slight weight. On this level Morante represents a
paradoxical case, as she is an author still much beloved by the
public and yet, still today, relatively unknown. Unlike the popular *La Storia*, *Menzogna e sortilegio* and *L'isola di Arturo*
(1957; *Arturo's Island*, 1959) are read by an élite, while her
poetry collections and short stories are basically ignored by the
public. Her last novel, *Aracoeli* (1982; *Aracoeli*, 1984), is still
viewed with considerable hostility.

But the real transformation of an author into a principal
interlocutor and essential point of reference, even when critics
have finally conferred canonical consecration, is effected by
future generations of artists who take the author as model. This
is not, however, a straightforward process. It may be the case
that artists who greatly admire a predecessor proclaim themselves his/her heirs, as an act of homage. But in many instances
such a declared legacy reveals itself to be no more than a shared
tendency, or indeed just a desire for a shared tendency; it is not
steeped in spiritual or emotional likeness, in a specific moral
universe, even while it adheres to specific and complex modes
of writing. In short, this legacy cannot re-create the intellec-

tual, artistic, and human universe put forward in the work of the chosen model artist. I think that cases of this kind are not infrequent with respect to Morante, and have created confusion when it comes to identifying more legitimate legacies. By this I do not mean that a theoretical affinity, and the desire for assimilation, are irrelevant when it comes to the cultural recognition of an author; but they are not adequate to the task of laying the foundations of a homogenous genealogy that carries the same imprint as the chosen model, or, rather, that is capable of emancipating itself from slavery to the given model, while at the same time maintaining the legacy and developing it into a tradition.

It is arduous to theorize from Morante's writing a recognizable and identifiable model, as is the case, instead, for other writers, like Alberto Moravia himself for whom we see a more clear legacy of his work in authors like Giorgio Montefoschi, Marco Lodoli, and others. What only improperly can be defined as Morante's "technique," then, is in fact an extraordinary storytelling ability, the art of constructing the "narrative cathedrals" that Berardinelli called her novels. It is thus an inherent quality that, particularly in times of minimalism, can hardly be replicated in its intent.

Morante's language, aside from some specific features such as the excursions into the vitality and expressive invention of dialect, appears ill-suited to facile reproduction. I believe that the explanation for this lies in the quality of metamorphosis exhibited by Morante's writing, its constant self-renewal, shifting from the nineteenth-century form of *Menzogna e sortilegio* to the measured terseness of *L'isola di Arturo*, to *La Storia*, marked by a demotic and low linguistic register, to the recuperation of disparate literary codes (ranging from Greek tragedy to early-twentieth-century experimentalism) in the *Mondo salvato dai ragazzini*, the baroque emphasis and the plurilinguistic texture of *Aracoeli*. Yet despite all this, it is still possible to identify a small group of recent Italian writers who, in diverse form and fashion, have inherited the Morantian legacy.

I should begin by stating that only the methodological part of my study can be considered in any way complete. While I have identified some of the lines along which recent artists have engaged with Morante's legacy, my map of the "heirs" would certainly appear to be partial and incomplete, as I limit my study to a few exemplary cases. Among such artists I would distinguish those whose poetics have manifested an affinity with Morante's work, with her way of understanding the role of literature and of the intellectual, and the ones whose works bear a closer relationship to her creative works in the concrete practice of writing. This is a convenient if somewhat artificial distinction, as the line between these two categories is inevitably blurred. Nevertheless, I believe that there is more than a partial element of truth in such a distinction, and that it is important to a study of Morante's canonicity in Italian literature.

Enrico Palandri

The first author is the novelist Enrico Palandri who, aside from acknowledging Morante's influence, is perhaps the only writer so far to have meditated with critical and acute judgment on the profound effect Morante had on a younger generation of writers. In 1979 Palandri published his first novel, *Boccalone*, an important work that took critics by storm to such an extent that they did not hesitate to mark this as the beginning of the final phase of the twentieth-century Italian novel. While it differs from Morante's novels in form, Palandri's work nonetheless deals with a theme very dear to the Roman writer: the adolescent who discovers the world, and discovers love:

> Maggio e settembre sono da sempre i mesi che preferisco; amo il sole e il cielo, i gatti, i tetti, e le belle facce che se la spassano sui gradini di san petronio o sdraiati sui prati dei giardini margherita.
>
> Vorrei raccontare uno per uno tutti i giorni di questo mese bellissimo, invece il ricordare scivola confuso su un pomeriggio in piazza maggiore, adesso provo a raccontare:
>
> costruivamo delle mongolfiere con giuliano, e poi le facevamo volare alte, cantando delle canzoni; un pomeriggio venivo da una di queste strane cose, che non so bene come chiamare, dove si faceva funzionare un po' tutto, saltando come i matti e urlando "vola!! vola!!," oppure, "brucia!! brucia!!"; ero molto allegro, nello stato di traboccamento amoroso in cui mette la primavera.
>
> Non è possibile calmarsi, o trattenersi, e il sesso, l'enorme energia del sesso che è capace di non farvi addormentare

mai, sfugge alle norme che ci si danno (norme invernali)
per affrontare le miserie e le paure della solitudine.
(*Boccalone* 11)

May and September have always been my favorite months;
I love the sun, the sky, cats, roofs, and the lovely faces that
hang out on the steps of san petronio or stretched out on the
lawns of margherita gardens.

I'd like to describe the days of this wonderful month one
by one, but my memory slips confusedly to an afternoon in
piazza maggiore, now I'll try and describe it:

We were making hot air balloons with giuliano, and we
made them fly up high, singing songs; one afternoon I was
coming back from one of these strange things; I'm not really
sure what to call them, where we made everything go, jump-
ing like madmen and yelling "fly!! fly!!" or else "burn!!
burn!!" I was feeling really good, in that state of overflowing lovingness that spring induces in you.

It isn't possible to calm down, or to control yourself, and
sex, the enormous energy of sex that is capable of never letting you go to sleep, escapes the rules that we give ourselves
(wintry rules) for facing the misery and fear of solitude.

The discovery of the world and of feelings takes place through
expressive means which are an appropriation, if distanced and
ironic, of the forms of high culture. It is not by chance that the
novel begins with the name of Torquato Tasso:

"cosa leggi di bello?" faccio io.
"l'aminta, di tasso."
"tasso?"
"già!"
Ero grato a daniele per le sue risposte quiete e cortesi,
senza malizia; nonostante la sua evidente compiacenza non
smettevo di temerlo; poteva sbottare da un momento all'altro in un "a te che cazzo te ne frega brutto scimmione puz-
zolente, pussa via!" o quel che è peggio trovare un altro
doloroso confronto nel mondo animale, più precisamente
collegato alle dimensioni della mia bocca; daniele invece è
delicato, magnanimo, non aveva probabilmente motivo per
innervosirsi, cosa che a me invece non manca mai, e rispon-
deva con puntualità alla trafila di stupide domande che gli
facevo; a un certo punto nella nostra conversazione semi-
seria sulla letteratura, vedo che si è fermato, ha fermato tutto (testa, parole e respiro), mi guarda sorridendo e con
questi pochi cenni ha spezzato la conversazione banale e io

ne sono davvero contento, mi guarda (io aspetto una rivela-
zione sconvolgente dalle sue labbra!) e mi domanda:
"ti interessi d'amore?"

ero emozionatissimo, volevo dire io quella cosa, era proprio ciò di cui avevo bisogno di parlare (è proprio ciò di cui
ho bisogno di parlare)

[...] si lanciò in una appassionatissima lettura dei versi
che trovava nel suo libro antico. io seguivo i miei pensieri e
ascoltavo tutte le belle parole. (*Boccalone* 12–13)

"reading something good?" I say.
"aminta, by tasso."
"tasso?"
"yeah, that's right!"

I was grateful to daniele for his quiet and courteous
replies, which had no malice in them; despite his evident
complacency I was still afraid of him; he could burst out
any minute with a "what the fuck's it got to do with you,
you stinking ugly ape, fuck off!" or, even worse, find another hurtful comparison within the animal kingdom, more
precisely to do with the size and shape of my mouth: but
daniele is delicate, magnanimous, he probably had no reason to get angry while I had plenty, and he gave prompt
answers to the string of stupid questions I was asking him;
at a certain point in our half-serious conversation on literature, I see he's stopped, he's stopped everything (his head,
words and breath), he looks at me with a smile and with
those few signs he breaks off our banal conversation and
I'm so pleased, he looks at me (I'm expecting a shattering
revelation to drop from his lips!) and he asks: "you interested in love?"

I was so excited, that's what I'd wanted to say, that's
exactly what I needed to talk about (that's exactly what I
need to talk about)

[. . .] he launched into a passionate reading of the lines
he read in his old book. I followed my own train of thought
and listened to all those beautiful words.

Nor is it by chance that the protagonist's most dramatic experiences are shaped by Shakespearian formulae:

Macbeth vede gli alberi che si muovono e circondano il
castello, la profezia delle tre streghe che si avvera, scende
dalla torre di guardia, parla della paura, macbeth non dor-
mirà mai più. (Shakespeare è molto intelligente, Roman
Polanski è un genio!). (*Boccalone* 108–09)

> Macbeth sees the trees moving and surrounding the castle, the prophecy of the three witches coming true, he comes down from his guard tower, he speaks of fear, macbeth will sleep no more. (Shakespeare is very intelligent, Roman Polanski is a genius!)

The entire novel is veined through with laughter, very similar to the tender humor that Morante reserves for innocent creatures, for the "Felici Pochi" ("Happy Few") and for animals. Just as tender, without falling into pathos, is the tone with which Palandri recounts his autobiographical hero's sudden initiation into love and pain. The strongly expressive vitality of *Boccalone* was, in fact, much appreciated by Morante, who developed a close relationship with Palandri.

Several years later Palandri was to reconsider an important relationship that marked not only his intellectual life but also his whole existence. He did so by putting forth the kind of moral and human education, rather than literary lesson, that Morante was inclined to impart to young artistic talents. She would discourage, as Palandri himself witnessed, forms of passive imitation that would have resulted in her eyes in an unbearable mannerism. Morante's teaching is recognized by Palandri in a passage that can correctly be defined as moral and that, at the same time, is a categorical indication of poetics: it's about being faithful to a task Palandri describes as "un impegno a tenere vicine le ragioni della scrittura e quelle dell'esistenza, a pensare la vita attraverso l'arte e a ragionare dei problemi della letteratura in una prospettiva che comporti responsabilità morali assolute" ("Alcune notazioni" 79; "a commitment to holding the reasons for writing close to those for existence, to think of life through art and work through the problems of literature in a perspective that brings with it absolute moral responsibilities").[4]

In Palandri's view, being a writer, for Morante, is neither technique nor job nor role but a way of dealing with reality: it is having faith that a better world, the one of art, can exist. A world that, while closely tied to that of daily life, cannot be confused with it.

Aside from Palandri, I would include Patrizia Cavalli and Gianfranco Bettin among the "moral" heirs of Morante. I call them "moral" heirs less because of their literary motifs or formal writing patterns, which are indeed quite different, than for their similar faith in art, the coherence between writing and existence she always manifested, the same attention to historical and social situations, and the conviction that artistic practice requires an absolute rigor that begins with the formal and technical, and ends in the ethical.

Patrizia Cavalli

The poetry of Patrizia Cavalli, in particular, manifests the same profound trust in the word, and in the images created by the word, that so marked particularly Morante's early writing. Cavalli's poems exhibit the same patient and craftlike attention to verbal expression, to the measure and rhythm of the phrase. And Cavalli, like Morante, remains substantially faithful to the themes she developed and illustrated in her first collection of poems: the role of the word, whose salvific quality is soon modified even while retaining its totalizing and essentializing quality.

> l'affanno delle mie parole,
> avvocatesca smania che m'impone
> di riprovare con nuovi verbi e nomi
> la costruzione logica esteriore
> —si ricomincia, su, ricominciamo—
> che a dirlo meglio è come dar le prove,
> se ci riesco poi passo la mano
> ("L'io singolare proprio mio" 220)

> the breathlessness of my words,
> an advocating desire which compels me
> to try again with new verbs and names
> the logical exterior construction
> —we start again, come, let us start again—
> which to put it better is like giving proof,
> if I succeed then I hand it on to someone else.

Also central is the body, sensual, narcissistic, or lovingly demanding, but in a stylistic sense serving to lower the excessive claims of the poet, whether spiritual, platonic-amorous or intellectual, within the tradition of the *Canzoniere* from Petrarch onwards.

Io scientificamente mi domando
come è stato creato il mio cervello,
cosa ci faccio io con questo sbaglio.
Fingo di avere anima e pensieri
per circolare meglio in mezzo agli altri,
qualche volta mi sembra anche di amare
facce e parole di persone, rare;
esser toccata vorrei poter toccare,
ma scopro sempre che ogni mia emozione
dipende da un vicino temporale.

("L'io singolare proprio mio" 229)

I ask myself scientifically
how my brain was created,
what I'm doing with this mistake.
I pretend to have a soul and thoughts
all the better to circulate among other people.
Sometimes it even seems to me I love
the faces and words of others, just a few;
being touched I would like to be able to touch,
but I always discover that every emotion of mine
is the effect of an approaching storm.

Above all, in Cavalli we see the representation of loss, particularly but not exclusively the loss of love, itself a mocking admission of the illusory nature of many objects of faith, lucid awareness of opportunities missed and perhaps not even sought—possibilities only insofar as they are worthy of regret:

Adesso che il tempo sembra tutto mio
E nessuno mi chiama per il pranzo e per la cena,
adesso che posso rimanere a guardare
come si scioglie una nuvola e come si scolora,
come cammina un gatto per il tetto
nel lusso immenso di una esplorazione, adesso
che ogni giorno mi aspetta
la sconfinata lunghezza di una notte
dove non c'è richiamo e non c'è più ragione
di spogliarsi in fretta per riposare dentro
l'accecante dolcezza di un corpo che mi aspetta,
adesso che il mattino non ha mai principio
e silenzioso mi lascia ai miei progetti

a tutte le cadenze della voce, adesso
vorrei improvvisamente la prigione.

("Il cielo" 103)

Now that all my time seems my own
and no-one calls me for lunch or for dinner,
now that I can stay and watch
how a cloud dissolves or fades
how a cat walks over a roof
in the immense luxury of exploration, now
that every day I can look forward only to
the endless length of a night
where there is no-one to call me and there is no more reason
to undress quickly to rest within
the blinding sweetness of a body that waits for me,
now that the morning never has any reason
and leaves me in silence to my own projects
and all the cadences of the voice, now
all of a sudden, I would like prison.

The complex syntactic and metric structure of Cavalli's lyrics constitutes a further element that brings her work near to Morante's writing, this despite Cavalli's exclusively poetic production and Morante's intense interest in the novel. The reach of her poetry expands the singularity of experiences and emotional responses into a system based on a breadth of construction that gives an epic-narrative pace to her lyrics, while simultaneously taking on the attributes of philosophical poetry.

Gianfranco Bettin

Filippo La Porta notices polarities of guilt and innocence, meekness and dominance (146) in the first novel by Gianfranco Bettin, *Qualcosa che brucia* ("Something's Burning"). These dichotomies constitute the pillars of the Morantian narrative and ethical world. With Bettin, the novel of the path to adulthood becomes a means of finding one's way through a reality in which even the more stable terms of antithesis have undergone a profound degradation, becoming unrecognizable. The family produces nothing but hatred and false values, as in the terrible episode of the little dog Volpe, punished and killed by a conspiracy of family and neighbors. Her crime? persistent begging for food:

> La signora Piera aveva già aperto la porta e stava scendendo le scale. La spiai con apprensione, e rimasi impietrito. Con fare circospetto, si stava avvicinando alla cagnetta con una grande pentola fumante fra le mani. Volpe la guardava col musetto rivolto all'insù. Forse sentiva odore di cucina; forse non era maliziosa, Volpe, e aveva d'istinto fiducia negli uomini. Infatti non scappò, rimase immobile, solo un po' scodinzolando. La signora Piera, in ciabatte e vestaglia, l'aggirò in silenzio, e con un piede accostò il portone, chiudendo la via di fuga. Quindi, con un gesto rapido rovesciò addosso a Volpe il pentolone d'acqua bollente. Un guaito straziante, ma breve, sfuggì alla cagnetta. Per un istante Volpe apparve come colpita da una micidiale scarica elettrica: balzò in aria, restandovi come sospesa, con gli occhi sbarrati e le zampette divaricate nel vuoto. Poi ricadde sul pavimento, con un rumore d'acqua pesante, afflosciandosi in un grumo di pelo fradicio e fumante.
>   [...] Mi aspettavo che qualcuno intervenisse a condannare quel gesto, e denunciare la donna per la sua ferocia. Invece, mio padre osservando l'accaduto disse: "Era ora che qualcuno si muovesse." (*Qualcosa che brucia* 54)

Signora Piera had already opened the door and was going down the stairs. I peered out at her apprehensively, and stood rooted to the spot. Warily, she went up to the little dog, a large, steaming saucepan in her hands. Volpe was watching her, muzzle pointing upwards. Perhaps she could smell cooking; perhaps there was just no malice in her, and she had an instinctive trust of men. In fact she didn't run away, she stood still, just wagging her tail a little. Signora Piera, in slippers and dressing gown, went round her silently, and with one foot pulled the door shut, cutting off her escape route. Then with a quick movement she poured the boiling water over Volpe. A brief but dreadful howl came from the little dog. For a moment Volpe looked as though she had been stuck by a fatal electric bolt: she leapt into the air, and seemed to hang there, her eyes wide and her paws flailing in the empty air. Then she fell over on to the floor, with a sound of heavy water, into a heap of wet and steaming fur.
    [. . .] I expected someone to intervene and reproach the woman, report her for her cruelty. But no, my father saw

Concetta D'Angeli

what had happened and said: "It was time someone did something."

The city in which the novel is set, Venice, far from being synonymous with artistic splendor, becomes a rag-tag collection of decidedly unpoetic locations, the site of corruption and marginalization:

> L'altra faccia di Venezia è una città vasta e senza bellezza, sparsa alla rinfusa in terraferma, in grandi quartieri, come un fitto, frastagliato arcipelago di pietra [...] Figurette magre di alberelli ornamentali costeggiavano le vie, mentre profili più robusti e slanciati di pioppi e di platani sbucavano, sparsi, da povere aiuole o da piccole zone incolte, quasi delle selve minuscole di sterpi, cespugli e rifiuti. Accanto alle case e ai bordi della strada, ovunque, spuntavano sagome basse e regolari di garage in lamiera e, lì attorno e sopra i marciapiedi, sostavano decine e decine di automobili e di moto (queste ultime, spesso, incatenate agli alberi). Sopra le nostre teste s'intravvedevano sospese le corde che reggevano lunghe file di panni, smossi appena da una corrente fiacca e fredda, e più in alto ancora, a perdersi nella notte, i grossi cavi d'acciaio dell'alta tensione, spioventi da tralicci poderosi e fitti come una foresta di bizzarri, elettrici totem. E su questo panorama, fin dove era visibile nel buio, un'enorme ombra rossa proiettava il bagliore immenso, mai spento, dei forni e dei camini industriali. (*Qualcosa che brucia* 162)

The other face of Venice is a vast and ugly city, scattered at random on terra firma, in large districts, like a thick indented archipelago of cement [. . .] The scrawny shapes of little ornamental trees lined the roads, while the outlines of more robust and shapely poplars and plane trees struggled to grow in inhospitable beds of earth or in the odd uncultivated corner, miniature woods almost of thorns, bushes, and rubbish. All around the houses and along the streets you could see the low, square shapes of tin garages, while around them and all over the pavements dozens and dozens of cars and motorbikes were parked, the bikes often chained to the trees. Over our heads you caught a glimpse of the ropes that held up long lines of washing, barely stirred by a weak, chilly wind, and higher up again, as far as the eye could see in the night, the huge steel high voltage cables, numerous and weighty as a forest of bizarre, electrical totems. And all over

> this panorama, as far as you could see in the dark, an enormous red shadow cast an immense glow that never faded, the glow of the industrial furnaces and chimneys.

What remains in the gaze of this boy now on the verge of adulthood, and quite reminiscent of Morante's Arturo faced with the first burning disillusions, is the courage to keep his gaze on the world around him with a level of attention that for Bettin will transform the ethical into a personal involvement in political and practical action:

> Volevo andarmene via, al più presto. Vittorio e Orso mi hanno aiutato, procurandomi un po' di soldi e un documento di identità. Quando ho saputo dell'uccisione di Malaria ho rotto ogni indugio. Questa non è più la mia guerra—ho deciso—e non sarà nemmeno la mia pace. (*Qualcosa che brucia* 234)

> I wanted to leave, as soon as possible. Vittorio and Orso helped me, getting me some money and an identity card. When I heard that Malaria had been killed I decided not to hold back any more. This is not my war any more—I decided—and nor will it be my peace.

Alongside this moral legacy, which Palandri rightly considers the most demanding legacy of the writer to her successors, some writers have picked up on and reworked thematic strands that Elsa Morante continued to unravel throughout her entire career. Such a thematic reworking generally excludes, however, Morante's later and more difficult production, whether *Il mondo salvato dai ragazzini* or *Aracoeli*; even while they explore the themes to which the writer persistently returns, they are written in a key of alienating desperation. This renders Morante's habitual themes almost unrecognizable and particularly impervious to those authors not inclined to the extremism of Morante's later narrative choices.

A thematic legacy may be the most immediately detectable one, but it is also the most dangerous for the author's "heirs," who risk losing their autonomous voice, drowned out by the richer tones of the model. The authors I analyze in my study are in most part exempt from this danger, safeguarding their own identity, even as they pay evident tribute to the literary term of reference. In this conscious mixture of imitation and autonomy, or rather in the personal rendition of an authoritative and respected lesson, we see an excellent example of the dialectics between personal originality and the constraints of tradition.

Mariateresa Di Lascia, Fabrizia Ramondino, Elena Ferrante

The recuperation of memory, particularly that of the family, is the main subject of the only novel by Mariateresa Di Lascia, *Passaggio in ombra*, as well as being one of the subjects most frequently explored by Fabrizia Ramondino who also, just as Morante did, traces memory through physical sensation in accordance with a tradition beginning with Saint Augustine. The bodily characteristic of the remembering process is particularly powerful in *Aracoeli*, where the tormented search for the mother by her son Manuele starts from the physical traces that the maternal body has left in the body of a badly aging man of forty-three. It is with these traces that Manuele begins "come un animale sbandato va dietro agli odori della propria tana" (1046; "like an animal gone astray returns to the smells of its own lair"), to find his way back through memory and geography to the remote El Almendral in Andalusia—and, perhaps, to his death. But the physically perceptible nature of memory can be drawn out in different ways from the whole of Morante's work, to the point of becoming a sort of reading of the world. This gives her writings, especially those of her later period beginning with *Il mondo salvato dai ragazzini*, a genuinely philosophical underpinning. To synthesize the ideas that patently weave through at least *Il mondo salvato dai ragazzini*, *La Storia*, and *Aracoeli*, we could state that Morante attributes a contradictory status to the body: placed at the vertiginous crossroads between earth-bound atomism and the provisional on the one hand, and on the other, the blind yet vital and eternal rhythm that drives the universe, the body retains the traces of our individual past. At the same time the materiality of the body lends it a remote, absolute, and eternal knowledge, the anonymous biological knowledge of the species of which it receives intermittent and flickering signals. It is from this firm rootedness in an implicit philosophical base that derive, in my view, the power and stature of Morante's images dealing with this theme. In Ramondino, however, the connection with the underlying philosophical concept has been severed, radically transformed; even while retaining the idea of memory connected with the senses, the proximity between her writing and that of her model becomes therefore less close and intense than the formal analogy might have us believe.

The family saga, difficult family relations, sometimes preceded by a distant but happy childhood, are other themes of Morante's to return in works by Di Lascia, Ramondino, and Elena Ferrante, along with a solitude that consumes the present and the past, and the problematic discovery as a child or adolescent, of the world external to the family. I consider these three writers to be the most significant representatives of the "thematic heirs" of Morante. Fundamental to their writing are those same topics of Morante's narrative, particularly *Menzogna e sortilegio:* along with childhood and the difficult passage to adulthood, in these writers we see represented a suffocating southern world, frequently and centrally dominated by powerfully fascinating female images encircled by male characters of dubious moral worth, often violent and tyrannical, but also sensual and disturbing. There is the presence of bodies ferociously alive who impose their needs and drives with the same overbearing, imperious southern nature that often frames these stories.

In her use of *Menzogna e sortilegio* as a model of reference, Ferrante's *L'amore molesto* (1992) is something of a separate case. Here, the search for the truth about the life and death of her mother becomes a cognitive anxiety along the lines of Morante's *Aracoeli,* in particular. The maternal figure, who appears as a mother who was loved too much and yet was not well enough known, becomes the focal point of a mystery left unresolved by Ferrante's novel but that functions as a centripetal force for settings, characters, and situations. The bewildered daughter who recounts the maternal mystery, and the world that shapes itself around it, are represented as through an oneiric screen that cannot, however, prevent them from appearing as real. Take for example the scene of the open-air film, where the father's jealousy and the fear exhibited by the small girl who is the protagonist take shape in hostile complicity:

Quando andavamo al cinema senza di lui, mia madre non rispettava nessuna delle regole che le aveva imposto: si guardava intorno liberamente, rideva come non doveva ridere e chiacchierava con sconosciuti, per esempio col venditore di caramelle, che quando si spegnevano le luci e compariva il cielo stellato le si sedeva accanto. Perciò, quando mio padre c'era, non riuscivo a seguire la storia del film. Lanciavo sguardi furtivi nel buio per esercitare a mia volta un controllo su Amalia, anticipare la scoperta dei segreti di lei, evitare che anche lui scoprisse la sua colpevolezza. Tra i fumi delle sigarette e il lampeggiare del fascio di luce sprizzato dal proiettore, fantasticavo atterrita di corpi d'uomini in forma di ranocchio che saltavano agili sotto la fila dei seggiolini, allungando non zampe ma mani e lingue viscide. (*L'amore molesto* 182)

When we went to the cinema without him, my mother ignored all the rules he had imposed on her: she looked around freely, she laughed the way she wasn't supposed to laugh and she chatted with strangers, with the sweet-seller for example, who came to sit next to her when the lights went down and the starry sky appeared. And so when my father was there, I could never follow the film. I would direct furtive looks in the dark, carrying out my own check on Amalia, expecting her secret to come out, stopping him from discovering her guilt. Between the smoke from the cigarettes and the beam of light that came flashing out of the projector, I had terrified fantasies of men in the form of toads leaping agilely beneath the row of seats, stretching out not claws but slimy hands and tongues.

Ferrante's narrative has indeed been defined as realistic by Goffredo Fofi (43–44) and would therefore appear to be out of kilter with the sumptuously fantastic universe of Elsa Morante. It seems to me, however, that the realism of Ferrante's first novel is limited to the stylistic and expressive level, where Morante's influence is basically minimal. More generally, for all three writers here discussed, Morante's lessons do not go beyond the thematic level; her valuable lessons on expression, which cannot be reduced to a mere formal fact, do not seem to me to find their true heirs among them. Even Ramondino's unquestionable linguistic skill does not demonstrate the versatility and renewal of Morante's prose. The style of these three authors nonetheless demonstrates a refined linguistic and stylistic sensibility, and particularly in the case of Di Lascia, an ability to restore a three-dimensional depth to objects and images through an operation of linguistic estrangement. The case of Di Lascia is perhaps the most pertinent, although we have just the one novel, *Passaggio in ombra*, published posthumously after her premature death.

The outstanding and specific analogy between *Passaggio in ombra* and *Menzogna e sortilegio* is represented by the narrating voice.[5] In both cases it is the young daughter, Chiara and Elisa respectively, who tells the story of the adored mother, of her own segregated and solitary life, marked by a precocious old age and a substantial renunciation of the will to live. Inevitably, the choice of the narrating voice determines also the orientation of the point of view. In the case of Morante's novel this serves to lend a kind of therapeutic power to the literary word, rigidly delimiting Elisa's life and any possible existential mobility, while conversely guaranteeing, through art, an escape from neurosis; the apparently greater openness of Di Lascia's novel, a sort of "unfinished" state in which the story narrated in the novel slowly fades away, is on the contrary a more rigid closure that harbors no metaphysical faith.

> Questo silenzio—che si lascia esplorare come un mondo mediano dove il passato s'incarna nella fantasmagoria del sogno—attraversa la sconfinata regione della salvezza. Se chiudo gli occhi ne intravedo i santuari imponenti, dove si celebrano—fra ricchezze tanto meravigliose da parere irreali—i riti incantati della MEMORIA e del FUTURO.
>
> Eccoli! Avanzano scambiandosi gli identici volti, coi corpi intrecciati in una danza sincronica: entrambi sono giovani, entrambi sono vecchi e quando l'uno è giovane, l'altra veste il suo volto vecchio; e quando l'altro è vecchio, quella prende il suo volto giovane. Come la favola che inizia dove finisce, come la vita che segue alla morte, come il giorno che nasce dalla notte: essi sono gemelli e l'una vive nell'altro.
>
> Con un sospiro, guardo la pallida luce del giorno che se ne va con la sua ombra lunga sulle mie pezze: nessuno più mi chiamerà, nessuno mi verrà a cercare. Forse riceverò ancora qualche lettera da Titina e rivedrò la mia balia Rosina; forse incontrerò mio padre e ci arrenderemo a un sorriso.
>
> Forse, mi dico, forse. (*Passaggio in ombra* 266)

> This silence—which lets itself be explored like a median world where the past takes shape in the phantasmagoria of sleep—crosses the endless region of salvation. If I close my eyes I can glimpse the imposing sanctuaries where, among riches so marvelous as to appear unreal, the enchanted rites of MEMORY and the FUTURE are celebrated.
>
> Here they are! They advance, exchanging their identical faces, their bodies intertwined in a synchronic dance; and when the one is old the other takes on his young face. Just like the fairy tale that begins where it ends, like life that follows death, like day that is born of night: they are twins and the one lives within the other.
>
> With a sigh, I watch the pallid light of day that fades away, its long shadow on my rags: nobody will call me any more, nobody will come to look for me. Maybe I will still get the odd letter from Titina and I will see my nanny Rosina again; perhaps I will meet my father and we will yield ourselves up to a smile.
>
> Maybe, I say to myself, maybe.

The reader is also struck by some formal analogies in the organization of the narrative material: for instance, the titles of the short chapters that mark out the narration, and some important turns of the plot. For instance, the love for the cousin, which in Morante's *Menzogna e sortilegio* is attributed to the mother Anna and occupies a large narrative and symbolic space, is lived in the first person by the protagonist of *Passaggio in ombra*. Even while it is more restricted in its narrative dimension, it is nevertheless useful to signal the level of alienated virtual existence that Morante's Anna ends up inhabiting and to which, precisely because of this love, Di Lascia's young Chiara also seems to resign herself.

> Dopo questi fatti non è accaduto più nulla che non abbia già detto, e la mia vita è trascorsa nascosta, in luoghi sempre diversi, dove finanche il tempo ha stentato a trovarmi.
>
> Deve essere stato per questo [...] che il mio aspetto è rimasto a lungo inalterato, mentre il tempo saccheggiava i volti e i corpi dei miei conoscenti, rubando loro inesorabilmente la luce della giovinezza.
>
> Così, mentre le poche persone che ho conosciuto e con le quali ho avuto ancora vaghi e discontinui rapporti, hanno mostrato i segni di tutte le età della vita—rughe profonde come ferite o tratti divenuti misteriosamente consapevoli—

> io sola non ho avuto età intermedie e sono stata un'assurda giovinetta che un giorno precipitò nelle forme della vecchiezza. (*Passaggio in ombra* 257)

> After this nothing else happened that I haven't already spoken about, my life went by hidden, always in different places, where even time struggled to find me.
>   It must have been because of this [. . .] that my appearance remained exactly the same for a long time, while time was ravaging the faces and bodies of people I knew, inexorably stealing away from them the light of youth.
>   And so, while the few people I knew and with whom I still have vague and irregular contact have shown the signs of all the ages of life—deep lines like wounds or features that have become mysteriously knowing—I alone have had no intermediate age, and have been an absurd girl who one day suddenly plunged into the forms of old age.

In both novels, and in connection with the beloved cousin, two epistolaries are present; the one in Di Lascia's novel functions more to move the plot forward than as the event of mystery that so enhances its role in *Menzogna e sortilegio*.

To these numerous instances of formal and structural similarities we can add the striking and more general parallels: the motif of childhood and the passage to adulthood with the discovery of one's own difference; the absolute love for the prematurely deceased mother; a difficult and intermittent relationship with the paternal figure; the presence of a quasi-comical female character (the prostitute Rosaria in *Menzogna e sortilegio*, Aunt Giuseppina in *Passaggio in ombra*) who replaces the deceased mother; the setting in Southern Italy. Further similarities, too, are not hard to find.

These similarities do not undermine the autonomous value of Di Lascia's novel, amply demonstrated by the critical praise it received on publication, the awarding of the Strega prize in 1995, and a wide public readership. In fact *Passaggio in ombra*, even while it exhibits analogies that verge on the embarrassing, retains a high level of autonomy with respect to *Menzogna e sortilegio*. Nonetheless, this novel appears somewhat superficial if compared with its model; it has lost the philosophical underpinning of Morante's narrative, the extraordinary relationship between writing and the informing poetics and vision of Morante's world. I venture to state that this is a limitation common to all of Morante's "thematic heirs"; and, since the stylistic aspects of Morante's writing also obey the necessary connection between inspiring thought and formal sign, I think this explains why the expressive solutions adopted by Morante appear to be essential, while the same stylistic solutions in the prose of other writers, who remain at the surface level, appear as dubious mannerisms.

Carmelo Samonà

Among the authors that we can consider as heirs of Morante in one way or another, there is one instance that deserves attention for the attempt to construct a form endowed with a particular and intense meaning. This is the case of Carmelo Samonà. The fact that he was a personal friend of Morante's and wrote about her, producing some particularly fine pages on her musical tastes, are more than external signposts directing us to his literary references. In proclaiming him an authentic heir to Morante, I do not even consider decisive the fact that his protagonists are all derelict and suffering, caught up in that most nobly and profoundly moral of human endeavors, which is nonetheless tragic and destined to failure, which is the search for knowledge. Nor is it decisive that his novels are nourished by rich layers of symbolism or even allegory open to different interpretations at a connotational level and with reference to the philosophical dimension that they adumbrate. I would like to point out, however, that along with the other characteristics already mentioned, these belong properly to the work of Morante, whether in the senseless voyage of Manuele in *Aracoeli*, in the tragic delirium of Oedipus in *Il mondo salvato,* or even in the luminous and tormented passage of Arturo from adolescence on the island of Procida to the adulthood of *terra firma*: these are all narrative situations that reproduce, at the same time, a cognitive process. As for Morante's ability to use a specific narrative level in order to confer concrete significance to a wider symbolic level of reference, this is an aspect of the multiplicity and cultural wealth of Morante's writing, which critics have long recognized (Fortini 240).

But it is with regard to the most difficult aspect of Elsa Morante's work that I would recognize Samonà as her heir: he, too, possesses Morante's ability to make the formal facts essential in that they are intimately connected with the underlying reasons for writing, and transform some technical, rhetorical, formal, and linguistic procedures into philosophical categories. I am thinking of Morante's use of dialect, or at least dialect forms, in *La Storia* and *La serata a Colono*. While before I signaled this novel as a survival of Neorealism, this is a superficial critical consideration that seeks to reconstruct a literary trend. A closer look reveals that dialect is in fact the language of the poor, of the illiterate, of the marginalized, of the innocent: those who are outside the mechanisms of culture and power, and thus exempt from the sins of culture and power. It is thus the language itself that besides bearing witness to connections with literary trends, and being useful to a stylistic aim of variations and a linguistic aim of expressive enrichment and revitalization, becomes the bearer of meanings and values that occupy a central position in Morante's universe and thought.

Analogous to the use of dialect is the use of parody, a widely used rhetorical strategy in Morante's work, charged with structuring a number of narrative episodes. It is also a term that as it reappears in nuanced, mutated, and altered form, demonstrates the transformations that Morante's writing and thought have undergone. In *Menzogna e sortilegio* the parodic game is an element intrinsic to literary writing and lies at the heart of Morante's recuperation of numerous situations borrowed from the nineteenth-century novelistic tradition; also, in the part dealing with the description of the epistolary of the cousin, it allows for the reproduction of some stylistic lapses typical of the love prose in feuilletons. In *L'isola di Arturo* parody is adopted, as in *Aracoeli*, in the double garb of a rhetorical figure structuring some narrative shifts, and as a term bearing a particularly significant value, central to the interpretation of the novel: used as insult against Wilhelm, Arturo's father, it marks in fact the reversal of the paternal myth, just as in *Aracoeli* it contributes to denigrating the memory of the mother. In the *mondo salvato dai ragazzini* a whole text, *La serata a Colono*, of note for being the only theatrical work by Morante, carries the subtitle of "parody"; it is indeed a rewriting of Sophocles' tragedy, with all the characteristics of parodification apart from the comic one. In *Aracoeli*, besides the frequent and significant reappearance of the term, the parodic allusion maintains that element of reductionism seen as definitive by manuals of rhetoric, and continues to exploit the possibilities of the double stylistic register that the figure contains, presupposing the juxtaposition of two visible languages and two visible levels of writing. But it also accentuates the shedding of the comic element, if not perhaps to reach a sort of grotesque estrangement that is a frequent stylistic feature of the novel, or to utilize, if only rarely, the effects of comic automatism or mechanized comic grounded in repetition. But above all, by relegating the technical and rhetorical aspect to the background, parody becomes a significant value in itself: that is, parody is a vehicle of philosophical significance, a reading of the world and of literature that the whole novel sets out to illuminate.

It seems to me that Samonà has successfully managed to incorporate this trait of Morante's work within his own writing in a manner both original and personal. In the case of both *Fratelli* and *Il custode*, the underlying theme determines the structure, which does not appears as a form that pre-exists the narrative, but gives the impression of being born along with it and thus suggesting rhythm, measure, and character.

Fratelli and *Il custode* are two long monologues articulated around specific philosophical problems; within these monologues there are few properly narrative situations. The seeming formlessness of the monologue is tightly tied into the center by the first-person narrating voice. This narrating voice, or rather this narrative and philosophical instance, has a very strong centripetal capacity that does not depend on a strong psychic identity, given that very little is known about the "narrators" of the two novels. These psychological elements can be deduced only from the attitude they adopt with respect to the intellectual problem they are trying to solve. The narrators use a cultivated, highly controlled language, distinguished by a spareness that recalls some "humanistic" forms of scientific prose, occasionally shot through with a momentary lyrical touch. The minutest of actions can find space in the novel, if they are functional to the illumination of the central philosophical problem. More than real characters, these narrators are philosophical cyphers, rhetorically personified, placed at the center of the narrative so that they can articulate and make manifest their problematics in a manner that can be correctly identified as narrative.

In *Fratelli* we see the relationship between a man and his mad brother, whom he attempts to watch over and cure. They live in an enormous ruined house, in which they play their theatrical games, they love each other, they search for each other, they hate each other, and they try to assault one another ... But behind this surface aspect, most certainly a narrative of tension and suspense, there is another layer inseparable from the story, which is the philosophical problem of the limits and capacity of reason that finds itself compelled to face an irreducible intellectual, cultural, and emotional alterity.

Da un momento all'altro un'oscura inquietudine ci sovrasta. Il rimprovero è scattato come una battuta fuori dal testo, il gioco si ferma, le nostre braccia, le nostre mani si sfiorano, trattenendo, con mosse ancora agili da commedia, un'attesa di minacce. Evito di guardare mio fratello negli occhi. Con un guizzo, come se restassi fedele al meccanismo del gioco, mi porto lontano da lui. Mi nascondo ancora nelle nebbie della finzione. E di nuovo ci rincorriamo. Ma sento che ora la corsa di chi sta dietro ha l'ansimare corto e ritmato di una caccia implacabile. E' vero, io sono quel nemico da eliminare per gioco, mio fratello insegue in me il rapitore della fanciulla; eppure ho la sensazione precisa che sta braccando, nei panni del personaggio, il mio corpo; sento che sta correndo ad annientare il nemico-fratello che l'ha accusato di disobbedire alle giuste leggi del tempo. Nel suo abbraccio, che subisco passivamente se mi raggiunge, avverto un'ambiguità di impulsi trafelati, tremanti: il palmo di una mano guadagna presto le mie guance, ed è per accarezzarle, ma le dita dell'altra frugano tra i miei capelli come per cercare una presa, mirando, irte ed ostili, a chiudersi a tenaglia sulla mia nuca. (*Fratelli* 48–49)

From one moment to the next an obscure sense of unease washes over us. The reproach was sharp, like a note out of tune, the game stops, our arms, our hands brush each other, and with the agile moves of a drama they still hold an expectation of threat. I avoid looking my brother in the eyes. Like a flash, as if I was sticking to the rules of the game, I move away from him. I am still hiding in the fogs of fiction. And once more we chase each other. But I sense that now the chase of the one who is behind has the short, rhythmic panting of an implacable hunter. It's true, I am the enemy who is to be eliminated in a game, my brother is pursuing in

213

me the one who has run off with the girl; and yet I have the precise sensation that within the clothes of the character he is hunting down my body; I sense that he is running to annihilate the enemy-brother who has accused him of disobeying the just laws of time. In his embrace, which I bear passively if he comes near me, I feel an ambiguity of trembling impulses: the palm of a hand soon reaches my cheek, to stroke it, but the fingers of the other hand are running through my hair as if to find a hold; hostile and rigid, they seek to close like a vice on the back of my neck.

The story's tension thus hinges on the need, driven by powerful affective and mental motivations, to decipher a logic that never lets itself be reduced to the shared, culturally dominant one as defined by Aristotle, and that has come down to us almost intact. The narrative suspense leads to a sort of reversal in the dense confrontation between the forces in play, until the crazy brother, enclosed in his arcane world and incapable of communication, manages to shake to the core the universe of agreed certainties, and his own silence, which seemed forced upon him, ends up by appearing an enigmatic choice and a cruel request:

"Brigante—gli dico—perché scappi proprio quando ti chiamo? So bene che sei tu ogni mattina a bussare alla mia porta e a sparire. Un giorno o l'altro perderò la pazienza, e invece di raggiungerti qua, sarò io a nascondermi in una stanza segreta e a rimanerci per sempre.

"Cercami—è la sua strana risposta: la voce è tremula e sorda, le parole, sillabate e staccate l'una dall'altra, ripropongono un vecchio invito.—Cercami di nuovo— aggiunge—anche se mi hai trovato.

E mi fissa a lungo coi suoi occhi di cane perché io pronunci la parola esatta che sembra aspettarsi da me. Io che ignoro quella parola, lo guardo a mia volta con espressione interrogativa restando come lui, per qualche minuto, in attesa. (*Fratelli* 35)

"Brigand," I say to him, "why do you run away when I call you? I know it's you every morning who comes to knock on my door and then disappears. One of these days I'll lose my patience and instead of coming to join you here, it'll be me who hides in a secret room, never to come out."

> "Come and look for me" is his strange reply: his voice is thick and trembling, his words, separated out from each other, offer the old invitation. "Come and look for me again" he adds, "even though you've already found me."
>
> He stares at me for a long time with his dog's eyes, willing me to pronounce the exact word he seems to be expecting from me. Not knowing what this word is, I look at him in my turn with a questioning expression and, like him, I stand there for a few moments, waiting.

The double register, narrative and philosophic/interpretative, functions perfectly, each endowed with complete autonomy; but it is clearly the philosophical in which is rooted not only the persuasive power but also the intensity of the narrative: it is a lucid and intellectual tension, a genuinely philosophical exploration, which entrusts to the more broadly expressive genre that is narrative, the rendition of the tragic loss and final defeat experienced by Western culture: "Vi sono momenti in cui mi sembra d'essere vicino a uno spiraglio di verità, di cogliere una trasparenza simile a un significato intero. Mi concentro, in questi casi, e arresto ogni movimento" (*Fratelli* 112; "There are moments in which I feel as though I am near a spiral of truth, as though I can grasp a transparency similar to an entire meaning. In these moments I concentrate, and cease any movement").

In *Il custode* a man segregated in a room, for unknown reasons, by invisible guards, tries to re-create the free spaces that are denied him, reconstructing the external world through fantasy, dreams, and the rare moments of physical experience available to him. Using the few clues to come his way, he builds up a picture of his guards and weaves a precarious and exhausting conversation with them:

> La molla della mia resistenza è un sentimento di sfida, non un calcolo di possibilità materiali. E i miei punti d'appoggio sono proprio gli oggetti da cui non posso fuggire: la branda su cui riposo; la finestra inutile; la porta dalla quale, attraverso uno spioncino, chiunque può osservarmi in qualsiasi momento senza essere visto da me; persino il breve tramezzo che mi nasconde, in un angolo della stanza, la miseria innocua di un cesso e di un lavandino.

> Col tempo, senza curarmi dei vantaggi immediati che posso trarne, ho cominciato a tessere intorno a queste cose una tela stranamente futile e intensa, dove i capricci della fantasia si alternano alle scoperte e alle deduzioni oggettive. Posseggo una piccola scorta di conoscenze che coincide appena, e a fatica, con la mia stanza, eppure afferro e rielaboro dentro di me orizzonti minutamente articolati, sonorità impercettibili che, prima, mi erano ignote. Posso, col pensiero, dilatare queste cose fino a costruire universi, benché l'ampiezza delle mie congetture contrasti con la povertà dei miei sensi; posso formulare ipotesi illimitate, benché non sappia neppure com'è il profilo esterno di questa casa e distingua solo a momenti il timbro di una voce da un frusciare di passi sull'impiantito. (*Il custode* 10–11)

The coil of my resistance is a sentiment of challenge, not a calculation of material possibilities. The things I lean on are exactly the objects from which I cannot escape: the camp bed I sleep on, the useless window, the door and its spyhole through which anybody can observe me at any time without me being able to see them; even the short screen which hides from view the harmless wretchedness of a toilet and washbasin.

Over time, and without thinking about the immediate advantages to be gained, I have begun to weave a strangely futile and intense web around these things, where the whims of fantasy alternate with discoveries and objective deductions. I have a little store of knowledge that barely and with difficulty coincides with my room, and yet I can grasp and rework within myself minutely articulated horizons, imperceptible sounds that before were unknown to me. With my thought I can expand these things outwards and construct entire universes, although the breadth of my conjectures is in sharp contrast with the impoverishment of my senses; I can formulate unlimited hypotheses, even though I don't even know what the outside of this house looks like and only now and then catch the vibration of a voice or the rustle of steps on the landing.

Here, too, narration springs from a philosophical problem, which has to do with the possibilities available to the human mind, limited by physical and rational ties, when it is forced to think and somehow experience the mysterious. In this case mystery is articulated and fragmented without becoming more knowable, in the impenetrability of other human beings, and in the impossibility of learning anything about them beyond the patchy and incongruous; and even more so in the obscurity that shields nature and animality, to be glimpsed only in minute and ungraspable flashes. And in the midst of all this incomprehensible limitedness, there is still an improbable yet never extinguished impulse to reach a metaphysical dimension that nothing, outside of impossible faith, authorizes us to postulate or to imagine.

Dying prematurely in March 1990, Samonà left a final, unfinished novel, *Casa Landau*, which was published at the end of the same year. The theme is the same as that which runs through the two previous novels—a desperate search around a mysterious nucleus. But this time the similarity with Morante is even closer. Not just because Casa Landau is a decrepit villa that boasts a glorious past long gone, and not just because it houses a ghost—images and situations that are a clear reference to *Menzogna e sortilegio* and *Aracoeli*. The strongest analogy seems to me the literary game that Samonà plays in this novel: in order to solve the indecipherable mystery that is in the air, the young protagonist turns to the great novels of the past, altering their plots to fit the situation he is himself experiencing in *Casa Landau*:

> Ogni giorno la mia casa palpitava di ombre, le strade della città si animavano di occhiate oblique, di voci rotte, affannate, che riecheggiavano a brani, a frammenti, parole, esclamazioni, intere frasi trasmigrate dai libri. Era una dura fatica, per me, raggiungerle col mio "secondo sguardo," *vederle*, ritoccarne gli esiti e qualche volta i destini intervenendo sui testi; ma era anche motivo d'orgoglio che stessero là da secoli, probabilmente in attesa, e che io solo riuscissi, con la mia fantasia, a chiamarle a raccolta e a rivestirle coi corpi e con le voci di persone viventi. (*Casa Landau* 57; emphasis in original)

> Every day my house palpitated with shadows, the roads in the city were alive with oblique glances, broken, breathless voices that echoed passages, fragments, words, exclamations, entire sentences that had migrated from books. It was a real struggle for me to reach them with my "second look," to *see* them, to redirect their outcomes and sometimes their

destinies by intervening in the texts; but it was also a source of pride that they had been there for centuries, probably just waiting, and that I alone, with my imaginative fantasy, could gather them up and clothe them with the bodies and voices of living persons.

In this sense the clearest analogy has to do with a less-known work by Morante, "Il gioco segreto," a fascinating story from the collection *Lo scialle andaluso*, where literature becomes the sole consolation of three unhappy brothers who are unable to establish a healthy relationship with reality: the creatures of their fantasy feed on books read in secret, finally coming to life, just as happens for the ghosts of the young protagonist in *Casa Landau*, who are also able to live if they are intertwined with the lives of literary characters:

> La stanza cominciò ad agitarsi. I volti (e i nomi) dei personaggi mi vennero incontro dalle pareti. Qualcuno era dietro la porta, un fruscìo delicato mi avvertì che una mano, due mani premevano per entrare. Mi sentivo proteso a un inveramento più forte di tutti quelli ai quali, fino ad allora, avevo creduto di assistere. (*Casa Landau* 64)

> The room began to move. The faces (and names) of the characters came toward me from the walls. Someone was behind the door, a delicate rustling alerted me that a hand, two hands, were pressing on it to come in. I felt that I was about to see a coming to life much more powerful than all the others I thought I had seen up to now.

The secret game can be interpreted as a mirroring of all of Morante's writing, or indeed of all literary writing possessing great aesthetic value. It can also be seen as the potentially vital fruit of all legacies. Tradition produces pieces of a mosaic that can be deployed as in a jig-saw puzzle, to give life to one's own writing. In her own work Elsa Morante used chivalric novels, lines from the *Divine Comedy*, Greek tragedy, German romantic poetry as well as Rimbaud, Dostoyevsky, and Kafka. But in using this great wealth, with the skill that games permit and indeed demand, she renewed the tradition that preceded her and rooted within it her own specific originality.

Notes

1. Speaking of which, I do not think it is mere chance that Italian writers seem mostly to appreciate Calvino's *Lezioni americane* (*Six Memos to the Next Millennium*) and, to underline the point, his last narrative works in which the critical consciousness of the writer comes to the fore.

2. Debenedetti's "L'isola della Morante" is probably still one of the most insightful studies on this novel. Most of Garboli's writings on Elsa Morante are now collected in *Il gioco segreto. Nove immagini di Elsa Morante*.

3. By Berardinelli one should look at least at "Il sogno della cattedrale. Elsa Morante e il romanzo come archetipo."

4. A revised translation of this essay appears in the present volume (257–67).

5. For a comparison between Di Lascia's novel and *Menzogna e sortilegio*, see the essay by Lucamante, "*Passaggio in ombra*: riprese, innovazioni e soluzioni tematico-strutturali in un romanzo morantiano."

Works Consulted

Berardinelli, Alfonso. "Il sogno della cattedrale. Elsa Morante e il romanzo come archetipo." *Per Elsa* 1–33.

Bettin, Gianfranco. *Qualcosa che brucia*. Milan: Garzanti, 1989.

Bloom, Harold. *The Western Canon: The Books and School of the Ages*. New York: Harcourt, 1994.

Cases, Cesare. *Patrie lettere*. Turin: Einaudi, 1987.

Cavalli, Patrizia. *Poesie (1974–1992)*. Turin: Einaudi, 1992.

D'Angeli, Concetta, and Giacomo Magrini, eds. "Vent'anni dopo *La storia*: Omaggio a Elsa Morante." Spec. issue of *Quaderni novecenteschi* 47–48 (June–Dec. 1994).

Debenedetti, Giacomo. "L'isola della Morante." *Saggi 1922–1966*. Ed. Franco Contorbia. Milan: Mondadori, 1963. 379–96.

Di Lascia, Mariateresa. *Passaggio in ombra*. Milan: Feltrinelli, 1995.

Ferrante, Elena. *L'amore molesto*. Rome: edizioni e/o, 1992.

Ferroni, Giulio. "Elsa Morante." *Storia della letteratura italiana. Il Novecento*. Turin: Einaudi, 1991. 547–61.

Fofi, Goffredo. "I riti della memoria e del futuro: il romanzo di Mariateresa Di Lascia." *Linea d'ombra* 104 (May 1995): 43–44.

Fortini, Franco. *Nuovi saggi italiani*. Milan: Garzanti, 1987.

Garboli, Cesare. *Il gioco segreto. Nove immagini di Elsa Morante.* Milan: Adelphi, 1995.

La Porta, Filippo. *La nuova narrativa italiana. Travestimenti e stili di fine secolo.* New edition. Turin: Bollati Boringhieri, 1999.

Lucamante, Stefania. "*Passaggio in ombra:* riprese, innovazioni e soluzioni tematico-strutturali in un romanzo morantiano." *Italian Culture* 15 (1997): 269–95.

Lukács, Gÿorgÿ. *Scritti sul realismo.* Turin: Einaudi, 1978.

Mengaldo, Pier Vincenzo. "Spunti per un'analisi linguistica dei romanzi di Elsa Morante." D'Angeli and Magrini 11–36

Morante, Elsa. *Opere.* Vol. 2. Milan: Mondadori, 1990.

Palandri, Enrico. "Alcune notazioni in margine a *Pro o contro la bomba atomica.*" D'Angeli and Magrini 79–90.

———. *Boccalone.* Milan: L'erba voglio, 1979.

Per Elsa Morante. Milan: Linea d'ombra, 1993.

Ramondino, Fabrizia. *Athénopsis.* Turin: Einaudi, 1981.

Samonà, Carmelo. *Casa Landau.* Milano: Garzanti, 1990.

———. *Il custode.* Turin: Einaudi, 1983.

———. *Fratelli.* Milan: Garzanti, 1978.

Sinibaldi, Marino. "'La storia' e la politica. Gli analfabeti degli anni settanta." *Per Elsa* 205–18.

Stefania Lucamante

Teatro di guerra

Of History and Fathers

This study of *Althénopis* and *Guerra di infanzia e di Spagna,* by the Neapolitan writer Fabrizia Ramondino, suggests that Ramondino's characters, family sagas, and even the ever-transient position she assigns to her narrators, could not properly be comprehended without taking into full account the suggestive presence of Elsa Morante's novels, and her particular sense of life as a large-scale baroque mise-en-scène.[1] The notion of war as a futile theater for demonstrations of power and authority is represented first in *Menzogna e sortilegio* through a subjective narrating I-eye, and later through *La Storia*'s omniscient narrator. I argue that, while not directly dealing with issues of philosophy and ethics, Morante and Ramondino propose in their works a literary revisitation of some of the tenets on which modern Western civilization is based, namely, war and the position of individuals, particularly children, within its orbit, based on a common conceptualization of human action in the terms perceived by Hannah Arendt in *The Human Condition.*[2]

Secondly, in Ramondino's works mnemonic data tend to overlap with fictional ones as they construct an obvious pattern of similarities with the empirical author's life.[3] This second instance also resonates with Morante's position vis-à-vis her texts, as eloquently illustrated by Marco Bardini in his volume on the Roman author.[4] Morante's working process was one in which her own life was transformed in the construction of fictional events that often acquired fablelike qualities of suspension from time and retrieval in the no-man's land of childhood. This essay, then, proposes to read Ramondino's texts in the context of a Morantian legacy.

221

Stefania Lucamante

Morante's Legacy

Twenty years after her death, Elsa Morante's presence in the Italian literary panorama represents what someone defines as the typical "artistic model," someone who, citing Harold Bloom, broke "the canon only by aesthetic strength" (29) with no extra-merits except the complexity of her work, which, considered almost anachronistic in her times, resonates strongly with contemporary thinking in its insistence on the (negative) notion of Power(s). Several publications in the 1990s have called for a proper reassessment of Morante's role in Italian and international contemporary literature. A famous essay by Amos Oz, "'Into Mother's Bosom': On Several Beginnings in Elsa Morante's *History: A Novel*," eloquently manifests how acclaimed authors inscribe the writer's work within a large corpus of novelistic writing with intellectual and ethical pursuits. While Oz's article argues for the extrapolation of more universalist issues from the novel *La Storia*, her collective work is considered to be a necessary point of reference for those writers interested in investigating family memories, in conjunction with a particular construction of identity under the shadow of an oppressive Southern Italian society. Pier Paolo Pasolini at an earlier stage of Morante's work,[5] and Goffredo Fofi later, both decreed non-existent the supposed "uniqueness" that would make her work isolated, not available to future intertextual references. In short, they rejected the concept of her work in the terms of an artistic "island" that Cesare Garboli always maintained in his criticism. On the contrary, both Pasolini and Fofi insist on the effectiveness of her model, vigorously arguing that she constructed a new path of influence within Italian literature. In the work of some authors, most evidently Mariateresa Di Lascia's *Passaggio in ombra*,[6] Morante's heritage is important in the reprise of the structure of *Menzogna e sortilegio*, for the ghost of her dense and suffocating family setting underlies every word the cyclothymic character of Chiara utilizes to narrate her personal history and that of her family. Morante's model thus emerges in what is perhaps the most apparent evidence of a by now affirmed "canonicity": structure, characters, setting, and undertones used in *Passaggio in ombra* are strikingly similar to those of *Menzogna e sortilegio*. Elena Ferrante's first novel, *L'amore molesto*, similarly employs Morantian undertones, particularly in the portrayal of the very intricate relations of a Neapolitan family. The shadow of the love triangle, a pattern evident in *Menzogna e sortilegio*, reappears here in all its ambiguity, casting doubt on the solidity of the Southern family institution. Family interrelationships present Morantian overtones: the beautiful mother; the problematic daughter who, like Elisa, spends much of her time in perfect isolation; her unspoken competition and sense of rivalry with respect to the mother figure she desperately loves certainly make of this novel, however different in its outcome as a thriller, a Morantian one.

The inclination to a lyrical writing style is another component and *trait-d'union* between, for instance, Di Lascia and Morante; this lyricism is also a feature of the work of Fabrizia Ramondino, suggesting a powerful inheritance from Morante. Ramondino is a particularly prominent heir of Morante's from both a formal and a thematic point of view, even if this influence is less obvious than in the case of Di Lascia or Ferrante.[7] Ramondino's masterful writing creates an epic of its own, independent of intertextuality, yet the rich texture of her writing is enhanced by a dialectical sense of the legacy of the older writer that suffuses Ramondino's pages. It seems to be an almost parallel, and yet entirely personal, journey through the intricacies of family relations, childhood memories, and the construction of identity. While Ramondino and Morante are equally intolerant of mannerism, of any possible literary calque, nonetheless Ramondino shares Morante's anti-conventional path of love for tradition and the past. Ramondino's most obvious influences (Cervantes, Leiris, Cocteau, Rilke, Benjamin, the anarchists of *L'isola riflessa* such as Rossi and Spinelli)[8] further suggest affinities between the two writers.

Fabrizia Ramondino's polished, refined style exhibits a commitment to a flexible and plastic language that incorporates linguistic elements from the Neapolitan vernacular as well as from other languages. Italo Calvino's lecture on precision finds an answer in her fixation on the "perfect" word constructing the image; her artful and unorthodox manner crosses almost intuitively the dangerous boundaries of the 1970s' and 1980s' feminist essentialism[9] and traditional European *bellelettrism.*

This acute and often unsympathetic writer, far from any stereo-typical conceptualization of *Napoletanità* and closer in attitude to Anna Maria Ortese and Clotilde Marghieri, examines a complex world, simultaneously eviscerating the most intimate problems of a community and submitting herself to profound self-scrutiny.

In Ramondino's works autobiographical writing develops along two vectors. Her nonfiction works document her interest in social issues mediated through a *flâneuse* who is ingeniously placed to connect the reflections on society and travel in a concise and yet lyrical form. In an opposite direction, her autobiographism practices the fictional genres of the novel and the short story through an existential itinerary in which personal data are felicitously combined with the datum of *inventio*. As in Gadda and Leiris, footnotes appear in the pages of *Althénopis*, making of this paratextual element one of her writing's most salient characteristics. They have an explanatory function but also serve as immediate evidence of how recollection works as "interpretation" of the past events. While Morante will eventually abandon the essayistic style that was one of the modes composing the texture of *Menzogna e sortilegio* for greater lyricism (although never entirely devoid of dramatic undertones, as in *L'isola di Arturo*) or poetry as in the case of *Alibi,* the essayistic approach pervades nearly all Ramondino's works.[10]

Morante's and Ramondino's works, with images at times charged with overtones of magic realism, could misleadingly be considered as connected to the separate world of imagination. Yet the visionary element and the descriptions of dreams, particularly in the case of Morante, only reveal the actual gravity of the human condition they narrate. These are fictional realities where the most urgent discourses, whether ideological, political, or aesthetic, make display of the pleasure of narrating stories, infantile anecdotes (the fablelike quality of narrative), and are never devoid of the poetic aspect that is indispensable to a revision of the role of psychology in the novel genre. Structurally, Morante's and Ramondino's works are purposefully devoid of the structural centrality that a chronological sequence of events would normally guarantee fiction. For through fiction we find reality or else, as Morante noted, "[u]n vero romanzo, dunque, è sempre realistico, anche il più favoloso" ("Sul romanzo" 50; "a true novel, then, is always realistic, even the most imaginative one"). Starting with the most obvious nucleus for normative laws, the family, Morante and Ramondino move on to expand their perceptions on human action, which far from being the work of one individual, is always that of many. An individual is apolitical, according to Arendt; only in the company of others is political action possible. Action and reaction thus take on a different meaning from political theories in fictional prose, and move toward the utopian social and ideological universe Morante, and later Ramondino, aim for. Both fundamentally and profoundly refuse to come to terms with history and politics, the disastrous effects of which it is for ordinary people to endure; thus they engage in a struggle with the Pirandellian mask as they attempt to unveil Reality against its imposed notions. In the unveiling of masks, the traditional role of the father as played in Morante and Ramondino's fiction determines a forced yet superficial submission of women and children to the laws of politics and statehood, Arturo's "CERTEZZE ASSOLUTE," that the power of literature manages (at least on a theoretical basis) to elicit and combat. But authority is a concept that cannot be peacefully accepted by the narrators, as not even the mother escapes from this act of moral rebellion toward authority at large in the work of both writers.

Autobiographical episodes in all of Ramondino's works are charged with essayistic annotations, interweaving fiction and history, as so eloquently characterized in *Time and Narrative* by Paul Ricoeur (188–92). In *Althénopis,* Morante's legacy is particularly traceable in the reinterpretation of childhood through the use of memory. The narrator, also the main character, a young Neapolitan girl, reveals the panorama of her broken yet strangely cohesive extended family, itself an allegorical version of Southern Italy. The narrative voices portray the decay of her social class through the telling of analeptic episodes that elicit continuous comparisons between life in downtown Naples after the war and that in Santa Maria del Mare, the village where her family took refuge during the war. In this fictional narrative about childhood in Campania in the aftermath of World War II, Ramondino reinscribes a blurred autobiographical aspect of her life, empowering the use of personal memory with the tools of fictional narrative. Its subjective facet permeates the whole work, thus becoming relevant to the hermeneutics of the text, a work too generically categorized as either *novel* or *autobiography,* the simultaneous presence of both impeding categorical statements in both generic vectors.[11] This oscillation is what Sidonie Smith and Julie Watson note in stating that, "(a)utobiographical writing surrounds us, but the more it surrounds us, the more it defies generic stabilization, the more its laws are broken, the more it drifts toward other practices, the more formerly 'out-law' practices drift into its domain" (xviii).

Althénopis adopts the specific properties neither of fictional writing, nor of traditional autobiography. In her double subjectivity as protagonist and narrator of her story, the protagonist investigates her past in order to understand the essence, fears, and neuroses of her adult self in the present tense of writing and remembering, which thus becomes an act of hermeneutics. The "formerly 'out-law practices,'" the intersection of autobiography and fiction as outlined by Smith and Watson, find their narrative medium in Ramondino's employment of focalization: the eye of a grown-up woman that retrospectively analyzes some of the most significant past events of her existence. The double use of autobiographical data in the novel *Althénopis*, whose title, indeed, means, "Old Woman's Eye," thus becomes apparent.

In her most recent work, *Guerra di infanzia e di Spagna,* Ramondino analyzes her pre-*Althénopis* years, thus filling an important gap for the comprehension of the construction of her identity. She does so both as a writer and as an individual who is subject to the nonsensical and yet tragic events of the Spanish Civil War as witnessed during her stay in Majorca (1937– 44), where her father was consul. While her Majorca appears similar to the one portrayed in some poems by Jean Cocteau, her revision of time in terms of history, parental relationships, and paternal authority appear in strict relation with tragic public events. In *Guerra di infanzia e di Spagna* tenets already elicited in *Althénopis* and other works such as *Storie di patio* and *Star di casa* return to be further examined.

Althénopis

I have previously spoken of the difficulties of attributing a precise genre to *Althénopis* (Lucamante, "Le scelte" and "Tra
romanzo e autobiografia"). Not only is there no paratextual element to identify the work as novel or autobiography; the name
of the narrating "I" in *Althénopis*, whether fictional or actual,
remains unstated. The editing process oversees memories in a
configuration of the past that subscribes to a particular form of
utopia. The degree of approximation by which one remembers
what time has *dis*membered can produce increasingly accurate
memories, but never precisely the same event in all its dynamics. In many artistic operations in the feminine, the subjective
authorial data assume characteristics fundamental to the development of the narration, particularly in that of entire family
genealogies that follow a matrilineal order. In the case of
Ramondino, then, the anamnestic moment prevails in the
process of recounting her family and her female relatives, her
turbulent relationship with the rich cultural heritage and geography of Naples, and her engagement in politics and diverse
social initiatives. The author's strategy of self-representation
introduces personal facts, easily comparable to her real life,
which are then deprived of the anticipated autobiographic
specificity provided by dates or personal names, sometimes
without providing the reader with other expected information,
including the fictional. While Arendt claims that finding refuge
in our own intimacy is essential, she also claims that there is a
specific, performative need to act *outside* the "room" of one's
mind, as *action* becomes such only in the presence of others
(131). As Emanuella Scarano noted in her reading of *Menzogna e sortilegio* (152–53), the character-narrator Elisa enacts
such performance in the intimacy of her room in the company
of her characters. Such need for action will find its most necessary solution in the divulgatory message of *La Storia*'s omniscient narrator. A work of art keeps its physiognomy regardless
of whether or not we know the name of the author (Arendt 132).

Althénopis was published seven years after *La Storia*. While
few years separate these two novels of war and childhood, a
certain structural difference is highly noticeable. In Morante's
novel, apart from the strongly autobiographical character of
Davide Segre and from inferences the narrator makes in the

course of her narration, there is no attempt at an intradiegetic narrative intervention. This strategy allows the omniscient narrator to present events according to a perspective that is entirely different from "official," institutionalized historiographic discourse. Facts that evidently coincide might bring us to the author's life, as they refer to the war period. However, they cannot mislead the readers about the message of the text. The scandal of war is the protagonist of the work, and is not to be disturbed by an intradiegetic narrator whose vicissitudes could distract readers from the main point of the *grand mal* ("great sickness") affecting us all. Useppe remains the central nucleus of beauty and innocence placed against a barbarian war; an intradiegetic narrator would have disallowed the universalizing tone that described the violence of "la Storia" and the despair into which it compels human beings. In *Althénopis,* recollection is configured as a hermeneutical act *tout court*: the selection of words to bring to mind images of the past serves as an interpretative act on time past, re-enacting an "event of appropriation" (the Heideggerian *Ereignis*) that takes place when man steps back for the understanding of the principles linking us to the Being (Heidegger 25). Genette's fitting metaphor of autobiography as a revolving door reshapes the very same boundaries of the paraliterary/literary genre, allowing personal data to build a fictional work, where the two realms are always intertwining, or weaving, the construction of an existence. Furthermore, in the act of reading, these elements drawn from the different worlds of autobiography and fiction allow the reader to double constantly the possibilities of entering the text while the author of the recollection attempts to assess the validity of childhood truths or myths, if they exist, when experiencing the act of writing/recollecting.[12]

The process of *Andenken* works, thus, both ways, for the narrator, likely to be identified with the author because of life experiences evoked in the text, and for the reader who inevitably reflects upon the *vraisemblance* of narratorial enunciations. The "non-naming" of the narrator in *Althénopis,* particularly as a child in the first and second parts of the book, is in part prompted by the necessity of reintegration-reinvention of yet another personality as opposed to the one at the origin of the investigation. This erasure, one of Ramondino's most interesting fictional games, corresponds to the "non-naming" of World War II in the book. War is always present but is defined because of its very absence in the narrative refiguration in the same way the narrator's presence is, because, as we shall realize at the end of the second part of the book, its definition of "senseless tragedy" will be found by the narrator. The reader learns by comparison, by reference to another object, and by the vicinity of the other object as related to the first, how the narrator has come to terms with historical and personal facts. It is not by isolation that the narrator learns of events, but by carefully excluding/including others within her life. Following the voluntary elision of her name, we are witnesses now to the elision of the *topos bellicum,* or post-*bellicum.* We witness the elision of a motif that, at least tangentially, should have affected the narrator's childhood years if only in mere chronological approximation. Eliciting curiosity by elision creates a strong contrast with the richness of details offered in the description of everyday life of *Althénopis*'s characters. "Elision" is also a term that reminds us of Elisa, the narrator and character of *Menzogna e sortilegio.* She who felt elided by the world of adults describes precisely that very world, but in her own words. The same decisional power about what needs to be related brings together the two young women, Elisa and her companion in *Althénopis,* in the construction of a fresco about Southern Italy. Far from being presented as the central theme as in the case of *La Storia,* the war topos is presented almost incidentally in *Althénopis.* The rhetorical figures that "find again" (metaphor) and "reset" (metonymy) in movement time lost are mindful of Proust's sense of time. The reader discovers otherwise its magnitude through a process elicited by the metonymic essence of the following motifs: the girl and the village; the war in *Althénopis* and its absence from the "place" where the little girl lives, the setting of the first part of the book in which the narrative is deceptively divided; the city and society; the village and the peasants; the space inscribed in the kitchen of the villas and the workers, the *salotti* and the minor aristocracy. The author's selection for such combinatory choices establishes once more the evidence that the tropes of metaphor cannot make memory relive without the metonymic imagery as Gerard Genette theorizes *à propos* Proust.[13] It is their relationship in these analogies that liberates their essence and reason for being in this spatial-temporal Elysium. Observing the topos of the complex relations between adults and children resuscitated in the analepses reconfirms the Proustian referent (also via Morante) that such relations reveal in the story.

Of History and Private Histories

In an article on Walter Benjamin's history theses, Maurizia Boscagli illustrates the theoretical similarities between the German thinker and Elsa Morante's treatment of history in *La Storia*. Boscagli claims that Morante "complicates" Benjamin's theories in the *Theses* through gender and gender oppression, but without fetishizing women "as the only object of history" (137). The critic notes how for both, history is first and foremost narration, "a cultural practice that takes shape in the always already colonized territory of language" (132). The practices by which Benjamin and Morante deconstruct the traditional tenets of historiography are interestingly both based on irrationality (Boscagli 132). While for Benjamin it is Jewish Messianism, in the case of Morante it is her use of an "irrational," "unorthodox religious discourse" that allows her to reject Italian bourgeois values and affirm the supremacy of a utopian system. Within her narrative discourse the oppressed position themselves within the interstices of official history. She is fully convinced, as Boscagli maintains, that "marginal history is a flash that could never be seen again, depending on who constructs and manages the circulation of this memory" (135). Boscagli sees Morante's *La Storia* as being "constituted by a series of intermittent *Jetztzeiten*, moments of historical rupture when the Other of history is made visible" (135) in which, while private and public discourses are apparently kept separate, there is the intuition that the latter strongly affect the former in a "contradictory relationship" between History and stories. Concetta D'Angeli's structural division of the novel's temporal levels reaches conclusions similar to Boscagli's, noting the impact of the time of narration on the remaining three levels.[14] With the time of narration, extensive compared to the scant pages introducing each year/chapter of the book, Morante establishes the priority for the time of the oppressed. She also invites us to consider the need for a "grey zone" within the system of characters that recalls Primo Levi's views in *If This Is a Man* and *The Drowned and the Saved*. Everybody is defeated by war, particularly the oppressed, whether these be women, children, or the young Gunther. After raping Ida in his brief stay in Rome, and without fighting the enemy, Gunther dies, his airplane attacked between Europe and Africa. Gunther rapes Ida, but, as an electrician back in Dachau, he also repairs her light. He both gives light and helps bring Useppe to light. A melodramatic aspect is added to the character of the "invader" as the book opens on this scene of rape in Ida's *caseggiato*. Morante acknowledges that war is imposed upon all sides in the conflict, that the consequences are lived by everybody, and that, even in exceptional events such as World War II and the *Shoah*, forgiveness needs to be applied to humans whose role was nothing but a walk-on part, as in the case of Gunther. She applies that Arendtian sense of forgiveness that should never be mistaken for weakness or failure to address juridically war crimes, but instead, as Sigrid Weigel puts it, should be seen as a "desire for forgiveness that concerns the unforgivable" (322). While it is the rulers who take decisions and bear moral responsibilities, there is here a strong defense for those who are forced, sometimes through indoctrination, to enter a conflict. The "oppressed" are those unable to construct their own destiny. Just like the innocent child of *Althénopis*, the child in *Guerra di infanzia e di Spagna*, and *La Storia*'s Ida Ramundo and Useppe, are all unaware of the role of History in their lives, or impotent before it, intent only on survival in the face of the rhetoric of Fascism(s). Gunther, too, suffers the imposition of History, dying after unwittingly spawning the divine creature Useppe. It is the ideological role of the authors to avenge the destiny of such characters.

The similarity between Morante's and Ramondino's conceptualizations of historical discourse is striking. In a progressive discovery and construction of the narratorial self through the process of recollection and destruction of childhood myths, the same concepts are maintained. The topic constituted by

Stefania Lucamante

Morante's personal dislike of the traditional conceptualizations of History, Country, and authority are reworked within the parameters of Ramondino's use of personal remembrance of childhood years. The rejection of a nationalistic fanaticism leading inevitably to war finds a path of fictional interpretation in *Althénopis* particularly through the complex, Morantian quality of the relationships established between children and adults during extraordinary wartimes, relations, and events whose role in the creation of neurosis is gradually untangled, evolving through the chronological period from the end of World War II, an age of decline and loss of security among the Italian Southern bourgeoisie and the minor aristocracy.

The antonymy between the city and the village offers a framework for the small girl's personality: she feels like an intruder in the *ville* ("the mansions"), where reason imposes itself on impulse, forbidding spontaneity of the *gioco* ("game") that is allowed instead in the square of Santa Maria del Mare. But not only this troubles her. The notion of never really *belonging* to any of these groups affects her coming of age just as much as her knowledge of things adults are only dimly aware of. Like Ramondino's adult characters, the little girl will always be an *outsider*. The narrator gives a positive meaning to her sense of displacement, which, she claims, brings knowledge:

> Noi ci trovavamo sempre in situazioni di mezzo, tra ricchezza e povertà, città e campagna, mare e villaggio, fortune e sventura; anzi di passaggio dall'una zona all'altra. Questo ci è servito a conoscere il mondo. (74n1)

> We always found ourselves in the middle, between riches and poverty, town and country, sea and village, luck and mishap; or passing, rather, from one to the other. This helped to give us knowledge of the world. (79)

Even before the creation of the divine Useppe, we witnessed a similar situation in Elisa's room, the narrator of Elsa Morante's *Menzogna e sortilegio*. Completely detached from a world she in fact tries to escape, and yet tries to analyze in the present of memory, Elisa begins by defining within structural family relations the discourse that the omniscient narrator will continue in *La Storia*. Useppe is divine and is untouched by his

gift: Elisa and the girl of Santa Maria instead share the awareness of the process by which children are the repository of
truth. Cruelly, they face a process of power and human limitations that escapes Useppe as a child and has been spared him
as an adult, since, like all martyrs, he departs the world early.
The discussion with History, a relativized History as perceived
by disempowered individuals upon which its effects are
imposed, both in the micropractices of their lives and also in
the events related to their families, rests thus on the shoulders
of the two young women. In the realm of exile of the *paese*
("little town") where she spent her childhood, the girl in
Althénopis experiences the ambiguous interchangeability between the elderly and the children that takes place when the
everyday life of individuals undergoes the cataclysm of war-
time: while the adults play roles in the *teatro di guerra* ("theater of war") the division created by age and needs between
children's lives and old relatives is canceled by the contingen-
cies of war. This phenomenon occurs against the adults' group,
busy with the art of living (or surviving), whose existence has
been drastically transformed during and because of the war, and
to which they try to adapt new masks, new impersonations of
roles they sometimes do not understand. While the children and
the elderly are not to be considered actors in the theater of war,
the adults perform and seemingly accept the roles imposed
upon them by Fascism(s). As in the emblematic case of the
narrator's father's existence, "l'attore brillante si era trasformato in una comparsa" (*Althénopis* 37; "the cabaret acting
had been transformed into a walk-on part"; *Althenopis* 43), personal and private lives undergo drastic transformations. Fear is
common to all, but the social ties, usually imposing and con-
straining Italians in their everyday relationship to the Other, do
not, in the village, force the city children—such as the narrator
and her siblings—to follow the rules established by the eti-
quette of their social class.

In this unexpected freedom, the certainties that usually
accompany such social ties vanish, perhaps forever. The very
metaphors that epitomize *adults* in the eyes of their children
are already lost, along with the traditional sense of reliability
and security society long decreed to be one of the main roles
played by adults. The adults who belong to the empowered

class, those who are supposed to provide the children and the elderly with some strength, are, in the narrator's eyes, those most in need. Against them, the characteristic Genettian "fetishism of the place" helps Ramondino's in the *romanzare* of life events: that is, to better articulate the concept of the *branco*, the cohesive group formed by the children that is striking and made even stronger by a "piacere proibito e cannibalesco," the cannibalesque and forbidden pleasure they find in food. These children are not considered individuals, but an inchoate group, a coalition against all odds, particularly against the world of the adults. This *branco* is offered to us much in the same manner that Morante presents us with the *Mille* of *La Storia*: it is the innocent and simple ones who recognized Useppe's benevolence, as one of *La Storia*'s epigraphs, a passage from the Gospel of Luke, recites:

> . . . hai nascosto queste cose ai dotti e ai savi
> e le hai rivelate ai piccoli . . .
> . . . perché così a te piacque. (Luca X-21)

> . . . thou hast hid these things from the wise and prudent,
> and hast revealed them unto babes . . .
> For so it seemed good in thy sight. (Luke 10.21)

In slightly different terms, the *branco* offers a wider spectacle of the rejection that the writer already felt unconsciously while living through those times, and that would grow stronger when entering the summer mansions of the Neapolitan *noblesse,* who were apparently unaware of changing times and events. The confusion of historical occurrences following the loss of a war has turned them into a generation of lost values and certainties, while innocent (yet implacable) youth registers tensions, incongruence, loss of values and restraint in the adults' behavior, an impression that will remain dormant until the narrator's act of remembrance. The rejection of war, of history, of the whole concept of homeland, is viewed by the narrator as just another natural consequence of the images and feelings unconsciously produced years earlier by the narrator's contradictory relationship with her parents. It is this awareness that constitutes the moment of revelation of her own empowerment against the horrors of war, against the History as narrated by her father, against an authority she has unconsciously rejected all her life and which ultimately will construct her adult identity.

"Un romanzo anche il più favoloso è sempre realista"

In the case of *La Storia* we witness textual evidence of the main theme in the fragmented pattern of the narrative structure that, despite a Manzonian division into rigid parts (and years, as in the Roman *Annales*), remains symbolically loose. We have the presumption of a "division" of temporal levels that, as shown by D'Angeli, constitute merely a pretext to allow an understanding of how interstitial levels are much more difficult to grasp than the "official" story. In *Althénopis*, too, the official story no longer holds, as subplots intertwine incessantly with episodes already encountered in preceding passages, constructing a fresco of a displaced country. In a play of mirrors, scenes are repeated as in kaleidoscopic impressive rendition of the *déjà vu* and the *déjà vécu* in yet another war, in yet another aftermath, endlessly repeating itself. While this mirroring process is not exclusive to *La Storia*, even if the issue of reflection of historical events on the lives of the fictional characters is unquestionable, the employment of this technique takes us back to Morante, and to *Menzogna e sortilegio*. The "fantastico doppio," the fantastic double of every scene we have already encountered, of every character in the first part of the story, comes back, repeated in muted forms in the second part, as the anaphoric-cataphoric chain "fin qui / d'ora innanzi," observed by Emanuella Scarano, as by Donatella Ravanello,[15] affirms. Elisa's "native disposition" to the lie, to melodrama and the theater, partly explains the replicas of scenes. It is from the Morantian "d'ora innanzi" that Ramondino begins to follow her *magistra*, while Di Lascia (and it is probably one of the most evident divarications of Morante's influence) abandons her at that point. Di Lascia prefers to keep Chiara in her world of ghosts and lies, within her room. While both authors construct characters who reveal a neurotic impatience in describing even the most disturbing symptoms of their illness, be it mental or intellectual, Ramondino's main character cannot hold such passion without a subsequent rationalization of the time "lost." She steps forward and reflects, in the *hic et nunc* of the narration. She needs to see events sifted through another period of time independent of the others who actually related the stories to her: "Le visioni, che sono verità rivelate, come le ossessioni, che sono verità non ancora rivelate, non si possono dimenticare; né però spiegare" (*Althénopis* 5; "Visions, which are revealed truth, like obsessions, which are truths not yet revealed, cannot be forgotten; nor yet explained"; 11). The love for theater and melodrama only further enhances the constant restagings. In *Althénopis* they reappear with a muted perspective as each time we are mindful of the endless repetition of historical events that enables us to connect the private and public in the story narrated. We witness a similar phenomenon of what Freud would call *Durcharbeitung* ("working through") for his patients' cases: bringing to memory traumatic events, later to be reconstructed in the narrative of disease on which he focused his research. It is the recollection pattern that determines *Althénopis*'s intentionally fragmented structure, symbolizing an experienced loss of psychological stability through her narrator's renewed role as historian of her own existence. Like Elisa's character (but also Di Lascia's Chiara), she is afraid of having developed a hereditary disease: this time, however, we could call it "class consciousness" that she does not want to acknowledge and fully rejects, as she rejects her own parents' values and inability to stand up against the regime. The loss of that security, also apparent in the female characters' diminishing roles in what appears to be a patriarchal society, mirrors itself in the loss of a linear and chronological order, and privileges for its form a loosely analeptic structure that collates relevant episodes in the life of the protagonist. Such a process is devoid of any consequential order, except the one dictated by her personal choice of object of reminiscence in her continuous "rectifications," in Paul Ricoeur's sense of the term, applied to the previous moments of her life. Far from an involuntary act of reminiscence, here events are carefully chosen in order to explain the present state of the narrating person. In this narrative structure, which pertains throughout the text, names, places, and things provide a powerful taxonomy of life in those times as the narrator describes what she, as a young girl, was used to cruelly judge. But didn't Elisa act in exactly the same way toward her parents?

> Le figure dei miei, che m'avevano circondato fin qui, e con le loro voci defunte mi descrivevano le proprie stanze antiche, la propria città di larve; confidandomi segreti e pensieri ormai da tempo sepolti; le triste figure dunque diventavano via via piú frettolose e roche, dileguavano una dopo l'altra. Onde finito è d'ora innanzi il mio privilegio d'assistere, sola spettatrice, a una commedia di spiriti. Non udirete piú da me la voce molteplice della dormiente. Una lucida insonnia s'impadronisce di me, e io, nella camera taciturna e spopolata, altro non potrò interrogare d'ora innanzi che la mia vera memoria. (*Opere* 1: 578–79)

> The faces of my people who have surrounded me until now, their dead voices which have described their old dwellings and their city of phantoms, confiding to me secrets and thoughts long since buried; these sad figures have become little by little more hurried and hoarse; one after the other they have faded away. From now on it is over, my privilege of witnessing, as a solitary spectator, a comedy of ghosts. You will no longer hear from me the many voices of sleep. A lucid insomnia has taken hold of me and, in my silent, deserted room, I can turn to nothing from now on but my own true memory. (*House of Liars* 348–49)

As in the case of Elisa, in fact, Ramondino's narrator can see *now*, or *d'ora innanzi*, ("from now on") how other characters experienced different kinds of loss through that skillfully refigured life itinerary (psychological, economic, and, in some cases, mental losses), and aligns them as evidence against her failed relationship with the mother and the assumed beliefs of the father.

The child in *Althénopis* lives in the magic world of Santa Maria del Mare. In this novel there appears to be room only for children and women, since men are at war, or, as they return, reveal a lack of principles and ethics and prefer to rely, instead, on their women. In the last part of the novel, the girl and her mother symbolically switch roles, as the latter is dying: the family heritage, including courage and strength, follows a matrilineal line; all the male characters are described as troubled in different ways. However, this shift to the matrilinear does not take place without a moment of grief for the lack of understanding between daughter and mother; the daughter has long before opted for the domain of Santa Maria del Mare ruled by the *nonna*, the grandmother, over the power of the city, ruled by the mother. This positive correspondence between female generations (even when it skips her mother's generation)[16] makes Ramondino's character different from Morante's, where such affinity exists only on sublimated, mystical, or symbolic levels.

The *nonna* is perhaps the strongest representative throughout Ramondino's works of the *naturalità* that reminds us of Morante's legacy. She possesses the same qualities that make of Nunziatina, Alessandra, Rosaria, Ida, and even the dead Aracoeli the most convincing characters in Morante's fiction. The maternal grandmother is a character still anchored to the past, a woman whose firm beliefs and values still enable her to retain certain convictions even "*in quei tempi di guerra*" ("during those times of war"). The relationship with her granddaughter is very distant from the stereotype evoked by tradition or summoned up in relation to small children. She is still able to charm, her posture dominates the street, while the narrator's heart still recalls that familiar and yet fascinating figure so strictly connected to the myth of a lost society. The *nonna* gives stability and reintegrates a different perspective on the concept of History—as likened to a religious, mythical world, similar to Morante's unorthodox religious discourse—in the story of this family, which would otherwise be lost:

> I nostri genitori erano atei, degli atei fatui, sicché la religione stessa ai miei occhi era peccato. La nonna apparteneva invece a un'epoca in cui si era riusciti a far *coincidere l'eternità della storia con quella della vita, sicché la storia trascorreva in progresso*—ma di questo si occupavano gli uomini—e la vita terrena in vita eterna—e di questo si occupavano le donne, in preghiera ai capezzali. (*Althénopis* 6; emphasis added)

> Our parents were atheists, atheists of a fatuous kind, so that religion itself was a sin in my eyes. Whereas Grandmother belonged to a period when it had been *possible to make the*

*eternity of history coincide with that of life, so that life went
by as progress*—but that was men's business—and earthly
life passed into eternal life—and that was the business of
women, praying at the bedside of the dying. (12)

The mother, in time of war, had vainly tried to elide all else
in the pragmatics of her everyday existence, concentrating stub-
bornly on the budget, oblivious to the presence of the *nonna's
naturalità*, of the children's Eden. Nature is presented to the
child in two ways: that of the mother, "natura minerale e
vegetale" (*Althénopis* 38; "mineral and vegetable nature"; 44)
and the other, "umorale e sudorosa degli amplessi, dei parti,
del latte e delle ragadi" (*Althénopis* 38; "moist, sweaty nature
of the marital embrace, of childbirth, of milk, and of rhapsody";
44), which we feel constituting the reign of the *nonna*, the only
survivor of a time in which "l'eternità della storia" ("the eternity of history") could still coincide "con quella della vita"
("with that of life") (*Althénopis* 6; *Althenopis* 12). The *nonna*
is forced to accept the bitter reality of history, namely, the wars
to which Mussolini led the country, while her granddaughter,
almost contingently, is forced by legal and blood relations, to
accept her deluded parents. The only possible link, it seems,
remains the one between the reality of the *nonna* and that of
the child, leaving out the parents' generation.

Aside from the father's role in her mother's periodic muta-
tions of personality,[17] the reminiscence of her father is filled
with melancholy and disdain. Compelling her to adulthood, he
represents all that she has come to loathe: obedience to a disruptive regime, obedience to the laws of a strange History that,
as in Alessandro Manzoni's *I promessi sposi*, is not the History
of humankind, but the History of the few imposed upon the
ordinary, helpless many. The revelation of her deception as a
child springs from her adult recollection of an early episode:

Di mio padre non avevo mai capito se facesse sul serio o se
recitasse. Anche la mamma gli diceva sempre di non fare il
buffone. Ora pareva un attore comico ora un attore drammatico. Questo enigma: recita, fa sul serio? gioca, non gioca? era per me affascinante. Ma al suo ritorno dal campo di
prigionia di Tangeri, quando ci raggiunse a Santa Maria,
l'attore brillante si era trasformato in una comparsa. Forse

era stato l'incalzare delle disgrazie di quegli anni: la caduta del fascismo e la sua caduta personale, lo squallore del piccolo impiego nel ministero e delle camere mobiliate nelle quali viveva nella capitale, la morte della madre, a cui era attaccatissimo.

Tutto era dunque finito tra me e loro, perché mi negavano le due uniche consolazioni dell'esistenza: la favola e il teatro. (*Althénopis*, 37; emphasis added)

I had never understood whether my father was to be taken seriously or whether he was acting a part. Even my mother was always telling him to stop playing the clown. At one moment he seemed a comedian and the next, a tragic actor. The enigma: is he acting, does he mean it? is he play-acting, is he serious? was fascinating to me. But on his return from the prison camp in Tangiers, whenever he joined us at Santa Maria del Mare, *the cabaret act had been transformed into a walk-on part.* Perhaps it had been the repeated blows of those years: the fall of Fascism; his own personal fall; the squalor of his lowly job at the Ministry and of the bedside he inhabited in the capital; the death of his mother, to whom he had been very deeply attached.

Everything was over between me and them because they denied me the only two consolations that life held: fairytales and theatre. (42–43; emphasis added)

In *Menzogna e sortilegio* Elisa attributes to her parents the irreversible fall of her dreams and illusions. The supreme instant of Morantian "smagamento," or disenchantment—derived by Elisa's awareness *a posteriori* of the childhood trauma of being rejected by the one we love above all—is located by Elisa in the painful textual involution of this passage:

Fu a questo punto ch'egli trasse di tasca due biglietti per l'Opera: si dava, al Teatro Lirico, l'*Aida* in serata di gala, ed egli aveva acquistato due posti di poltrona. Invitò dunque mia madre a vestirsi per lo spettacolo, che incominciava alle nove; e, per la prima volta in quella sera, nell'invitarla apparve agitato e sofferente, dal timore d'un rifiuto. [. . .] Intanto, io chinavo il capo sulla tavola, sentendomi la gola soffocata da un nodo: ché la festa si concludeva, per me sola, nell'abbandono e nell'invidia. Gli altri andrebbero al teatro, ed io rimarrei sola a casa. Alla parola *teatro* i miei sensi tutti all'unissono si destavano, suggerendo alla mente grande spazio, brulicare di splendori, voci strane e corali, odori d'incenso. Un tumulto quasi di foresta, e una religione di cattedrale; l'esaltazione della favola, il gioco fattosi cosa divina. Tutto ciò per *loro*, mentre io resterei sola nella piccola casa, con questo sapore di sale in bocca. (*Opere* 1: 661)

Then he took two tickets from his pocket; there was a gala performance of *Aida* at the opera house, and he had bought two orchestra seats. He told mother to dress for the performance which began at nine and for the first time that evening, when he asked her, he seemed painfully afraid she might refuse. [. . .] Meanwhile, I had dropped my head to the table, stifling, with a knot in my throat, for the celebration was ending for me and I could only feel deserted and envious. The others would go to the theater and I would stay home alone. (*House of Liars* 400)[18]

In this passage of the novel, Elisa remembers the evening her parents went to the theater, leaving her behind. Although placed in a profoundly altered context, the words of *Althénopis* resonate with Elisa's remembrances, and both recall the Proustian theater of memory. The consolation of theater is denied to both protagonists who, in turn, create one of their own. To the theater of war of the parents—both personal and public—from which children are excluded, Morante and Ramondino oppose instead a different notion, charged with a metaphoric significance. The theatrical aspect (D'Angeli, "Le maschere" 56) of literature foresees a "contiguity" of territories in which created images take form by metonymy. Characters isolated by the theater of parents live within other enclosed spaces in which their "favola" (the process of creation of an entirely different existence and system of beliefs other than the one projected by the parents) can take shape.

Childhood appears at the door of memory through these "consolazioni": the "favola e il teatro" that the pessimism and sense of defeat of the parents would forbid them: Santa Maria del Mare, an actual terrestrial Paradise in the eyes of the little girl, cannot but be found, precisely according to Morante's views, by the children. Parents are absent, unworthy of this mythical Edenic paradise. The author remains convinced of their wrongful participation in a conflict whose only attributes are the blood uselessly shed, and the thirst for power that has provoked it from time immemorial.

The sheer existence of the mother and of the father, and their generation of "lost causes" (*cause perse*), force acceptance upon the generations of the *nonna* and the daughter, but only to a certain degree. In general, male characters in *Althénopis* do not hold a position of respect; they are vulnerable, passive, and largely pitiful. To demonstrate the matriarchal character of the family, not only numerically but for the prevailing mentality, the narrator writes:

> La riuscita e il successo nel mondo venivano invece visti con sospetto, perché quello che contava era l'essere nati in quella famiglia e non diventare qualcuno. Ma non si trattava di arroganza da nobili; un civico e nel contempo religioso sistema di valori che veniva definito signorilità, era considerato proprio della famiglia e si opponeva al regno della volgarità e dell'utile. Solo per un [*sic*] ascesi intellettuale, spirituale o religiosa ci si poteva elevare al di sopra della famiglia. Questi atteggiamenti erano certo dovuti al fondamento stesso della rendita; ma anche al senso civico ereditato dal padre; o forse soprattutto al fatto che era una famiglia di donne. Gli uomini infatti vi morivano presto, o non contavano. (*Althénopis* 109)

> Achievement and success in the world were looked on with suspicion, for what counted was being born into the family, and not becoming someone. This was not aristocratic arrogance: a system of values, both civic and religious, and known as gentlemanliness, was considered a rightful property of the family and was set against the world of the vulgar and the useful. Only by going beyond an intellectual, spiritual or religious flight, was it possible to rise above the family. This attitude without doubt was based on landed income but it also derived from a sense of civic duty inherited from their father; or mainly perhaps from the fact that it was a family of women. The men died early and, in effect, didn't count. (*Althenopis* 113)

The emblematic figure of the father enjoys very little respect in the narrator's eyes because of his own acknowledgment of individual and political defeat, because of his past collaboration with the Fascist Party as a Consul in Majorca, and partly for personal reasons. It is almost as if she holds him responsible for her difficult, yet inevitable growth. Moreover, the implacable narrator's eye blames him for the mother's attempt to resume an *antebellum* lifestyle every time he comes back from the far away *Capitale*, center of corrupted power, recasting her in a role she never rationally accepted as her duty, even while the husband was consul in the far away island, and that now, in the aftermath of the lost war, appears even more anachronistic. But not only that. In the following passage, the *Erzählendes Ich* eloquently describes a conversation between herself as a child and her father, while visiting an historic house on the slopes of Vesuvius, Villa Murat. The subject of the discussion, the father's plans for the daughter's future:

> Davanti a quella lapide, mio padre mi esortava a fare la bibliotecaria *da grande e a studiare la storia*, e piú sordo si radicava in me il rifiuto per quel futuro di custode di spettri e di pietre. Come poteva conciliarsi—pensavo—la fronte alta e bianchissima di nostro padre, la bella curva nero-argento dei capelli, la forma leggermente aquilina del suo naso, con la fatua ironia dei suoi occhi, ma soprattutto col suo ventre gonfio, quasi flaccido, e con quel suo gesto, che avevo intravisto, di pisciare in un piccolo orinale, vestito della sola giacca del pigiama, sotto la quale appariva, penzolante, la maglia di lana!
>
> E quando mi parlava di Murat ai fuochi e al fumo dei combattimenti o allo splendore della reggia di Althénopis, si sovrapponeva l'immagine di un signore in *déshabillé* che pisciava impacciato. (*Althénopis* 50; emphasis added)

> Standing in front of the slab, my father would exhort me to become a librarian *when I grew up and to study history*, and revulsion at a future as guardian of stones and spectres rooted itself in me even more stubbornly. How was it possible—I asked myself—to reconcile my father's high, extremely white forehead, the silvery-black wave of his hair, the shape of his slightly aquiline nose, with the fatuous irony of his gaze, in particular with his swollen, almost flaccid belly, and the thing I had glimpsed him doing, his pissing into a small chamberpot with nothing on except a pyjama-top, a woollen vest hanging down beneath.

> And when he talked to me about Murat in the fire and smoke of battle, or about the splendour of the royal palace

> in *Althénopis*, the image of a half-naked man awkwardly pissing would overlay what he was saying. (*Althenopis* 56; emphasis added)

The image of her father imposing on her the importance of a job as historian returns also in her latest *Guerra di infanzia e di Spagna*:

> —No, non diventerai ballerina. Diventerai bibliote-caria!—E questa *biblioteca* cui alludeva mio padre mi appariva come una vasta tomba regale nella quale mi vole-vano rinchiudere viva, affinché custodissi quello che resta-va, una volta che avevano finito di risuonare le chiacchiere festose, il canto e la musica, il fruscio delle danze. (324; emphasis in original)

> —No, you will not become a dancer. You will be a librarian!—And this *library* to which my father alluded would appear to me as a vast royal tomb in which they would bury me alive so that I could watch over all the remains, once the happy noise of the chatting, the singing and the music, the rustling of the dances had ceased.

It seems that females only have access to knowledge as custo-dians of male knowledge, reified in the canon that makes the entrance of specific books in the *biblioteca* possible. While try-ing to live the myth of childhood itself, although in desperate situations, whether war or its immediate aftermath, she is forced to accept reality because of the parents' intervention, their very existence, and in the remembrance of the shuttered past this still causes pain. As her parents have participated as public functionaries, or as wives of public functionaries in the ignoble theater of war, they are judged by the daughter's necroscopic eye as an integrated part of that historical period. Anger lies in her memories of her father's attempts to force her into a different path from her vocation of writer. In his minimal appearance on the novelistic stage the father is a somewhat wretched figure, not only because of the career he intends his daughter to pursue, but because of the very sense of estrange-ment and intolerance of the young girl for a figure endowed with scant meaning for her, forced by his public position to fol-low rules she considered strange at the time, and that now she can finally condemn in her full understanding of their tragic importance. The father, also one of the very few male figures in this novel of women, relies on her sense of curiosity as well as on her already evident intellectual capacities to instill in her a love for history, in making a mission of her future occupation, the preservation of male myths. But even at this early age, as if intuitively, she cannot be compelled to study History and to love her country (*La Patria*), as she is already intimately aware that studying History can still signify perpetrating the power of the Fathers. She is aware that History is a dangerous form of knowledge that is produced and governed by power, as Foucault aptly registered. Of the famous speech at Villa Murat, the young girl realizes the tragic, and yet grotesquely comic, aspects of Man's ambitions, juxtaposing the image of her father's noble profile with his image while relieving himself. The first man in her life, her father, is also the object of irony and sarcasm, precisely as in the case of *Menzogna e sortilegio*'s Elisa for Francesco. The sense of repulsion provoked by her father's projects for her future continues to accompany her throughout life, a memory hardly worthy of respect, which she ridicules, and which recalls the rejection of what Virginia Woolf long ago called the "dominance of the professor."

Morante's concept of History is completely shared by Ramondino. It is a pessimistic opinion of History that entirely shapes Morante's concept of *homeland* and *war*, as well as the futility of war conflicts, aptly put in words such as "History endlessly repeating itself ad infinitum in space and time."[19] The emblematic subtitle of Morante's novel *La Storia, Uno scandalo che dura da diecimila anni* ("A ten-thousand-year-long scandal") could be taken, in fact, as a verbal representation for Ramondino's narrator's post-analepsis revelation; both in Morante's third novel, *La Storia,* and Ramondino's *Althénopis,* the conviction prevails that History, as the Fathers want it, cannot be anything but a scandal, a needless, useless tragedy, along with the authors' corollary inclination to believe that History needs to take another stance altogether, departing from images of Power. The connection created in the book between the fatherly figure, the Fascist emphasis on Patriotism, and the war conflict only reconfirms Gayatry Spivak's view in "Political Interpretations" that "'Patria,'"[20] "is not merely masculine in gender but names the father as the source of legitimate identity" (130). While the term *patria* in Italian is not masculine in gender, Spivak's concept holds true: the word relates directly to the Father's sense of ownership, "of legitimate identity" that both authors reject entirely as devoid of value. Power is also, according to Morante "the dishonor of human beings. *Power* takes shape through human society immediately, one that has been universally and always founded on the opposition *masters* and *servants*—abusers and abused (Morante, *"Piccolo manifesto"* 7). Foucault was only eager to make manifest this concept derived by Nietzsche. Against any utopian conceptualization, individuals are constituted as effects of power.[21]

The rejection of power in traditional terms is what *Althénopis*'s narrator had already unconsciously decided in visiting Villa Murat with her father: by declining the unwanted destiny of passively preserving and recording the historical events of a History in which she does not believe, and of which she has intuitively realized the danger of normalizing the hegemony of male power in the construction of an ethics for war, it has now become reality. The established link, or rather the one she wants to establish in her memories, is that between her *nonna*'s reality/*naturality* and her own, entirely bypassing her own parents' generation, and constructing a matrilinear autobiographical line of a different kind, from which she reworks the very issue of power as unfitted for her vision of the world in its traditional conceptualization, where "knowledge of the world" does not entail destruction and acquiescence to horror, but an opposition of values.

Through a process that could annihilate the memories of her youth, of her father, and her mother, gynealogy[22] ideally reconnects the daughter to a world where such matrilinear continuity would overturn the sense of History and historical discourse as perpetrated by men, and yet find a reason for mediation; as Spivak comments, women cannot find meaning without a wide series of differentiations, of which the most important is man and the values a male discourse has created, particularly in the course of historical events ("Feminism and Critical Theory"; 77–92). Far from proposing a peaceful relationship with the maternal authority to be counterpoised to the paternal, both writers trace instead a formidably antagonistic

relationship between daughter and mother figures. Such ago-
nic love (it is love) is crucial to the development of this sense
of loneliness, helplessness, and ultimately cyclothymia that
transpires from Morante and Ramondino's female characters
in all their novels in their struggle to reach a world where love
could eventually be experienced not in terms of isolation,
dependence, and addiction (the Morantian *morbo*) but for
higher causes. Already in the 1981 novel, for Ramondino's
character there is no connection with the mother, whose distance is carefully defined at every possible moment. In *Guerra
di infanzia e di Spagna*, the relationship manifests in a fictional
and significant manner Rosi Braidotti's statement that the
"mother is not only a biocultural entity, but a discursive field"
(61), a concept that in Ramondino's fictional narrative is primarily linked to language and our being in the world in connection with the mother: these coordinates, along with other
"official" ones (name, birth, locations) position the protagonist
within the present reflections on her identity and perception of
reality. In "The Cicatrice," a title of Morantian memory,[23] we
witness "fights" between mother and daughter as the tension
between them becomes as spectacular as in a circus. Transformed into a tiger, the daughter attacks the mother. Rivalry
and competition construct this difficult relationship that is less
caring than antagonistic. When the girl is locked in a *stanzino*
("backroom") by her rational mother, who thought that "[o]gni
persona infatti e ogni cosa doveva stare al suo posto" (*Guerra*
143; "everybody and everything, in fact, had to stay in their
rightful place"), she realizes the difference between that institution in her mother's house vis-à-vis her grandmother's house.
For the mother the *stanzino* was a symbol for order and rational thinking in obedience to established patterns of life. For
the grandmother it represented her *own* ideal place in which to
find spiritual peace, "stare in pace a fare penitenza e pregare"
(*Guerra* 144; "stay in peace to remit sins and pray"). This
conceptualization of space can be reconnected to Elisa's room,
where she was a "monaca della menzogna" (a "nun of the lie")
of others, but which is also the same room in which she
unveiled the mysteries of her house, a house of "liars," that is.
A lie is also what history means to the *nonna*, and her grand-
child will almost unconsciously follow her belief.

The child of *Guerra di infanzia e di Spagna* knows, as do
Morante's children, that the stories parents tell are not always
"true": often it is the most surreal and visionary path, such as
the one presented by the *nonna*, that reveals the "reality" of
life:

> Avevo poi altre ragioni per non volere che la fiaba fosse
> assimilata alla vita che i miei genitori conducevano. [. . .]
> Mi sembrava inoltre che l'esistenza che noi conducevamo
> fosse molto lontana da quel felice epilogo e che in essa ope-
> rassero quotidianamente tali incantesimi e malefizi da ren-
> dere impossibile ancora ogni scioglimento. (46–47)

> I had other reasons not to want the fable to be absorbed into
> my parents' life. [. . .] It seemed to me that the existence we
> lead was very far from that happy ending and that in it there
> were spells and witchcraft at work such as to make any
> solution still unthinkable.

The *scandal* of History will reach the protagonist even
though she was spared the terrible experiences in the city, living, as she was, in a place that "did not exist on the map." Both
Santa Maria del Mare and Majorca are places that, like Eden,
cannot be found except by the worthy ones. In fact, the *paese*
of Santa Maria is spared by the Americans and by the bombs,
not because the Americans felt pity for them, but because Eden,
being the time of childhood when pain is felt without its exact
knowledge, is *not* going to be found on their military maps
(*Althénopis* 34; 39). Only when the American GIs arrive in
Santa Maria del Mare will she leave the village to go to a now
desolate and destroyed Naples. Her eye will eventually come
to be the "eye of an Old Lady" symbolized by the word
Althénopis in which *Parthenopis*, ancient name for Naples, was
distorted at the sight of its desolation by the German soldiers
during their occupation.

Later, years later, a name can be given by the narrator in one
of the footnotes—an element that accentuates the essayistic
tone of the text, furthering its distance from the genre of the
novel—to all these past public events, along with the more personal ones. The paratextual element of the notes often has the
scope of self-eliciting *Erklärungen* to her own fears as a child,
which, as Freud writes, are completely different from those

experienced at a later stage by the individual, and are strictly related to—if not produced by—the anguish of the adults sur- rounding the child. Only at a later stage of life will there be an understanding of certain phenomena of unconscious rejection, all the fears she could not explain, or express as a child, and now object of her introspection and comprehension in the retelling of past events:

> Ho saputo poi che questo stato si chiama "pavor nocturnus" e si accompagna in genere a costituzioni gracili e nervose. Ma nessuna scienza dei dottori è riuscita mai a convincermi veramente che quel timore fosse infondato, essendosi poi rivelato che le cose da temere erano assai piú inquietanti di quelle che io temevo allora. *(Althénopis* 81n1)

> I have since learnt that this state is known as "pavor nocturnus," night terror, and generally goes along with frag- ile and nervous constitutions. But no science of the doctors has ever really managed to convince me that those fears were unfounded, since it was later revealed that the things truly to be feared are a great deal more disquieting than what I was afraid of then. (86n1)

Myth is unveiled through the *Andenken*. But the more it is rec- ollected, the more time reveals that its purity outlives wars, undesirable relatives, death. It forms a special *Dichtung* of rec- ognition that departs from autobiography as well as from a tra- ditional view of history in a fusion created by Morante, who is tellingly defined by many as the "poet-novelist." The woman's point of view assimilates myth to reach the realm of her dis- quieting and yet poetic family. She reaches it while looking for remembrances, while searching for her authentic identity. She does so in the rebuttal of those voices of authority that would shape the world but could not shape the course of her exist- ence, which, in spite of her father's attempts, she linked to the magic of her *nonna*'s archaic sense of Nature, to the *naturalità*. Mastering a new knowledge of History, which is entirely futile when perceived in the way her father did when he tried to persuade her to become a priestess of knowledge, means giv- ing a name—*pavor nocturnus*—to fear. These are the unex- pressed fears against a symbolic order that conceived History, as her father did, for the past ten thousand years. Realizing their nature constitutes the metaphoric ransom from an extinct age, that of childhood and dependence on authority.

The "danger" of confusing two genres, novel and autobiography, aside from a certain impossibility of severing the two constitutive parts of fiction writing, as Paul de Man affirms, activates instead an innovative practice of reading in *Althénopis*, within which one can easily situate the attempt of Ramondino to intertwine the reality of her own life with the fabulous one of a mythical world in the telling of the adventures of a soul by the most varied narrative means. Means and expressions that originally belonged respectively to autobiographic writing and to novel writing, but here they are presented as hardly divisible. Ramondino's narrative sign declares the importance of Walter Benjamin and Hannah Arendt's considerations about the power of the narrator over history: the one who narrates stories has also the power over the actors of making History. However, as in *La Storia*, there are some "paradises within history." It is possible and hopeful to find images of intellectual and human ransom that, as Morante's poetics in *La Storia* eloquently show, can interrupt the scandal of History and "prevent the abasement that creates unreality" (Morante, in D'Angeli, "Il paradiso" 234). These are "the wings that break the gravity of the human condition, bringing a different form of temporality in which one finds a divine sense of grace and freedom. These are the wings of poetry that is able to reconstitute the density of evil" (D'Angeli, "Il paradiso" 234). Both writers oppose their own vision, based on the possibility of human action to counterpose the cultural model given by such theater, thus establishing a literary form for expressing a new and post-Foucauldian interpretation of what power entails. New capacities can thus be attributed to the art of writing. Their own form of acting in the "literary" decrees a desire, utopian perhaps, to operate positively within their conceptualization of *teatro e favola* while eliminating the very bases for a tragic *teatro di guerra*.

Notes

1. I would like to thank Cristina Della Coletta and Giancarlo Lombardi for their attentive reading and important observations.

2. My study relies on Diana Sartori's articles on Hannah Arendt's conceptualization of authority, "*Tu devi*. Un ordine materno" and "Nessuno è autore della propria storia: identità e azione."

3. An earlier version of the first part of this study, devoted to the notion of autobiography, is published as "Le scelte dell'*autofiction:* il romanzo della memoria contro il potere della Storia," *Studi nove-centeschi* 56 (1998): 367–81.

4. The critic defines in his book a critical discourse that follows Morante's process of maturity. His contribution significantly frees Morantian criticism from some stereotypes that only negatively parallel her personal life to her works. Bardini eliminates in fact the topos of the identification of every literary concept to the actual compatibility of Morante's relations, whether friends or family. He reminds us of the danger of exegesis that leans heavily on a form of biographical criticism of Romantic heritage. While it would be often irresistible to draw from Morante's existence and real characters of her life to comment upon some of her characters (a particular conceptualization of maternity, protean and yet always linked to the *naturalità* of the mothers) it is nevertheless a dangerous pattern that ultimately limits the meaning of her work.

5. See for this, the Introduction to the present volume.

6. For further reference, see also Lucamante, "*Passaggio in ombra*: riprese, innovazioni e soluzioni tematico-strutturali in un romanzo morantiano."

7. Ferrante derives from Morante particularly the notion of viscosity of the body, the fluids that connect us to nature. Such a notion is present in her novels, *L'amore molesto* and *I giorni dell'abbandono*. It actually "constructs" both main characters and their reactions to life and events in general. Naturality and *Southerness* thus find a common thread starting from corporeality. Menstruations are also seen in both as the connection to nature. Also the scene, common to both writers, of female characters drowning at sea, in which the sea is clearly a welcoming, nurturing mother after a life on earth of obstacles—*la mère–la mer*. Nora, Ida's mother in *La Storia*, drowns herself. Amelia, in Ferrante's first novel, and the unnamed character of *la poverella* in the second, drown in the waters near Gaeta.

8. Morante's legacy is one that cannot be detected in traditional paths of influence. Also, there are many biographical affinities between the two authors. Aside from writing, both writers worked in scriptwriting, Morante with Pasolini, Ramondino with Mario Martone. This new parallel should be mentioned, as Martone is frequently considered the heir of Pasolini. Both worked in theater, Morante with *Serata a Colono*, Ramondino with *Terremoto con madre e figlia*. They were interested in cinema: Morante collaborated extensively with Pasolini on his films, while Ramondino repeated her experience with Mario Martone for *Morte di un matematico napoletano*, a movie on the last week of Renato Caccioppoli.

Stefania Lucamante

9. As in the case of Morante, in fact, Ramondino was not until recently interested in "women's issues." But, while Morante died without leaving any statement about the awareness of gender issues, in her *Passaggio a Trieste* Ramondino seems absolutely aware of the consequence of having ignored it for too long. For Ramondino Trieste reveals itself to be the place in which finally it is right to "descend" into the particularity of gender, in which finally it is correct to understand oneself as woman. Revising Freud, studying Melanie Klein, after years of social and artistic engagement, the author realizes what she had not understood before for a "veiled lack of esteem of women in general" and this in spite of the many physiological experiences, "lived with aristocratic detachment" as if someone else, not her, was living them.

10. It could be argued that the only work of Ramondino's that can be considered an actual novel is *Un giorno e mezzo*.

11. Such as—for instance—the ones made by Maria Marotti "Filial Discourses," likely to be perceived only in the last of the three parts composing the book

12. De Man's widely cited statement in his "Autobiography as De-Facement" reminds us also that, "[a]utobiography, then, is not a genre or a mode, but a figure of reading or of understanding that occurs, to some degree, in all texts. The autobiographical moment happens as an alignment between the two subjects involved in the process of reading in which they determine each other by mutual reflexive substitution. The structure implies differentiation as well as similarity, since both depend on a substitutive exchange that constitutes the subject. This specular structure is interiorized in a text in which the author declares himself the subject of his own understanding, but this merely makes explicit the wider claim to authorship that takes place whenever a text is stated to be *by* someone and assumed to be understandable to the extent that this is the case. Which amounts to saying that any book with a readable title page is, to some extent, autobiographical" (70).

13. "Il va de soi que le 'rapport' à poser entre 'deux objects différents' est le rapport d'analogie qui dégage leur 'essence commune.' Ce qui est moins évident, mais qui paraît à peu près indispensable pour la cohérence de l'enoncé, c'est que ces deux objets différents font partie de la collection des objets qui 'figuraient' (ensemble) dans le lieu à decrier: autrement dit, que le rapport métaphorique s'établit entre deux termes déjà liés par une relation de contiguïté spatio-temporelle" (*Figures III* 60; "It goes without saying that the 'link' to be made between 'two different things' is the analogical link disclosed by their 'common essence.' What is less clear but seems essential for the coherence of this pronouncement, is that these two different objects are part of the collection of objects that 'figured' [together] in the space to be described: in other words that the metaphoric link is established between two terms already bound by a relation of spatio-temporal contiguity").

Genette adds: "Sans métaphore, dit (à peu près) Proust, pas des veritables souvenirs, pas d'histoire, pas de roman. Car c'est la métaphore qui retrouve le Temps perdu, mais c'est la métonymie qui le ranime, et le remet à sa propre fuite et sa propre Recherche. Ici donc, ici seulement, par la métaphore, mais dans la métonymie—, ici commence le Récit" (*Figures III* 63; "Without metaphor says Proust (more or less), there can be no real memories, no story, no novel. For it is metaphor that recaptures Time past, but it is metonymy that revives it, that sets it in search of its own evanescence. Here, then, and here only, by metaphor, but in metonymy—, here begins the narrative").

14. These times are (1) the official one (history of those who are responsible for the "scandal" as Elsa Morante defines it), (2) the parallel time of everyday people's history, (3) the temporal level of Ida and Useppe's story (see D'Angeli, "Il paradiso" 216).

15. The presence of Freudian patterns of representations of events is a frequent pattern for Morante as well, as Elisa Gambaro points out in her analysis of *Diario 1938* in the present volume (21–44).

16. The narrator's recollections bring evidence of her mother's seclusion from her: "Imparai un anno a scuola il significato e l'uso delle parentesi; a me pareva che la mamma, chi sa quando, forse quando eravamo partiti dalla bella isola, o forse molto prima, quando non ero ancora nata, si fosse messa tra parentesi. La chiudevano anche come due parentesi i muri di quella casa, che parevano fatti di tempo; da una parte il giorno in cui eravamo arrivati, dall'altro quello del giorno in cui saremmo partiti" (*Althénopis* 39; "At school one year, I learnt the use of parentheses; it seemed to me that Mother, who knows when, perhaps when we left the beautiful island, or perhaps even long before I was born, had put herself in parentheses. Even the walls of that house enclosed her like parentheses seemingly made of time: on one side there was the wall of the day we came, and on the other the wall of the day we would leave"; 45).

17. This has been discussed in psychoanalytical terms by Adalgisa Giorgio.

18. The rest of the text is missing in the American translation, thus only confirming the problems due to such an incomplete and unfair translation of *Menzogna e sortilegio.*

19. I have translated this emblematic sentence, taken from an essay that Ramondino wrote for the character of Useppe, the innocent child in Elsa Morante's novel *History* ("Useppe e sua madre").

20. The term is quoted in its original Italian.

21. "It's not a matter of emancipating truth from every system of power (which would be a chimera, for truth is already power) but of detaching the power of truth from the forms of hegemony, social, economic and cultural, within which it operates at the present time" (Foucault 133).

253

22. Graziella Parati defines the term: "Gynealogies are genealogies that women autobiographors create to recuperate the silenced voices of their mothers, but they are also constructions that open themselves to revision and expansion toward a nonseparatist concept of women's personal narratives" (12).

23. This is, in fact, a part of *Menzogna e sortilegio* in which Edoardo "marks" Anna with a scar of her face as a sign of his "intervention" upon her physical appearance that decrees his own "power" over her.

Works Cited

Arendt, Hannah. *The Human Condition*. Chicago: U of Chicago P, 1958.

Bardini, Marco. *Morante Elsa. Italiana. Di professione, poeta*. Pisa: Nistri-Lischi, 1999.

Boscagli, Maurizia. "Brushing Benjamin against the Grain: Elsa Morante and the *Jetztzeit* of Marginal History." Marotti 131–44.

Braidotti, Rosi. "Mothers, Monsters, and Machines." Ed. Katie Conboy, Nadia Medina, and Sarah Stanbury. *Writing on the Body: Female Embodiment*. New York: Columbia UP, 1997. 59–79

D'Angeli, Concetta. "Le maschere delle mie futili tragedie." *Cahiers Elsa Morante* 2 (1995): 56–75.

———. "Il paradiso nella *Storia*." *Studi novecenteschi* 21. 47/48 (June–Dec. 1994): 215–35.

de Man, Paul. "Autobiography as De-Facement." *The Rhetoric of Romanticism*. New York: Columbia UP, 1984. 70.

Ferrante, Elena. *L'amore molesto*. Rome: Edizioni e/o, 1992.

———. *I giorni dell'abbandono*. Rome: Edizioni e/o, 2002.

Fofi, Goffredo. "I riti della memoria e del futuro: il romanzo di Mariateresa Di Lascia." *Linea d'ombra* 104 (May 1995): 43–44.

Foucault, Michel. *Power/Knowledge: Selected Interviews and Other Writings 1972–1977*. Trans. and ed. Colin Gordon. New York: Pantheon, 1980.

Genette, Gerard. *Figures III*. Paris: Seuil, 1972.

Giorgio, Adalgisa. "A Feminist Family Romance: Mother, Daughter and Female Genealogy in Fabrizia Ramondino's *Althénopis*." *The Italianist* 11 (1991): 128–29.

Heidegger, Martin. *Identity and Difference*. Trans. J. Stambaugh. New York: Harper, 1969.

Lucamante, Stefania. "*Passaggio in ombra:* riprese, innovazioni e soluzioni tematico-strutturali in un romanzo morantiano." *Italian Culture* 15 (1997): 269–95.

———. "Le scelte dell'*autofiction*: il romanzo della memoria contro il potere della Storia." *Studi novecenteschi* 56 (1998): 367–81.

———. "Tra romanzo e autobiografia: il caso della scrittura di Fabrizia Ramondino." *Modern Language Notes* 112 (1997): 105–13.

Marotti, Maria. "Filial Discourses: Feminism and Femininity in Italian Women's Autobiography." Marotti 65–86.

———, ed. *Italian Women Writers from the Renaissance to the Present: Revising the Canon*. University Park: Pennsylvania State UP, 1995.

Morante, Elsa. *Diario 1938*. Introd. Alba Andreini. Milan: Adelphi, 1995.

———. *History: A Novel*. Trans. William Weaver. Steerforth Italia: South Royalton, 2000.

———. *House of Liars*. Trans. Adrienne Foulke. Editorial Assistance Andrew Chiappe. New York: Harcourt, 1951.

———. *Opere*. Ed. Cesare Garboli and Carlo Cecchi. Vols. 1 and 2. Milan: Mondadori, 1988 and 1990.

———. "*Piccolo manifesto*" *ed altri scritti*. Milan: Linea d'ombra, 1988.

———. "Sul romanzo." In *Pro o contro la bomba atomica*. Ed. Cesare Garboli. Milan: Adelphi, 1987. 41–73

Oz, Amos. "Into Mother's Bosom: On Several Beginnings in Elsa Morante's *History: A Novel*." *The Story Begins: Essays on Literature*. Trans. M. Bar-Tursa. New York: Harcourt, 1999. 65–87

Parati, Graziella. *Public History, Private Stories: Italian Women's Autobiography*. Minneapolis and London: U of Minnesota P, 1996.

Pasolini, Pier Paolo. "L'isola di Arturo." *Il portico della morte*. Ed. Cesare Segre. Rome: Ass. Fondo Pier Paolo Pasolini, 1988. 167–70.

Per Elisa. Studi su "Menzogna e sortilegio." Pisa: Nistri-Lischi, 1990.

Ramondino, Fabrizia. *Althénopis*. Turin: Einaudi, 1981.

———. *Althenopis*. Trans. M. Sullivan. Manchester: Carcanet, 1988.

———. *Guerra di infanzia e di Spagna*. Turin: Einaudi, 2002.

———. *L'isola riflessa*. Turin: Einaudi, 1998.

Stefania Lucamante

Ramondino, Fabrizia. *Passaggio a Trieste*. Turin: Einaudi, 2000.

―――. "Useppe e sua madre." *Per Elsa Morante*. Milan: Linea d'ombra, 1993. 185–98

Ricoeur, Paul. *Time and Narrative*. Vol. 3. Trans. K. McLaughlin and D. Pellauer. Chicago: U of Chicago P, 1984–88.

Sartori, Diana. "Nessuno è autore della propria storia: identità e azione." *Diotima. La sapienza di partire da sé*. Naples: Liguori, 1996. 23–57.

―――. *"Tu devi*. Un ordine materno." *Diotima. Oltre l'uguaglianza. Le radici femminili dell'uguaglianza*. Naples: Liguori, 1995. 5–30.

Scarano, Emanuella. "La fatua veste del vero." *Per Elisa* 95–171.

Smith, Sidonie, and Julie Watson. *De/Colonizing the Subject: The Politics of Gender in Women's Autobiography*. Minneapolis and London: U of Minnesota P, 1992.

Spivak, Gayatri. *In Other Worlds: Essays in Cultural Politics*. London and New York: Methuen, 1987. 118–33.

Weigel, Sigrid. "Secularization and Sacralization, Normalization and Rupture: Kristeva and Arendt on Forgiveness." Trans. Mark Kyburz. *PMLA* 2.117 (Mar. 2002): 320–23.

Enrico Palandri

Narrative and Essays

The Ethical Commitment
of Elsa Morante

In speaking of Elsa Morante, it is difficult to draw a line
between her commitment to the foundations of writing and to
those of living itself.[1] Thinking about life through art, and
working through literary problems in a perspective that implied
absolute moral responsibility: these two positions are axiomatic in her work, and will brook no deviation or approximation.

Within this commitment we can recognize a questioning of
the relationship between thought and writing that goes back to
the most ancient formulations central to Western culture, such
as the seventh letter of Plato. In this letter, Plato explains that
nothing of what he has written can represent his thought. A certain level of mistrust in the possibility of language to represent
reality is deeply embedded in our tradition, whether in the form
of analytical thought dealing with structural shortcomings of
expression (from Cicero to Leibniz), or in religious attitudes
seeking control of expression through censorship. Morante
inherits this broad sense of sacredness around the poetic word
prior to the rise of the bourgeoisie in the eighteenth and nineteenth centuries: the word is inspired in a manner that is divine,
transhistorical, and transcendent. She adds to it a romantic and
individualistic vision of the poet as a solitary beacon, a
Prometheus in fatal combat with the gods, spoken by the poetical world rather than speaking it.

This stance later created many problems for Morante. In the
secularization that characterizes our times, the novel-reading
public sees art as a substitute for religion. Since Fra Cristoforo,
Cardinal Borromeo, and the atypical ending of Stendhal's
Chartreuse, characters inspired by a religious ethos have been
few and far between. With due exception made for Alyosha
Karamazov, they have also been of relatively slight literary

257

weight. The bourgeoisie has other problems and other models: Bovary and Bezuchov, Zeno Cosini and Gregor Samsa fulfil their novelistic destiny within the fabric of relationships with other characters rather than in a transcendental surge. The reality of this fabric is then questioned by the inadequacy of the social context to express all their humanity; something is left over that dooms them to a kind of incommunicability and loneliness, but does not find a solution in the otherness of religion. Religious reflection is thus reduced to a metaphysical nostalgia, a bare trace of the problems that dominated medieval Europe and still preoccupied Dante and Tasso. Modern writers feel increasingly less compelled to tackle these problems; while they still recur in Alessandro Manzoni's *I promessi sposi*, here, too, social questions are already more important than religious tension, explicitly fundamental only to the episode of the *Innominato*.

Morante registers with extraordinary intensity this shift of focus from transcendental aspiration to material and social contexts. Like Pasolini she, too, has her roots in a lower middle class only recently emancipated from an archaic world, where a pre-modern vernacular mythology has been suddenly and sharply eroded by the onset of industry, with its language and its values. Saints' names have disappeared from calendars, the day is no longer tolled by the bell in the local belfry but by the siren that marks the change of shift in the factory, the cycle of the seasons has been relegated to second place, distances have shrunk. More so than Pasolini, Morante is willing to speak in the language of this transformation. She seeks neither dialect nor any kind of mixed genre; she writes the novel, or rather the Novel; she appropriates the Word within the bourgeois drawing room, at the heart of the social group responsible for this change. More than anyone else she explores the split between these two worlds. The first world is where truth is the reality evoked by Plato, divine and yet close to man, attainable through thought but untranslatable into words and where art, just like any other language, is on a lower plane, aesthetic, related to the feelings, as the etymology of the terms *aesthetic* ("to feel") suggests, and in opposition to the pure conception of the soul that has no need of language. The second world on the other hand is that of the bourgeoisie, which in the material aspect of art, in feeling, in the textuality of the artistic object, seeks to reify what it feels has been lost in Olympus and on Golgotha; it seeks the gods who have fled the temples spoken of by Heidegger, it seeks what in reality it no longer believes in, having substituted history for the inscrutability of an unbearably silent divinity.

The style in which Morante's essays are written, somewhat weighed down by the *pesanteur* that Cesare Garboli notices in the preface to the 1987 reprint of *Pro o contro la bomba atomica*, and more generally Morante's stance toward the essay writing with which she counterpointed the writing of novels, are two of the points where we might attempt a comparison between her narrative writing and her essay writing. It is first of all in the voice she uses to address theoretical issues that we can contrast two different modes of being a writer. Her baroque, rich vocabulary gives way to a rather pedagogical prose, as if a lowering of the tone were deemed necessary for the sake of clarity. But is it simply a lowering of the tone or does her voice betray a more complex and hidden ambition? Are there other factors that account for this transformation of her style?

For Morante, art is both secularization of the sacred and the verification of human experience; in her vision of the world art is more than expression, or the techniques adopted by an artist to express himself or herself. Indeed, when expression becomes recognizable in a particular technique, in something empirical and extrinsic that can then be imitated, Morante is immediately suspicious of manner; and by mannerism, which has a decidedly negative nuance in her vocabulary, she means, above all, the derivative or unnecessary forms of expression that no longer have roots in life but are prompted by extrinsic elements, fraudulent aesthetic ambition, mimicry, desire for wealth, and so on. Sometimes a *mannerism* in her vocabulary simply means education, the use of techniques that have been handed down rather than forged directly by experience. In education, social divisions, whether in the name of gender, class, or geographical origin, are imprinted onto individuals, quelling the universalism that is within each one of us. But above all, mannerism is falsification, the non-true because artificial, and it is this that attracts her polemic.

Morante exploits the contrast between these two ideas of language (the reality of language versus its manners) in *L'isola di Arturo*, juxtaposing constantly the legendary, invented names Arturo makes up to describe the world around him, with the reality of things. Poetry and prose. The pleasure of reading this book is also sharing the sense of simultaneous superiority and nostalgia the mature Arturo has for his former self and yet, secretly, approving an absolute superiority of the child and his poetry over the mature man, where language will become a form of mistrust. To some extent this duality in language is exploited throughout her work, either by using the sensitivity of children and their lack of realism, or simply by implying a more sober description of the world beyond the one she offers.

For her there is a natural narrative inventiveness, and a fraudulent one. In the authors she reads she seeks an authenticity in which she perceives the continuation of fundamental moral values, the voices of the gods, which struggle to make themselves heard above the din and clamor of our world. From a theoretical point of view, at least, she finds herself in a position diametrically opposed to that of Baudelaire and the Symbolists, with their exaltation of the artificial. On a theoretical level, it is worth repeating, because when a poem or a single phrase of Baudelaire's convinces her, Morante sets aside any theory in the name of a deeper meeting of minds. For her, objection or approval based on aesthetic principles finds its correlative in ethical condemnation or total admiration. Criticism and theory must know when to give way to an intuitive and deeper knowledge.

In parallel fashion, being an artist, for her, is not simply gaining mastery of an art form, whether music, painting, or the novel. To be an artist is to be part of a specific human destiny that should be lived as a mission. But if art is more than the sum of its parts, how then can it be defined? Elsa Morante never gives a simple answer; rather, she poses the question constantly, in more or less direct form. If it is not possible to say what God is, we should certainly not let ourselves be satisfied with a technique. In speaking of books, she seeks to stand against those who in her opinion reduce to a formula that which of its very nature is in continual tension, and who thus throttle the life out of a book.

Real and unreal, antithetical terms that dominate Morante's linguistic universe, are the moral development of these two aesthetic poles (mannerism versus authenticity) and are aligned by her in a system of parallel values: art on the one side, the bomb on the other; on one side the poet, the joy of the creative imagination, on the other a dark mimicry, the turncoats, the conformists; on the one hand individual and romantic adventure, on the other hand groups, formalisms, literary movements, schools, -isms.

The neo-positivist climate of semiotic and narratological criticism so fashionable in the 1960s and 1970s left Morante cold. She cared little for an approach that sought to establish in style, in language, or at least in discrete elements, a terrain that could be delimited scientifically and laid out for examination. It is very likely out of a spirit of polemic with the "gruppo '63," with Pasolini even, or at the very least with the literary theories that marked the phase of the neo-avant-garde, that Morante writes in *Pro o contro la bomba atomica:*

> [. . .] e che sorta di linguaggio dovrà adoperare [lo scrittore]? Dialetto, industria, quale koinè? quale stile, quali semantemi, quale carattere tipografico? Pro o contro le maiuscole? Pro o contro la punteggiatura? Ma lasciatelo scrivere come gli pare, ché tanto il primo inventore dei linguaggi è stato sempre lui! (116)

> [. . .] and what sort of language should [the writer] adopt? Dialect, industrial, which koiné, which style, what semantics, which type face? For or against capital letters? For or against punctuation? Just leave him alone to write as he pleases, since he has always been the primary inventor of language!

Nonetheless it would be misleading to imagine that Morante's resistance to the climate that dominates critical reflection in the 1960s and 1970s was in any way naïve. Morante was an attentive, voracious reader, and each of her novels springs from a profound conception that determines style and material in a coherent manner. Rather, it is the hieratic tone of the essays that reveals Morante's diffidence toward any attempt to separate writing from living, attempting to turn the former into an objective discipline and living into a subjective matter, into a private affair that can withdraw from the gaze of others. Thus she challenges the boundary between what is public in a writer (books, projected public image) and what is deemed to be private, making these two sides constantly interact. Style in itself is not credible; according to Morante, we constantly gaze beyond. We are interested in the private sphere of authors; we want to know not out of sheer moral voyeurism, but because, since the text is made up of infinite surfaces, there is always a deeper and more meaningful level that emerges when we read. A good reader brings out these deeper levels of meaning. However, Morante was not keen on reading, or developing her analysis of the work of others. Of a book she would say simply "it's good," rather than engage in lengthy discussion. Of course a rich and engaged reading implies different strata, but she would warn against the complacency of academic readers more interested in displaying their cultural education than in grasping the reality of texts through possibly a single word or expression. She behaved with books as with lovers, where a smile out of context or some empty sweeping statement can forever alienate one from the other.

It also seems to me significant that Morante was somewhat reluctant to collect and publish these essays in a single volume, almost as if she glimpsed the fact that the relationship between her theories and her narrative works could only remain allusive; far from explaining her creative procedures, her essay-writing bore witness to the almost unnatural effort that poetry makes when it reflects on itself. She feared that by explaining her way of reading she would end up like a critic, satisfied with intellectual speculation rather than engaged in the dangerous but creative art-life adventure.

The characteristic features of literary criticism, which passes judgment on a new work with all the rhetorical authority of tradition, produce a potentially damaging tension in Morante when she tries to play that role which divides her, putting her in opposition to herself. She reacts by asserting the indivisible and unquestionable nature of her own opinions. Because art is life and life is art, she cannot afford to "think about them," as if one could theoretically speculate on the possibility of having a different destiny. We are one thing and within it, and books are part of it. One cannot be both inside and outside; one is either art and wholly with it or else an objectifier, "un operatore," as Carla Benedetti would say today. Morante seems to suggest that there is nothing external to her own persona; she is whole and indivisible.

Moreover, in these essays we sense the unease of the author who addresses a public made up, in part, of academics: to their judgments she offers here not her work but its motivating force, her theoretical reflection, her readings. And here, almost as if she feared being surprised among the tools of her trade, she appears more defenseless. By her attitude even more than by her style, which verges on the sermon, she shields the delicate ethical and aesthetic equilibrium that is so important in her creative work: love of beauty, love of truth, love for what is good, hedged about by the threat of darkness, which bursts through giving us a glimpse of chaos, the difficulty of articulating pain and silence in words. Somewhere in between essays and prose, her diaries are enlightening in this respect; they seem to indicate, just before the writing of *Menzogna e sortilegio*, the splinter that will oppose these two directions. It would seem that for her, analytical discourse can only humiliate, while art can rescue and restore.

The essays are, then, to be read with a key. While they are richly suggestive and illuminating for readers who have already had access to her poetic world, the essays do not explain, nor do they attempt to persuade; rather, they enunciate in apodictic manner their own theses. Narrative has already achieved hegemony over any other form of writing since *Menzogna e sortilegio,* giving it thus a specific interior configuration. The essays are from that moment onward a sort of doodle in between novels; they do not push her to pursue new directions and hardly interfere with the close identification her first novel has created between language and personal reality.

There is no theoretical elaboration, no adherence to a trend or current, no meeting with her generation that can any more alter the route of her journey. Literature for her is a nucleus of values and reality that is beyond time. It embodies itself in historic forms of expression but cannot exhaust itself in any one work, neither is it contradicted by the partial results that it inevitably achieves. Elsa Morante is an artist who listens for this nucleus of reality as her characters in their fabulation are turned toward an absent mother or father.

Turning toward an absent mother or father assumes for her, then, a theological significance. All her novels are generated by the interrogation of the space left empty by an absent or inadequate parent, by the impossibility of filling this void. The private genealogies of Elisa, Arturo, Useppe, and Emanuel are, finally, the novel itself; beginning with a recognition of origins, the narrative goes ever deeper in a search for meaning that generates in a flight-line the private world of the characters, the world of the novel and finally the world itself. Sacralization and secularization are, then, not stylistic registers or instruments through which to deal with an object, but the place in which the ideal generative principle and the textual aspect of Morante's world enter into open conflict. The intonation of Elisa, Arturo, or Emanuel is a turning toward parents who are partly biographical, partly imaginary, partly literary. Here emerge the eternal wounds and questions: we have a father and a mother, but who were they really? Are they the people who have generated us physically? Those whom we have read? Those we have met and who have shaped us? Or perhaps those we have never met and whom we tacitly reproach for our incompleteness?

Novels operate within this state of restlessness by secularization, searching out content from this dark place of origin, beyond time, between the divine and mystery, to bring it into art, among men and women, and into language. The enchanted and wonderful world intuited by children, the creations of fantasy, are revealed to be a hard and prosaic world when they are ripped away from a vital relationship with that world. We move from the enchanted tone of *L'isola di Arturo*'s opening pages (the stars, the marvelous island with its celebrated toponymy), toward the realistic epilogue unfolded by the prisoner, who undermines the heroic figure of the father. The same thing happens in *Aracoeli*, where mother and father are pursued in a humiliation that gradually acquires more realist tones. The process repeats itself from novel to novel, with shifting nuances. The infantile world is presented as an overflowing baroque garden, with abundant use of adjectives and complex syntax. As the narrative unfolds a splintering takes place through which emerge, with ever more insistent rhythms, comedy and the realistic business of being an adult, increasing the sense of distance from the fablelike beginning.

In her essays Morante takes the opposite path: beginning with lay questions about a character such as Andrei Bolkonski or on the function of art, she is gradually caught up by a prophetic tone, in sacralization. Writing essays, for her, is a dialogue with an essential mystery, and a mystery that she does not wish to be solved. Rather, she wraps the explanation and the question in a shroud of empathy with the authors, trying to be there, with him or her, possibly within him or her. In other words, she contrasts any process of objectification, of creating otherness. From this point of view it is worth remembering that Morante, in the private anecdotal world she shared with her friends, had reconstructed her own genealogy with two fathers. Having more than one father was important to her, because it opened up a speculative horizon on her own origins. The remote origins of her characters, the enchanted tone in which Arturo connects himself through his name with King Arthur or the constellation of Boote, the Herdsman (see Della Coletta's article in this volume, pp. 129–56), the African adventure with which the insignificant German soldier imagines his own destiny at the beginning of *La Storia*, and so on, are in many ways analogous to her own two private fathers: origin as destiny is something remote and mysterious that goes beyond the immediate and obvious horizon of dates and places and social position and gives rise, in the narrative exploration, to speculative fantasy. A before and an after that in the shadows acquire their own richness: to contemplate and interrogate a character is, for Elsa Morante, to cross over the surface of naturalism and plunge into its secret heart; to share doubts and questions, and to live like Arturo, or Elisa, or Iduzza, in a state of ignorance as to one's ultimate course, which is the only one to avoid becoming fixed by the external gaze. Again, as in Plato, to be aware of an ultimate impossibility of words to represent.

Certainly the characters belong to a comedy that unfolds among men and women, but they are observed against the light of the absoluteness of their human nature, which presents them·

Enrico Palandri

in limine, on the threshold of a transcendence that can take place only through the novel.

Like all of her own biography as she recounted it to friends, Morante had deliberately co-opted her two private fathers into the business of making novels. The dreamlike mystification of her own youth was part of a conscious attempt to have her own private life serve as a mirror that, in multiplying and deforming hypotheses, led her to transcend her personal sphere, where the real energy sprang from, in order to stage her own thematics in a theater of fantasy. In other words, to make literature out of herself as well.

Morante was, anyway, fully aware that between desacralization and secularization she had chosen, and given the best of herself in, the nonsacred, in the novel. It was her anticonformism, subversion, the tension of youth, recalled perhaps in her mature and older years, which had given the best fruit. Only unwillingly did she reveal the shadow of this approach, the reflective side that took her back to mysterious and confused origins that she kept at bay with her art. No wonder, then, that she wanted the essays to remain concealed.

Despite the frequently noted eccentricity of her work with regard to the literary currents swirling around her (with a baroque novel such as *Menzogna e sortilegio,* published at the height of Neorealism, and a novel that in many ways recalls Neorealism, such as *La Storia* in the 1970s), Morante was anything but isolated. On the contrary, only to the most superficial glance does her idiosyncratic view of literary movements, and frequently of the people who attached themselves to these movements, alienate her from the context in which new generations of writers with whom she came into contact were developing their own ideas about literature. This strange rigidity around her own talent made her peculiarly solid in her contact with others and leaves Elsa Morante, curiously enough, central to the twentieth century in Italy. In her case it is not so much openings onto the new that characterize her narrative journey, but on the contrary, the radicalization of what constituted her own self. It is by defending her own intricate fabric of public and private, of writing and being, that she has so successfully achieved a form, eschewing the objectifying process of analysis. Rather than explore her poetical world, these essays serve her purpose of concealment of the space necessary to create.

Notes

1. This article was previously published in Italian as "Alcune notazioni in margine a *Pro o contro la bomba atomica*," by Enrico Palandri, in C. D'Angeli and G. Magrini, eds., "Vent'anni dopo *La storia*. Omaggio a Elsa Morante," spec. issue of *Studi novecenteschi* 21.47–48 (June–Dec. 1994): 79–90. It is reprinted here in translation with permission.

Works Cited

Garbole, Cesare. Preface. *Pro o contro la bomba atomica*. By Elsa Morante. Milan: Adelphi, 1987.

Walter Siti

Elsa Morante and
Pier Paolo Pasolini

This article traces the intense, reciprocal, fertile, and troubled
relationship between Elsa Morante and Pier Paolo Pasolini.[1] In
analyzing the several aspects of Morante's presence in the work
of Pasolini, I have deliberately enmeshed three elements: (1)
the level of empirical people, (2) the level of psychic "self-im-
ages," and (3) the level of literary characters. This last item
should subsequently be divided into (a) characters appearing
with the same name as their empirical referent and requiring
an immediate comparison with the extra-textual world, and (b)
autonomous characters, in which the reference to empirical persons is cryptic and of little bearing for the comprehension of
the text.

The first mention of Elsa Morante in the work of Pier Paolo
Pasolini is to be found in his letters. In a letter dated June 22,
1954 (*Lettere 1940–1954* 667),[2] Pasolini recommends
Morante's *Lo scialle andaluso* to Leonardo Sciascia, for a
series that was also to include the works of Giorgio Bassani
and Natalia Ginzburg; Pasolini had first read *Lo scialle
andaluso* when it appeared in *Botteghe Oscure* in 1953. During
these years, Pasolini was seeking entry into the influential literary circles of Rome, attempting to insert himself into the
"cultural politics" of the day. To recommend *Lo scialle
andaluso* to the high-profile Sicilian writer Sciascia, however, transcended such politics, while Pasolini's reading of
Morante's work also suggests a deepening understanding
between the two artists.

Writing from Bari on January 18, 1955, Pasolini announces
his intention to invite Alberto Moravia and Elsa Morante to dinner at his parents' house: "Prima di tutto la mamma faccia
l'esame di coscienza e veda se si sente di affrontare con calma

il nuovo tour de force. Poi, il babbo dovrebbe telefonare subito a Elsa Morante e chiederle se per domenica sera lei e Moravia sono liberi e disponibili" (*Lettere 1955–1975* 13; "first of all, Mother should take a good look at herself and see if she feels up to facing this new tour de force comfortably. Then, Dad should quickly phone Elsa Morante and ask her if she and Moravia are free for dinner on Sunday"). The tone of the letter suggests that the planned dinner was somewhat formal, making it likely that Pasolini's personal acquaintance with Moravia and Morante was still a recent one.

On an intellectual level, a hint of textual coincidence between the incipit of Morante's poem "Alibi," "Solo chi ama conosce" (Morante, *Opere* 1: 1392–95; "Only who loves knows"), and the incipit of Pasolini's "Il pianto della scavatrice," "Solo l'amare, solo il conoscere / conta" (Pasolini, *Tutte le poesie* 1: 833; "Only loving, only the knowing / Counts"), appears to offer further confirmation of the blossoming relationship between the authors. The suspicion becomes almost a certainty when we compare this line from "Alibi," "povero come il gatto dei vicoli napoletani" (Morante, *Opere* 1: 1394; "poor as a cat from the back streets of Naples"), with the line "povero come un gatto del Colosseo" in Pasolini's "Il pianto della scavatrice" (*Tutte le poesie* 1: 836; "poor as a cat from the Coliseum"). The dates claim "Alibi" to be prior[3] to "Il pianto della scavatrice," while Pasolini seems to have engaged in a private micro-allusion bordering on homage. The image of the cat will soon, in fact, become a recurring pattern of symbolic recognition between the two artists.

On December 21, 1957, Pasolini published a review of Morante's second novel, *L'isola di Arturo* (*Arturo's Island*) in *Vie nuove*. While he comments very favorably on the novel, he also criticized some formal elements of the work. He believes, for instance, that Morante could easily have cut half of the first 150 pages; she should have drawn only a general picture of the period preceding the arrival of Nunziatella on the island of Procida, omitting the descriptions of the islanders and the island. For Pasolini, the image of the island rendered in these pages becomes too superficial and sketchy. In his review, the artist stresses how Morante's writing should have focused, rather, on Arturo's life. The experimentalist Pasolini appears uneasy with Morante's "slow pace," choosing to use her novel as a means of honing his own views on Neorealistic polemics, presenting it as an example of an "expanded realism" enriched by fabulous and magic undertones. Perhaps unsettled by an implicit comparison with Italo Calvino, Pasolini is ill-disposed toward the nineteenth-century "residues" of the book and fails to see the essential link between realistic *minutiae* and the fantastic exuberance of the imagination. He approves, though, the "ingenuity of the lexical verve" and a "delicious diligence of scholastic *pensum*." Pasolini observes the "candid respect towards the most traditional linguistic and communicative institutions," which Morante always dispenses generously to her readers. Being the excellent stylistic critic he was, he links these traits to a "practical and cognitive inferiority complex, that she [Morante] transcends with the help of a humbly amorous creature." In the Morantian pages of *L'isola di Arturo* we witness a "dilation of greatness, of the importance and of the goodness of the world" (Pasolini, *Portico della morte* 167–90).

As Cesare Garboli and Carlo Cecchi recognize in "Fortuna critica," Pasolini picks the "path of adulation [. . .] hiding within Morante's fabulous technical skills" in his review of her second novel (in Morante, *Opere* 2: 1673). He cannot bring himself to state explicitly, although he comes very close, that Morante's masochistic love is twofold: it allows her to transform the defects of loved beings into qualities of excellence and it also determines her attitude toward the average or mediocre language of the narrative institution. For instance, the less than perfect Italian translations of the great European novels that she read did not diminish Morante's love for them, and this stance represents perhaps the foremost example of her attitude toward loved things and beings. An adoring humility is thus transformed into pride, for it is only by loving that we can share the goodness of what we love. In my view, however, Pasolini is unaware of the degree of irony that such a position can bring with it: the same irony that there is, for instance, in saying ostentatiously to somebody "your most humble servant."

We can be quite sure that Pasolini's acute observations, which range from stylistics to psychology, contain some level of reference to his own life and work: "too much love" is such a conspicuous leit-motiv of his own poetry that it is difficult not to think of it as a quotation when we find it in *Aracoeli*, even if we don't recognize it as a motif that already lies behind Elisa in *Menzogna e sortilegio*. But in Pasolini the awareness of exclusion provokes a fermentation of love into hate and a consequent fissure of the world: on the one side, one loves; on the other, one hates. For Pasolini there is, however, a twist: it is impossible to love those he feels are socially superior to him: his love is never "from below." He cannot accept any inferiority without a counterpart. His eroticism is competitive, not of a begging kind, "[e]lemosina ardita / ei domanda alla gente: / se qualcuno consente / com'è bella la vita" ("boldly begging, / he asks people: / if anybody agrees / how beautiful life is"; Penna 84). Although he feels it foreign to himself, the topic of holiness fascinates him and will make him liken Morante to the poet Sandro Penna.

By 1961 the friendship between Morante, Moravia, and Pasolini had become so close that they organized a trip to India together. Morante, in truth, joined them for only a short part of the trip. Still, it is bizarre that in the notebook Pasolini wrote, entitled *L'odore dell'India* (*The Smell of India*) *(*Moravia's notebook exhibited an interesting opposition of terms and was called *L'idea dell'India* [*The Idea of India*]), Morante is present only in the third chapter. She appears explicitly connected with the theme of charity. The two go together to visit Mother Theresa of Calcutta: then they lodge a little poor boy in an institute in spite of Moravia's rational warning, given the enormous number of wretched children, about the futility of such a gesture: "Elsa, aggressiva e dolce, mi si volle unire, attratta dall'assurdo" (Pasolini, *L'odore dell'India* 50; "Elsa, aggressive and sweet, wanted to join herself to me, attracted by the absurd"). The feeling of brotherhood between them is cemented in the sense of a shared belonging to the race of those who believe, in "come ideale, quello di svuotare l'oceano con un ditale" (*L'odore dell'India* 51: "emptying the ocean with a thimble as an ideal in life").

In 1961 Elsa Morante plays the part of a prisoner in *Accattone*. While Elsa was motivated by her own desire to act and be among friends, her dark, proud face was certainly the main reason for such a choice on Pasolini's part. Moreover, these are the years in which the ideological thread in Pasolini's work, which was to lead to a parallelism between intellectuals and sub-proletarians, was becoming evident, a parallelism geared to a possible anti-bourgeois allegiance. In this sense the episode of the soccer match in "Pietro II," in which one could imagine Pasolini's intellectual friends taking the place of the boys, exemplifies a linking of working-class and intellectual endeavor:

> Correndo Giorgio ha la faccia di Carlo Levi,
> divinità propizia, facendo una rovesciata,
> Giannetto ha l'ilarità di Moravia, il Moro
> rimandando, è Vigorelli, quando s'arrabbia o abbraccia,
> e Coen, e Alicata, e Elsa Morante, e i redattori
> del Paese Sera o dell'Avanti, e Libero Bigiaretti,
> giocano con me, tra gli alberetti del Trullo [. . .].[4]

> Running, Giorgio has the face of Carlo Levi,
> propitious divinity, as he takes a dive,
> Giannetto has the light joy of Moravia, the Moor
> Passing back the ball, is Vigorelli when he gets angry or embraces,
> and Coen, and Alicata, and Elsa Morante, and the editors
> of Paese Sera or of the Avanti, and Libero Bigiaretti,
> play with me, among the little trees of the Trullo.

Linking his intellectual friends to the boys has a further, private motivation, that of drawing the separate fragments of his own life into unity. In the same "Pietro II," in the section dated "Wednesday, March 6 (night)," the line "come dice un verso orale di Elsa Morante" (*Tutte le poesie* 1: 1154; "as a spoken verse by Elsa Morante goes") appears. Morante's example, with its "poetics of creatures" is particularly significant here, and is coherent with Pasolini's future theory on the *cinema di poesia*. The main tenets of this theory are that poetry takes place in reality, before taking on any other form, and that a form of "lived" poetry, rather than a written one, can indeed exist. This holds true despite Pasolini's long-standing interest in oral poetry, which dates back to the 1940s. It should be mentioned that the "spoken verse" in question is "che ha per sé un amore infelice" (*Tutte le poesie* 1: 1154; "which has for itself an unhappy love"). This formulation needs to be changed only slightly to evoke the "innamorata non ricambiata di se stessa" ("the unrequited lover of herself") that appears in a satirical portrait composed in 1950 by Morante in "I tre Narcisi" (*Opere* 2: 1473). A man like Pasolini, who always placed himself under the sign of Narcissus, could not but feel put on the back burner by an implacable accuser of Narcissuses such as Morante, implacable to the point of ambiguity.

When on April 30, 1962, Morante's close friend Bill Morrow committed suicide, Pasolini shared deeply in her grief, commemorating the "povero ragazzo che è volato due volte" (*Tutte le poesie* 1: 1337; "the poor boy who flew twice") in "Poesia su una poesia," a poem composed only fifteen days after Morrow's death, dated May 14, 1962. There is some irony in this verse and it will recur in 1968 when, in his review in verse of *Il mondo salvato dai ragazzini*, Pasolini spoke once more of the young man's death and continued lamenting for his loss, adding that "un intero clan piange per la sua camiciola" (*Tutte le poesie* 2: 39; "an entire clan cries for his shirt").

In 1963–64 Morante was invited to select the music for Pasolini's *The Gospel according to Matthew*. She also collaborated in the casting of actors, and indeed it is difficult to define the limits of her contribution to the film. It is worth mentioning that two of the most typical and "scandalous" gestures of the Pasolinian Christ, who is both impulsive and violent, the expulsion of the money lenders and the cursing of the fig tree, are the same biblical episodes cited by Davide Segre in the speech in the hostelry, in Morante's *La Storia*. The first episode is the expulsion:

> Si gettò, allora, alla ripresa con un nuovo respiro dopo l'ultimo salto dell'ostacolo: "Volevo dire, insomma," proferí a voce ancora più alta di prima (almeno cosí a lui parve), che "solo un uomo puro può scacciare i mercanti e dirgli: *la terra era il tempio della coscienza totale, e voi ne avete fatto una spelonca di ladri!*" (*Opere* 2: 945; emphasis in original)

> He rushed on with renewed breath, after leaping over the last hurdle. "What I mean, in other words," he declared in a voice even louder than before (at least so it seemed to him), "is that only a pure man can drive out the money lenders and say: the earth was the temple of total consciousness, and you have made of it a den of thieves!" (*History* 657)

The second episode is the story of the fig tree:

> Si racconta che un cristo (non importa quale, era un cristo) una volta camminando per una via di campagna ebbe fame e andò per cogliere un frutto da un albero da fico. Ma siccome non era stagione, l'albero non aveva frutti: nient'altro che foglie incommestibili . . . E allora Cristo lo maledisse, dannandolo alla sterilità perpetua . . . Il senso è chiaro: per chi riconosce Cristo al suo passaggio, è sempre stagione. E chi non riconoscendolo gli nega la propria frutta col pretesto del tempo e della stagione, è maledetto. Non si discute. (*Opere* 2: 951–52)

> They tell of a christ (it doesn't matter which one; he was a christ) who once was walking along a country road and he was hungry, so he went to pick a fig from a tree. But since it wasn't the right season, the tree had no fruit; only inedible leaves . . . And then Christ cursed it, damning it to perpetual sterility . . . The meaning is clear: for anyone who recognizes Christ as he passes, the season is always right. And the man who doesn't recognize him denies him his own fruit with the excuse of the time and the season, and is cursed. There is no arguing. (*History* 663)

A typical feature of Pasolini's film is the identification of the Christ and the poet, as opposed to the "moralisti di sinistra" ("leftist moralists") of the *Quaderni piacentini*. It is important to remember that in *Pro o contro la bomba atomica* Morante describes how the poet is evangelically sent to earth to "bear witness to reality" (*Opere* 2: 1546). The two artists share a sense of the religious dimension of reality, together with the idea that the divine takes the part of the humble, because they alone are not distanced from reality. It is Morante who coins the term *unreality* (*irrealtà*) to indicate an image of the world filtered through the false values of "pseudo-cultura o, come dice più esplicitamente la mia amica Elsa Morante, dell'irrealtà" (*Le belle bandiere* 219; "pseudo-culture or, as my friend Elsa Morante puts it more bluntly, of unreality"). In subsequent works Pasolini will appropriate the term in statements such as, "che io e Elsa Morante chiamiamo 'irrealtà'" (*Il caos* 87; "what Elsa Morante and I call unreality."

In 1964, after receiving "Poesia in forma di rosa," Elsa Morante composes an ironic text entitled "Madrigale in forma di gatto" ("Madrigal in the shape of a cat"). Morante's text is a calligram contained within the silhouette of a cat and signed "un gatto che non crepa" ("a cat that doesn't die") and is an allusion to a hemistich in "Una disperata vitalità" ("A desperate vitality"). Pasolini defines himself in "Una disperata vitalità" precisely as "un gatto che non crepa" (*Tutte le poesie* 1: 1183; "a cat that does not die"). The partly fatuous, partly revealing, game of the reciprocal mirror images, of the elective brotherhood between the artist and Morante, begins in this period. In the rhetorical form of the *laudum*, a series of anaphoras modeled on the "discorso delle beatitudini," Morante does not spare him ferocious accusations:

> beati [. . .] i vari equivoci dell'egoismo le mascherate degli
> stracci
> le carità pretestuose le immondizie deificate
> i pregiudizi di casta l'alibi storicistico
> le complicità attuali, l'adorazione ai padri farisei, la paura della
> castrazione
> il candido tradimento il pianto vantone.
> (In *Lettere 1955–1975* lxxxiv–xc)

> blessed [. . .] the many misunderstandings of egoism the
> masquerades of rags
> the acts of charity only pretexts the deified garbage
> the class prejudices the historicist alibi
> the current connivances, the adoration of the Pharisees, the fear
> of castration
> the candid betrayal the boastful cry.

In essence, Morante accuses Pasolini of false love, of hypocrisy, exhibitionism, ideological bad faith, but all appears redeemed by his candor, by the felicitous narcissism to which Morante juxtaposes her own self-hatred:

> e lui beato ignorerà gli altri peccatori al bando della rosa
> e al bando di se stessi
> non protagonisti del mondo
> non leggenda di se stessi
> soli senza nessun addio.
> Agonie senza nessun pianto e nessuna rosa.
> (In *Lettere 1955–1975*: lxxxiv–xc)

and he the blessed one will ignore the other sinners ostracized
by the rose

and ostracized by themselves
not protagonists of the world
not legend of themselves
alone without any farewell.
Agonies without any cry and any rose.

The complaint of "adoration of the Pharisees" alludes to a specific moment of discord that resulted from a failed payment by Arco Film to some of Elsa's friends, who had participated in the *Gospel*. Pasolini volunteered to pay them out of his own pocket, but Elsa writes to him:

> E tu sai benissimo che il pagare di tua tasca (o io di mia tasca) qui non significa niente, giacché quelli di Arco Film non desiderano altro, perché così si crogiolano meglio nella loro merda. Perciò anche se tu fossi miliardario (e purtroppo non lo sei) non potrei accettare i tuoi soldi né per Willliam né per Giacomo (come difatti non li accetto e te li unisco qui). L'ombra che tu dici sulla nostra amicizia lo sai benissimo non è il *debito* tuo, che fra l'altro non esiste; ma 'l'adorazione ai Padri Farisei' come ti avevo già scritto nella poesia. Ma non è vero che questa è la prima volta che c'è quest'ombra. (Morante, in Pasolini, *Lettere 1955–1975* clxxiii, n58; emphasis in original)

> And you know very well that paying out of your own pocket (or out of mine for that matter) doesn't mean a thing since the people at Arco Film want nothing more, so they can wallow all the better in their own shit. Therefore, even if you were a millionaire (and sadly you are not) I could not take your money either for William nor for Giacomo (and in fact I'm not taking it, and I'm returning it with this letter). As you know full well, the shadow you mention which has fallen over our friendship is not your *debt*, which, besides, does not even exist; but the "adoration of the Pharisees" as I already wrote you in the poem. But neither is it true that this is the first time we see this shadow.

As we can see, the same accusations of complicity with the *Padroni* (the "Pharisees") rebound between the two: the accusations take on different forms as Pasolini reproaches Morante for a linguistic complicity that is hidden and unconscious, while she upbraids him for a more material and concrete complicity: cowardice in the face of the cultural industry, with a severe psychological twist whereby the fear of the Fathers prevents him from loving people as people.

The bond between Morante and Pasolini was strongest during the central years of the 1960s, particularly from an ideological point of view. These are the years of Pasolini's farewell to historicism. Faced with the shift toward neo-capitalism, he no longer believes in revolution but rather in rebellion and subversion *tout court*. The contradiction between individual aestheticism and collective discipline that he developed while reading Antonio Gramsci's theories is now on the wane. Also fading is the concept of class betrayal, so closely linked with this contradiction. The chaos of "new prehistory" summons forth, rather, his previous inclination to a desperate and extreme heroism. Pasolini's heroism is analogous to Morante's ethical anarchism to which the issue of "barbarie" ("the barbarian") is strictly related. In the elaboration of his new "atonal" metrics, Pasolini takes on board the work of the beat-generation poets, Allen Ginsberg, Larry Ferlinghetti, and his passion is shared, if not prompted, by Morante.

Sub-proletarian anthropology begins with Pasolini, as do the observations on a certain sub-proletarian "aristocraticism"; the insistence on the happiness of the disinherited, and his attempts at the "comic" come instead from Morante, as in the example of *Uccellacci e uccellini* and *La terra vista dalla luna*. It would be hard to say the extent to which Morante is indebted to Pasolini's obsession-motif of boys dying in the very moment in which they try to rebel against society, when she invents and begins to construct the "victim" character Useppe in *La Storia*.

Their reciprocal influence as far as Greek tragedy is concerned appears almost impossible to untangle. Morante's interest is perhaps more ethical and political as she was particularly fascinated by the work of Simone Weil, while Pasolini's interest is more formal and allegorical. In 1968 Pasolini invites Morante to translate a Greek tragedy for the Stabile Theater in Turin. She chooses the *Philoctetis* (in Pasolini, *Lettere 1955–1975* 644), and in 1969 she helps select music for the sound track of *Medea*.[5]

Pasolini published a review in verse of *Il mondo salvato dai ragazzini*. The review appeared in two parts in *Paragone*, one in the October 1968 issue and the second in the April 1969 issue (*Tutte le poesie* 2: 35–44, 45–54).[6] The text places itself in a direct relationship with "L'enigma di Pio XII" (*Tutte le poesie* 2: 17–25), the start of which is the famous passage from the first Letter to the Corinthians, which states that charity is the most important among the three theological virtues. Faith and hope, states the Pope in a relatively free interpretation of Saint Paul's statements, are the virtues of those who can govern themselves, while charity is the virtue of those who require guidance. Establishing a nexus between charity and institutions, the Pope declares that while faith and hope are the virtues of the progressive bourgeoisie, charity is the virtue of the ignorant peasants; while faith and hope are allies of the good liberal will, grace stands on the side of charity. This is the basis for Pius XII's justification of his own decision to side against the urban and cultivated Jews, favoring instead the peasant followers of Hitler.

Elsa is Jewish, "col Talmud nella pancia" (Pasolini, *Tutte le poesie* 2: 35; "with the Talmud in her belly"); she sides with faith and hope, against charity. She does not want to understand that love for the humble would mean accepting the ruling of the I.M. (the "Unhappy Many"), of their mediocrity and their need for demagogy. Elsa's idealism is at fault, in Pasolini's review, in that it does not take sufficient account of political quietism. She has, however, the saving grace of democracy. She respects society even as she contests it: humor is her way of venerating institutions, a humble peasant laughter from which she cannot distance herself. Herein lies her mystery: that in her apparent turning away from charity, there is in fact a great deal of charity. The quality of Morante's charity is of a specific kind, manifesting itself not through accepting the dictatorship of mediocrity but in laughing with it. Humor as charity, this is grace. Sacrificing one's own intellectual doubts, to laugh like the simple people—this is grace.

Both Pasolini and Morante are out of harmony with the world. But while he is the prisoner of anxiety, she goes further: she loves whoever rejects her without asking for anything in return, like a mother's love. It is this that allows her the mystery of humor and the ability *to lose herself in the characters.*

Her voice is not competitive: unlike Pasolini, who is first and foremost a lyric poet, she gives her characters the *gift* of a voice. In her characters she resolves the paradox of being enslaved to the world and simultaneously its mistress, because she is slave to a world she herself has created. This remains the blind spot of Pasolini's review, the unspoken border of which Pasolini himself cannot be aware. This nexus is in fact made implicit in the text by sheer contiguity, by the relationship between Elsa's humor and the fact that she suggested to Pasolini his best character, Ninetto: "l'idea di Ninetto a te dovuta / [. . .] / *è superiore al Pazzariello*" (*Tutte le poesie* 2: 45–46; emphasis in original; "the idea of Ninetto that I owe to you / [. . .] / is superior to the Pazzariello"). But we should remember how Ninetto is a trans-textual character, placed between literature and life; he does not speak, he is described. In a comment whose humor is only superficial, Pasolini avers that with Ninetto he has added sexuality to the Pazzariello. In other words, he cannot renounce a competitive form of eroticism, an idea of possession calqued on paternal imitation. He does not entirely consume sacrifice: he could say, paraphrasing Dino Campana, "per essere santo non sono abbastanza vile" ("to be a saint I am not coward enough").

In his second review of *Il mondo salvato dai ragazzini*" ("The World Saved by the Kids"; Spring 1969), Pasolini was to admit that his previous assessment had been wrong: in a metahistorical perspective the *ragazzini* ("kids") are the heroes of death. If we love their levity we must "adempier[c]i al di fuori di ogni amore" (*Tutte le poesie* 2: 280; "fulfill ourselves beyond every love"). For the moment, however, in 1968, Pasolini is thinking of the historical *ragazzini,* of those who should make the revolution. In a prose review Pasolini even maintains that the book could be the political manifesto of the new left. Historically, then, Elsa is perhaps wrong to identify the "ragazzini" who are lay-bourgeois (in Pasolini the Gramscian idea of the "power block" remains strong despite everything).[7] The textual solution to this discord with Elsa is a bizarre compromise that does not in fact solve anything: in reality, they are not two fathers but grandfathers, and when they are still at a tender age the bourgeoisie can make up with their very youth for the equivocation of class.

What divides them deep down is that, while Pasolini's relationship with the petite bourgeoisie has always and fundamentally been one of rejection,[8] that of Morante is one of unhappy adoration, or enamored parody. Furthermore, this is the source of her need of realistically specific details, which Pasolini disapproves or does not understand. Morante does with the feuilleton what Kafka does with nightmares: she decks it out realistically.

The most apparent point in common is their shared love for the *ragazzi* ("boys"). They both link this attraction to an ideological choice, be it one of subversion or of revolution. It is not surprising, then, that the discrepancies between them concern their diverse complicity with the bourgeoisie, their way of loving, the nuance-abyss separating the *ragazzi* from the *ragazzini*. After 1969 the passionate arguments between the two artists, arguments that were intended to add a profoundly dialectical dimension to their intellectual friendship, begin to feel burdened by senile inflexibility, and are transfixed in rising levels of rancor. He feels tortured by her intransigence; she feels let down. In Pasolini's 1969 "Poesie in una lingua inventata," the project of a poem entitled "Morant" appears. In this poem a line goes as follows: "la delusione che io le ho dato non decidendomi a diventare né un santo né un grande poeta" (*Tutte le poesie* 2: 1291; "the disappointment I gave her in making an effort to become neither saint nor great poet").[9] And there is a further poem beginning "Tu crodis, Basilissa . . ." (with the Basilissa being Elsa Morante) in which Pasolini reiterates his provocative rejection of rigor, of sacrifice, of memory, and praises vitalism: "tu crodis, Basilissa ke la sbissa sedi corùa, / [. . .] eh ben! la sbissa no è corùa: ma cor su l'erba de or. / [. . .] / eu esprim il sol col sol, il mar col mar, / il cùarp col cùarp, / e la sbissa cor, Basilissa" (*Tutte le poesie* 2: 1292; "you believe, Basilissa, that the snake has gone, / [. . .] / oh well! The snake has not left but runs through the golden grass. / [. . .] / I mean the sun with the sun, the sea with the sea, / the body with the body, / and the snake runs, Basilissa").

The 1970 "Canzone N.1," "Canzone N.2," and "Canzone N.3" (*Tutte le poesie* 2: 355–57, 358–59, 360) realize the project anticipated in "Morant": she is too demanding, he does not want to deal with fate, as he only "vuole pace" (*Tutte le poesie* 2: 355; "wants peace"). Pasolini wallows "nell'idea che c'è tempo" (*Tutte le poesie* 2: 355; "in the idea that there is time"): rather than regaining it, he prefers to abandon himself to time. In *Petrolio* he will speak of "la recherche comme à la recherche," and the Proustian ghost will haunt him intermittently throughout his career. It is not by chance that *Petrolio* remains unfinished, as, in order to realize the Proustian dream, one would have to "die to one's own life." This, Pasolini cannot do.

Even as he begs her not to let the tension of expectation slacken, as one finds delight in "knowing that much is expected from his own future," he still declares that he has not the strength of faith but, rather, faith in strength: a kind of vital force, of "efficienza, appetito, Ninetto" (*Tutte le poesie* 2: 358; "efficiency, appetite, Ninetto"). Mentioning Mozart, "il Mozart che lei mi ha regalato" (*Tutte le poesie* 2: 357; "the Mozart she gave me"), signifies a mixture of seduction and apology, as he writes in "Il poeta delle Ceneri": "io sono un piccolo-borghese, e non so sorridere . . . / come Mozart. . ." (*Tutte le poesie* 2: 1266; "I am a petit bourgeois, and I don't know how to smile . . . / like Mozart. . ."). Also, "umorismo e fretta: ecco il segno / della mia vecchiaia" (*Tutte le poesie* 2: 359; "humor and haste: here is the sign / of my aging"). In the idea of having disappointed Morante, there is also the underlying regret of having disappointed his own heroic idea of homosexuality. In a letter in verse that she wrote him in 1971, Morante tries to distance herself from the role of "Demanding Queen" she feels pinned to by Pasolini:

> a ogni modo (anche se NON "a scanso di equivoci") / io qui m'affanno a comunicarti / quello che tu vuoi negare: in somma che / non rimprovero NIENTE A NESSUNO / e tanto meno a te [. . .] l'Elsa che tu vuoi conoscere / e cioè dico la pura la / inconcussa Oh Dio / essa è concussa invece e impura. (*Lettere 1955–1975*: clxxxvi–clxxxvii)

> in any case (even if NOT without misunderstandings) / here I have an urgent need to tell you / what you want to deny: which is that / I have NOTHING to reproach ANYBODY for / you least of all [. . .] the Elsa that you want to know / the pure Elsa that is / the one with a stable and perennial

truth I mean My God / she is instead not perennial, she is impure.

The wrenching crisis to which the 1972 "Hobby del sonetto" bears witness brings about what could be considered the most serious crisis in Pasolini's relationship with Elsa. She watches him suffering like a dog because Ninetto is getting married, and she stands by Ninetto's side. The one who guaranteed him his vitality is now the one who is leaving. This time Elsa seems to be the bearer of the values of *caritas*, of a merciless charity, supporting Ninetto's right to fall in love with a girl and telling Pasolini that the only way to love is to desire what is best for those we love, asking nothing in return.

In the sonnets entitled "Hobby del sonetto," Pasolini tries to defend himself from the deadly conjunction of conformist common sense with a heroic moral. He accuses Elsa of being banal, even though he knows that Elsa's truth is higher. But he cannot bear to remain alone with his own diversity. So he states in "Hobby del sonetto" (paper 87): "Non c'è chi non veda in questo amore / tutto ciò che c'è di bello e la sua convenzione. / Tutti vi parteggiano, e nel loro cuore non hanno alcuna pietà dell'uomo rimasto solo" (*Tutte le poesie* 2: 1207; "no one sees in this love / but beauty and its convention. / Everybody participates in it, and in their heart do not have any mercy for the man left to himself").

In "Hobby del sonetto" (paper 82), he openly accuses Morante of lending her higher reasons to Ninetto's conformist ones, to whom he writes: "quelle parole del tuo diritto le ha pronunciate / Elsa Morante, e tu, che sei così più saggio / di noi due, te ne sei impossessato / una volta per sempre" (*Tutte le poesie* 2: 1202; "those words about your right / it was Elsa Morante who pronounced them / and you, who are the much more wise / of the two of us, you have taken hold of those / once and for all"). Finally, in "Hobby del sonetto" (paper 84), Pasolini tries to oppose Ninetto's "duties" to his own duty of sacrifice: "è vero che l'amore dev'essere santo, / Elsa aveva ragione, e altro non si deve volere / che la felicità di chi si ama. Ma è vero anche / che non c'è diritto a cui non si opponga un dovere. / [. . .] / Elsa non ha capito certamente che / io potevo morire; o ero così debole da desiderare / d'essere consolato"

(*Tutte le poesie* 2: 1204; "it is true that love must be sacred, / Elsa was right, and nothing more could be wanted / if not the happiness of those we love. But it is also true / that there is no right without an opposite duty. / [. . .] / Elsa certainly did not understand that / I could have died; or that I was so weak as to wish / to be consoled"). At the moment in which he must confess the defeat of his own vitalism, Pasolini projects onto Morante the ghost of the Consoling Mother.

In April 1972, at the Automobile Club d'Italia (ACI) in Rome, Pasolini gives a lecture with the mysterious title "E.M." The title is a joke alluding to Morante's initials but also to Moral Extremism or Metapolitical Extremism. These are in fact the qualities that characterize Elsa Morante and that have been the qualities of the 1968 "grandchildren." The lecture sketches a utopian allegiance among the different grievances of the grandchildren and grandfathers against the true winners, who are the opportunistic technocrats of the generation in between. Finally, however, he condemns the old ones (including Elsa and himself) because they have arrived, even unwittingly, at a position of Power: "accuso i vecchi d'avere fatto la volontà della vita" (*Conferenze dell'ACI*, file XXI; "I accuse the old of having followed the will of life").

In note 3d of *Petrolio*, entitled "Prefazione posticipata (IV)," the protagonist goes to Sicily to visit a girlfriend. Even if Pasolini tries to put us off the track, and while some physical traits do not correspond, others are unmistakable: "il viso era il viso di una giovane gatta" ("the face was the face of a young cat"); unmistakable are, above all, the psychological traits: "padrona del proprio pensare, per quanto il suo fondo potesse essere passionale, viscerale e tempestoso" (*Petrolio* 25–27; "mistress of her own thinking, even though deep down she could be passionate, visceral and tempestuous"). Unmistakable also is the girlfriend caught in a gesture of charity toward a poor child "e anche un bruttino, per quanto lei lo considerasse bellissimo" (*Petrolio* 25; "and rather ugly with it, even though she would consider him beautiful"). This is a character *à clef* and clearly alludes to Elsa Morante.

The female character is so taken up by her acts of charity that she pays no attention to him. She never listens to him, not even later: in the fifteen years of their friendship, she refuses to listen to him "by ideological choice." He harbors a secret of enormous historical value, and she might be the only one to be able to give it away because she "si è messa nella condizione di non avere sostanzialmente niente da perdere" (*Petrolio* 27; "has put herself in the condition of basically having nothing to lose"). Beyond the fiction, the complaint against Morante is, I believe, that she has never given herself over to his side in militant political struggles, that she has disengaged herself from ideology out of an excess of sublimity.

> E poiché quella persona inutilmente cercata e pregata era uno scrittore, se ne deduce facilmente come nei libri di quello scrittore, per quanto pieni e completi in se stessi essi fossero, mancava in realtà qualcosa: e ciò li destinava, di conseguenza, a una fatale ambiguità. (*Petrolio* 27)

> And because that person vainly sought and implored was a writer, one can easily deduce how in the books of that writer, rich and complete as they were, something was in fact always missing: and this would consequently destine them to a fatal ambiguity.

Pasolini publishes in *Tempo* a review of *La Storia*. Here, too, the review appears in two parts, respectively published in the July 26 and August 2 issues of the magazine. The review is basically an attack, and Pasolini's aggressive pen allows the anger of a denied affection to surface between the interstices of the text. The aggressiveness is in part self-punishing: Pasolini points to the "mannerism" of her work that critics had constantly attacked in his own. He punishes in her the sins that he himself committed: making fun of the "lunga celebrazione della vitalità, dell'innocenza, della joie de vivre dei poveri di spirito" ("long celebration of vitality, of innocence, of the joie de vivre of the poor in spirit"), "napoletani o sottoproletari romani, figurarsi" ("Neapolitans or Roman sub-proletarians, you can imagine"), "una vita esaltata e strumentalizzata in quanto tale" ("a life exalted and manipulated as such"; *Descrizioni di descrizioni* 353–62). He uses Morante's novel, in short, as a scapegoat, and the review as a kind of recantation; we should not forget that it was written less than one year before his "Abiura alla trilogia della vita."

This self-destructive push leads him to find the most extraordinary character in the book, Useppe, unbearable. That does not mean, of course, that Pasolini's critical thinking has ceased to exist. Of Davide Segre, for instance, he makes linguistic observations that are absolutely right: "il ragazzo si presenta come bolognese, in realtà è mantovano ma parla una specie di veneto" (*Descrizioni* 358; "the young man introduces himself as if he were from Bologna, in reality he is from Mantua but speaks a sort of Venetian dialect"); the character is an ill-laid mosaic of diverse empirical persons, and this absence of fusion is denounced precisely by the language that Davide speaks, intellectualizing and non-existent: "non c'è un angolo dell'Alta Italia in cui 'cadere' si dica 'cader'" (*Descrizioni* 360; "there isn't one corner of Northern Italy in which the Italian word for 'to fall' is truncated").[10] The suspicion remains that Pasolini is particularly harsh here in his critique, because he feels that Davide Segre is in part constructed as his fictional caricature. The purpose of caricaturizing Pasolini is manifested in Davide's obsessive idea that the bourgeoisie is infesting the world and with his neurotic insistence on his own bourgeois being. It is actually the objectivity of Morante's novelistic structure (as the character is faced with other voices) that relativizes and ridicules his emphatic hatred: "'e vabbè, t'avemo capito!' [. . .] 'a te i borghesi te stanno sui coglioni'" (*Opere* 2: 932; "'All right, all right, we get it!' [. . .] 'the bourgeoisie give you a pain in the ass'"; *History* 646).

Pasolini's reflections on the work become more intimate and closer to his own deep mental paths when he analyzes Morante's contradictions between Oriental knowledge and anarchic and subversive ideology: if everything is play, what does it matter who the victims are? The theme of play will be his in the *Trilogia*, not in opposition but as a flight before history; reversed, the same play (of the four Masters) will be the concentration camp history in *Salò*, where no life is possible. The contradiction in Morante dissolves once more—although Pasolini cannot see this—in a maternal movement: nothingness looks at life with the sweetness with which a mother looks at her child threatened by evil—and this is, in the book, the centrality of Useppe.

The protagonist of *Aracoeli* (1982) declares himself at some point to be "un canuto Narciso che non crepa" (*Opere* 2: 1172; "a white-haired Narcissus who does not die"; *Aracoeli* 101): the quotation from the hemistich of "Una disperata vitalità" is too precise not to be openly allusive. Also, let's look at the calendar: Manuele arrives at El Almendral, an arid and desolate place, the last possible of the stations of the cross, the place he chooses to re-enter the maternal womb—in sum, the reconjunction with the mother, on Saturday, November 1, 1975. On that night Pasolini died.

The protagonist of *Aracoeli* is in part and in a manner compatible with the needs of the novel form, a portrait of Pasolini. It was Morante's way of interpreting death, and to console herself for that death: the deformed kittens, the female cats who eat them, are just some of the clues. Some of the psychological discoveries that the protagonist makes about himself are psychological data that belong to Pasolini, such as when he interprets his own hatred as a masked envy, or when he realizes that he has always loved his father more deeply than his mother. This is a father who resembles Pasolini's empirical father, as Aracoeli (mother-girl-bird) resembles Pasolini's mother, Susanna.[11]

One would almost be tempted to say that Morante performed an experiment, in Zola's sense of the term: what would it have been like to be a Narcissistic *niñomadrero* homosexual who loathed his own body just as she did at that time? To juxtapose the autobiographical data of both in a single coherent character would be the most fitting way to enhance the sense of affinity, which had always been characterized by a loud crash of intelligence: when the protagonist tells his mother he has sinned in intelligence, the mother answers: "ma, niño mio chiquito, non c'è niente da capire" (*Opere* 2: 1428; "but niño mio chiquito, there's nothing to be understood"; *Aracoeli* 292). If the structural mechanism underscores the image of brothers, the thematic content elicits a maternal image, of a mother as "impure" as Aracoeli. The two ghosts, who could not discipline themselves for over twenty years, are placed in the novel in two different stylistic spaces.

There is a story by Morante in which a child wishes to become a saint and renounces his dream for love of his mother.

After he gives up his dream, the two lead a mediocre life while she is "convinta che lui sia destinato a qualcosa di grande" ("convinced that he is destined to something great"). The story is *Lo scialle andaluso*. It is as if Morante wanted to reply to the "Canzoni,"[12] as she would want to tell Pasolini "I myself am a disappointing mother, I am not a Basilissa, I am only a failed dancer."

Notes

1. This article was previously published in Italian as "Elsa Morante nell'opera di Pier Paolo Pasolini," by Walter Siti, in C. D'Angeli and G. Magrini, eds., "Vent'anni dopo *La storia*. Omaggio a Elsa Morante," spec. issue of *Studi novecenteschi* 21.47–48 (June–Dec. 1994): 131–48. It is reprinted here in translation by permission.

2. See also the letter dated May 30th.

3. The poem "Alibi" was written in 1955 and was published in *Tempo presente* in January 1957; "Il pianto della scavatrice" dates to 1956 and was published in the *Contemporaneo* in June 1957, now in *Tutte le poesie* 1.

4. "Pietro II" is a diary in verse form, written in 1963 during the shooting of *Ricotta*. The episode I refer to is in the section dated "Wednesday, March 6th, (evening)" (*Tutte le poesie* 1: 1151).

5. Her musical contribution is not limited to the two films in which she is explicitly present in the credits. Pasolini was to seek her advice for all his movies. See the article by Carmelo Samonà, "Elsa Morante e la musica," from which the following quotation is drawn: "Si deve ai suoi appassionati interventi, credo, una certa accentuazione espressionistica che la musica conferisce al racconto pasoliniano, e, in particolare, quella drastica convergenza di registri umili e alti che è come il segnale d'una poetica, e in cui sembra di vedere uno sguardo d'intesa fra i due artisti ogni volta che le immagini e la melodia si congiungono. Penso, e mi tornano alla memoria i commenti della scrittrice—ad alcuni esempi famosi: l'attacco del coro 'Wir setzen uns' della *Passione secondo San Matteo* nel momento della tragica zuffa di *Accattone*; le prime battute della 'Marcia funebre massonica K 477' durante alcune apparizioni di Cristo nel Vangelo; l'adagio introduttivo del Quartetto 'delle dissonanze' K 465, accoppiato—in una trascrizione per fiati—al rustico Tiresia dell'*Edipo re*; e ancora un altro adagio, dal Quartetto K 458, ne *Le mille e una notte*, per dare maggior risalto (questa almeno, sembrava essere l'intenzione) alla purezza e alla grazia di alcune sequenze amorose" (15; "We have her passionate interventions to thank, I believe, for a particular expressionistic rhythm with which music endows Pasolini's tale, and, in particular, the drastic convergence of high and low registers which is the mark of poetics, and in which we seem to see a look of understanding pass between the two artists each time images and melody come together. I am thinking, and I have in mind here the comments of Morante, of some famous examples: the beginning of the chorus 'Wir setzen uns' of the *St Matthew's Passion* in the moment of *Accattone*'s tragic scuffle; the first bars of the 'Funeral March K477' during some appearance of Christ in the 'Gospel,' the introductory adagio of the Quartet K465, coupled, in a transcription for wind, with the rustic Tiresias of *Oedipus*, and another adagio, from Quartet K458, in *A Thousand and One Nights*, to give greater emphasis [or at least this seemed to be the intention] to the grace and purity of some of the love scenes").

6. Originally the text was collected in *Trasumanar e organizzar*.

7. Originally published in *Tempo settimanale* (27 Aug. 1968), now in *Il caos* 51–52.

8. Implacable, Morante would always reproach Pasolini with his neurotic ambivalence, to which his reply comes in "Coccodrillo," "sì, Elsa, li odiavo perché li amavo, hai ragione" (*Tutte le poesie* 2: 230; "yes, Elsa, I hated them because I loved them, you are right").

9. The alternative poet/saint is in reality Pasolini's own ghost that he projects onto Elsa Morante as in the case of "Il poeta delle ceneri": "Ma la professione di poeta in quanto poeta / è sempre più insignificante [. . .] / Non sa, egli, dialogare con la realtà? / [. . .] / Perché non la contempla in silenzio, /—*santo, e non letterato?*" (*Tutte le poesie* 2: 1277–78; emphasis in original; "But the profession of poet as such / is more and more insignificant [. . .] / Doesn't, he, know how to dialogue with reality? / [. . .] / Why doesn't he contemplate it in silence /—*man of god, and not man of literature?*").

10. This last statement serves to show how different the mimesis of spoken dialect is for the two authors. For Pasolini it has a philological basis, while for Morante it is primarily "auditive." In this instance, I am not so sure that the dialectology in dictionary style of Pasolini is even right: Perhaps the young men who no longer know dialect and adapt it starting from Italian, really say "to fall" truncated, but it is also true that probably they would not have said it back in 1945.

11. Young Pasolini saw analogies between Andalusian and Friulan. We need only think of the importance of García Lorca for "La meglio gioventù" and "L'usignolo."

12. Pasolini did not send the "Canzoni" to Elsa Morante, but she received them from Graziella Chiarcossi around 1980.

Works Cited

Fusillo, Massimo. *La Grecia secondo Pasolini*. Florence: La Nuova Italia, 1996.

Garboli, Cesare, and Carlo Cecchi. "Fortuna Critica." Morante, *Opere* 2: 1651–81.

Morante, Elsa. *Aracoeli*. Trans. William Weaver. New York: Random, 1984.

———. *History: A Novel*. Trans. William Weaver. Steerforth Italia: South Royalton, 2000.

———. *Opere*. Ed. Cesare Garboli and Carlo Cecchi. 2 vols. Milan: Mondadori, 1988–90.

Pasolini, Pier Paolo. *Le belle bandiere*. Ed. Giancarlo Ferretti. Rome: Riuniti, 1978.

———. *Il caos*. Ed. Giancarlo Ferretti. Rome: Riuniti, 1979.

———. *Descrizioni di descrizioni*. Ed. Graziella Chiarcossi. Turin: Einaudi, 1979.

———. *E. M. Conferenze dell'ACI, Fascicolo XXI*. Rome: Automobile Club, 1972.

———. *Lettere 1940–1954*. Ed. Nico Naldini. Turin: Einaudi, 1986.

———. *Lettere 1955–1975*. Ed. Nico Naldini. Turin: Einaudi, 1988.

———. *L'odore dell'India*. Parma: Guanda, 1990.

———. *Petrolio*. Turin: Einaudi, 1992.

———. *Il portico della morte*. Ed. Cesare Segre. Milan: Garzanti, 1988.

———. *Tutte le poesie*. Ed. Walter Siti (with editorial help of Maria Careri, Annalisa Comes, and Silvia De Laude). 2 vols. Milan: Mondadori, 2003.

Penna, Sandro. *Tutte le poesie*. Milan: Garzanti, 1977.

Samonà, Carmelo. "Elsa Morante e la musica." *Paragone Letteratura* 37 (1986): 13–20.

Filippo La Porta

The "Dragon of Unreality"
against the "Dream of a Thing"

On Morante and Pasolini

> Contro la bomba atomica non c'è che la realtà.
>
> Against the atomic bomb we have nothing but
> reality.
>
> Elsa Morante
> Pro o contro la bomba atomica

In reconsidering the extraordinarily nuanced and multiform oeuvre of Elsa Morante in all its variety, I propose to demonstrate the following thesis—that an understanding of the writer is impossible without an understanding, or at least an interpretation, of her concept of "reality." In *Il mondo salvato dai ragazzini*, the writer's real ethical and political manifesto, when she describes the F. P. (*Felici Pochi*; "Happy Few") we read: "pure quando siano volgarmente intesi brutti / in REALTÁ sono belli; ma la REALTÁ / è di rado visibile alla gente" (*Opere* 2: 137; "even when they are vulgarly thought of as ugly / IN REALITY they are beautiful; but REALITY / is seldom visible to people"). And just a few pages later, in her discussion of the I. M. (*Infelici Molti*; "Unhappy Many"), she is at pains to underline that they do not see happiness because they have in their eyes "la cispa dei troppi fumi di irrealtà" (*Opere* 2: 139; "wisps of the dense smoke of unreality").

In order to understand her concept of reality we need to extend our critical perspective to authors who played a significant part in her development, whether through their writings or through personal contacts: Pier Paolo Pasolini above all, Simone Weil, and Carlo Levi. It seems to me appropriate to articulate these reflections around the following points:

(a) The concept of reality that we find in Morante finds its source in Simone Weil, a writer almost feverishly read and

290

studied by the Roman writer, as demonstrated by the *Cahiers* in her personal library. The following may serve as a synthesis of what Morante gleaned from these readings: that which is "real," however painful, conflicting, or frustrating is, for Weil, always necessary, and as such always preferable to that which is unreal (in other words the gratuitous, irresponsible, only apparently free space of the abstract imagination).

(b) Such a concept of reality (and unreality) is shared by both Morante and Pasolini, and in the incessant and continuous dialogue between the two writers the concept is further refined.

(c) This positive prejudice in favor of reality generates a whole series of oppositions between values and their corresponding negative values. In brief: above all, it is life (which obviously includes death) that is real, the concrete, lived present, happiness (always precarious, and carrying within it the possibility of unhappiness), love for what *is* (and not for that which could or should be), the full acceptance of the chance and unpredictable nature of life. Unreal on the other hand is power, with all its strategies, the eye to personal advantage, the belief that we can expel everything "negative" from our lives, the illusion that objects can be manipulated and controlled, making use of other people, and finally the cold and inhuman "perfection" of any social utopia (while in order to combat unreality, Morante herself will adopt myth and fable).

(d) This "positive" concept of reality, although indebted to the great tradition of Italian realism (see, for example, the essays of Carlo Levi, a writer who profoundly influenced both Pasolini and Morante), could today be better understood by an American public, for profound social and cultural reasons. Or rather, it is that in the American tradition we find an idea of reality that is always in conflict or at least in a critical relationship with certain "derealisation" that belongs to the imaginary of advertising and to the mass culture of the United States.

Simone Weil: If the Real
Does Not Exist Then All Is Permitted

In Morante this "positive" idea of reality descends directly from Simone Weil's *Cahiers*, which Morante was poring over and underlining throughout the 1960s. We should remember that for Weil, joy was nothing other than "the feeling of reality." Concetta D'Angeli has described and explained very clearly the influence of Weil on Morante, in the character of Davide in *La Storia*, for example, but also in that of Useppe, the sacrificial victim; but she has not dwelt further on the implications of the concept of reality. Morante was to write the following, in a tone that echoes the most limpid passages of Weil: "la realtà, e non l'irrealtà, rimane il paradiso naturale di tutte le persone umane, almeno finché [. . . n]on siano diventate, cioè dei *mutanti* [. . ..]" (*Pro o contro la bomba atomica* 110; emphasis in original; "reality, and not unreality, remains the natural paradise of all humans, at least as long as [. . .] they have not become *mutants* [. . ..]"). According to Weil what matters the most is to define the real, as her entire reflection hinges on the question of reality, our inability to grasp it, its precious value, in the face of everything that seeks to alienate it, even in the name of something noble—utopia, political ideology, the idea of the future, the imaginary in general, which for her is always a corrupting influence. We might even say that for Weil the real "enemy," from the existential and moral point of view, is this very *imaginary* (where indeed there is no need nor contradiction), unreality, dream, fantasy: "*La perte du contact avec la réalité c'est le mal, c'est la tristesse*" (*Cahiers* 1: 137; emphasis in original; "The loss of contact with reality—there lies evil, there lies sorrow"; *Notebooks* 1: 28) while "joy is the feeling of the real." The far point of Weil's reflection brings us to a paradoxical equivalence of reality (necessity) and good in which "Est bien ce qui donne plus de réalité aux êtres et aux choses, mal ce qui le leur enlève" (*Cahiers* 1: 102; "That which gives more reality to beings and things is good, that which takes it away from them is evil"; *Notebooks* 1: 8), and similarly of unreality and evil. The result is unexpectedly monotone, precisely in that "tout y est *équivalent*. Rien de réel; tout y est imaginaire. Le mal est monotone [. . .] comme des dessins où tout serait inventé, ou des fictions tout à fait inventées par des enfants" (*Cahiers* 2: 54; emphasis in original; "[. . .] everything in it is *equivalent*. Nothing real; everything in it is imaginary. Evil is monotonous [. . .] like drawings in which everything has been invented, or the fictitious happenings entirely invented by children"; *Notebooks* 1: 180). This last concept is one Weil holds dear and to which she frequently returns. We have here almost an ontological foundation of ethics. Weil's invitation to "de-create" ourselves, to empty ourselves, in fact allows someone or something else to be, to manifest himself/itself. Paraphrasing Dostoyevsky, we might say that for her, if "the real does not exist everything is allowed." And evil in fact is exactly the opposite: to expand, to fill a gap in oneself by creating emptiness in others, whether through the imagination or through the future. Weil's paradoxical love for necessity is founded on an aesthetic vision of world order that is historic and platonic in origin enriched by Hindu influences, to be reached only through the fullness of joy. For her the Beautiful does not coincide simply with the Good, but it is certainly capable of creating good, because we desire a beautiful thing simply to be what it is; in other words, we want to invest it with reality, not improve or modify it through the imagination, whether it is a friend or a work of art. In this sense the "Beautiful" cures us of any utopian dream. When Weil goes to work in a factory for a year she doesn't mitigate the "tragic aspect" of the workers' condition but this does not prevent her from recognizing in a letter to a former school pupil that she has "di essere sfuggita a un mondo di astrazioni e di trovarmi fra uomini reali—buoni o cattivi, ma di una bontà e cattiveria autentiche" (*Piccola cara* 53; "escaped from a world of abstractions to find myself among real men—good and bad, but whose goodness and badness is authentic").

Morante and Pasolini:
Wonderful Barbarians . . .

In speaking on the concept of reality in one of his dialogues with Jean Duflot, Pasolini states that "[l]'ambiguità risiede soprattutto nel significato che Lei dà alla parola barbarie: Quando ne parlavamo, Elsa Morante ed io, le davamo il significato di meraviglioso barbaro [. . .] la barbarie primitiva ha qualcosa di buono" (Pasolini, *Saggi politica* 1487; "Ambiguity lies above all in the significance you attribute to the word barbarism. When Elsa Morante and I were discussing this we gave it the meaning of marvelous barbarian [. . .] primitive barbarian has something good and pure"). Pasolini's reference to the positive use of the word *barbarian* shared by himself and Morante is counterposed to the other concept of *irrealtà*, "unreality," fundamental to the whole of Pasolini's work. In a dialogue from 1968 with Franco Citti, first published in the column "Il caos" Pasolini argues: "Tu in quale realtà vivi? Nella realtà che è nel cuore dei puri o nella realtà che è ingiustizia (e che io e Elsa chiamiamo 'irrealtà')?" (*Saggi politica* 1149; "What reality do you live in? In the reality which is in the hearts of the pure or in the reality which is injustice (and which Elsa and I call "unreality")?" What should we then understand here by "unreality"? If we believe that for Pasolini the less "interested" barbarian is the more primitive—and therefore the more real—it is then, following this line of argument, we should note as "unreality" all that which presents itself as being "interested," such as calculation, a manipulative relationship with people and things, bourgeois good sense and "reasonableness." Referring back to the Greek myth so dear to Pasolini, we could say the *non-recognition* of Dionysus and of what he represents, in more or less direct form (in other words the irrational, the ontological necessity of death, of unlimited Eros, "potentiality which does not have a way of satisfying itself," the emptiness over which every City is suspended). Then this unreality— which in Elsa Morante's words was precisely the "dragon of unreality" (against which the work of the Writer sets his sword) reveals itself as a most insidious enemy. It might coincide with the society of consumerism and the superfluous—which tries so anxiously to fill that emptiness—it might wear the garb of literature itself (reduced to tired convention, to chic consumerism and as such stripped of all power)—and in fact Pasolini writes that Morante's aim "non è la letteratura, ma un ideale etico-fantastico, a cui la letteratura è asservita" ("is not literature, but an ethical-fantastical ideal to which literature pays service")—or again it might identify itself with culture, when culture becomes a leviathan of a superstructure, used in a demagogic and intimidatory fashion.

Culture as Unreality:
About the Illusions of the Avant-Garde

In this respect we should recall a particularly "prophetic" attack made by Pasolini in 1966 on Umberto Eco, who "conosce tutto lo scibile e te lo vomita in faccia con l'aria più arrogante e te lo vomita in faccia con l'aria più indifferente: è come se tu ascoltassi un robot" *(Saggi politica* 1605; "knows all there is to be known and vomits his knowledge in your face with utter indifference: it's like listening to a robot"). Against this arrogant robot-intellectual, so fully immersed in the noisy media unreality enveloping his novels, Pasolini sets the figure of a normal "erudite American" in this article entitled "Un marxista a New York." Unlike Eco, Pasolini "non si considera mai padrone della sua sapienza, è quasi spaventato dalla sua cultura" *(Saggi politica* 1605; "does not ever consider himself master of his own knowledge and is almost alarmed by his own culture"). And perhaps one of the reasons for the runaway international success of Eco's *The Name of the Rose* lies precisely in his giving his readers the illusion that they feel themselves to be "masters" of their culture, with little responsibility and less effort, and in satisfying their inexhaustible need for social promotion and for the "university." In the same article, which is an interview with/portrait by Oriana Fallaci, Pasolini appears wandering alone around the streets of New York, "cercando l'America sporca infelice violenta che si addice ai suoi problemi" (Pasolini, *Saggi politica* 1597; "looking for the dirty violent and unhappy America which suits his own problems") but also, as an "independent Marxist" *(Saggi politica* 1605) completely seduced by the "metropolis" as to him New York appears as "una città magica, travolgente, bellissima. Una di quelle città fortunate che hanno la grazia" *(Saggi politica* 1598; "a magic, overwhelming, extraordinarily beautiful city. One of those fortunate cities touched by grace"). He is of course drawn to the most precarious and risky areas, to Harlem, but also to Greenwich Village, identical to "come glielo descrisse Elsa Morante" *(Saggi politica* 1604; "the way Elsa Morante described it to him"). The writer is drawn, above all, to the new American Left—a new left that has never been able to establish itself in Italy—nonideological, nonviolent, libertarian, tolerant, full of grace, outside any "unreality." And he brings an anecdote to bear on this point. On Tenth Avenue there is a pro-Vietnam march going on. Suddenly three young men get out of a car and, guitar in hand, strike up a protest song while the demonstrators look daggers at them but offer no insults or hostile gestures. Pasolini comments: "Questa è la cosa più bella che ho visto nella mia vita. Questa è una cosa che non dimenticherò finché vivo" (*Saggi politica* 1606; "This is the most beautiful thing I have ever seen. I will never forget this as long as I live").

A Gnostic in Love with Reality:
Pasolini's "Contradiction"

Imbued as he was with classical culture, myth, and Greek tragedy, Pasolini believes with Plato that in the final analysis Reality—which is certainly not neat and contained as in the Parmenidean model—coincides with the Good, and beauty thus has the task of revealing it to us. Theological digression: in this, Pasolini confirms himself as a real ancient Greek and as a Gnostic. By all means, the Gnostics believed also that the world was the creation of the devil, in a moment of corruption and temporary fall from the drop of divine knowledge. And yet this fall constituted a voluntary gesture of love, as we see in the myth of *sophia* in Valentino. Nonetheless, in Pasolini a Gnostic repulsion toward the world of feeling and the natural body coexists in a traumatic manner with an absolutely physical, earthly sense of happiness. We might recall that in the long short story "Romans" (published posthumously in 1994), which constituted a narrative nucleus, subsequently cut, of *Sogno di una cosa* (written, in its turn, in 1947–48 and published in 1962), the homosexual priest don Paolo, obsessed by sin and the flesh, notes in a page of his diary: "E' il corpo l'origine di tutto e bisogna farlo sparire" (*Romanzi e racconti* 2: 228; "It is the body which is the origin of everything and it should disappear"). Gnostic also seems to be the other Pasolinian idea that at its root the positive principle—of good, of life—is the same as the negative principle—of evil, of death (Eros, with its demons and fantasies that can never be satisfied, or the terrible Furies, who always need to be transformed and sublimated into the benign Eumenides . . .).

Pasolini's highest aspiration remains that of making reality express itself—with no mediation—of making things speak. And as such, his shift to the cinema and his abandonment of the word—always and already metaphoric—was inevitable. In order to express reality, in fact, cinematographic language uses not a series of symbols but reality itself, as he repeatedly theorized. The writer declared at the same time that his experience as a film director signified a refusal of the Italian language, of a rhetorical and bookish culture, of a cultural tradition. Almost a secession, an internal exile, a flight from the fatherland; and of those who in his judgment are the authors of three recent masterpieces, Eugenio Montale, Carlo Emilio Gadda, and Elsa Morante, he observes that there is little of Italian in their work: "il loro tipo di cultura si è formato altrove, in un terreno franco, europeo" (*Saggi politica* 1620; "their form of culture is shaped elsewhere, in a European territory, a sort of *terrafranca*"). And yet this pathos toward reality, if we look at it closely, reveals itself at heart to be typically Italian, tied to the great realist tradition that began with the Renaissance.

Realism and the Great Italian Tradition (A Digression into Literary History)

Nineteenth-century critic Francesco De Sanctis wrote in his history of Italian literature about Ariosto:

> E non è che cerchi effetti di luce o di armonia straordinari o lusso di colori e accessori: non ci è ombra di affettazione o di pretensione; ci è l'oggetto per se stesso, che si spiega naturalmente. Il poeta fissa l'esteriorità nel punto che è viva [. . .] non la scruta, non l'interroga, non cerca dal di dentro, non la palpa, non la maneggia per vederla abbellire [. . .] Non c'è il poeta, ci è la cosa che vive, e si muove, e non vedi chi la muove, e pare si muova da sé. Questa sublime semplicità nella chiarezza della visione è ciò che il Galilei chiamava a ragione la divinità dell'Ariosto. (521)

> It's not that he seeks effects of unusual light or harmony, or luxurious colors and accessories; there is not a glimpse of affectation or pretension; there is the object itself, which explains itself naturally. The poet fixes its exteriority where it is most alive [. . .] he doesn't scrutinize it, he doesn't interrogate it, he doesn't search inside it, he doesn't handle it, he doesn't manipulate it in order to beautify it [. . .] we see not the poet, we see the thing which lives, and moves, and

> we do not see who moves it, it seems to move by itself. This
> sublime simplicity and clarity of vision is what Galilei
> rightly called the divinity of Ariosto.

This is unlike, say, Angelo Poliziano whose octaves seemed to
De Sanctis more studied, in which he sees "e si vede l'intenzione dell'eleganza" (521; "the effort toward elegance").
Besides, the imagination of the author of the *Orlando furioso*
is in no way imitable because he is entirely devoid of manner.
Ariosto, as De Sanctis maintains, is "*tutto obliato e calato nelle
cose*" and "ha un ingegno poroso" (521; "entirely submerged
within the thing"; "has a porous mind"). Nor does contemporary art, despite all intentions, seem to offer any real resistance
to this invasion of reality. We might remember Pasolini's poem
"Picasso" in *Le ceneri di Gramsci*, where we read that in the
Spanish painter's canvasses we do not see "il brusio del
popolo" (*Bestemmia* 1: 95; "the hustle and bustle of the
people"). And in fact, avant-gardes often are guilty of a sort of
identification with the aggressor, precisely in their giving in to
infirmity and chaos, "[l]'informe [presente nelle estetiche
contemporanee] è il contrario della poesia, com'è il contrario
della vita," Elsa Morante declares in "Il poeta di tutta una vita"
(*Pro o contro* 35; "the informal [present in contemporary aes-
thetics] is the opposite of poetry in the same way it is the opposite of life"). According to Morante, in fact, poetry and life
want to give a form, an order to things of the universe,
"traendoli dall'informe e dal disordine, e cioè dalla morte" (*Pro
o contro* 35; "saving them from the informal and chaos, from
death, that is"). Both Morante and Pasolini express a clear
choice in favor of realism, even if this is to be understood in a
broad sense. Pasolini came to maturity reading the essays of
Erich Auerbach on realism in western culture. In his view even
an expressionist writer such as Gadda could be considered "realist." In "Sul romanzo" Morante reminds us that "un vero
romanzo, dunque, è sempre realista: anche il più favoloso" (*Pro
o contro* 50; "a real novel, then, is always realist; even the most
fantastic") and that even Edgar Allan Poe in his work represents "la sua psicologia reale di uomo vivente" (*Pro o contro*
50; "his real psychology as a living being"). While in the work
of James Joyce, adds Morante in the same essay, we do not

find a search for a recognizable poetic truth in all things real that is to be laid bare for others (*Pro o contro* 67).

Evil or the Desire to Possess

For Pasolini as for Morante the opposition between real and unreal is more significant than any other opposition, even that between life and death. For him the greatest expression of unreality is the typically bourgeois claim or illusion that we can possess reality, in other words control it, guide it, turn it upside down (and so often the present is exchanged with the future, which is far more malleable. In his controversial and incomplete posthumous novel *Petrolio*, a flood of a novel that sets out to explain Power and in some ways a competitor to Morante's *La Storia*, possessing is equated with Evil (we always possess only partially, never completely). On the other hand, Pasolini maintains in the same novel that "essere posseduti" (*Romanzi e racconti* 2: 1548; "being possessed"), however much it might imply pain and humiliation, is Good, "vita allo stato puro, cosmico" that "viene quando vuole e se ne va quando vuole" (*Romanzi e racconti* 2: 1548; "life in its pure, cosmic state" that "comes when it wants and goes when it wants"). The one who is possessed is aware that something takes him over and reduces him to "un nulla che non ha altra volontà che quella di perdersi in quella diversa Volontà" (*Romanzi e racconti* 2: 1548; "a nothing with no other desire than to lose himself in that different Will"). This is what the writer has his character experience, as over the course of the novel he changes sex and becomes a woman. Power, we read in *Petrolio*, cannot achieve "real discourse" in that it needs notions that are "directly translatable" into facts and action; indeed it is born of the illusion that we can govern the world. He returns to the theme of possession in his final interview for *Tuttolibri* with Furio Colombo in November 1975, in which the writer speaks of power as "a system of education" that aims to ensure that "tutti vogliono le stesse cose e si comportano nello stesso modo" (*Saggi politica* 1725; "everybody wants the same thing and everybody behaves in the same way"). The same social opposition to this system is clear: "Io ho paura di questi negri in rivolta, uguali al padrone, altrettanto predoni, che vogliono tutto a qualunque costo" (*Saggi politica* 1727; "I fear these blacks who are in revolt, equal to their masters, just as grasping, who want everything at whatever price"). At one point Pasolini, mindful of what he himself calls his "descents into the inferno," turns directly to his most courteous of interviewers, Furio Colombo, in Pasolini's eyes exponent of the establishment and of the ruling class, accused of not seeing clearly the "fallimento sinistro di un intero sistema sociale" (*Saggi politica* 1726: "sinister failure of an entire social system") and he pronounces his judgment in more strident tones: "Ma state attenti. L'inferno sta salendo da voi [. . .] con la scuola, la televisione, la pacatezza dei vostri giornali, voi siete i grandi conservatori di questo ordine orrendo basato sull'idea di possedere e sull'idea di distruggere" (*Saggi politica* 1728–29; "But beware. Hell is rising up toward you [. . .] with your schools, television, your subdued papers, you are the great conservatives of this appalling order based on the idea of possession and on the idea of destruction"). It is the "idea of possession" that signifies the murderous illusion of control, of predictability, while in the *Divina Mimesis*, a work from the mid-sixties, he had read that "la Realtà si rivela quando le pare" (*Romanzi e racconti* 2: 1104; "Reality reveals itself when it wishes to do so"). No, for him not only can the real not be possessed, but we must accept to the last degree its anguishing precariousness and instability, while at the same time being fully aware that it is exactly this which gives shape to our experience (of joy or pain, satisfaction or frustration). There is nothing else. In general Pasolini declares himself interested, like every other artist, in what is concrete, because only "solo ciò che è concreto è autentico" (*Il caos* 56; "only what is concrete is authentic").[1] On this same page we see the influence of existentialism on the writer's intellectual development, an influence documented by various letters (in particular, Schopenhauer, who seems to have been one of the philosophers most dear to Elsa Morante). Concreteness always passes through the singular, in this case the relationship of the writer with the individual reader, real precisely in that he is empirically verifiable, free, and autonomous. Unsurprisingly his concept of unreality contains a sense of forcing, an extremist option of a moral nature. And so everything that has to do with power, injustice, hidden purposes, politics (by extension we might even say "reason" in the bourgeois sense of utilitarian reason, interested solely in how things can be used, no matter how easily observable within social life), is considered as unreal. But what can we set against power? What can we set against the "inferno"? What type of happiness or existence?

A Happiness That Leaves No Traces

As we have seen the *Infelici Molti* fail to see happiness because of the "dense smog of unreality." So, happiness and reality are in some way connected. In an interview with Davide Lajolo in 1971, Pasolini clarifies his position that "la felicità consiste prima di tutto nel non pensare mai al futuro" (*Saggi politica* 1693; "happiness first of all is never thinking of the future"), adding that hope is always "retorica, meschina, ricattatoria e ipocrita" (*Saggi politica* 1693; "rhetorical, shabby, a hypocritical blackmailer"). Even the hope of the protestors, of the disobedient young who are so similar to the bosses and who seem to live a subcultural form (subculture that now puts itself forward as culture) of revolution: the "presente può essere ingiusto e infelice, ma è solo nel presente che si sperimenta e si vive totalmente il reale" (*Saggi politica* 1694; "the present may be unjust and unhappy, but it is only in the present that the real is experienced and lived totally"). And on the alienating characteristic of hope, a few years previously in the column "Il caos," he had explained how charity, almost always neglected, is "thinkable also in itself," while the other two theological virtues—hope and faith—are, without charity, not only unthinkable but monstrous, "quelle del Nazismo erano fede e speranza senza carità" (*Saggi politica* 1122; "what Nazism presented us with were faith and hope without charity"). And again, in the same column, he proposes an analogy between the events of 1968 and the conditions that surrounded the Protestant revolution, precisely in that on the horizon he glimpses the possible supremacy of charity in "un rapporto reale con la realtà" over the other two theological virtues (*Saggi politica* 1129; "a real relationship with reality"). Furthermore Pasolini explains to students at Lecce, two weeks before he dies, that for him happiness is "sorridere e cantare e inventare linguisticamente tutti i giorni una battuta, una spiritosaggine, una storia" (*Saggi letteratura* 2836; "smiling and singing, a daily linguistic invention, witticisms, stories"), an aptitude that he used to find in the unskilled bicycling workers of Rome, who by now are "pallidi, nevrotici, seri, introvertiti" (*Saggi letteratura* 2836; "pale, neurotic, serious, introverted"). The happiness the writer speaks of is made up of smile and song and melts away like the snow in the sun; it leaves no traces; it constructs nothing. It is an immediate adhering to life, to an entire culture concretely lived, which, as we know, means also adhering to the mysterious fount of life, to the inevitability of death (the fleeting song and smile are not stable, you cannot possess them . . .). And for Morante, too, happiness has nothing to do with History— defined as a nightmare that has lasted ten thousand years. On the one hand, it is ephemeral, untouchable, without memory, and immediately dissolves into the air like the verses that Useppe sings in *La Storia*. On the other hand, it always seems to contain within it an obscure presage of death. Whichever, it is something very real.

The Bourgeoisie as Unreality

In the final analysis, Pasolini's very death can be interpreted as an allegory of the victory of the dragon of unreality (or, to put it another way, a new humanity gloomily homologized, the idolatry of money and hyperconsumerism, the passive and always frustrated adhesion to abstract models of life) over any concrete, tangible "dream of a thing." And this is what is addressed in Morante's awesome crepuscular novel *Aracoeli*, ideally dedicated to the poet-friend who vanished a few years before: the world can no longer be "saved," but only kept at a distance. For Pasolini, but for Morante also, unreality can be equated with the bourgeoisie itself, the same bourgeoisie that he declares his desire to speak against with violence, in his weekly column "Il caos" in *Tempo*. Once more: readers in English-speaking countries might balk at this surprising equation bourgeoisie = unreality. After all, historically, the bourgeoisie is by definition productive, active, hardworking, and extraordinarily "real." But the fact remains that in this case the bourgeoisie implies less a social class than an evil, a "sickness."

What sickness might this be? And why is the bourgeoisie always abstract, in his view? For the simple reason that we saw before, which has to do with the desire to possess (and the illusion of possessing) and with the negation of the present.

"All the Saints Are Demons"
(On Carlo Levi and His Influence)

> L'arte italiana non può dunque essere un
> ornamento esterno [. . .] essa è per sua natura
> realistica . . .
>
> Italian art cannot therefore be an external ornament
> [. . .] it is by its very nature realistic . . .
>
> Carlo Levi
> *Le mille patrie*

I mentioned before the decisive influence of Carlo Levi on Morante and on Pasolini. In the 1950s the great writer and painter developed his idea on reality (also exemplified in his novels), which is different from Neorealism. For Carlo Levi, realism, unlike every form of naturalism, does not presuppose an already given image of reality, since it "crea la realtà per la prima volta nell'atto dell'espressione" (*Prima e dopo* 31; "creates reality for the first time in the act of expression"). On another occasion he suggests adopting the "unmistakable" criterion of truth for all the art that he defines as "Contadina" ("peasant"), as compared with "Luigina" art (in other words petit-bourgeois, vacuous, aestheticising). An art then which by naming things for the first time makes them exist, "la poesia è l'invenzione della verità" (*Prima e dopo* 51; "poetry is the invention of truth"). For him, and this is the crux of the matter, reality presents itself as something unstable, slippery, on the brink of disappearing, constitutionally ambiguous. "Ogni cosa è doppia. Tutti i santi sono demoni" (*Prima e dopo* 29; "Every thing is double. All the saints are demons"), says to him in prophetic tones an old Lucanian peasant with white whiskers, wrapped in a black cloak. And in fact in the south of Italy (of the world?) all the saints are demons, good mixes with evil, life intertwines with death, and each event comes back to haunt one. Let us then attempt to focus on Levi's very particular concept of reality. Above all, even if reality pre-exists us it acquires form, visibility—we might say "truth"—only when we manage to name it for the first time, to remove it briefly from its changing and shifting nature. Only poetic expression, which is potentially present in each of us, is capable of this much. Furthermore this reality expands to embrace the cosmos, the whole, the mysterious equivalence of the Good and the Necessary (remembering Weil). In short it comprises its own opposites and it is unallowable to select or to attempt to censure one side. Nor can we, according to Levi, fool ourselves at being able to constantly draw it from the literary word. The literary word perpetually makes the effort of giving a name to things, knowing though that before language a submerged world is opened. A dark world that will never be able to become entirely transparent. How much reality escapes our own words: Pasolini's films gave finally a voice to the under-proletariat; the immobile civilization of the South (or that of the Third World), the archaic and magic residues of any possible Modernity, the obscure vital bottom in each of us. Many truths, invisible or buried, to which we can only give a trembling poetic expression, are not entirely rationalizable. Levi appears to us as an almost classic essayist, so rich with his love for a "humble Italy," but with a luminously poetic look toward reality, a look that, as we read in one of his essays of the 1950s, all the people he met in his life had, if they had within themselves something true.

How to Defeat the Dragon?

Let us turn back to Morante, for whom the writer, the novelist-poet, is associated with the figure of the hero, the solar protagonist who in myth and fairy tale takes on the dragon of the night. But how? Simply by offering us a mirror capable of reflecting real life (which, it goes without saying, contains within it contradiction, anguish, deformity, tragedy) just like the mirror that Geppetto finally gives to Pinocchio when he becomes human, "Ecco, invece, quello che tu sei" (*Pro o contro* 107; "Look, this is what you really are like"). Knowing what we are like can, in certain circumstances, be depressing and hardly edifying, but Morante reminds us in her essay "Pro o contro la bomba atomica" that all great art makes no attempt to coat reality with sugar, but rather draws all the movements of nature into the dimension of the real, thus recognizing them as natural and therefore as "innocent" (*Pro o contro* 108). The point is to realize what this real dimension is. When reading Morante's short stories of the 1940s, particularly her childhood anecdotes, until recently excluded from publication and now collected in *Racconti dimenticati*, one can enjoy a Spanish and almost unconsciously baroque suggestion (Morante's last novel, *Aracoeli*, amply returns to Spain). I would dare to say that such a suggestion is almost Hispanic by the way of those statues and sinners, almost in the mode of Carlo Levi in Lucania, with those opulent cakes, those votive offerings often linked to perfidious jokes and an obscure sense of guilt, those sumptuous and sensual metaphors, those precious similes in which gums are likened to a velvet case and the eyes to a sapphire tiara, the sense of death incoming and the dead more in general. Particularly significant is the almost musical sense of theater and the world intended as a stage. We should be mindful also of the intense and blinding chromatics: the colors of the children's faces (purple, gold, vermilion), the colors of drapes and carriages and, finally, remember the beloved Charles Lindbergh who, for Elsa as a child, "volava per me, per me conquistava le palme" (*Racconti dimenticati* 238; "for me he would fly the skies, for me he would conquer the palms"). The universe where the little girl moves about is crowded with, aside from children, ghosts, angels (unaware of being so), fake devils, and populated by mysterious voices, bewitching epiphanies, visions of Renaissance gardens, and by forgotten islands with little homes and pianos. All of her female fantasies seem to generate themselves within little female dresses. Particularly in one of her stories, which she names "Il Sogno del carovaniere" (*Racconti dimenticati* 230; "The Dream of the Caravan Driver"), the fantasy appears more clearly: an oasis glowing in the desert, that is, an image ripped from a box of almond candies. This is the suggestion of a fablelike and exotic world, meridian and of burning contrasts but also pertaining to the most prosaic and familiar reality. I believe that already these early works define Morante's idea of

"Reality." On the one hand, fantasy seems to devour everything in a despotic and untameable way. But if we look at it closely, imagination only hides reality, which reveals itself in her own essence, always unattainable, magic, mysterious, an internalized "real maravilloso." In her youthful anecdotes, still quite fablelike in tone, Morante does not stage yet the figure so dear to her, the one of the hero whose task is fighting the dragon of unreality. However, we can uncover here how, according to Morante, "real" is what springs from a genuine love (for people and things), from an original desire without an object, from passion for the very existence, for being itself. "Real" is, then, the world transfigured and made more lively by a free imagination: and because it is free, this kind of imagination can influence and modify us, even with the knowledge that it will always somehow escape us.

The English language (and culture) allows us perhaps to penetrate the ambiguity of such a concept of reality. At times, in fact, we are forced to delve into the most impure and antiliterary universe, such as the media one, in order to understand the truth of a writer. We have to go where the very debris of the language is deposited in an inert and yet eloquent manner. In the United States a slogan has been coined—"Coca-Cola is the real thing." That is to say, it is the true, the good thing. A slogan, I should say immediately, that is incomprehensible to Italians, almost enigmatic. If, for example some advertising executive in our country were to have the bright idea of launching the slogan "La pasta De Cecco è la cosa reale" ("De Cecco pasta is the real thing") people would not understand and would most likely think of "reale" in the sense of "royal" rather than "real." Let's take another example, the English expression "Get real!" meaning "Be serious!" This, too, is somewhat mysterious for Italians, accustomed over the centuries to "reciting," to the wearing of more or less ephemeral masks. It seems to me that for deep-rooted cultural reasons, Americans share what we have called a *positive* inclination toward that which is real (think also of the American anti-intellectual, pragmatic tradition). An inclination that, for very different reasons, they share with ancient Greeks and that, as we have seen, was nurtured by both Morante and Pasolini. What's more, the mass culture of Italy offers us continual images of reality that are totally unreal (or to be more precise, hyper-real), where in the place of reality we find its packaged representations and simulations, pleasing and stripped of any conflictual or tragic aspect. It was in fact about the Disney documentaries on nature that Carlo Levi commented "qui nessuno muore: in questo regno della morte c'è tutto fuorché la morte, cacciata e nascosta da un eterno, sorridente balletto" (*Specchio* 77; "nobody dies here: in this kingdom of death there is everything except death, which has been chased away and concealed by an eternal grinning ballet") and as such they constitute the document of "un mondo di uomini che hanno terrore di vivere e morire, e che accettano di deformarsi per nascondersi" (*Specchio* 77; "a world of men who are terrified to live and to die, and who agree to deform themselves in order to hide themselves"). Perhaps, immersed in this mass culture, in this phantasmagoric universe of publicity and the media, we have all become "mutants" (in the sense that Weil used the term before Pasolini and Morante), and as such attracted by artificial paradises, without feeling and without pain, the virtual, in which to hide ourselves. But, attempting to paraphrase the Coca-Cola slogan for Pasolini and Morante (and for Carlo Levi before them) "the real thing" is life itself, which is by definition not docile, which never lets itself be "possessed" in any way, as the bourgeoisie has attempted to claim over the years and which includes within itself its own opposite (death, the negative) against any New Age style elbowing toward an unreal and deceptive happiness. In the novel *White Noise* by Don DeLillo, inspiration in the 1980s for so much cyberpunk literature, an average Yankee housewife agrees to be a guinea pig in order to try out (potentially harmful) chemicals that do away with the fear of death, which she can no longer bear to live with. For the housewife, not accepting death is equivalent to not accepting life. In the end she will have to give in to what Morante called "the dragon of unreality" that television, ads, and an obsessive pursuit of happiness make manifest to her everyday. That is the dragon of unreality!

Pasolini was struck by a passage in a letter from Karl Marx to Arnold Ruge in which Marx refers to the "sogno di una cosa" ("dream of a thing") that the world has had for some time and that it should come to terms with. This "dream of a thing," an

Filippo La Porta

expression that Pasolini planned to use as a title for an early novel, is not a suggestive, insubstantial utopia to be brought about in the future. Rather, it is nothing other than the recognition of reality in its entirety, to be lived and experienced in its totality.

Notes

1. This essay does not appear in *Saggi sulla politica e società* and the quotation is taken from the 1979 eponymous volume edited by Gian Carlo Ferretti.

Works Cited

D'Angeli, Concetta. "La presenza di Simone Weil ne *La Storia.* "Per Elsa Morante*. Milan: Linea d'ombra, 1993. 109–35.

DeLillo, Don. *White Noise*. New York: Viking, 1985.

De Sanctis, Francesco. *Storia della letteratura italiana*. Vol. 2. Florence: Salani, 1935.

Levi, Carlo. *Le mille patrie*. Rome: Donzelli, 2000.

———. *Prima e dopo le parole. Scritti e discorsi sulla letteratura*. Rome: Donzelli, 2001.

———. *Lo specchio. Scritti di critica d'arte*. Rome: Donzelli, 2001.

Morante, Elsa. *Opere*. Ed. Cesare Garboli and Carlo Cecchi. Vol. 2. Milan: Mondadori, 1990.

———. *Pro o contro la bomba atomica e altri scritti*. Ed. Cesare Garboli. Milan: Adelphi, 1987.

———. *Racconti dimenticati*. Turin: Einaudi, 2002.

Pasolini, Pier Paolo. *Bestemmia. Tutte le poesie*. Ed Graziella Chiarcossi and Walter Siti. Vol. 1. Milan: Garzanti, 1993.

———. *Il caos*. Ed. Gian Carlo Ferretti. Rome : Editori riuniti, 1979.

———. *Romanzi e racconti*. Ed. Walter Siti and Silvia De Laude. Vol. 2. Milan: Mondadori, 1998.

———. *Saggi sulla letteratura e sull'arte*. Ed. Walter Siti and Silvia De Laude. 2 vols. Milan: Mondadori, 1999.

———. *Saggi sulla politica e sulla società*. Ed. Walter Siti and Silvia De Laude. Milan: Mondadori, 1999.

Weil, Simone. *Cahiers*. Vol. 1 and 2. Paris: Plon, 1972.

———. *The Notebooks of Simone Weil*. Trans. Arthur Wills. 2 vols. New York: Routledge, 1976

———. *Piccola cara* . . . Trans. Maria Concetta Sala. Genoa: Marietti, 1997.

Contributors

Marco Bardini is an associate professor at the University of Pisa. He has published several articles on Morante, and has authored *Elsa Morante. Italiana. Di professione, poeta* (Pisa: Nistri-Lischi, 1999).

Concetta D'Angeli is an assistant professor at the University of Pisa. She is co-editor with Giacomo Magrini of the monographic volume of *Studi novecenteschi* entitled "Vent'anni dopo la Storia: Omaggio a Elsa Morante," *Studi novecenteschi* 21.47–48 (1994), in which are collected all the papers of the homonymous conference D'Angeli organized in Pisa earlier that year. D'Angeli has authored *Leggere Elsa Morante: Aracoeli, La Storia e Il mondo salvato dai ragazzini* (Rome: Carocci, 2003) and *Forme della drammaturgia: definizioni e esempi* (Turin: UTET, 2004). With Guido Paduano, D'Angeli is also the author of *Il Comico: dalle origini a oggi* (Bologna: Il Mulino, 1999).

Cristina Della Coletta is an associate professor at the University of Virginia. She is the author of *Plotting the Past: Metamorphoses of Historical Narrative in Modern Italian Fiction* (West Lafayette, IN: Purdue UP, 1996), as well as articles on a variety of contemporary novelists.

Nicoletta Di Ciolla McGowan is a senior lecturer at Manchester Metropolitan University. She has published widely on contemporary women's fiction and popular culture, and is the editor of Francesca Duranti's *Left-Handed Dreams* (Market Harborough: Troubador, 2000).

Elisa Gambaro is a researcher at the University of Milan. She has published articles on Franco Fortini, on Elsa Morante and Katherine Mansfield. Her most recent study, "Ragazzi allo schermo," in *Tirature 2005: giovani scrittori e personaggi giovani*, ed. Vittorio Spinazzola (Milan: Il Saggiatore, 2005), 36–41, deals with contemporary Italian narrative.

Filippo La Porta is a critic for *L'Unità*, *il manifesto* and *La repubblica. Musica!* He is the author of *La nuova narrativa* *italiana: travestimenti e stili di fine secolo* (Turin: Bollati Boringhieri, 1995; 2nd ed. 1998), *Non c'è problema: considerazioni morali su modi di dire e frasi fatte* (Milan: Feltrinelli, 1997), *Manuale di scrittura creatina* (Rome: Minimum Fax, 1999), *Narratori di un Sud disperso* (Naples: L'Ancora del Mediterraneo, 2000), *Pier Paolo Pasolini* (Florence: Le Lettere, 2001), *L'autoreverse dell'esperienza: euforie e inganni della vita flessibile* (Milan: Bollati Boringhieri, 2004).

Stefania Lucamante is an associate professor at The Catholic University of America. She is the author of *Elsa Morante e l'eredità proustiana* (Fiesole: Cadmo, 1998), *Isabella Santacroce* (Fiesole: Cadmo, 2002), and numerous articles on the contemporary Italian novel. Lucamante is also the editor of *Italian Pulp Fiction: The New Narrative of the "Giovani Cannibali" Writers* (Madison and Teaneck, NJ: Fairleigh Dickinson UP, 2001).

Enrico Palandri is writer-in-residence in the Italian Department at University College, London. His many novels include *Boccalone* (1979); *Le pietre e il sale* (1987), translated as *Ages Apart* (Vintage/Ebury, 1989), *Allegro fantastico* (1993), *Le colpevoli ambiguità di Herbert Markus* (1997), and *Angela prende il volo* (Milan: Feltrinelli, 2000); *La via del ritorno* (Milan: Bompiani, 1990), translated as *The Way Back* (London: Serpent's Tail, 1993). He has translated Eudora Welty, George Grossmith, and McLiam Wilson. Palandri has also authored *La deriva romantica: ipotesi sulla letteratura e la scrittura* (Novara: Interlinea, 2002).

Hanna Serkowska is an associate professor at the University of Warsaw. She has published *Le radici medioevali di Federigo Tozzi* (Warsaw: Uniwersytet Warszawski, 1994), *"Uscire da una camera delle favole." I romanzi di Elsa Morante* (Cracow: Rabid, 2002), *Rzecz o Elsie Morante* (Cracow: Universitas, 2004), and several articles on modern and contemporary Italian novelists. She is currently editing a Polish collection of essays, *Writing in Progress: Italian Contemporary Writers from A to T,* ranging from Alda Merini to Andrea Camilleri.

Walter Siti is a professor of contemporary Italian literature at the University of L'Aquila. He is the author of two novels, *Scuola di nudo* (Turin: Einaudi, 1994), and *Un dolore normale* (Turin: Einaudi, 1999). He is also the author of *Il neorealismo nella poesia italiana (1941–1956)* (Turin: Einaudi, 1980). More recently, Siti has directed the publication of Pier Paolo Pasolini's collected works in two volumes (*Novels* and *Short Stories*) for the Meridiani Mondadori (Milan, 1998) and the short-story collection *La magnifica merce* (Turin: Einaudi, 2004).

Sharon Wood is a professor of modern languages at the University of Leicester. She is the author of *Woman as Object: Language and Gender in the Work of Alberto Moravia* (London: Pluto, 1990), *Italian Women's Writing 1860–1994* (London: Athlone, 1995). She is also the editor of *Italian Women Writing* (Manchester UP, 1993) and, with Letizia Panizza, of *A History of Women's Writing in Italy* (Cambridge: Cambridge UP, 2000), as well as numerous articles on modern Italian literature. Wood has also translated novels and stories by Susanna Tamaro, Romana Petri, Alessandra Montrucchio, and Gabriella Maleti, as well as *The Black Hole of Auschwitz* by Primo Levi.

Index

Index

Venus, 150
Verdi, Giuseppe, 122
Viareggio Award, 2, 117
Vinci, Simona, 13
Vittorini, Elio, 131

Walker, Alice, 184n8
war, 2, 4, 80, 81, 131, 152, 153,
    221–49 *passim*
Warren, Robert Penn, 117
Weaver, William, 18n1
Weigel, Sigrid, 231

Weil, Simone, 116, 182, 191, 277,
    290–93, 304, 307
women scholars, 21
women writers, 21, 28, 47, 129
Wood, Sharon, 14, 40–41n5,
    154n14
Woolf, Virginia, 245

Zambrano, Aracoeli, 183n1
Zampolini, Anna Maria, 165, 168
Zola, Emile, 67, 286